CHILDREN *of* PARADISE

CHILDREN

of PARADISE

THE STRUGGLE FOR THE
SOUL OF IRAN

LAURA SECOR

RIVERHEAD BOOKS

New York

2016

RIVERHEAD BOOKS
An imprint of Penguin Random House LLC
375 Hudson Street
New York, New York 10014

Copyright © 2016 by Laura Secor
Penguin supports copyright. Copyright fuels creativity, encourages
diverse voices, promotes free speech, and creates a vibrant culture.
Thank you for buying an authorized edition of this book and for
complying with copyright laws by not reproducing, scanning, or
distributing any part of it in any form without permission.
You are supporting writers and allowing Penguin to
continue to publish books for every reader.

Verses from Mohammad Mokhtari, "From the Other Half," in English
translation are reprinted by permission of Arcade Publishing,
an imprint of Skyhorse Publishing, Inc.

ISBN 978-1-59448-710-1

Printed in the United States of America
1   3   5   7   9   10   8   6   4   2

Book design by Marysarah Quinn
Map by Jeffrey L. Ward

FOR GEORGE, CHARLIE, AND JULIA

CONTENTS

IV RESISTANCE

ISLAMIC REPUBLIC OF IRAN

RUSSIA

KAZAKHSTAN

GEORGIA

*Caspian
Sea*

UZBEKISTAN

ARMENIA   AZERBAIJAN

TURKEY

TURKMENISTAN

Ardabil•

Tabriz•   •Rasht   Tonekabon
           (Shahsavar)

Shaft•   •Amol

Qazvin•   *Alborz Mountains*

Karaj•   ★ **Tehran**   •Semnan   Mashhad•

Hamadan•   Shahr-e Rey•

Kermanshah•   •Qom   *Kavir Desert*

IRAQ

Khorramabad•

IRAN

Baghdad★   Isfahan•   Ardakan•   Birjand•
                •Yazd

Karbala•   AFGHANISTAN

Najaf•   •Ahvaz
          Khorramshahr•
Shatt al-Arab •Abadan   Kerman•

          Shiraz•

KUWAIT   •Bushehr   PAKISTAN

                Persian Gulf   Bandar-e Abbas•

BAHRAIN—|

          QATAR

SAUDI
ARABIA   *Gulf of Oman*

          UAE

0 Miles   500   *Arabian Sea*

0 Kilometers   500   OMAN

© 2016 Jeffrey L. Ward

AND ITS NEIGHBORS

Preface

I WAS A CHILD when Iranian students overran the U.S. embassy in Tehran and took its personnel hostage for 444 days. It was the first international news event to enter my consciousness. On television, Tehran appeared to be a city of unmoving traffic and mobs of very riled-up young people burning American flags. I had urgent vocabulary questions. What was an embassy? What was a hostage? But the images and emotions I understood. Somewhere on the other side of the world, there was a forbidden country entangled deeply and inextricably enough with my own to produce a hostility that stunned the anchors of the network news.

For Americans of my generation, Iran was the object of fearful caricature, the world's first Islamic theocracy, with a dour ayatollah at the helm. Iran was a foreign policy conundrum to be solved and a black box whose contents were all but unknowable. After 1979, Americans seldom traveled there, and press reports of any depth were surprisingly rare. When I became a journalist, such places intrigued and compelled me. The privilege of being a correspondent, after all, was to go places where one didn't belong. Iranian visas were notoriously difficult to come by; in 1999 a *New Yorker* story by the journalist Robin Wright portrayed Iran as a country so compelling that I realized I'd one day have to try to get one.

I knew that Iran's recently elected president, Mohammad Khatami, had pledged to reform the country's autocratic regime. But I hadn't imagined that behind the frozen images from 1979 lay a vibrant, soul-searching country. Student activists, who still used looted American embassy letterhead for copier paper, defended newspapers from censorship, and philosophers reached for new theories to reconcile liberal rights with an Islamic state they'd helped coax into being. One of the lead hostage takers in 1979 had become a proponent of democratic reform and now devoted his time to traffic issues on Tehran's city council. It was as arresting a reversal as it was unlikely. Revolutionary ideology had limits, the city councilman explained. It could not solve mundane urban problems. Behind this simple assertion, I was certain, was a universe of context: two decades of experience in the life of a nation and the life of that man, but surely also a shift in the intellectual climate that made it possible to speak of democratic change and of the city council as its humble instrument.

I had never been to the Middle East. I was a writer and editor at *Lingua Franca* magazine, which covered intellectual life and academic politics, and at the time I was working on a story of my own about the former Yugoslavia. The dissident intellectuals in my piece had followed what seemed the opposite of the Iranian trajectory, from reformist critique within communism to a ferocious and exclusionary nationalism that tore their country apart. Here again was a country after my heart, as I had come to know it—one where ideas mattered, and where history was so compressed as to be indistinguishable from the biographies of the people who made it. I was pretty sure my editor at *Lingua Franca* had read the *New Yorker* piece, too, when he looked up from editing mine to remark offhandedly that he expected the two of us to reconvene in his office one day to work on a story about Iran.

I started to collect all the scholarly books about Iran that crossed the magazine's transom. There would be time, and other subjects, before I got to them, but Iran was the dream story for a writer who loved the things I loved.

. . .

I STARTED VISITING IRAN IN 2004. The atmosphere was more oppressive than I'd imagined. The excitement over reform had obscured the conditions that rendered such political relaxation so necessary. What I encountered probably would have been familiar to anyone who visited the old Soviet bloc in days gone by, and it was undoubtedly less severe than in many neighboring countries. Still, this was a closed country, and no honest accounting for its politics could fail to acknowledge the fact.

Even ordinary Iranians made the practical assumption that their phones were tapped and e-mails read. Sensitive meetings were best arranged through elaborate chains of in-person contacts. Some of my interview subjects were routinely followed; others received harassing phone calls or were forced to report continually to the men who'd interrogated them in prison. A merchant I met in the bazaar slipped me a note to see him privately, which I did, on a busy street corner, where, sotto voce, he explained the layers of political control within his workplace.

Anxiety was a way of life in Iran, and you couldn't report on the country without sharing in it. Iran was not a place where one undertook any kind of opposition, even loyal opposition, lightly. And yet, to my never-ending amazement, this was also a country with a civic spirit that refused to die. The engagement of the Iranian citizenry, against all odds and in the face of pervasive surveillance and often violent repression, suggested lessons for the complacent democracy from which I came.

By the time I started going to Iran, the reformist experiment was apparently over. Many Iranians I met spoke of people like the hostage takers turned reformers and the outgoing President Khatami with bitter disappointment, as vehicles for little more than dashed hopes. I would spend the next ten years and five visits trying to piece together the story of how reform had coalesced, fallen apart, and surged forth as the Green Movement in 2009—what it stood for, where it fit into the stream of the country's consciousness, and what Iran was left with in its wake. This was a story that spanned the revolution itself as well as the three convulsive decades that followed. What Iranians lived in that time—what they channeled through their intellectual salons and prison letters, their dreams and childhood memories—felt to me like an epic novel, replete with calamities and reversals, crescendos and epiphanies, and a sweeping arc of history that cut through its core.

In Tehran in June 2005, I met a young blogger who had recently been released from a harrowing stint in prison. I wrote about Roozbeh Mirebrahimi's ordeal with the Iranian justice system in *The New Yorker* that fall. When he arrived on American shores a year later, speaking not a word of English, he came to live with my husband and me until he got settled and his wife, Solmaz Sharif, also a journalist, could join him.

We had strange days, sitting at my kitchen counter of a morning and comparing the Persian and English words for objects we could point to: garlic, banana, pepper. How easy, but inadvisable, it might be to say "chicken" when you meant "kitchen," and vice versa. We stayed up late at night with a dictionary between us, talking about Iranian politics, the one subject that could pull Roozbeh so far out of his shell that he became determined to communicate. The more fluent he became, the more I yearned for another fluency—in the history of Iran's revolution and its aftermath—that would allow me to truly absorb his life's story.

Roozbeh seemed to share an originary trauma with nearly every Iranian I got to know inside or outside the country. He spoke of a forbidden graveyard in his home city and of his childhood fascination with its provenance, which no adult would explain. The revolutionary decade had been a violent one: street battles, bomb blasts, political executions, the brutal war with Iraq, and, finally, a seemingly senseless state-sponsored massacre of political prisoners. The country ostensibly moved on. But for Iranians who were children then as much as for those who were old enough to fear for their lives or question their own complicity, the 1980s were a repressed memory that gave the country no peace. This book is in part an effort to explain that graveyard and Roozbeh's troubled presence on its periphery.

．　．　．

IN THE UNITED STATES, we tend to greet the swings of Iranian electoral politics as definitive pronouncements on the country's character, and to allow our own foreign policy debates to color the Islamic Republic as fundamentally fearsome or benign. We risk overlooking the soul of the matter, the experience of politics as it is lived, by those who hold the highest stakes in its outcome. Iran is not a happy place, but it is a supremely dignified one—a country that has wrested its destiny from the designs of great powers, experimented with a form of government never before seen on earth, and kept that experiment alive with a spirit of constant questioning that has threatened dissidents' very lives. Wherever Iran goes, it will get there first, and get there on its own terms.

What follows is not the history of the Islamic Republic of Iran. That would be presumptuous if not impossible for a foreign reporter to write. This is a book about real people, some more famous or more admirable than others, but people whose complex and imperfect lives illuminate the passages through which they've traveled. There are no American protagonists and no American policy prescriptions. It is a book about Iranians, and it is *a* history—a hidden history, for the most part, of a powerful and protean current in the political and intellectual life of a nation. How many Iranians' aspirations this current carries we can't know for sure. Ten years ago reformists were fond of saying that 80 percent of the country thought as they did and only 20 percent supported the regime. When I last visited Iran in 2012, I heard hard-liners quote exactly the reverse proportion. Public opinion is unmeasurable under conditions of fear. But what is clear is that deep schisms rend Iranian society just as they do its political class. The more I've gotten to know Iran, the more I believe this inner conflict all but defines it and serves as the engine of its fate.

I
—

REVOLUTION

LITTLE BLACK FISH

ON A COLD WINTER NIGHT, at the bottom of the sea, a wise old fish gathered twelve thousand of her children and grandchildren and told them a story.

Once upon a time, she began, a little black fish lived in a mountain stream with its mother. From dawn until dusk, mother and child swam in circles, in and out of crevices, following each other until night fell and they went to sleep in their home under a mossy rock.

One morning before sunrise, the little fish woke its mother and announced that it was leaving. A single thought had come to possess its mind: Where, the little black fish wanted to know, did the stream end?

The mother laughed. "My dear," she said, "a stream has no beginning and no end. That's the way it is. The stream just flows and never goes anywhere."

The little black fish was certain that this could not be true. Despite threats from its elders, and to the awe of its peers, off it went, down the waterfall and into a pond, where the only creatures in sight were tadpoles.

The tadpoles told the little black fish that they came from nobility and that they were the most beautiful creatures in the world. The world, they said with confidence, was the pond where they swam. Their mother, a frog, chided the black fish, calling it a "worthless creature" for leading her young astray.

Undaunted, the little black fish swam on, outwitting predators and overcoming many obstacles on its way to the open sea.

There the fish found a school of brave, indomitable fish like itself. So powerful was this school of fish that it foiled fishermen by dragging their nets to the bottom of the sea.

At last the little black fish had found its true place in the world. Before joining its brethren, it went for a swim along the water's surface, where it could feel the sun on its back. The fish knew that it was vulnerable to predators there, but by now it also understood that its own mortality was a trifle. "What does matter," the fish told itself, "is the influence that my life or death will have on the lives of others."

Just then, a heron swooped and swallowed the fish. Inside the heron's stomach, the little black fish heard someone crying. It was another fish, tiny and young, who missed his mother. The little black fish thought quickly. It would swim around to tickle the heron's stomach, the black fish told its tiny companion. When the heron laughed, the tiny fish should leap out of her mouth. The little black fish would stay behind and kill the heron with a dagger made from a blade of grass.

And so the little black fish tickled, and so the tiny fish leapt. From the safety of the water, the tiny fish watched the heron writhe and shout, beating her wings as she fell to her death. But the little black fish never emerged.

The grandmother fish had finished her story. She and eleven thousand nine hundred and ninety-nine of her spawn went off to sleep. One little red fish lay awake. She could not stop thinking about the sea.

So GOES THE CHILDREN'S STORY that inspired a generation of Iranian revolutionaries. *The Little Black Fish*, by Samad Behrangi, was published in 1968, the year its twenty-nine-year-old author spent a hot week at the end of August touring villages near the Aras River in the north of Iran. He was collecting folklore with a friend, something he had done often in the remote rural villages of his homeland. One day he waded by the shore of the river to cool himself while his friend swam. The young writer was not aware of it, but the Aras was known locally for its fierce current, which easily lashed him from the spot where he stood. Behrangi could not swim. He cried out, but by the time his friend reached him, he had vanished into the river's depths. The author of *The Little Black Fish* drowned, his body pulled five kilometers downstream, where it was found three days later.

Behrangi had spent a decade traveling to poor villages, distributing books he'd purchased himself to needy children. He was not a religious man but a man of the left, moved by the depth of rural poverty. He noticed something on these trips: Iran was not only an unequal country, but a country alienated from itself. Iranian elites were steeped in the ideas, the culture, the mores of Europe and America. But the country's interior was nothing like those places.

Iranian teacher-training texts, Behrangi noted in an early essay, came overwhelmingly from America, and they focused on concerns, including childhood obesity and school lunch programs, that were laughably inapplicable to Iranian village life. When Iranian children were taught English—a language Behrangi also studied—their textbooks referenced hot dogs and baseball, cultural markers that were meaningless to the children of rural Iran. Iranian teachers ought to focus on the pressing needs and cultural realities of Iranian children, to come up with their own pedagogy to fit their real context.

Behrangi wrote short stories in the form of folktales in order to avoid censorship, but within them he embedded revolutionary exhortations, even to the violent overthrow of the ruling class with its American affectations. If *The Little Black Fish* strikes today's Western reader as dark for a children's book, that was not Behrangi's concern. "I don't desire that aware children read my stories only for pleasure," he wrote. "We must lead our children away from building hopes on false and empty visions, toward creating hopes based on a correct understanding and interpretation of the harsh realities of society and on how to struggle to eliminate those harsh realities."

Eleven years after his death, when Behrangi's countrymen dragged the fisherman's net to the floor of the open sea, many of them cited his story as their inspiration. It was a parable of courage and sacrifice, and of the refusal to be blinded by convention or confined by fate. At the time of Behrangi's writing, in 1968, Iran seemed, to some, like a plebeian mountain stream that just flowed and never went anywhere; to others, like a haughty, noble frog pond that did not even know the stream that fed it. The germ of revolution was to refuse to be bounded by the accidents of birth, the fear of predators, or the riverbanks of fate.

NOBODY ASKS ANYMORE why Iran had a revolution in 1979. Western powers had robbed Iran of its resources and made puppets of its leaders. Iranians suffered political repression and glaring inequality. Iran's religious leaders and its merchant class saw the culture and economy they held dear slipping away, displaced by arrangements suitable to foreigners. With all we now know, the Islamic Revolution of 1979 seems overdetermined. But what we forget, or underestimate, or maybe never knew, is that the Iranian Revolution was not a simple act of refusal—of modernity; of the West; even, in the end, of absolute rule. It emerged in impassioned, ambivalent dialogue among passionate, ambivalent people. And the state it produced is passionately ambivalent, too.

Outside Iran, we have come to associate the Islamic Revolution with the severe, otherworldly face of Ayatollah Ruhollah Khomeini and the return of theocracy in the twentieth century. Behind and within this story is another history—of a revolutionary impulse as complexly modern as the society that produced it, and which has yielded a culture of civic engagement as imperishable as the quest of the little red fish. To the extent that the postrevolutionary state has tried to deny the multiplicity of its origins and to suppress the engagement of its people, its course has followed an arc of tragedy.

The story of Iran's Islamic Revolution and the republic it spawned is not only—perhaps not even primarily—a story about religion. It is a story about politics and identity, about social division and cohesion, about the forces that move history everywhere in the world. It is also the story of individuals who have quested ceaselessly, pressing against seemingly impermeable barriers, for the open sea.

IRANIAN REVOLUTIONARIES sometimes describe their revolution, in terms resonant with Behrangi, as the convergence of many streams of thought and activism. Some of these streams were religious. Others were secular. Where the basin widened, the religious and secular ideas became, if not indistinguishable, inextricable. That did not occur right away. But when it did, history happened, and has been happening ever since.

To make a myth of Samad Behrangi's eerily resonant death by drowning was nearly irresistible. The man who did so was Behrangi's friend and champion in Tehran's intellectual circles, Jalal Al-e Ahmad, an essayist active against Iran's autocratic king, Shah Mohammad Reza Pahlavi. Al-e Ahmad had hosted Behrangi at his Tehran salon, and he wrote affectionately about the teacher, storyteller, and folklorist he called his younger brother. It was Al-e Ahmad who floated the legend that Behrangi was murdered by the shah's secret police, even persuading the friend who was with Behrangi the day he drowned to keep quiet about the details of the accident.

That fall Al-e Ahmad wrote in an essay, "Now we must mourn in our agony for this younger brother and eulogize him? And anyway, how many Samads do we have? . . . No, it's no good. Now it's better if I . . . instead of mourning this younger brother's death or carrying a cane, start a rumor that Samad, just like that *Little Black Fish*, has made his way through [the] Aras to the sea so that he may reappear one day."

With Behrangi, Jalal Al-e Ahmad was one of the most important fish in the secular stream. His most famous work was an extended essay called *Westoxication*, published underground in 1962. *Westoxication* excoriated Iranians for what Al-e Ahmad saw as their self-loathing worship of the West. This plague ate away at Iranian industry, culture, power, and self-esteem. The machine, invented in the West and controlled by the West, was devastating Iranian pastoral life. The old arrangements, economic and social, had been upended, but the new ones, devised elsewhere and evolved to suit an alien history and culture, made no sense for Iran's largely rural people. There was no use trying to rewind modernity; the only hope was for Iranians to seize control of the machine themselves, to bring it to their villagers not as a replacement for their labor but as a tool for their betterment.

Westoxication would become the foundational text of revolutionary Iran's anti-Americanism. But it was a cry less of hatred than of anguish. That Iran had borrowed too heavily from the West, that it had adopted an alien intellectual tradition that lacked roots in local culture or history—that Iranians consequently saw themselves as inferior to Westerners, and saw themselves through the eyes of Westerners who looked down on them—was a nearly inevitable critique at that time. But Western influence on Iranian philosophical thought was too deep to cast off completely, its attraction too profound. Iran was enmeshed as though in a relationship with an abusive lover, self-loathing bound up with the contempt in which it was held. For the very fact of loving its abuser, Iran hated itself.

The solution to this problem was not obvious. The Western intellectual tradition was intertwined with the Persian one from its root. The Shiite seminaries of Najaf and Qom taught the same ancient Greek philosophy that lay at the foundation of European thought. Generations of Iranian students abroad soaked up European ideas and brought them home. Iranian thinkers had built on, around, and against these schools of European thought. Al-e Ahmad himself ended his anti-Western manifesto by appealing to the works of Albert Camus, Eugene Ionesco, and Ingmar Bergman. Was there really any such thing as a separable Western tradition? If so, was it something alien, adapted from and to foreign cultures and different circumstances, or was it, even so, as much an Iranian birthright as a French or German or American one? The Iranian thinkers of the 1960s embodied this dilemma. In their effort to create a native, Iranian intellectual language and political ideology, they drew on Western sources, because those sources were as natural to them as the native ones—as available, as meaningful, as useful.

Jalal Al-e Ahmad died in 1969. And when he did, perhaps the most influential thinker of all stood ready to carry the revolutionary relay to its finish. Ali Shariati would fashion an ideology that was the stuff of a generation's dreams: militant, transcendent, and inalienably, authentically, Iranian.

SHARIATI, a charismatic orator and Islamist ideologue in the eastern shrine city of Mashhad, had met Al-e Ahmad earlier that year. Younger, wilder, more imaginative—already holding sway over rooms of students who sat, hypnotized, well after the bell that marked the end of class— Shariati must have known at some level that the light Al-e Ahmad carried would soon pass into his own hands. When the author of *Westoxication* died, Shariati wrote, "I completely forgot all the memories, ties, friendship, intimacy and harmony that existed between me and dear Jalal. His face faded away in my memory and instead another loomed. It was my own face! It was as if I had heard the news of my own death."

Shariati called for casting off what he saw as the courtly, superstitious, passive Islam of the clergy and reviving what he considered the true Islam—one that was militant and justice-seeking, and which contained the answers to nearly all of man's problems. He married the language and concerns of Iran's secular opposition to the identity of its Shiite masses. He might as well have split the atom.

Shariati's charisma was legendary. He habitually arrived late to his lectures, smoked while he spoke, and held forth for as many as six hours at a stretch. But the oratory was so powerful that one of his students told his biographer, "During his lectures, you would be so carried away with his performance that you wouldn't even feel the chair you were sitting on." Even some of his bitterest critics, today, wax sentimental at the mention of his name. As it turned out, he was a dangerous man, they say. But oh, you should only have heard his voice.

Shariati was born in 1933 to a traditional lower-middle-class family in a northeastern desert town not far from the Turkmen border. His father was a local religious teacher who founded an important Islamic center in the city of Mashhad. In many ways Shariati's thinking would follow a clear line from his father's. Shariati's father spoke of shaking off superstition and passivity to make religion into a more active force in Iranian life. He modeled for Ali the study of Western ideas as well as Islamic ones: the capacity to swim in two streams, one traditional and religious, the other modern and rationalistic, in order to speak a single language to a divided society—perhaps even to his divided self.

According to his biographer, Shariati was a rebellious, indolent student. He skipped class, dashed off his homework just before school, and disrupted lectures with sly remarks and practical jokes. Although he achieved little in school, he spent his free time reading from his father's two-thousand-volume library. One of his early teachers described Shariati as "a student who is more educated than all his teachers and lazier than all his classmates."

Shariati read Lenin and Dostoyevsky alongside Persian poets and Sufi dervishes. He would later take a particular interest in a school of Sufis known as the "self-blamers," who deliberately committed public acts of immoral behavior in the hope of being ridiculed and humiliated. Their public disgrace was meant to stiffen their inner resolve; for a devout Muslim, it was a perverse form of self-sacrifice. Although Shariati dabbled in it only briefly, it was an uncanny fit for his sensibility, which all his life would draw him to play games with mirrors, to invent alter egos and revel in contradictions, to oscillate between a public life in lecture halls teeming with acolytes and one of mystical, melancholy, self-lacerating solitude.

The early fifties were a time of political awakening, not only for Shariati, but for Iran. Following decades of repressive, autocratic rule, a young and diffident new king, Mohammad Reza Pahlavi, had assumed the throne during World War II, in 1941. When the war ended, the young shah presided, by his passivity, over a brief window of relative openness that lasted from when Shariati was twelve until he was twenty. During these years,

Britain continued to direct Iranian politics with a heavy hand and to treat the new shah like a despised vassal. But a labor movement stirred, and so did the parliament. Intellectuals, journalists, clerics, and politicians cast off the deferential silence the previous shah had imposed on them and filled the public space with lively debates and new political parties.

Through the ranks of the newly energized parliament rose a liberal nationalist named Mohammad Mossadegh, who promised the Iranian people the rule of law and freedom from the interference of foreigners. Specifically, Mossadegh proposed that the oil industry should come under Iranian national ownership and control. Iran, a country awash in the world's most valuable resource, should not suffer the humiliation of poverty while enriching foreigners. As prime minister from 1951 to 1953, Mossadegh effectively wrested Iran's oil industry from Britain's grip and outmaneuvered Mohammad Reza Shah at every pass, rendering the king nearly powerless despite his foreign backers and titular role. In 1953 the United States, fearing the prime minister's relations with the communist Tudeh Party, helped Mossadegh's domestic enemies topple him with a CIA-supported coup.

Mohammad Reza Shah emerged from that crucible a hardened, brittle man. Fearful of court intrigue and insecure before his people, he grew ever more obsessive and tyrannical. He took an axe to the knees of his most effective opposition, the Tudeh and the nationalists, and would soon go on to crack down on the clergy as well. He turned the country's oil industry over to an international consortium that split its profits with Iran but did not allow Iranians to audit its books or serve on its board of directors.

Under Mossadegh, it had seemed possible that Iran would evolve along its own track, influenced by leftist and liberal ideas that originated in the West, perhaps, but defined by a powerful sense of national pride, the drive to own its own resources and command its own fate. Now the wind sweeping Iran from the West seemed both cruel and irresistible. Either one capitulated to it, as the shah had done, or one found some object to wrap one's fists around—something supple yet firmly enough rooted to hold one's weight against the storm.

. . .

THESE WERE THE CIRCUMSTANCES of Shariati's late adolescence. He joined a religious group that supported Mossadegh on the grounds that monarchy was incompatible with Islam. At teacher-training school he became an activist for Mossadegh, and he continued these activities even after the coup, when they became dangerous. By that time Shariati had graduated and started work as a primary school teacher; he also substituted for his father from time to time as the main speaker at the family's Islamic center. Once during those years, his biographer recounts, Shariati was caught in the dead of night scrawling pro-Mossadegh graffiti on city walls. He was forced to lick the graffiti clean, until his tongue was swollen and black.

Amid the lengthening shadows of the late 1950s, the nationalist movement spent or crushed, Shariati retreated into Gnosticism, a mystical search for illumination based on the view that divinity resides within humans, who must somehow liberate their better nature from the debased material world—the "stinking mud," as Shariati called it. He wrote poetry and attended poetry circles while he studied literature at the University of Mashhad. He attended the same poetry circle as a young Mashhadi cleric named Ali Khamenei.

Shariati won a scholarship to Paris, where he studied sociology in the late fifties and early sixties and joined a circuit of politically active Iranian students abroad. During those years he grappled ferociously and publicly with his country's vexed relationship with foreign influence. In one essay Shariati lamented that Iran's modern, educated elite belittled itself by elevating foreign ideas. While these Iranians rejected their own history and imagined a future modeled on the West, he wrote, the common people, wedded to local tradition, embraced the past and felt the future didn't belong to them. Shariati diagnosed the problem astutely: "A futureless past is a state of inertia and stagnation, while a pastless future is alien and vacuous." And so he set about inventing both a useful past and a utopian future.

To construct a new originary myth, Shariati mined the Western philosophical tradition for its best and most revolutionary ideas and then attributed them to a larger doctrine that was authentically Iranian—namely, Shiite Islam. But Shiism, as it was practiced in Iran, was politically quietist, more given to ritual and tears than to heroic uprisings. And so Shariati had to reinvent it. Shariati's Shiism was revolutionary and militant; it encouraged the overthrow of despots; it was moved by dialectics and promoted a classless society. It was humanistic, in the sense that it required no clerical mediation between the individual and God. Indeed, the clerics were to be blamed for obscuring this true Shiism from the Iranian people. According to Shariati, Islam guaranteed individual liberties, including freedom of religion; it supported universal economic equality; and it could even be used to defend Darwin's theory of evolution.

It was not that all these ideas were compatible with Islam; rather, according to Shariati, they originated from Islam and from the lives of the Prophet and the twelve imams, beginning with Ali, whom Shiites recognize as his successors. To Shariati, collective memory was something malleable. To remember was an act not of excavation but of self-creation in the present tense.

Shariati's special genius was to deliver a modern, revolutionary creed to religious Iranians not as Western dogma but as their deepest birthright. And yet, to judge from an essay he called "My Idols," Shariati's formative influences were those he found in Paris. Among them were two French scholars of Islam, as well as the anticolonialist thinker Frantz Fanon and the existentialist philosopher Jean-Paul Sartre. Shariati had traveled far from his homeland in order to find it. His sources were French, but they served the purpose of solidifying, in his mind, the need for Iran to turn inward.

Shariati called for a return to an authentic Islam as an answer to modern problems. But the Islam he defined as authentic was not one any textual scholar had seen before. Rather, it was the outgrowth of modern experience and of European influence reconsidered—an alternative history Shariati had all but created and then claimed to have liberated from suppression. As the scholar Ali Mirsepassi has written, "Shariati's work was a type of revivalism: out of the dialogue he produced between Shiism and Western ideology, he 'revived' Islamic tendencies which perhaps never existed, but spoke to people's contemporary needs." Curiously, the Western ideologies that he brought into this dialogue were the two great atheistic doctrines of his day: Marxism and existentialism.

Shariati is alleged to have once admitted that if he were not a Muslim, he would have been a Marxist. And yet, for all its attractions, Marxism carried some European biases Shariati could not abide. First, it was not only irreligious but antireligious, a tendency Shariati found wholly at odds with the spiritual yearnings and convictions of his people. In the West, he noted, criticism of religion had led to freedom of thought and the growth of science. But in Islamic societies, religion was the last line of defense against imperial domination and cultural decay. Second, Shariati was still a nationalist. He did not want Iranians to dissolve their struggle into that of the international proletariat or, worse, to fuse their fate with that of the Soviet Union, which Shariati knew to be as exploitative and heartless a foreign empire as the capitalist West. So Shariati did not sign on to the international Marxist agenda. Instead, he borrowed from Marxism the ideas he liked best, and claimed them for an authentic Shiism, which he called the Shiism of Ali.

Existentialism, the fashionable creed of postwar France, made perhaps the stranger and more problematic bedfellow. But it resonated with the work of Iran's great philosopher of the sixteenth and seventeenth centuries, Mulla Sadra, who argued against Aristotle for the primacy of the concrete world over the categories and attributes accorded to it by human judgment. To the existentialists of postwar Europe, this metaphysical insight—that existence precedes essence, in the phrase they coined—became a moral one. The human will acted on a world divested of intrinsic meaning; individuals had the freedom and the responsibility to forge meaning by their choices and actions.

The idea of the emancipated individual was an intoxicating one. And yet, Shariati looked at secular, even nihilistic, postwar Europe and worried about where such ideas might lead. Shariati and other pre-revolutionary

Iranian thinkers abhorred the sterility of European modernity, with its lax public morality, heartless economics, and abandoned traditions. Iran had a different experience, different hungers. Like an older Europe, it was moored to its religion, morally and socially; but, unlike that Europe, it had witnessed all of post-Enlightenment European history, wrestled with its ideas and absorbed its innovations, looking upon some of its outcomes with envy and others with aversion.

In the end, Shariati envisioned a limited freedom for Iran. Although it was the religious duty of Iranians to cast off despotism, their liberated country, as Shariati envisioned it, would provide righteous guidance, which would allow Iranians to subordinate their will to the will of God. Shariati likened Iranian political subjects to children in need of kindergarten. He argued for a "directed democracy" led by a leader so perfect and so incontestable that he would embody and produce the utopian revolutionary society. Such a leader could not be constrained by the whims of an unenlightened public.

This view suggested Plato's *Republic*, with its designation of the philosopher king. Far more strikingly, it would resemble Ayatollah Ruhollah Khomeini's theory of the rule of the Islamic jurisconsult, or *velayat-e faqih*, which the elderly cleric elaborated a few years later in Najaf in the early 1970s.

WHEN SHARIATI RETURNED from Paris in 1964, he went to teach at the University of Mashhad. Many of his students came from the upper and upper-middle classes, which leaned to the left and took little interest in religion. Shariati made it his project to lure young minds to an Islam that he laid before them as a rival to the left and a purveyor of the students' most treasured ideals: social justice, reason, scientific progress, the refusal of despotism. At the same time, for young people from the traditional classes, burned by the condescension of the secular elites, Shariati supplied the stuff of empowerment. They were not backward practitioners of an outmoded faith: they were the revolutionary vanguard.

Shariati made enemies among the clergy. He did not believe that clerics were really needed to mediate between man and God. Islam should be open to multiple, competing interpretations, he insisted. When Jalal Al-e Ahmad visited Mashhad in 1969, he tried to persuade Shariati that intellectuals and the clergy needed to work together to defeat the shah. At a meeting during that visit, Al-e Ahmad extended his hand to the only cleric in the room—Ali Khamenei—as a gesture of that cooperation.

Shariati did forge a brief and fateful alliance with one clergyman. In Tehran, Iran's vibrant, sprawling twentieth-century capital, Ayatollah Morteza Motahhari had helped found an institution where modernist clerics—those who believed in a dynamic Islam that could be interpreted to meet contemporary needs—could gather, deliver lectures, and build a new community of believers. That institution officially opened its doors in 1967 as Hosseiniyeh Ershad, a marble-fronted complex in northern Tehran that included, under its graceful blue-tiled dome, a lecture hall, library, and ornately mosaic-covered mosque. Its founders purposely situated the Hosseiniyeh in Tehran's north so that it would be insulated from the conservative clerical establishment that clustered around the city's bazaar and its traditional southern quarters. The new thinkers who lectured at Hosseiniyeh Ershad meant to reach the city's secular elite, who tended to live in the north, and to draw them away from Marxism, toward Islamic modernism.

Ayatollah Motahhari and his inner circle, including a young cleric named Ali Akbar Hashemi Rafsanjani, delivered nearly all the institute's lectures until 1969, when Shariati, originally at Motahhari's invitation, came to Tehran to speak regularly at the Hosseiniyeh. Shariati would quickly overshadow Motahhari and Rafsanjani as Hosseiniyeh Ershad's main draw. As one observer later recalled, when Motahhari spoke, the lecture hall was often only half full; but for Shariati, the crowds spilled from the grand hall into "the staircases, the yard, and even the basement." Shariati's lectures were anticlerical and openly political; he spoke of cultivating a "revolutionary society." It was not long before Hosseiniyeh Ershad became known above all as the place to hear Shariati—and as a hotbed of revolutionary Islamism.

Motahhari was uneasy with this development. He worried that Shariati was using religion to political ends and putting Hosseiniyeh Ershad at risk. Along with Rafsanjani and the other clerics who had once made Hosseiniyeh Ershad their home, Motahhari left the institute. More conservative clerics began to call Hosseiniyeh Ershad a house of infidels and to question Shariati's piety. For Shariati was not merely a believer seeking answers in the texts; he was a prospector, extracting the meanings that served his purposes. He took great liberties with Islamic history and theology. And his purpose, it appeared more and more, was mobilization—indeed, the fashioning of Islam into a mobilizing ideology. More than once, Shariati bluntly explained that what Marx could not inspire Iranian peasants to do, Islam could.

As the intensity of opposition to the shah mounted, so did the intensity of Shariati's rhetoric. In the mid-1960s, Shariati had stopped short of preaching revolution. In 1965, Shariati said, "Our society is neither intellectually nor conceptually prepared for what should come after the shah. Rushing events could be disastrous." This was a view Shariati would espouse frequently, when he wasn't calling for its opposite—violent and immediate revolt. Was he dissembling, making a public show of quiescence for fear of SAVAK, the shah's brutal intelligence and security apparatus, while secretly nurturing his militancy? Perhaps this bipolarity was simply true to Shariati's intellect and character. He was too passionate to adopt a moderate view of anything, but too mercurial to cleave to his passion, and so he embraced opposites, sometimes successively, sometimes simultaneously.

Only in 1971 did Shariati take a decisive radical turn. That year, armed militants attacked a gendarmerie post in the village of Siahkal. The militants became popular heroes. The shah, awake now to the restiveness of the country, cracked down. Iran's already capacious prison system expanded seemingly overnight. The very year of Siahkal, a grim new prison complex sprang up on Tehran's northwestern outskirts. Run by SAVAK, Evin Prison would quickly earn a reputation surpassing Qasr, the notorious Tehran prison of the day, as the site of the monarchy's cruelest tortures and the country's new Bastille.

Now Shariati bent to the force he had helped unleash and began exhorting his crowds to rise against the state. He called the militants martyrs and said that "the martyr is the pulsing heart of history." By 1972, Hosseiniyeh Ershad had become a prime recruiting ground for a band of Islamic leftist guerrillas known as the Mojahedin-e Khalq. Shariati was neither the leader nor even a member of the Mojahedin, which had promoted armed revolt since the mid-1960s; but the underground group's ideology—leftist, Islamist, anticlerical, and given to violence and martyrdom—overlapped significantly with his, which made his work good propaganda and his followers easy recruits. SAVAK was displeased.

On November 10, 1972, Shariati gave a lecture about existentialism that would be his last at Hosseiniyeh Ershad. According to his biographer, Shariati knew that the police would raid the institute the following week; that there would be clashes between the students and the police; and that he and his associates would likely be arrested. And so this orator who once said, "Wage jihad and kill if you can, if you cannot, accept martyrdom and die," fled with his father to the north of Iran. On November 17, the police surrounded Hosseiniyeh Ershad while the students occupied the building in protest. They staged a prayer session in the unfinished mosque, chanted slogans well into the night, prayed, and wept.

For a year Shariati hid. SAVAK's men searched for him in vain. They did, however, find his books. They found them in the homes, the hands, the minds of Islamist militants everywhere they looked; they arrested people for the simple crime of their possession. Finally, they arrested Shariati's elderly, ailing father and kept him in prison as a hostage. If Shariati turned himself in, then—maybe—his father would be released. Shariati pondered this proposition for two and a half months. At last he surrendered, but his father was held for almost a year more.

Shariati was held for eighteen months without a trial. According to SAVAK sources cited in his biography, he wrote two tracts in prison at his captors' behest. One claimed that no similarity existed between Islam and Marxism—that the two creeds were in fact irreconcilable. Such was the monarchy's official line against the left and particularly against the Mojahedin; political prisoners in the early 1970s were forced to parrot that argument in public recantations. Shariati's other prison essay, "Return to Self," was a celebration of Iranian national greatness.

According to the SAVAK file, Shariati handwrote these essays in prison; intelligence agents typed them and gave them to *Kayhan*, the country's largest newspaper, for publication. But the authenticity of the SAVAK file is disputed, and Shariati's defenders are adamant that Shariati remained independent to the end and that he penned these works outside prison as a result of a genuine change of heart. Whatever the truth about the two tracts, after his release, Shariati followed them with "Return to Which Self?"—which sounded the same themes and called for the opposition to back away from revolutionary action. He left for England in May of 1977.

ABDOLKARIM SOROUSH WAS LIVING in London when he heard, through a mutual acquaintance, that Shariati was to be smuggled into the United Kingdom. Soroush was a lay theologian and a student of chemistry from a scrappy neighborhood in the south of Tehran. In London he attended meetings of the expatriate Iranian student opposition. The students discussed Shariati's books at these meetings as though they were textbooks at a study group.

Soroush admired Shariati, but he was also skeptical. There was a little too much Marx in Shariati, he thought. At the time, Soroush preferred Khomeini. But when he learned that Shariati was headed for Southampton, he relished the opportunity to exchange ideas with the great man face-to-face. He made an appointment to meet the celebrated orator in June of 1977.

Just before Soroush arrived in Southampton on June 20, Shariati was found dead of a heart attack in the doorway of his room. His daughters had arrived from Iran the night before. They were dressed in black, Soroush told an interviewer decades later, with their backs "pressed to the wall like frightened sparrows."

In photos taken throughout his life, Shariati was clean-shaven, with closely cropped hair under a slightly receding hairline and dark eyes at once sharp and brooding. He had a round face and a glint of humor in his gaze, a gleaming smile of even, white teeth. He nearly always wore a jacket and tie in the Western style. If the jacket had fit more closely, if the shirt had been more carefully pressed, Shariati could have been a banker rather than a charismatic revolutionary thinker and spiritual seeker. And so Soroush's description of Shariati's body is arresting: "He had long hair, down to his shoulders. I had never seen Shariati looking so imposing. He looked very serene."

Shariati died on the very eve of Iran's revolution, to which his ideas were indispensable. He embodied the anguish of his country at the fulcrum of its twentieth century, and he furnished a common point of origin for two generations of thinkers. They began in his thrall and ended in argument with him. They built their house to his design, and by the early 1990s they came to see it as a prison.

Among scholars, Shariati is variously described as a visionary and a charlatan, a revolutionary hero and a collaborator, a lyricist and a fabricator, even a plagiarist. But to many Iranians, Shariati is the little black fish who charted the course of freedom and cut the heron down from the sky. Much of his work survives in the form of lectures transcribed by his students, but he also wrote books, some of them works of mysticism, others peopled by a baffling array of fictive characters presented as real people— a scholar whose work he plumbed, but whom he had entirely invented; a lover who is not known to have existed.

Shariati was not yet forty-four when he died, but he was a heavy smoker and under considerable stress. Iranian revolutionaries would immediately and forever after claim that he was murdered by the shah's secret agents abroad, but no evidence exists to substantiate this notion. After an autopsy, his body was transported to London, where his associates were to perform burial rites before flying the body to Damascus for interment.

Islamic funerary rites are typically performed by close relatives of the same sex as the deceased, and Shariati had none around him in Britain. And so four young men from the revolutionary movement washed Shariati's body in the ritual fashion, wrapping it in the traditional white burial shroud. They were Ebrahim Yazdi, Sadegh Ghotbzadeh, Mohammad Mojtahed Shabestari, and the chemistry student who had come that day to see him, Abdolkarim Soroush.

Yazdi and Ghotbzadeh would go on to be important figures in the first postrevolutionary governments of Iran. Shabestari, a young cleric who led prayers at a mosque in Hamburg at the time of Shariati's death, would later become one of the leading clerical voices for religious reform in the 1990s.

As for Soroush, he would go on to become a lay theologian of far-reaching influence. Like Shariati, he would argue for a living Islam, flexible enough to accommodate contemporary ideas and concerns if not to become their vehicle. Like Shariati, too, Soroush would attract legions of young acolytes who sought to reconcile their anger at the Iranian state with their fealty to Islam. By the early 1990s, Soroush was Iran's leading lay theorist of Islamic reform—Shariati's heir apparent and one of his most potent posthumous critics.

TWO

ISLAMIC REPUBLIC

*So our city will be governed by us and you with
waking minds, and not as most cities now,
which are inhabited and ruled darkly as in a
dream by men who fight one another for
shadows and wrangle for office as if that were a
great good, when the truth is that the city in
which those who are to rule are least eager to
hold office must needs be best administered and
most free from dissension, and the state that gets
the contrary type of ruler will be the opposite
of this.*

By all means, he said.

—PLATO, *The Republic*

IN 1963, in the city of Shiraz, Alireza Haghighi was born between worlds.
His aristocratic mother had married a bazaar merchant who bled her of her
fortune and took another wife, leaving mother and son to a hardscrabble
life in the city's southern slums. There the neighbors were gruff, poor, and
devout. Alireza's mother grew remote in her piety. From her, Alireza learned
to read the Quran in Arabic, something none of his peers could do. She

tolerated no television, nor any other Western affectation. Alireza was a solitary child, and lonely but for the books he turned to for knowledge of humanity and of the world.

He was a hungry patron at the local library, where he checked out *The Count of Monte Cristo* and read it in one night, to the librarian's disbelief. After school he prayed at the neighborhood mosque, Masjed-e No. The mosque, too, had a library, and it was there that Alireza discovered Samad Behrangi. *The Little Black Fish* spoke to him of the isolation of poverty and the occlusion of wealth. He felt himself swimming in both the mountain stream and the open waters, his gaze constantly forced on the confusing disparity between his life and the lives of his rich, secular, cosmopolitan cousins, whose homes were as lavishly appointed as Alireza's was bare. He did not know it then, but he inhabited the very cleavage in Iranian society that would produce a revolution and its continuous aftershocks. He resolved to educate himself somehow. He had the intelligence and drive, and he had no father looming over him, pressing him into a family business or dictating the course of his education. He would compete with his cousins by the power of his mind.

In the south of Shiraz, there was no obvious haven for a restless intellect. But there was a shrine, in short walking distance from Alireza's home, and a mosque surrounded by trees. At Masjed-e No, Alireza escaped the rough manners and profane language of his neighborhood and entered into a sort of polite society, one that prized courtesy, helpfulness, sensitivity to suffering, and Islamic morality. The refinement of the clergy mirrored the refinement of his educated cousins, but within the moral boundaries of his mother's faith. For Alireza, the mosque was father and teacher, political conclave and spiritual home. In the waning decade of the shah's rule, the mosque crackled with talk of social justice, an end to tyranny and to the inequality it was Alireza's birthright to stare down.

He dreamed of becoming a clergyman. At fifteen he left high school to study at the nearest seminary. When the seminary's headmaster, Ayatollah Hashemi Dastgheib, talked to the students about the Quran, Alireza, his mind alight, would pepper the old cleric with questions. Why did the Quran say this? Why did it not say that? One night the ayatollah pulled Alireza aside. The seminary was not the right place for him, he explained. All the other students were from rural villages. Only Alireza was from Shiraz. It would be better for Alireza to return to his high school, earn his diploma, and then come back to study religion. From this conversation Alireza understood that his questions had been received as impertinence, that he had inadvertently undermined the authority of his elders and was being asked to leave.

Although his clerical ambitions dimmed, Islam remained one of Alireza's two great loves. The other was cinema, a forbidden fruit from the West, secreted away from him in movie houses from which his mother forbade him entry and which he could not in any case afford. One of his neighbors had fashioned a homemade zoetrope, through which he would feed reels of Hollywood films while Alireza peered into the lighted box with just one eye. Like this, Alireza became entranced with cinema. He tutored neighborhood children, helping them with their schoolwork in exchange for bouts of television or glimpses of American movies. Years later, when he saw *Cinema Paradiso*, the 1988 Italian film about a movie director's childhood obsession with cinema, Alireza felt it told the story of his life. Movies, he had determined as a boy, were a keyhole through which he could see the contents of other people's minds, the very grain of life and love in worlds far away.

Had he lived in Tehran, had he been five years older, Alireza might have spent long evenings under Shariati's spell at Hosseiniyeh Ershad. But it was 1977, near the time of Shariati's death, when his works and those of Ayatollah Ruhollah Khomeini began to circulate in Alireza's Shiraz. When Shariati died, Alireza was fourteen. He knew just enough to eagerly accept when a friend's brother, who was a university student, offered to take him to the memorial service and demonstration on campus marking the fortieth day after Shariati's death.

The events of that day would brand themselves on Alireza's memory, but not because of Shariati. When he arrived on campus, the friend's brother vanished almost instantly into the crowd, and a policeman stopped Alireza, still a slender boy, to demand his university ID. He thought quickly. He told the officer he was there to find his high school teacher, because he was looking for his grade. The officer struck him, and Alireza fell to the ground. Nobody came to his aid.

The police waved him to a spot behind a line of police cars and fire trucks near the Eram Garden, by the Faculty of Law. In that spot was another young man who had gotten into trouble. His name was Ahmad Meftahi. Some six months later, Meftahi would be murdered by the shah's police. After the revolution, Alireza's high school would be renamed for him. But that afternoon Meftahi and Alireza watched in silence as students spilled toward a dormitory where the memorial ceremony would be held. It was a place, a moment, heavy with tension, the anticipation of violence, the electricity of a cause deeply felt. And just then, in the road alongside Alireza, a young man pulled up in a Citroën.

"Mehri!" the man called. It was his girlfriend's name. "Mehri! Come here."

The young man saw Alireza and the outpouring of students, most of them in modest religious dress. "Why are all these people here?" he asked.

"For Shariati," said Alireza.

"Shariati?" said the young man. "Who is Shariati?"

Mehri had broken through the crowd and approached the window of the Citroën. The young man kissed her, a long kiss hello, something Alireza had never seen anyone do in public.

At fourteen, there was a lot he had never seen. He had never been to a party, apart from the weddings of his rich cousins. He knew little of youthful levity and still less of the cosmopolitan adolescent culture of his day, charged with adrenaline and sexuality and revolt. Between his poverty and his mosque, he had spent even his childhood in serious discussions, in books and prayer. And now, in the movie rolling in Alireza's mind, there at the Eram Garden was a brightly lit scene, a footloose young man and his girlfriend in a Citroën, and the somber boy by the side of the road, feeling in himself something monastic, the drive into politics as abstemious and serious as his lost calling to the clergy. Some people, he understood in that moment, came to a scene like this one at the University of Shiraz for politics. Some people came for life. For Alireza, politics would have to *be* life, his source of meaning, his intoxicant of choice. Otherwise a person would give up, would fall instead for the girl and the car and the afternoon sun. There might not even be a price to be paid.

That night the Islamic Revolution began in Shiraz. At Masjed-e No there was a ceremony for Shariati, and as the crowd departed, it sent up a chant: "Hail to Ayatollah Khomeini." It was the first invocation of the exiled cleric at an Iranian demonstration—the first, it would turn out, of a great many. There was no mention of the shah, only of Khomeini. When the police attacked the crowd, Alireza and Meftahi slipped away. The demonstrators surged toward Capri Cinema, the city's movie house, shattering its plate glass window with rocks.

To many of the demonstrators, the cinema was a symbol of licentiousness, Westoxication, and corruption. To Alireza it was the location of a 70-millimeter film festival he'd planned to attend the next day. Capri had already shown *Ryan's Daughter* and *Ben-Hur*; Alireza wanted to see *Spartacus*. When he arrived that morning, there was a line for tickets, but the posters of John Wayne and Barbra Streisand that had long graced the cinema windows now winked through broken glass. The moviegoers asked the owner what had happened.

He could have said, "An Islamic revolution has begun." In just a month or two, the demonstrations would spread to Tehran, and in the years of revolutionary and postrevolutionary violence to follow, some 195 of Iran's 525 movie houses would be demolished. But that morning in northern Shiraz, none of this was even thinkable. The cinema owner ventured a guess: "Some drunks must have gotten into a fight."

OF ALL IRAN'S REVOLUTIONARY THINKERS, Ayatollah Ruhollah Khomeini was the least ambivalent. He wrote and thought with a vigorous clarity, the lines of his logic clean and straight. He had the discipline of a philosopher, the certitude of a man of the cloth, the soul of a mystic, and an ambition whose patience and magnitude would one day astound the world. With his deep-set eyes and chiseled features, Khomeini was a man with a commanding physical presence. From beneath his great black eyebrows— he had a habit of arching only one of them—his gaze beamed a cold, dignified intelligence that seemed to encompass things unseen.

Khomeini was born near the dawn of the twentieth century, and he lost his father, a provincial cleric, when he was only five months old. His mother and then his brother raised him. As a teenager, Khomeini helped build bunkers for World War I and learned to fire a rifle. He entered the seminary at seventeen. By the time he was thirty-four he had completed his advanced clerical studies and begun publishing treatises on everything from poetry to politics, jurisprudence to mysticism. Like Shariati, Khomeini was inflamed by the situation in which he found his country, and he saw his religion as a source of resistance and power.

Shiism, the world's second-largest Islamic sect, emerged in the seventh century as the creed of those who believed that the rightful leader of the Muslims was the Prophet Mohammad's first cousin, Ali, and after him, the line of his descendants. The Prophet had twelve such successors, whom the Shia called imams, each of them infallible and endowed with divine wisdom. But worldly adversity and tragedy diverted the imams from their rightful paths, as the Muslim community was not united in accepting their divine leadership. The twelfth imam went into occultation, meaning that his presence on earth would be revealed only at God's appointed hour.

Shiism was the most hierarchical branch of Islam, often likened to the Catholic Church. Shiite clerics were ranked in their prestige, from the *mojtahed* fresh out of the seminary to the grand ayatollah, who had not only achieved the most distinguished level of scholarship but who had answered the call of his students and followers to publish a compendium of his fatwas on a broad range of practical matters. Ordinary Muslims could select from among these grand ayatollahs a *marja al-taqlid*, or source of imitation, whose religious injunctions he pledged to follow. Ruhollah Khomeini became a *marja* in 1963, the same year he catapulted to political prominence as an opponent of the monarchy.

In a 1944 book called *Revelation of Secrets*, Khomeini argued that the only legitimate government was an Islamic one guided by the clergy. That year he called for clerics and their followers to rise as militants. The shah, Khomeini believed, had sold his country to foreigners, who would not only pillage its resources but corrupt its very soul. For unlike Shariati and the religious modernists, Khomeini did not have mixed feelings about Western cultural influence: rather, he was averse to it. In 1963 the shah unveiled a reform package that included female suffrage and permission for non-Muslims to hold public office. These two measures, Khomeini protested, were against Islam. In fact, they were a cover to allow Bahais, members of a post-Islamic religious minority, to infiltrate the government and ensure its fealty to Israel. What the shah called the White Revolution, Khomeini viewed as American reforms.

Although the White Revolution was probably not evidence of it, the shah's subservience to the United States was hardly subtle. The Iranian monarch had become obsessed with building his military, whose equipment and advice all came from the United States. A growing community of American businesspeople, particularly from the defense industry, took up residence in Iran. In 1964, as part of a deal with Washington, Iran's parliament passed a bill that made American military personnel and their families living in Iran immune from criminal prosecution. Khomeini thundered:

> If some American's servant, some American's cook, assassinates your marja in the middle of the bazaar, or runs over him, the Iranian police do not have the right to apprehend him! Iranian courts do not have the right to judge him! The dossier must be sent to America, so that our masters there can decide what is to be done! . . . Let the American President know that in the eyes of the Iranian people, he is the most repulsive member of the human race today because of the injustice he has imposed on

our Muslim nation. Today the Quran has become his enemy, the
Iranian nation has become his enemy. Let the American government know that its name has been ruined and disgraced in Iran.

The shah had Khomeini arrested and put down the ensuing protests
with bullets, leaving as many as four hundred dead and sending Khomeini
into exile in neighboring Iraq. But the ayatollah's words had resonated
deeply with an offended public, and his rough treatment at the shah's hands
only burnished his prestige.

During his years of exile, Khomeini elaborated his political vision,
which he had first intimated decades earlier. God could not have meant for
Muslims to live in darkness during the occultation of the twelfth imam.
But all the world's regimes, Khomeini noted as early as 1941, had been
established by force of arms. They had no claim to legitimacy or justice.
Only a government of God could possess those virtues. In the absence of
divine rule, one had only to look around, "from the streetsweeper to the
highest official," to see the prevalence of "disordered thoughts . . . self-
interest, lechery, immodesty, criminality, treachery, and thousands of associated vices." Such, one might think, was the human condition. But
Khomeini believed that man was capable of higher states. He believed it
first as a mystic, committed to a spiritual path to personal perfection, and
then as a matter of politics. A just and divine government, under clerical
guidance, would elevate its subjects and deliver them from the disorder
and darkness to which they were prone.

A series of lectures Khomeini gave in Najaf, Iraq, and published in 1974
became his treatise on the subject, called *Islamic Government*. In it Khomeini argued for a state that would have neither a constitution nor legislation beyond the revealed word of God. In the absence of the twelfth
imam, the duty of guiding such a nation must fall to its most esteemed
Islamic scholar, or *faqih*, who would be uniquely qualified to interpret the
divine texts.

Khomeini wrote: "The governance of the *faqih* is a rational and extrin-
sic matter; it exists only as a type of appointment, like the appointment of

a guardian for a minor. With respect to duty and position, there is indeed no difference between the guardian of a nation and the guardian of a minor." Khomeini's view of the people as infantile and incapable of judgment dovetailed with Shariati's rationale for "directed democracy" and with Plato's for the philosopher king of his *Republic*, who would rule in his wisdom over citizens as benighted as cave dwellers. The Platonic elements were not accidental. Few places on earth have preserved the ideas of the ancient Greek philosophers with more reverence than the Shiite seminaries of the Middle East, where Aristotle and Plato have exerted a far-reaching influence on Islamic scholarship.

During the very years Khomeini spent painstakingly setting forth this vision, he attracted an enormous following among young Iranians who hardly acknowledged it. What they thrilled to was Khomeini's assertion of a proud and defiant national identity and an indomitable will to resist tyranny. His letters and declarations, written in a more vernacular language than *Islamic Government* and distributed more widely, carried these messages. They recalled the man who had stood up to the shah in 1964. They inveighed against the two empires, in the East and in the West, that had conspired to inflict the state of Israel on the Muslim world as its oppressor. The Universal Declaration of Human Rights was a deception—"the opium of the masses," Khomeini pointedly wrote—its signatories concerned exclusively with the rights of superpowers. Only Islam would protect the rights of Muslims. Khomeini was cruder and more direct than Shariati, but his identity politics struck familiar chords. That could hardly have been accidental. For Shariati, far more than the clergy, had rallied Iran's youth away from the secular left in favor of Islam. While most clerics denounced Shariati for his anticlericalism, Khomeini shrewdly said nothing and opened his arms to Shariati's followers. Political Islam gathered like a perfect storm.

Demonstrations like the one Alireza witnessed in Shiraz broke out across the country. The more brutal the shah's response, the more determined the protesters became, until the shah declared martial law in the fall of 1978 and rolled tanks through city streets. The country was slipping from the monarch's hands. Iraq, no longer able to shelter the man at the center of the maelstrom next door, pushed Khomeini to emigrate. When the Kuwaitis refused him entry, the ayatollah resettled in France.

Khomeini abided patiently, outspokenly, in a white stucco house in a town called Neauphle-le-Château, where he dispensed wisdom beneath an apple tree during the last months of the shah's reign. He expressed no desire, then, for direct clerical rule. The clerics would offer "supervision" behind the scenes, but the executive affairs of state were best left to technocrats. The liberal nationalist circle that had once surrounded Mossadegh coalesced around Khomeini now. The Freedom Movement of Iran, a long-standing group of nationalist Islamic liberals headed by an engineer named Mehdi Bazargan, practically became the ayatollah's entourage. These nationalists held no brief for *velayat-e faqih*. Their presence in the ayatollah's inner circle suggested that Khomeini was willing to accommodate the revolutionary movement's complexity, and that those who did not favor clerical rule had nothing to fear from placing Khomeini at the movement's center. The nationalists, in turn, worked tirelessly on Khomeini's behalf, assuring the shah's Western allies that the coming transition would be liberal and democratic should they let the shah go. The nationalists even forged a relationship with the American embassy in Tehran and acted as intermediaries among Khomeini, the Americans, and the shah's army, which had to be persuaded to stand down.

THE REVOLUTIONARIES HAD ATTACKED one of the things Alireza loved most—cinema—in the name of the other thing he loved most—religion. It was a scene that stayed with him for decades to come, but it did not anger him or alienate him or tear him apart. Alireza was moderate by temperament, and political to the core of his being. What he thought was that attacking the cinema was an ill-chosen tactic, that it would have a negative effect on the feelings of the people, but that, while he would not join in it, he was powerless to stop it. Together with the throwers of those rocks, he attended demonstrations every day against the shah, mesmerized by the pulse of history come alive—history that he absorbed from the air and exhaled into the burgeoning crowds. He became a character in one of the European novels he'd read and loved: Ignazio Silone's *Bread and Wine*, about Italian peasants resisting fascism in the name of both religion and the left. In Shiraz, the pavement and the walls and the cypress trees throbbed with meaning.

Still, Alireza stood apart from himself. He was as much a creature of history, he mused, as its agent. If he'd been born in Israel, maybe he would be an Orthodox Jew. Ideas, he suspected, chose their bearers as much as their bearers chose them. Because he could think this thought, he decided, he would seek to understand the views of Iranians unlike himself, and to choose from among their creeds the one that most truly captured his revolution. He went to meetings of half a dozen communist groups. His rich, secular relatives belonged to these groups; some were Stalinists, others Trotskyists or Maoists. For the first time Alireza found himself at the center of a competition among his cousins, each of whom wanted credit for recruiting their poor relation from the south of Shiraz to his or her particular leftist cause.

Alireza enrolled in a Marxist indoctrination seminar at the university. He read Marx alongside his religious texts and searched for inconsistencies. After a while the exasperated seminar leader told him there would be no more time for his questions in class, and he could bring them only afterward. The atmosphere was much the same at the meetings of the Mojahedin-e Khalq youth organization, which Alireza attended in the mornings, also as part of his effort to open his mind to all the revolutionary strains. The Mojahedin was the Islamic leftist guerrilla group that recruited from among Shariati's followers at Hosseiniyeh Ershad, but by the time of the revolution it had coalesced around a charismatic leader named Massoud Rajavi. His were the only books to be read or discussed at the meetings. Alireza stopped attending.

The only place where Alireza felt at home was at meetings of a splinter group of Shariati's followers, an organization composed mainly of self-styled intellectuals who adhered to Shariati's vision of a militant Shiism committed to social justice. Egalitarian and radical, this group took so seriously Shariati's claim that clerical intercession was unnecessary for true believers that it did not embrace *velayat-e faqih*. Divine wisdom, its thinkers argued, was accessible to all educated people.

In Shariati's Shiism of Ali, Alireza thought he had found an answer to the authoritarianism and intolerance he'd encountered both among leftists and in the seminary. But in the long run his membership in this group of Shariati's followers, though brief, was a bad bet for Alireza. It made him an outsider when the mainstream of revolutionary Islamism emerged victorious in 1979 and consolidated power in Khomeini's hands through a series of bloody upheavals in the decade that followed. And although Alireza escaped the fate of the group's leadership and most of its followers, who were imprisoned or executed throughout the turbulent 1980s, his involvement would forever strike a black mark against him, rendering him effectively alone even when he worked inside the government. It was a government, a system, a country organized around informal networks of membership and ideological affinity. There was nothing more precarious than failing to belong.

In the heady days of the revolution, however, Alireza was in his element. For the first time in his sober youth, the hottest social commodity was intellect, and particularly knowledge of the two competing discourses of the day, Marxism and Islamism. The handsomest man Alireza knew was his friend Bahram. Before the revolution, when Alireza walked down the street with Bahram, young women found excuses to approach his dashing friend. But Bahram was not an intellectual or a militant of any stripe, and after the revolution the girls gravitated instead toward activists and theorists, revolutionaries and scholars. Bahram implored Alireza to help him win back the young ladies who had deserted him. They staged conversations for the ears of pretty Marxist girls. Bahram would opine about Marxism, and Alireza, whose intellectualism and political commitment were known, would pretend to be impressed. Bahram found two or three girlfriends this way. But what Alireza would remember in the years to come was that, in the narrow circle of his life in those days, Bahram was the revolution's earliest critic. Ideology, Bahram complained, had made people

hostile. It distorted the most basic human relationships. Handsome Bahram couldn't find a girlfriend, and everywhere people hated each other for
ideology, which meant they hated each other without knowing why.

THE REVOLUTION THAT HAD BEEN so long in coming unfolded blind-
ingly fast. Martial law availed the shah nothing. A general strike paralyzed
the country. Riots broke out. The shah bobbed and weaved. He appointed
a conciliatory prime minister; replaced him with a general; and replaced
the general with a prime minister meant to bridge the country's now inevitable transition. The shah left Iran on January 16. The rapturous, eighty-
four-point-type newspaper headline entered history: *"Shah Raft."* The shah
has left. Iranians danced in the streets. On February 1, Ayatollah Khomeini, at that moment the undisputed leader and symbol of the revolution,
touched down at Tehran's Mehrabad Airport. *"Imam Amad,"* the newspapers reported: The imam has come.

With him, to the euphoric and riotous country that welcomed him as its
savior, Khomeini brought the virtue and the menace of his clarity. Iran may
have been an ambivalent country, wracked by impulses at war with themselves and one another. But Khomeini was nothing if not consistent. "The
government I intend to appoint is a government based on divine ordinance,
and to oppose it is to deny God as well as the will of the people," he
informed the nation on February 2, 1979. He disowned all revolutionary
forces but his own. "Those who imagine that some force other than Islam
could shatter the great barrier of tyranny are mistaken," he intoned in June.
"You who have chosen a course other than Islam—you do nothing for
humanity."

In France, Khomeini had already appointed a small and secretive revolutionary council to run the affairs of state until a government could be established. The council included a circle of hardheaded and ambitious clerics
loyal to Khomeini and committed to the notion of *velayat-e faqih.* These figures included Ayatollah Mohammad Beheshti and the mid-ranking clerics
Ali Khamenei and Ali Akbar Hashemi Rafsanjani. Within a week of the

revolution, together with other members of the council, they formed a political party called the Islamic Republican Party. It was a juggernaut.

The Islamic Republican Party controlled the mosques, the state broadcasting agency, and other media organs. It could depend on not only Khomeini's personal charisma, which was incalculable in 1979, but an impressive array of coercive instruments. Suspicious of the loyalties of the shah's army, Khomeini had ordered the creation of a paramilitary force that would protect him and the Revolutionary Council. It was called the Revolutionary Guard Corps. The Islamic Republican Party also possessed its own network of club-wielding thugs, known as Hezbollah, to harass its opponents. Ayatollah Beheshti helmed the country's powerful new Islamic judiciary, and clerics close to him headed revolutionary tribunals all over the country, ordering the summary executions of "counterrevolutionaries": officials from the old regime, Kurdish separatists, political opponents, and other undesirables. In the first twenty-eight months of the Islamic Republic, without recourse to evidence or legal argument, these tribunals would execute 757 people for "sowing corruption on earth." This was more than seven times the number of political prisoners executed in the last eight years of the shah's regime—and it was only the beginning.

Khomeini and the radical clerics behaved as though the revolution belonged to them alone, but surely they knew that their position was not as secure as they pretended. Among the Iranians who had brought the shah's regime to its knees with demonstrations and general strikes were secular leftists, nationalists, liberals, and Islamic leftists who did not believe the clerics should rule. The nationalist Islamic liberals who had surrounded Khomeini in Paris were perhaps the weakest of these groups, the least likely to seriously challenge the clerics in a power struggle. But they were also the most useful in assuaging the anxieties of former Western allies. And so Khomeini felt secure in naming Mehdi Bazargan, a moderate nationalist intellectual, prime minister of a provisional government in early 1979. Many of the radical clerics were uncomfortable with this choice. They feared that Bazargan would be the Trojan horse through which American power and influence would reenter revolutionary Iran.

Bazargan was a visitation from another era, a mild septuagenarian whose time had either already elapsed or not yet come. He wore thick-rimmed, square-lensed glasses and a visible tension in the set of his jaw. He was an engineer, a contemporary of Shariati's father and a former official of the Mossadegh government, which had appointed him to head the briefly nationalized oil industry. Back then he had criticized Mossadegh's nationalists for their irreligiosity. To effectively oppose the shah, he argued, required the participation of the clergy and the traditional classes, and so he started the Freedom Movement, an opposition party that wedded nationalism and liberalism to Islam.

He was a democrat. From the seven years he spent in Paris, Bazargan had drawn the conclusion that religion thrived in secularly administered, scientifically advanced societies, and he believed that popular sovereignty, not coercion, would in time lead to a state in conformity with Islamic values. But he sustained a pragmatic alliance with the clerics. When Khomeini and other clerics opposed women's suffrage in the early 1960s, Bazargan is thought to have privately disagreed, but he chose to take a politic, rather than moral, stand: in a country where no one's vote counted for much, his Freedom Movement declared, suffrage was meaningless, for those who had it as well as those who did not.

Still, unlike many of the radicals of his day, religious and otherwise, he defended freedom of speech, the rights of minorities, and private property; he did not much care for the language of Third World revolutionary movements, with their emphasis on colonialism and exploitation, terms he found divisive and too easily wedded to Soviet ambitions. He was a technocrat. At the University of Tehran he told a crowd, "Don't expect me to act in the manner of [Khomeini] who . . . moves like a bulldozer, crushing rocks, roots, and stones in his path. I am a delicate passenger car and must ride on paved and smooth roads, and you must smooth them for me."

There were no smooth roads in revolutionary Iran. Nor was Bazargan any match for the popular utopian ferment or the machinations of the Revolutionary Council. It would be more than three decades, well after his death, before the Islamic Republic's first prime minister found a constituency.

During his premiership, he confronted a country where many citizens were armed, but the security forces had ceased to function. The Revolutionary Council took control of these impromptu militias, called them *komiteh*s, and marshaled them to its agenda of Islamization—an agenda Bazargan did not share, and on which he was never consulted. The *komiteh*s policed the populace for improper Islamic dress, Western music, pictures of uncovered women, and forbidden interactions between the sexes, among other moral infractions. Khomeini defended their work, arguing that an Islamic state had a duty to intrude on private life for the betterment of its subjects.

Iran had two governments: the legal one Bazargan headed, and an extralegal network of grassroots revolutionary committees, militias, and clerical tribunals backed by firing squads, all of which were loyal to Khomeini and the Islamic Republican Party. Bazargan's government tried and failed to secure command of the Revolutionary Guards, tried and failed to bring the revolutionary tribunals under the supervision of the ministry of justice. As Bazargan told the Italian journalist Oriana Fallaci, "In theory, the government is in charge, but in reality, it is Khomeini who is in charge. He with his revolutionary council, his revolutionary committees, and his relationship with the masses."

In Plato's utopian Republic, the philosopher would be king not only because he was wise, but because he was unwilling. The luminosity of his intellect was a condition to which he was born; it, and not ambition, would impel him to serve his countrymen, even against his natural inclination to withdraw into scholarly seclusion. In Khomeini's Islamic Republic, however, the radical clerics ruled "darkly as in a dream, fighting for shadows and wrangling for office." The most important and politically difficult task they faced was to lay an enduring foundation for their own rule, and so the battle over the revolutionary state's constitution reached a pitch for which Bazargan was hardly prepared.

Not two months after the overthrow of the shah, on March 22, 1979, Iranians had been presented with a public referendum: Would the future state be an Islamic Republic, or not? No definition was provided; no alternative presented. "Yes" carried the day by 98 percent. But what was an

Islamic Republic? Who would decide? In June, Bazargan and his allies set forward a draft constitution that was liberal and largely secular, based on the constitution of France's Fifth Republic. The draft was to be reviewed and ratified by an assembly of experts on Islamic law. Elections to this assembly were rife with irregularities, including violent attacks on opponents of *velayat-e faqih*. With Ayatollah Hossein Ali Montazeri as its chair and Beheshti as his deputy, the assembly was packed with members of the Islamic Republican Party or sister parties. They wrested the constitution from the prime minister's hands and rewrote it, adding elements derived from Khomeini's theory of the state. The result was an innovative and profoundly contradictory document whose internal tensions would define the country's future.

Most governments derive their legitimacy from a single source. Iran's would rest on two: popular sovereignty on the one hand, and the sovereignty of God on the other. Like most compromises, this one frustrated both sides. Iran would become, to a degree Khomeini had never envisioned, a republic. It would have an elected president and a parliament that could pass legislation. Far more than under the shah, it would require its people's participation and assent. But at the same time, a cleric would supervise the country as its Supreme Leader and the vice-regent of God on earth. The Leader would command the armed forces. He would control the instruments of internal security and foreign policy. He would appoint the chief of the judiciary as well as a Guardian Council, made up mainly of clerics. The laws passed by the parliament, and the candidates for the parliament, would be subject to the approval of this Guardian Council, which would function as an arm of the Leader.

Bazargan appealed to Khomeini in protest. The proposed constitution, he objected, would subject the country to a ruling class of clerics and poison future generations against Islam. But Khomeini did not respond.

"Now the Constitution makes some provision for the principle of the governance of the *faqih*," Khomeini would tell an interviewer three months later. "In my opinion, it is deficient in this regard. The religious scholars have more prerogatives in Islam than are specified in the Constitution, and the [clerics] . . . stopped short of the ideal in their desire not to antagonize the intellectuals!"

ON THE OTHER SIDE OF THE WORLD, Shah Mohammad Reza Pahlavi had become a desperate fugitive. He passed through Egypt, Morocco, the Bahamas, and Mexico, everywhere fearful of assassins from the new regime and stalked by an even more proximate concern for his safety: a lymphatic cancer the shah had discovered five years earlier and kept secret not only from the Iranian people but from his own family. His aides reached out to American intermediaries in September 1979, when his condition took a critical turn.

The United States admitted the shah for medical treatment on October 23, 1979. It did so over the objections of the top man at its Tehran embassy, who warned that admitting the shah would be "seriously prejudicial to our interests and to the security of Americans in Iran," unless the shah first renounced any claim to the Persian throne. But others close to the White House insisted that Washington owed a debt to the deposed king; the man was gravely ill, and hardly a country in the world would take him.

There were reasons for that. Khomeini wanted the shah extradited to Iran to stand trial for crimes against his people. But even more than they wanted to see him face the firing squad, many Iranian revolutionaries simply didn't want the shah in the United States. They feared a reprisal of the 1953 coup: perhaps the shah had gone to his North American ally not for medical care but to regroup with his CIA sponsors and plan his return to the throne.

On November 4, 1979, some four hundred revolutionary students breached the walls of the gigantic American embassy compound in central Tehran. The students, under the direction of a group calling itself Students Following the Imam's Line, stormed the embassy and took some fifty-one Americans hostage. Their demand was that the United States extradite the shah.

Khomeini had not ordered the embassy seizure; by all accounts it took him by surprise. But over Bazargan's objections, the ayatollah gave the students his blessing. The Islamic Republican Party folded the hostage takers into its apparatus, ensuring their political prominence for decades to come.

As much as the seizure of the American embassy would set the course of the Islamic Republic's foreign policy, it was also a brutal gambit in Iran's domestic politics. The radical clerics were through with Bazargan. To force him out, they had only to turn up the political temperature past the point that was tolerable for a man of his temperament. The hostage taking accomplished this. It also allowed the Islamists to seize the anti-imperialist ground from under the secular left, spectacularly outflanking Iran's opposition of longest standing.

Bazargan had favored cordial relations with the United States. He and members of his government had maintained contact with the American diplomats in what they considered the ordinary course of their duties. Now their foreign policy was finished and they had lost control of the domestic situation entirely. Bazargan tendered his resignation. In his final televised address, Bazargan shared with the public his fear that in the future, the sovereignty of the Iranian people might be supplanted by the rule of the clergy.

A month later, the new constitution, complete with *velayat-e faqih*, was ratified by a popular referendum in which fewer than 16 million Iranians voted. Khomeini publicly averred that he would exercise his vast authority only rarely, and only to prevent deviation from Islam. In actuality, the decade that followed would consolidate one of the more unaccountable and autocratic regimes of its time.

THE ISLAMIC REPUBLIC OF IRAN held its first presidential election in 1980. Ayatollah Khomeini cast his weight behind an independent candidate, Abolhassan Bani-Sadr, a self-styled radical Islamic economist with a Groucho Marx mustache. Bani-Sadr had assisted Khomeini in France and then served on the Revolutionary Council. He won in a landslide, for lack of any convincing opposition.

The new president was not the high-minded liberal Bazargan had been.

He was a man of his extreme times, determined to stand up to his political enemies whatever it took. His brazen self-confidence almost immediately rankled the clerics of the Islamic Republican Party. "The president should be in charge," Bani-Sadr declared, and he spoke of "the final defeat" of the clergy, the dissolution of the *komiteh*s, and the elimination of competing power centers.

Ayatollah Beheshti and the Islamic Republican Party were determined to stymie Bani-Sadr and to convince Khomeini that the elected president was an enemy of the state. The president's antagonists declared Bani-Sadr power-mad, "egocentric," and an "enemy of the clergy." They called him "Bazargan with a different face," grumbled about incipient liberalism, and admonished the new president to go "along with the revolution." They used their parliamentary majority to isolate Bani-Sadr within his own cabinet, appointing nearly all the ministers from their party's own ranks and forcing the president to take a prime minister who locked him in constant battle.

As if Bani-Sadr didn't have enough problems, on September 22, 1980, Iraq invaded Iran. The two countries had irritated each other for some time with provocations and minor conflicts. But now Saddam Hussein decided to take advantage of Iran's isolation and revolutionary upheaval in his quest for control of the Shatt al-Arab waterway. This was no minor border skirmish. The Iraqi dictator sent twenty-two divisions into Iranian territory in one of the biggest military operations since World War II.

There was no international outcry. American officials would later recall greeting the outbreak of the Iran-Iraq War with something close to schaden-freude. Iraq was a Soviet client and Iran was all but at war with the United States, so long as it held American diplomats hostage. The embassy seizure had placed the Islamic Republic beyond the pale of international concern. But Iran's revolutionaries understood the global silence differently. If they had always suspected that the international order was stacked against them, now they knew it.

War did not unite Iran's political factions so much as it further divided them. Bani-Sadr argued that the students should release the American hostages so that Iran could buy spare military parts from the West. He called for an end to the ideological purges in the army, which needed its commanders more than ever. But to Bani-Sadr's great frustration, the hostage crisis dragged on and the military purges continued.

Bizarrely, by the lights of most constitutions, Iran's president became the outspoken leader of its opposition. He rallied liberals and parts of the left to his side, along with the Mojahedin-e Khalq, whose ranks were swelling with young people, many of them teenagers. Bani-Sadr used his newspaper to decry the revolutionary regime's violence—its reliance on torture, censorship, assassination plots, and more. "This is not a republic of which I am proud to be president," he concluded. He even asked Khomeini to assure him that if anything should happen to him, his wife and children would not be hurt. Khomeini did not respond directly. But in time he cautioned the president that he should distance himself from the Mojahedin.

The Mojahedin were the best leverage Bani-Sadr had, and he was not willing to give them up. Starting in February 1981, demonstrators clashed in the streets, with hezbollahis, as pro-regime militants were often called, armed with clubs, knives, and pistols arrayed against the Mojahedin and other supporters of the president. When Khomeini appointed a commission to settle the matter, it was stacked against the president and stripped Bani-Sadr of his remaining authority. The clerics shut down Bani-Sadr's newspaper, arrested his aides, forbade him to give interviews to the foreign press, and finally, in June, removed him from the presidency with a parliamentary vote of no confidence.

"I am very sorry," Khomeini said when the warrant was issued for Bani-Sadr's arrest. "I tried to avoid . . . such a dismissal." But "there were [foreign] hands at work and wolves among these people who did not allow us to avoid what we had intended to avoid."

The Islamic Republic's first elected president became a fugitive inside Iran, his whereabouts unknown. The prime minister who had been Bani-Sadr's adversary now governed. The revolution, the clerics told the public, had been won in order to build an Islamic state that was neither liberal nor democratic. Bani-Sadr, meanwhile, signed a covenant with the Mojahedin, pledging to overthrow the government and replace it with a "democratic Islamic Republic."

Iran erupted in something very like a civil war. The Mojahedin and allied leftists fought the Revolutionary Guards behind barricades made from burning buses, tires, trees, and barrels, holding out up to eight hours at a stretch. These were not the genteel liberals of Bazargan's cadre; they included revolutionary street toughs, bomb makers, and assassins.

On June 27, 1981, a bomb planted in a tape recorder exploded at a crowded southern Tehran mosque where Ali Khamenei was speaking, permanently injuring his right arm and damaging his voice through wounds to his neck and throat. "Thank God the enemies of Islam are made up of idiots," Khomeini said by way of consolation. "They drive the people to stronger unity with whatever schemes and intrigues they hatch." Another bomb exploded in a Tehran square and a third, found on a city street, was defused.

But the most spectacular attacks came the next day, on June 28, when the Islamic Republican Party convened for its weekly meeting. Two bombs, never claimed by any of the opposition groups, exploded in the party headquarters, one in a garbage can near a podium where Ayatollah Beheshti was speaking, and the other in the audience. The explosion brought the two-story building to the ground, twisting the steel beams of the roof and killing at least seventy officials and functionaries, including Beheshti himself. Two months later, on August 30, a bomb ripped through the office of the prime minister during a meeting of the defense council, killing the prime minister and four others.

For the clerics, who had also recently put down a coup attempt from inside the armed forces, coexistence was definitively impossible. Bani-Sadr and the Mojahedin had to be eliminated from the political scene, and to do it the Islamic Republican Party unleashed a campaign of terror. Days after the blast that killed the prime minister, the judiciary authorized mass arrests and began executing oppositionists by firing squad. Firefights between the Mojahedin and the Revolutionary Guards intensified, particularly in the south of Tehran. Bani-Sadr and the leadership of the Mojahedin escaped to France, but altogether an estimated 2,665 of their followers—Mojahedin, Kurdish nationalists, leftists, and nationalists—were executed between June and November 1981. The deaths, declared the chief prosecutor, "are not merely permissible; they are necessary."

ALIREZA HAGHIGHI WAS A SURVIVOR. One after another in those years, the young men he knew seemed to vanish. Some were executed, others killed in battle. He had a friend who was a brilliant physics student. After the revolution, this friend joined the Revolutionary Guard. A former SAVAK officer was brought in to educate his unit; outraged, Alireza's friend left the Revolutionary Guard and joined the Mojahedin in search of a truer radicalism. He was killed in the turmoil surrounding Bani-Sadr. This young scientist had been used, Alireza felt, and disposed of. None of the armed factions cared about his education, his talents, his future promise.

Alireza was only sixteen when the revolution came. He intended for university to catapult him out of southern Shiraz, through his activist milieu, and into the center of the new mainstream. But the year he earned his high school diploma, there were no universities to enter. Starting in 1980, at Khomeini's behest, hezbollahis seized the university campuses to purge the faculties and student bodies and Islamize the curricula. The universities were closed for three years. Along with his entire cohort, Alireza found himself at loose ends. He might have studied abroad, but his mother could not afford it. He might have volunteered for the war, but his father beat him to it and asked Alireza instead to mind his shop while he was at the front.

And so Alireza disappeared into the Shiraz bazaar. Over his father's objections, he set up a desk in the shop and stocked it with books. Between customers, he read. The war was transforming Shiraz in ways Alireza did not approve of. Young men from Abadan, an oil-producing border city besieged in 1980, poured into Shiraz looking for girls, even while Iraqis occupied their homes. Alireza suspected that they cared little about the war. One knew a true revolutionary, he theorized, by his choices. Revolution was like love: between love and self-interest, the true lover chose love. But the young men who took war and revolution as seriously as Alireza did were mainly hezbollahis, foot soldiers of *velayat-e faqih*. From them, too, Alireza felt distant. He still belonged to the group of intellectuals inspired by Shariati. It was a radical group, both Islamist and egalitarian, but it was occupied mainly with producing newspapers, a voluminous literature penned by an industrious few.

Alireza had not vested himself in history only to pass his youth in the Shiraz bazaar. In 1979, Khomeini ordered the creation of a vast volunteer militia, called the Basij, to be made up of men above and below the age of conscription, as well as of women. Alireza was still seventeen in 1980, a year younger than draft age for the regular army, and so he reported to a training camp for the Basij. The instruction was part physical, part ideological. The war with Iraq, Alireza believed, transcended the factional politics that divided him from the Hezbollahis who populated the Basij. But those running the training camp saw things differently. One recognized Alireza and accused him of infiltrating the Basij only to spy on it. Alireza was expelled.

He joined the navy. To enter the military during wartime allowed him an honorable discharge from that other war—the one among political adversaries who saw their young followers as cannon fodder. From the navy base, politics unfolded vaguely and afar. Alireza and the other enlisted men could not go into the city or mix with civilians, and they read only the official newspapers. Later he would imagine that if he had not been on that base in 1981, he might have been arrested or worse. Instead, he shipped out to the front just in time to see the end of the war's decisive battle at Khorramshahr.

It was Khorramshahr, just fifteen kilometers north of Abadan on the Shatt al-Arab, that Iraq first besieged in September 1980. The city fell after thirty-six days of heavy artillery pounding, a battle that quickly became revolutionary legend as a ragged Basij and Revolutionary Guard force unsuccessfully defended the city from within its mosque. Under Iraqi occupation, Khorramshahr was a ghost town, half razed, graffitied, and bullet-scarred. Iraqi soldiers used photos of Khomeini for target practice. It was the fall of 1981 before the Iranian armed forces broke the yearlong siege of Abadan and then, at the end of a monthlong campaign in May of 1982, regained Khorramshahr.

Alireza arrived in Khorramshahr on the last day of battle. He stayed a month in the broken city. With Khorramshahr, Iran had successfully repulsed the Iraqi invasion just a year and a half after it began. Khomeini was in a good position to wrest a favorable peace from the Iraqis, who might have slunk back to Baghdad without further hope of annexing Iranian territory. Iran might have turned, then, to its internal troubles: political violence, social unrest, an economy in free fall. But that was not Khomeini's choice. Instead, the Islamic Republic went on the offensive, resolving to topple the Baathist regime of Saddam Hussein. Six more years of war would ravage the two countries.

Alireza returned to the navy base, and from there to civilian life. He had other obligations. His mother had fallen and broken her pelvis. At the hospital in Shiraz, Alireza was certain she would be neglected, a poor woman with little recourse. He would need to sit at her bedside to be sure she got proper care. But since the revolution, the hospitals were segregated by sex, and he was not technically permitted to stay in the women's section. And so he struck a deal with the nurses, one that allowed him to split his time between his father's shop and his mother's bedside, where he sat reading Gabriel García Márquez—and tending to all the patients on the ward when they buzzed, while the nurses talked and laughed among themselves.

One day, by chance, Alireza ran into the mosque librarian who had introduced him to *The Little Black Fish* when he was a child. The librarian was surprised to learn that the pious boy who had devoured books with such intensity now worked in the bazaar. The librarian served on one of the committees that oversaw the universities after the revolution; he had connections Alireza scarcely understood. He offered to shepherd Alireza's university application through the correct political channels. Alireza applied in cinema and in political science, and he was accepted in both.

To study cinema would have been a dream, a luxury. But Alireza chose politics at the prestigious University of Tehran. It was a fateful choice that he would sometimes regret in later years. To study politics in Iran was to be subject, always, to ideological scrutiny, even while it was to practice a profession in which every housewife, taxi driver, and corner grocer considered himself an expert. But politics lay at the core of his being. He had chosen it, time and again, over everything else.

Alireza was a true believer in his revolution, as radical as he was devout, and he had a shrewd head for politics. But as a teenager he bet on the wrong horse—Shariati over Khomeini—and this set the course of his life. Shariati, for whom streets were named in the Islamic Republic, whose use of Islam as an ideology had made the epoch, and whose clarion call for social justice Khomeini even co-opted for himself, was at once unmentionable and beyond criticism. The clerics knew only too well the power Shariati had unleashed. They rode it like a wild bronco they would eventually put down.

A man like Alireza would work for the bureaucracy of state but never be wholly trusted by it. He would circle political factions but never be absorbed by them. When trouble came, there was no one to fight for him or to vouch for him. He was canny enough to look out for himself. By middle age, Alireza was an exile in Canada, still loyal to a revolution he had never owned or disowned, despite all the revolutionary ardor in his heart.

IN THE FULLNESS OF TIME, Bani-Sadr and the paroxysm of violence that ended his tenure would trouble Iran's center of power less enduringly than the story of Bazargan. The Islamic Republic's first prime minister was politically overmatched, but he stood for an idea that did not fade so much as grow stronger with time. He seemed to believe that there was, or should be, room for people like him within the new Islamic state, and that the rule of law was not incompatible with the revolution Iranians had wrought.

Toward the end of the Bani-Sadr period, in the month of March, the Revolutionary Court opened a trial for Bazargan's former deputy prime minister, Abbas Amirentezam, at Evin Prison. The trial would return Bazargan to the national stage, this time as a furious and uncompromising voice for the opposition.

Based on documents they found in the embassy, the hostage takers had accused Amirentezam, a debonair diplomat fluent in English, of meeting with American diplomats and of harboring doubts about the course the revolution had taken. The trial was a gruff, informal affair, dispensed in a nondescript chamber hastily converted into a courtroom, where Bazargan, a witness for the defense, was the only attendee wearing a tie. A prison official in a brown T-shirt called the court to order by commanding those assembled to praise God. Amirentezam, and the eighty members of the audience, rose and chanted, "God is Great. Khomeini is our leader. Death to Saddam, the infidel." A court official in blue jeans read from the Quran.

The judge, a cleric named Mohammad Mohammadi Gilani, turned to Amirentezam and asked, "Did you ask for a defense lawyer?" When Amirentezam said he had, the judge snapped, "Mr. Bazargan gave evidence and spoke on your behalf. You don't need a defense lawyer."

Bazargan, loyal to his deputy to the end and clearly pained by his own experience in government, followed by Bani-Sadr's unfolding drama, delivered a stinging performance there in the weeks that followed. The allegations against Amirentezam—that he was conspiring with the CIA against Khomeini—were baseless, said the former prime minister. It was true that Amirentezam had had contact with the American embassy, but it was entirely in line with his duties and authorized by the prime minister.

"If anyone has to be tried," Bazargan told the court, "it should be myself."

In the postrevolutionary tumult, Iran's counterintelligence apparatus had been in disarray, so Bazargan had dispatched men to the embassies of both the United States and the Soviet Union to ask each superpower to supply intelligence about the other. "The Americans gave us plenty of information," said Bazargan, mainly about Iraqi troop movements near the Iranian border and internal affairs in Afghanistan. "The Soviets gave us nothing." (The Soviets, it would turn out, were talking not to Bazargan's government but to the clerics.)

The Amirentezam trial became a battle of the newspapers, with the vast publicity machine of the regime continuing to excoriate the former official as a spy for the imperialists, a traitor whose crimes were punishable by death, and Bazargan's small newspaper, *Mizan*, publishing detailed accounts of Amirentezam's courtroom objections. The accused had not seen the documents being used against him, nor had they been translated into Persian for the public to know what they contained. The indictment against Amirentezam was published in its entirety by the state media, but Bazargan's and Amirentezam's courtroom statements were expunged from the published record. *Mizan* reported that a frustrated Amirentezam told the court, "They have turned me into a devil . . . and you must know that here I have been referred to as an enemy of God, the Prophet, the Imam and Iran . . . They are lies and there is no document to support them. Let me defend myself."

Bazargan's rhetoric grew even hotter. He called the radical clerics "opportunists and criminals" who had "no conscience," and he declared, "The time has come when each of us must publicly pronounce his decision to do all he can, with the help of Allah, to redeem the country from this holocaust."

The editor of *Mizan* was arrested, the newspaper permanently shuttered on June 7, scant days before Amirentezam was sentenced to life imprisonment for espionage. Amirentezam would go on to serve twenty-seven years—longer than any other Iranian political prisoner and as long as Nelson Mandela. His smuggled letters and memoirs would provide vivid testimony to the conditions in Iranian prisons over the course of three decades, and his story would inspire some members of a generation not yet born when he first entered Evin.

The tale of Iran's movement for liberal reform ought to begin with Bazargan, but it does not. The men who would become the reform movement's protagonists, its ideologues, its adherents, and even its bureaucrats behind the scenes were Bazargan's antagonists. They had no interest in the moderate, technocratic, liberal strain of revolutionary thought. Rather, they were Shariati's children, utopian, ecstatic, extreme. They believed in the Shiism of Ali, in universal social justice and emancipation through Islam. Most aligned themselves with the radical clerics, Khomeini, and the Islamic Republican Party, even as these forces consolidated single-party rule. They little imagined that one day they and their friends would find themselves in shoes that looked suspiciously like Bazargan's, or that some of their own children would look past them for wisdom, to men like Amirentezam.

THREE

THE PERIOD OF CONSTANT CONTEMPLATION

MOSTAFA ROKHSEFAT'S MEMORY always returns to a scene that is inexplicable to him in retrospect. He is at a bookstore in front of the University of Tehran. The revolutionary hour approaches. He is an undergraduate student, active against the shah, affiliated with the militant Islamist left. He sees another young man there, also an activist, a member of the armed opposition. In those days the militants survived on the prudence of their silence. SAVAK walked among them. They did not share their names or addresses even with one another. But that afternoon, with that particular young man, Mostafa introduced himself, and against every rule, every instinct of their movement, he and Hassan exchanged addresses. They would become literary collaborators and great friends until Hassan's untimely death in an accident.

Mostafa came from the Shariati wing of the revolutionary movement. Hosseiniyeh Ershad was the only place he knew where he could extinguish his thirst in all its complexity—for answers, for dignity, for pride. He was the fifth of seven sons of a carpet and lumber merchant at the Tehran bazaar. The family was comfortably middle-class yet traditional in its habits, its values, its Islam. They lived in one of Tehran's most religious neighborhoods, called Maydan-e Khorasan, not far from the city-within-a-city that was the bazaar.

Of the Rokhsefat boys, only Mostafa took an interest in the life of the mind. But the secular leftism that was fashionable among intellectuals of that day did not stir his passions, and Mostafa was a young man of strong feeling, quick to anger and to intimacy, unshielded by his formidable intellect from the searing heat of his emotions.

The times—adolescence and the late 1970s—called for radicalism. Mostafa knew Mehdi Bazargan personally through neighborhood connections, but the Freedom Movement was too stodgy and moderate for Mostafa's tastes. He preferred the charged lyricism of Shariati, the righteousness of Khomeini. To live in the prism of their words was to refuse to be subject, either to the shah or to the irreligious ideologies of elsewhere. Decades later, Mostafa would return to those texts and wonder how he had ignored, or even embraced, their invitation to tyranny.

For all its luminary novelty, the Islamist movement lacked a literature, and it was that absence that Mostafa found himself discussing with Hassan on the afternoon of their unlikely bookstore encounter. Iran's great novelists and poets were largely leftists. They disdained religion as the superstition of the peasantry, and they looked down on the literature of the Arab and Muslim world because of its religious content. Instead they looked to Russia for inspiration. Russian novels, banned under the shah, circulated furiously in Tehran's underground press, distributed hand to hand, within white covers.

Mostafa and his new friend dreamt of building an institution that would cultivate a rightfully modern, even avant-garde literary voice for the movement of Islamic radicals to which they belonged. They brought this idea to a poet they knew. The poet informed them that this association already existed in the form of a literary circle around a mid-ranking Mashhadi cleric named Ali Khamenei. The circle had thirteen prominent members. Mostafa and Hassan, instead of starting their own circle, orbited Khamenei's.

They met a charismatic and eccentric cleric during that time. Mohammad Reza Hakimi did not wear clerical robes or turbans. Instead, his bald head glistened above its frenetic white fringe and wiry beard, and he dressed in long, loose, pajama-like shirts. Ferocious passions coursed through him and took root in those he taught, like electricity seeking the quickest route to the ground; he was given to poetic rhapsody and mystical visions, musical language and urgent persuasion. Hakimi had ties to nearly all the major clergymen of his time, including Khomeini and Khamenei. He was protégé, mentor, muse. There were grand ayatollahs who would lecture only if Hakimi was in the room to take down their words. Shariati made Hakimi his literary executor, with the exclusive power to posthumously edit his words.

Hakimi drew close to Mostafa, in whom he saw potential for religious learning. Mostafa must come to Qom and take up Islamic study, Hakimi urged. Only by joining the clergy could Mostafa accomplish anything. It was not a choice; it was a necessity, a calling. To be recruited by someone of Hakimi's stature was a great honor, but Mostafa balked. He made regular trips to Qom, less than two hours' drive from Tehran, and he thrived on the vigor and abstraction of its intellectual life. But he did not think he wanted to be a cleric, and the more he hesitated, the more Hakimi insisted.

With Hakimi, Mostafa was a man perpetually in arguments, frustrated, and seized with regrets. Hakimi mirrored Mostafa's heat and idealism, but this affinity only heightened his anxiety and self-reproach. And Hakimi's was not the only pull on Mostafa in those years. The Mojahedin had recently suffered a rancorous split. Some of its members turned to secular Marxism-Leninism, and they trained the attentions of their recruiters on Mostafa. Despite the unifying promise of Shariati's Islamism, to be Shariati's follower was to have a foot in each of two rapids coursing through a fervid landscape. There Mostafa stood.

To be called for military service at that moment was almost a reprieve. In his barracks Mostafa read a book called *Dialectic Conflict*. It was a refutation of Marxism by an obscure young scholar named Abdolkarim Soroush who had found favor with Ayatollah Khomeini. In his book Soroush criticized dialectical reasoning as rigid, resistant to revision, and too abstract to yield insight about societies as they actually existed. Soroush professed humility about the limits of human knowledge, and a stubborn preference for the rational over the visionary.

Clarity broke over Mostafa like a summer storm. Soroush dulled the lure of Marxism and cooled the fever Shariati once stirred. His authorial voice was the antithesis of Shariati's or Hakimi's—in fact, it was everything Mostafa thought he didn't want. It was neither sublime nor enraging so much as it was restrained, analytical, and painstakingly precise. Soroush wrote about religion and politics—the very soul of history—but he wrote not like a guru but like a philosopher. For the first time Mostafa understood that his intensity did not thrive on a matching intensity. What it required was the balm of dispassionate logic. Because of Soroush, Mostafa forked from Shariati and the Mojahedin decisively toward Khomeini.

At Khomeini's victorious command, Mostafa walked off his base into the giddy final days of revolt. He was one of the millions of Iranians who showed up at Mehrabad Airport to greet Khomeini's flight home. And he spent the early revolutionary years in sympathy with the radical clerics of the Revolutionary Council and *velayat-e faqih*. His utopia was in the making. He would not disrupt this by quarreling with its triumphant mainstream. But Soroush had planted seeds in his intellect that would flower in ways neither Mostafa, nor even Soroush, could foresee.

The poetry circle Mostafa had joined in the late 1970s did not become the nucleus of the new Iranian literary scene the way he'd expected. Instead, it fractured, a microcosm of the revolutionary movement itself, its thirteen luminaries spanning the establishment and its adversaries. Some members, including Khamenei, had grown very powerful overnight. Others were Islamic radicals whose early influence was soon eclipsed, their parties fully outlawed by 1982. Mostafa, once the young acolyte in a circle of eminences, now groped through the wreckage of their alliances.

The revolution still belonged to him, its certainties steadfast and gleaming. His dream was to strike the timbre of the revolution's voice, to fix the colors and the symbols that would announce Iran as the birthplace of a modern, religious avant-garde. To nurture such an intellectual milieu,

Mostafa believed, Iran's revolution required an arts corps to match its corps of Revolutionary Guards.

From the shards of the poetry circle, Mostafa chose his allies and began to build a network into which he ushered militant painters, poets, novelists, graphic designers, and filmmakers. The days were heady and long. He circled Tehran collecting cameras, equipment, books, and supplies. He founded an institute, which he called Howzeh-ye Andisheh va Honar-e Islami, the Center for Islamic Thought and Art. The word *howzeh* also meant seminary, a play on words that pleased Mostafa. His institute would give Islamist Iran's art world not only a cultural identity but a physical location, a productive hive. He got some funding from the Office of the Supreme Leader. But in the end Mostafa fell back on his own resources, selling his car to finance the work of his artistic army.

Howzeh produced theater and films; it hosted a weekly poets' circle, held exhibits and writers' workshops, and mobilized young artists and graphic designers to create the posters that would define Iran's revolutionary aesthetic. The posters combined the bold colors and stark iconography of the left with a Shiite imagery of blood, suffering, and martyrdom. Iraq, Israel, and the United States loomed demonically as skulls and serpents, giant masks splintered by the righteous. Posters announced events and festooned demonstrations, mourned the war dead and incited young men to battle; they celebrated the victory of Islam, in gore and tears, over the corruption of the shah and the perfidy of empire; they indoctrinated, educated, seduced, and threatened, and they adorned every Iranian consulate in the world.

It was during this time that Abdolkarim Soroush, the anti-Marxist religious philosopher whose work had spoken so lucidly to Mostafa as a conscript, returned from London to Tehran. Between meetings and events at Howzeh, Mostafa attended Soroush's lectures and seminars. He felt a strong tug of kinship toward the older philosopher, who came from Mostafa's neighborhood and shared its customs and habits of mind. Soroush had even gone to school with Mostafa's older brothers.

The calm and clarity Mostafa had admired in the writings was all the more compelling in person. On the rare occasion when Mostafa was moved to question Soroush's logic, the answer came without vitriol; it was elegant and convincing. More and more, Mostafa gravitated toward Soroush, and as he did so, he drifted from the magic and turbulence of Shariati and Hakimi, the lodestones of his youth. The drift inevitably brought conflict, and not only with Hakimi, who thought Soroush's way of thinking was a threat to the very roots of belief. For Mostafa suffered the hazards of an independent mind. He was a builder of movements who recoiled from movements.

Howzeh grew so large and successful that, by 1981, the Islamic Republican Party wanted to fold it into the government. Khamenei repeatedly sent a mediator to Mostafa, inviting him to join the party, even offering him a position in charge of art and cultural affairs. It was not a far-fetched idea. In the clashes on the streets, Mostafa and the members of his Howzeh aligned themselves with the hezbollahis. They opposed Bani-Sadr and the Mojahedin; some of the artists even volunteered as security guards for local buildings during the turmoil. Mostafa was loyal, he held the line, but something in him chafed at the thought of belonging, of yoking culture so nakedly to power, of circumscribing intellectual independence—his own and that of his colleagues. He said no to the Islamic Republican Party. And in return, it choked off his funding, accusing him and his artists, incredibly, of supporting Bani-Sadr and the Mojahedin.

Mostafa quit. His brainchild fell into the hands of the Islamic Republican Party, effectively ceasing to exist as he had conceived it, and he contemplated moving abroad. But he had not exhausted his vision. Revolutionary Iran was still, now more even than before, the cradle of a new culture, one that married Islam to the art and philosophy of the late twentieth century, the politics of revolution, and Iranian national identity. There was so much work still to be done.

Under the Shah, Iran was home to the largest newspaper company in the Middle East. Now that newspaper, *Kayhan*, belonged to the revolutionary state. One of its top executives was a mid-ranking cleric named Mohammad Khatami, who happened to know the family of Mostafa's friend Hassan. With Khatami's support, in 1984 the friends started a cultural supplement under the Kayhan umbrella called *Kayhan-e Farhangi*, with Mostafa as its editor. It was independent of the Kayhan newspaper group in all but name.

Now at last Mostafa began to realize his dream. In *Kayhan-e Farhangi*, Mostafa and his coeditors published interviews with prominent revolutionary intellectuals, who explained their ideas in their own words. The supplement suggested the existence of a vibrant scene of religious luminaries, and Khatami gave the editors a good deal of latitude. *Kayhan-e Farhangi* reached out to Soroush, inviting him to have his picture on the supplement's cover and an interview in its pages. Soroush refused, but he agreed to write essays for the supplement. Mostafa disseminated these essays to a broader audience than Soroush had ever known.

THE MAN WHO WOULD BECOME known as Abdolkarim Soroush grew up, like most Iranians, on poetry, the folk literature of his country, a canon that crossed social boundaries to a degree shared not even by Islam. Born in 1945 to a merchant family near the traditional, lower-middle-class Tehran neighborhood where Mostafa Rokhsefat also lived, Soroush did not have a single relative with a university education. But his father loved the thirteenth-century poet Saadi, a native of Shiraz who witnessed and wrote of the sufferings of Muslims displaced by the Mongol invasion. Every morning, after he performed his morning prayers, Soroush's father would read Saadi aloud at the top of his voice. Soroush listened to these verses as he ate his breakfast before school. It was his first exposure to literary and intellectual life, and the only one that would come directly from his family home.

Soroush's father may not have been an educated man, but he could see the intellectual potential in his young son. He strained the family budget to send Soroush to Alavi High School, an institution known in equal measure for its high academic standards and its traditional piety. In a country that prized scientific achievement as the key to social mobility, the Alavi school was particularly distinguished by its possession of laboratories for chemistry, physics, and biology. Its headmaster had a background in both physics and Islamic philosophy, subjects to which the young Soroush also warmed. But Soroush found the school's efforts to combine the two disciplines—by deriving scientific principles from religious texts—at once tantalizing and unconvincing. He argued as much with himself as with the headmaster; Islam, science, and philosophy were like puzzle pieces he knew must somehow interlock but whose master pattern remained obscure to him. Properly conjoined, surely they would explain the universe, but they repelled one another like incompatible magnets. They rattled in his pocket, calling him to ambition and frustration and at long last to understanding throughout the adult journey of his intellectual life.

The Alavi school, like most institutions of learning or religion in Iran, was awash in oppositional politics during Soroush's high school years, the early 1960s. Soroush's closest friend, an enthusiastic early member of the Mojahedin, invited Soroush to join the guerrilla struggle against the monarchy. But Soroush was not one to step in darkness, as he would later put it, and his friend had invited him to plunge into an obscurity beyond his daring. He told his friend that society did not need only revolutionaries. It needed many different kinds of people: physicians, poets, carpenters. Couldn't Soroush be one of those?

It was not that Soroush was uninterested in politics. He was an avid if critical reader of the political literature of the Mojahedin, the Marxists, and other groups opposing the shah's rule. But the Mojahedin were radical: they questioned the authority of the clergy and absorbed the ideology of the European left. Soroush was more conservative on both scores. He had admired Ayatollah Khomeini from the time of the senior cleric's arrest in 1962—so much so that the young Soroush went to see the ayatollah upon his release from prison. Moreover, his temperament was scholastic, his mind suited more to the rigors of abstract logic than the raptures of ideology and self-sacrifice, the intrigue of conspiracy. By the end of high school, Soroush's friend had disappeared into the Mojahedin's most secretive inner circle. He would follow the guerrillas into battle against the shah and against

Khomeini; later he would follow the Mojahedin's leadership to France and then Iraq, his friendship with Soroush long estranged.

Soroush, meanwhile, matriculated at the University of Tehran, where he studied Islamic philosophy and science side by side. He read Motahhari and Bazargan, electrified for a time by their insights; in Mulla Sadra he found a critique of Aristotelian essentialism that he would carry with him always; he pored over the Sufi poetry of Rumi; and when Shariati began lecturing at Hosseiniyeh Ershad, just as Soroush was called up for his two years of military service, he attended as often as he could. It was during these years, too, that Soroush read Khomeini's treatise on Islamic government and came to consider himself one of the ayatollah's followers. In later years he would be a fierce critic of *velayat-e faqih*. But during his student days he thought the elderly cleric came closer than anyone else to unifying the crucial visions of philosophy, mysticism, and jurisprudence.

Soroush was an earnest and humble student. But between the realms of his curiosity a chasm stretched, and nothing in Islamic philosophy helped to bridge it. There should be, he thought, a discipline of thought to link the empirical to the unseen, a metaphysics that could explain, for example, the enormous disparity between past and present scientific understandings of the world. As a scientist, he yearned for answers to questions Shiite Islamic philosophy did not ask. After a yearlong stint as a laboratory supervisor overseeing food and drug research in the southern Iranian town of Bushehr, Soroush gathered his poetry books and a volume of Mulla Sadra's and made for England to do his graduate work in 1973.

Compact, bearded, placid, and wry, Soroush was a man at once solitary and sociable, an intellectual wayfarer who carried nearly all his resources in his mind but was not averse to the company of others. He was animated by a fierce, even combative intellect, its edges softened somewhat by his penchant for metaphor and quotations from Sufi poetry. Where Shariati's retreat into Gnosticism seemed to emanate from psychic anguish, Soroush's peculiar combination of mysticism and cool rationalism produced in him a sort of serene detachment. And yet, in his youth, Soroush's hunger for the mastery of ideas was feverish. He spent his first year in London studying analytical chemistry. But he wanted also to ground himself in the Western philosophical tradition and to improve his English, so he bought a copy of John Passmore's survey, *A Hundred Years of Philosophy*.

There was, he understood, a universe of thought he had yet to uncover. To the extent they dealt at all in twentieth-century thought, Iranian philosophy departments had absorbed some of the ideas of the continental European philosophers, particularly the French and Germans. These were the grand visions of the Western tradition, the ones that moved like tectonic plates beneath a convulsive Europe, and their appeal to a politically inflamed Iranian intelligentsia was unsurprising. Iranian universities all but ignored the parallel Anglo-American tradition of analytic philosophy, which tended to emphasize logic, language, and epistemology—the questions of what human beings knew and how they knew it.

The analytic philosophers did not write of the "World Spirit," of Being or Nothingness or Time. Rather, they bored into the minute problems of human apprehension with mathematical precision, and without the soaring rhetoric or thunderbolts of insight that yoked continental philosophy to the aspirations and anxieties of its time. By comparison, analytic philosophy could seem arid and trivial, and Iranians had seen no reason to import it. And so it was in Passmore's book that Soroush discovered a school of thought to which he'd had no exposure, and which was by far the better fit for his scientific mind. It was from Passmore that Soroush first heard of Karl Popper's contributions to the philosophy of science. Other theorists had puzzled over the problem of induction: How exactly did scientists draw general conclusions from specific observations? Popper rejected even the existence of such a problem. Science did not start from observations and build toward generalities. Rather, the human mind tended already to generalize, often wrongly. The job of science was to test these generalities by making specific observations. That was why scientists subjected their assumptions to empirical tests.

A theory was scientific, according to Popper, if it could be disproved. The statement "All tigers are carnivorous" could be disproved by the discovery of just one tiger that was not carnivorous. That was what made it a scientific—testable—hypothesis. On the other hand, a theory was unscientific if all possible observations could simply be adduced in its support: Marxism, for instance, and psychoanalysis too easily explained all outcomes as further support for their theses.

There was a humility at the heart of this view, and it appealed to Soroush. The human mind did not apprehend truth at a glance—not through observation, not through totalizing theories, however brilliant, and not by induction. Perhaps it did not perceive truth at all. Rather, the scientist toiled at sweeping cobwebs from a well in the hope of an ever clearer—but never unobstructed—view of what lay at its bottom. He arrived not at the truth but at an ever lesser falsity. And the so-called pseudosciences Popper railed against—from Marxism and psychoanalysis to astrology—could not hope for even that much.

Soroush's link to Popper was forged with Passmore's seven-page summary and with this simple and lasting principle of the scientific method, known as falsifiability. His affinity for Popper was deep; it was not an accidental convergence of opinion on one or even several matters, nor an instrumental appreciation for the uses of an idea, although at the start he may have seen it that way. Soroush came to share the basic skepticism of Popper's outlook, his impatience with obscurantism or magical thinking of any kind, his love of transparent prose and logical argument. He would later say that he learned from Popper how easy it was to philosophize and how difficult to speak with true academic rigor.

Soroush approached the psychology department at his university and explained that he wanted to study the theoretical foundations of science. For the first time he was told that the discipline of his imagination indeed existed. It was called the philosophy of science, and Soroush should bring his query to that department at Chelsea College at the University of London. That was where Soroush continued his studies. There, in the 1970s, Soroush read Kant and Hume unmediated by the Iranian religious thinkers, like Ayatollah Motahhari, in whose work he'd first heard of them. He delved into linguistic philosophy and positivism, the works of Paul Feyerabend and Imre Lakatos and Popper, whose close friend and scholar

Heinz Post was one of Soroush's professors. Simultaneously, he studied chemistry.

It was the philosophy, in its headiest, most abstract forms—epistemology, metaphysics—that consumed Soroush. It infused all he ate and saw and breathed; it was the impulse that moved his limbs and animated his tongue; he wrote a whole book (albeit a short one) while sitting in the waiting room of a doctor's office, reversed a lifetime of his own thought in a day. Privately he gave this time in his life a name: it was the Period of Constant Contemplation. To his sorrow, Rumi's poetry, which he'd always loved, lost its resonance for him in those years; but while he would find his way back to Rumi later in life, other changes were hard-won and lasting.

The Islamic philosophy Soroush had studied in Iran included theories of the mind and soul, but it had not touched on the question of whether human knowledge could truly apprehend the essences of things. His course of study in Britain pressed precisely on this question, challenging many of his assumptions. As Soroush would explain later, as a man of faith, he had been educated to believe that man was immersed in an ocean of certainties, floating from one to the next. But as a student of philosophy, he came to see that instead a person drifted from conjecture to conjecture, doubt to doubt.

With certainty, the determinism he had understood to be inherent to Iranian Islamic thought also crumbled in Soroush's hands. Islamic scholars believed that the will of God ordered the world and its events. Humans fulfilled their divinely ordained destinies. The problem of free will—could people then be independent, rational agents, or were they merely vehicles for the will of God?—bedeviled Iran's philosophers, theologians, and jurists. Even Khomeini, Soroush would note, remarked once that if the hidden imam were one day to appear before him, he would be sure to ask him how to solve the problem of free will.

One day, in Soroush's class on epistemology, the British philosopher Donald Gillies proffered a hypothetical scenario. We are all sitting in this room, doing our own jobs, he said. But suppose that a very powerful magnet is surrounding us. We know nothing about this magnet, but because it is there, the behavior of everything in the room will change. We think it's natural. But if we knew about the magnet, then we could see that these actions are actually unnatural, even violent.

This was the thought experiment that changed the very flavor of the air Soroush breathed. What about the whole universe? he wondered. What about the planet Earth? And if we were surrounded by unknown fields of energy, what, then, of our experiments? We thought they showed us what was going on in nature. But maybe nature itself was influenced by forces of which we were not aware. Maybe, when we spoke of causes and effects, we isolated the wrong causes or were blind to factors that were just as necessary in producing their effects. This was the beginning of Soroush's turn toward indeterminism and away from dogma. To embrace indeterminism, he understood, was to open a whole new universe—in morality, in epistemology, even in politics.

POLITICS, FOR THE COMMUNITY of Iranian oppositionists in exile, led nowhere more directly than to Shariati. Soroush admired and learned from Shariati's work, but he was also troubled by what he saw as Shariati's manipulation of the religious narrative. To make Shiism revolutionary, Shariati had chosen certain heroes from among its pantheon—most important, Imam Hossein, who died resisting his oppressors in Karbala. But Imam Hassan, who had chosen the path of peace with the same oppressors, Shariati passed over in silence. Soroush was uneasy with this selection. Among the twelve Shiite imams, Hossein was uniquely militant. But Shariati had made the exception the rule, rendering Hossein's martyrdom the soul of a revolutionary Islam. To Soroush, this indicated that Shariati was more committed to mobilizing his listeners than to seeking truth, whether historical or theological. Shariati's aspirations for Iran, and his hatred of injustice, were noble. But he disparaged democracy, which was problematic, and he sacrificed truth for dogma, which was unforgivable. Years later Soroush would tell an interviewer, in reference to Shariati, "We always have a duty to break idols."

Back in the seventies, Soroush fought Shariati on Khomeini's behalf.

He was waging a battle against the ideas of the left, which he saw as threatening to religion. Shariati, he felt, had borrowed too much from Marxism. Soroush devoured volume after volume of Marx in an effort to build a case against the German socialist on behalf of Khomeini's Islam. And so he was thrilled to discover that a powerful weapon against both Marx and Hegel—and thus, too, against Shariati—had existed all the while, untranslated into Persian. It was Popper's *The Open Society and Its Enemies*, which Soroush read in 1974.

Popper had been a Marxist in his youth, but eventually abandoned both Freud and Marx for Einstein, whose theory of relativity dazzled him not only with its brilliance but with its daring: here was a theory that predicted events that seemed wildly improbable, one that could be definitively refuted through experiments. Freud and Marx, on the other hand, left no such exposed flank, and Popper's respect for them plummeted by the comparison. Popper retained real feeling for Marx, particularly for the humanitarian impulse behind his concern for the economically disadvantaged. And yet, *The Open Society and Its Enemies* was nothing short of a scorched-earth attack on Marxism and its progenitors.

Published in 1945—eight years after Popper, whose parents were Jewish, fled Austria in anticipation of the Anschluss—Popper's two-volume magnum opus traced what he believed was a lineage of totalitarian political thought from Plato, through Aristotle, to Hegel and Marx. Along the way, he made a passionate brief for the liberal state, where he envisioned individuals engaged in free, rational dispute and whose institutions were designed to hold the power of the state in check. Liberalism promised a state as imperfect as human science, justice as occluded as truth. But an open society contained the tools for its own betterment, Popper believed, for it allowed the free exercise of the rational mind. Ideologies that made utopian promises, by contrast, tended to produce men in chains and hell on earth.

Soroush had no interest in the affirmative part of Popper's view. He was not, at that time, a liberal. He saw in *The Open Society* merely a cudgel to use against Hegel and Marx in the name not of liberalism but of utopian Islam. And Popper's loathing for Hegel was particularly satisfying under the circumstances. Popper believed that Hegel's "oracular" style of writing—bombastic, consisting of pronouncements rather than arguments and thus hostile to rational challenge—had done much to mystify and evacuate European philosophy. Worse, in Hegel's work Popper saw seeds of Nazism: the belief that might made right, a romantic tribalism, and a call for blind submission to authority.

But Popper hated dialectics most of all. Critics would argue that Popper oversimplified and misunderstood Hegel's theory, which suggested a corkscrew motion to logic or history by which a thesis and its antithesis yielded a new truth. To Popper this was plainly irrational, a sort of sterile hocus-pocus that dazzled the young. Upon finding contradictory evidence, scientists and logicians jettisoned their hypotheses and concocted new ones. But in Hegel's dialectic, as Popper crudely understood it, contradictions did not disprove theories; rather, the two contradictory theories were married, subsumed within a synthetic truth. Here was an unfalsifiable idea—one that purported to explain everything and its opposite and so explained nothing while stopping inquiry in its tracks. Soroush would draw on this critique to counter the dialectical thinking of Iranian Marxists and Shariati enthusiasts.

Of still more interest to Soroush was Popper's case against Marx. Popper rejected historical determinism, or the belief that history was governed by iron laws whose outcomes were predictable, as bad science as well as bad politics. Historical determinists, Popper observed, tended to overread general trends, like the trend toward the advance of technology or toward increasing class polarization, interpreting them as laws, vectors of inevitability. But trends were not laws. They could halt or reverse without warning. There was no science to support the assumption that technology would advance indefinitely or that the poor would grow ever poorer, the rich ever richer. Rather, it was a basic human fallacy—the inductive fallacy, with which Popper had tried to do away in the philosophy of science—to believe that what we observed one day and the next, we would also observe the following day. History depended on an untidy welter of variables, the consequences of which were often unintended and unforeseeable, and the agents of which included individuals, who exercised free will. To argue that those individuals were preprogrammed by their national identity (Hegel) or their social class (Marx) to behave as they did or value what they valued was reactionary, for it was to turn history and politics over to irrational forces, "banishing the power of cool and critical judgment and destroying the belief that by the use of reason we may change the world."

Popper's critics have argued that what Popper called Marx's historical "prophecy" was not integral to Marxism—that Popper focused exclusively on *Capital*, while in his early and late writings, Marx was not a determinist at all. In Europe, whole schools of post-Marxist thought emerged from the internal debates among Marxists about the role of human agency and free will.

Nonetheless, Popper's dispute with the Marxists of his day was a substantial one. Many Marxists believed that political freedoms, like the freedom of expression or association, were mere formalities when economic inequality enslaved people. Popper saw it the other way around. No kind of justice, certainly not economic justice, could be rendered in a state under opaque, autocratic control. "The dogma that economic power is at the root of all evil must be discarded," Popper wrote. "Its place must be taken by an understanding of the dangers of *any* form of uncontrolled power."

The antidote to uncontrolled power, in Popper's view, was democracy. Marxists would argue that the sort of rational free choice Popper celebrated in a democracy was an illusion so long as the underlying economic structure remained unchanged. But Popper believed that the state consisted of institutions, and that its decency or cruelty was entirely bound within the design of those institutions. He wrote: "It is high time for us to learn that the question '*who* is to wield the power in the state?' matters only little as compared with the question '*how* is the power wielded?' and '*how much* power is wielded?'"

Those words would stay with Soroush after his return to the newborn Islamic Republic, and through the decades to follow. But Popper's distinction between the *who* and the *how* of power wielding could not have been further from the spirit of Soroush's times than they were when he read *The Open Society and Its Enemies* in 1974—and marshaled its critique of Marxism to the defense of Ayatollah Khomeini.

SOROUSH PUBLISHED MANY ESSAYS during his Period of Constant Contemplation, but his most significant works during his London years were his books. First there was *What Is Science? What Is Philosophy?* and then *Philosophy of History*. His attacks on Marxism were useful for the Khomeinists, who saw the secular left as their greatest adversary, with the equally leftist Mojahedin close behind. In his book *Dialectic Conflict*, Soroush argued that the theory of dialectics made empirical claims in the guise of abstractions and it should stand or fall based on its empirical truth. He looked at the history of science and could find in its unfolding no example of dialectical progression. If history could not actually be shown to have traveled in dialectical fashion, what use was the theory that it always did so? Echoing Popper, Soroush described the dialectic as a theory that, like air, fit all locks and opened none of them.

Dialectic Conflict was the book Mostafa Rokhsefat read in the barracks and that turned him definitively from the Mojahedin to what would become the mainstream of the revolutionary establishment. And Mostafa was not alone. In just the first two years after the revolution, to Soroush's knowledge, the book sold some one hundred thousand copies in Iran.

Finally, Soroush wrote a book in London that brought him to the attention of the great theologians of his day, including Motahhari and Khomeini himself. This was a study of Mulla Sadra's metaphysics, which he tried to enrich from his readings in the philosophy and history of science. The book was thick with footnotes citing Einstein, Wittgenstein, and Saint Augustine. Although it earned him the highest accolades at the time of its publication, Soroush would later speak of *The Restless Nature of the Universe* with something close to embarrassment, as a failed effort to reconcile irreconcilables, written during a period of his life when he had left one station but not yet arrived at the next. "The author of that book," he reflected in 2010, "is long dead." In 1979, however, the book catapulted the young scholar into the Iranian scholarly elite. According to popular lore, it was Ayatollah Motahhari who pressed a copy on Ayatollah Khomeini, himself a scholar of Mulla Sadra. Khomeini took a personal interest in Soroush after that.

Soroush returned to revolutionary Iran in September 1979, without having completed his doctorate, to chair the department of Islamic culture at Tehran's teachers' college. He was quickly pressed into the service of the new regime, which, starting with Khomeini himself, viewed the brilliant young lay theologian as a potentially effective propagandist. Soroush went on state television to debate a prominent spokesman for the communist Tudeh Party, drawing on Popper's critique of Marx even as he spoke for an authoritarian theocracy. When Bani-Sadr was driven from office, Soroush crowed over the Khomeinists' victory, concluding that "we are pleased now that the pain of having such an undesired president is over. . . . Like a healthy body that excretes its putrid parts, people have egested him." The people, he wrote during the reign of terror that followed Bani-Sadr's ouster, had been blessed by the coming of a beautiful spring to an arid land. They should submit to and be grateful to the Islamic Republic: "Otherwise, God forbid, they will suffer retributions if they show no gratitude towards God's benevolence."

As one later critic put it, Soroush denounced the "masked dogmatism" of the Tudeh Party and the Mojahedin even as the state he served met their challenge with its own flagrant dogmatism—dispatching gangs of club-wielding hezbollahis into the streets, setting bookstores and movie theaters on fire, and assaulting women who wore "improper" hijab. Years later, his critics, particularly those burned by his attacks on the left, would cry hypocrisy or opportunism. But it seems at least as likely that Popper's ideas had resonated with Soroush for a reason, just one that was obscure to him as yet, and which would rise like a vapor from the peculiar alchemy of historical events and personal conviction. For as unlikely as it looked in 1981, it would be fewer than five years before Soroush really did become a proponent of the open society, a turn that would take many of his colleagues, including those on the left and within the Mojahedin, far longer, if they made the transition at all.

FROM 1980 TO 1983, Soroush was associated above all with the closure of Iranian universities, a development that would have appalled Popper no end. This association was a misunderstanding, Soroush would later protest. It was the revolutionary students, he insisted, who closed the universities in April 1980, when the campuses, like the streets, were inflamed with politics and stray arms. Iranian universities had long been bastions of the secular left, and more recently the Mojahedin. Khomeini's followers felt themselves vastly outnumbered. This situation was intolerable to them. As the Islamic Republican Party strong-armed its rivals out of government, its allied students not only seized the American embassy but made a violent bid for control of Iran's academic institutions, attacking the campuses in gangs of hundreds and then thousands of club-wielding militiamen. When the students inside held out, the Revolutionary Committees opened fire on them. Students and faculty fled Iran's bloodied campuses, leaving them shuttered for what would turn out to be three years. These were the opening salvos of Iran's Cultural Revolution, which took its sinister name from Mao's far more dramatic campaign in China.

The Cultural Revolution came to mean three things to Iranians. First, it was shorthand for the three fallow years during which Iran lacked a higher education system altogether. Second, it was a term of art for the purging of Iran's professoriat and even its students, all of them harshly vetted for political orthodoxy from the early through the late 1980s. Finally, it connoted the complete overhaul of the country's educational curriculum in line with the state ideology. Two months after the initial university takeover, in mid-June, Ayatollah Khomeini made the Cultural Revolution official by appointing seven men to serve on a committee he called the Cultural Revolution Institute, charged with "restructuring . . . higher education based on Islamic culture." There would be no room in the restructured universities for "conspirators and other agents of foreign powers," by which surely he meant both the pro-Soviet left and the Western-oriented liberals.

Soroush would recall that the institute's members included the prime minister, whose political activities preoccupied and exhausted him to the point where he simply fell asleep in the institute's meetings; the minister of justice, who was interested only in writing regulations, attended few meetings, and eventually left; a hardline ayatollah who hung back because he was a seminarian with no experience of university life; a prominent writer who was ill and housebound; and, in the end, only three active members. These were an American-educated professor of education, a hardline member of the Islamic Republican Party named Jalal ad-Din Farsi, and Abdolkarim Soroush. They were tasked neither with closing the universities nor with purging them. Rather, the institute's job was to reopen the universities—with the caveat, of course, that Khomeini had pledged to reopen them only when they'd been brought into line with the state ideology and scoured of foreign influences. And so the institute was concerned mainly with revising the university's curriculum.

Soroush was not an obvious choice for this task. In speeches in 1981 and 1982, he described the ideal Islamic society as an open one that would have the confidence to respect academic freedom and to absorb ideas from both East and West. The notion that intellectual freedom was in any way inimical to religious truth was a false one: "We should neither limit social liberties for the sake of the Truth, nor should we use our freedom to spread myths and fallacies as the Truth," Soroush proclaimed. Moreover, he made a heartfelt brief for leaving the hard sciences alone, to be proven or disproven by their own methods. Science, he famously expounded, was wild and had no homeland.

But the powerful Ayatollah Beheshti argued that the same could not be said for the humanities, which were shaped by underlying philosophies and could therefore be Islamic or un-Islamic. If the underlying philosophies of the humanities were Western, Soroush countered, that was only because they were produced in the West, by Westerners. The way to deal with this was not to tamper with other people's humanities but for Muslims to produce canons of their own in these fields, which would then necessarily take on an Islamic cast. Ayatollah Khomeini listened carefully to both sides, then sent the members of the Cultural Revolution Institute to Qom, where clerics would advise them on reforming the humanities.

The institute dispatched a team of university lecturers to Qom to collaborate on some new textbooks. The professors worked with clerics at the seminary of the very hardest-line ayatollah, Ayatollah Mohammad-Taghi Mesbah-Yazdi, popularly known as Mesbah, an exponent of the use of violence to silence dissent. The lead intermediary for the university, and a friend of two decades to Mesbah, complained to Soroush that Mesbah was impossible to work with: "After a few sentences, it comes down to fisticuffs." The resulting textbooks, with names like *Islamic Psychology* and *Islamic Sociology*, were expensive flops that did little to alter the course of the humanities in Islamic Iran.

Other changes did take a toll, however. In the long run, censorship and forced ideological conformity would make the humanities such a political minefield that most of the country's best students would shun them in favor of hard sciences and engineering. Meanwhile, faculty purges deprived some seven hundred qualified scholars of jobs in the period from 1982 to 1983 alone and created an atmosphere of paranoia, ideological rigidity, and physical insecurity on the campuses. The student body was rife with spies, so much that professors had to tread carefully when answering provocative questions and had always to wonder whether inquisitive students were there to be educated or to collect intelligence.

Soroush credits the Cultural Revolution Institute with tempering the worst of the era's extremism, with publishing faculty work during the period of closure, and with making it possible for the universities to reopen in 1983. Soroush was personally responsible for introducing a philosophy of science curriculum in Iran and even making it a requirement for graduation. The purge committees, according to Soroush, did not report to the institute and were merely analogs of those that existed throughout the country in nearly all government bodies.

Moreover, the Khomeinist students—zealous, doctrinaire, extreme, and often violent—had grown nearly unstoppable, thanks largely to their backers in government. Many professors forced out of the universities were not officially purged so much as driven from campus by the students. According to Soroush, the institute, too, viewed these revolutionary students as an excessively empowered nuisance, and it spent much of its time trying to persuade them to deal with problems in more mature ways. The students, according to Soroush, wanted to keep the universities closed indefinitely, or for twenty years; the institute sought to reopen them.

Still, one of those radical students, Sadegh Zibakalam, has suggested that when pressed morally, Soroush abdicated. Zibakalam, who went on to become a prominent political analyst and to apologize publicly for his role in the Cultural Revolution, claims that his own conscience began to prick him during the purges, and he brought his concerns to Soroush, whom he knew to be the most sensitive and tolerant member of the institute. And yet, he claims, Soroush threw his hands up: "He did not shed any tears over this issue, appeared unflustered, and left the matter behind nonchalantly . . . as if these events were happening in Afghanistan and they were not the children of this country walking away from their homeland." Soroush would later claim that Zibakalam had exaggerated both his own importance and Soroush's, and that he had conveniently failed to level this charge of indifference at the other members of the institute who were perhaps more powerful than Soroush, and certainly more sympathetic to the purging.

But at another level Soroush knew, at the very least, that he was keeping poor if not deeply culpable company. His fellow institute member Farsi, for one, was a close friend of the notoriously cruel prosecutor and warden of Evin Prison. Soroush had the impression that after a day's work, Farsi went directly to Evin. What took place in these meetings? Did Farsi introduce the radical students to the prosecutor, and if so, to what end? Whom did they denounce, and what happened to those souls? Soroush did not pursue these thoughts. But there were scenes he could not avoid or explain, moments when he grew uneasy in Farsi's company. At an open meeting the institute held with faculty at Soroush's suggestion, a professor gave voice to his concerns and criticism. In conclusion, the professor declared that the institute wished to make trouble for the professors, and that the professors would not surrender. "No," Soroush remembers Farsi responding coolly, "we do not create trouble for anybody. If somebody is a troublemaker, we will kill him."

And yet, perhaps typically, Soroush, far more than his consistently hardline colleagues, would be scrutinized for decades regarding his activities in the early postrevolutionary period. That was partly because, as his stature rose, the consistency of his moral character became a subject of national concern. But it was also because Soroush refused to apologize. He himself had not harmed anybody, he would insist as late as 2010. Had he lent his legitimacy to the forces of violence and repression? Might he have used his proximity to power to protect those more vulnerable than himself? Should he have spoken up for those he disagreed with when they were treated brutally, as he himself would one day be? Soroush built a wall around his period of complicity, and to his critics he often replied: *Why are you asking me? The men to the right and left of me were worse.* Ordinary Iranians who found in his writings relief from the sweltering closeness of authoritarian thought and practice could not have the satisfaction of making their author into an uncomplicated moral hero as well. So went not only Soroush's story but that of the Islamic Republic.

Soroush tendered his resignation from the Cultural Revolution Institute in 1983, the year it was expanded to include nearly twenty members, many of them high-ranking clerics. He was the only member ever to resign from this institution, which still functions today. There was no longer any need for its work, he concluded; and in any case, his reservations about the undemocratic turn of the country's politics at last got the better of him.

WHEN MOSTAFA ROKHSEFAT PUBLISHED Soroush's essays in *Kayhan-e Farhangi*, they were a sensation. Soroush may not have offered recourse to embattled faculty when he had Khomeini's ear, but in the realm of ideas he was a warrior. He was a fierce defender of rationality in irrational times, willing to stand alone against an establishment that could not silence him so long as Khomeini was alive. He argued for humility at a time of grandiosity, for incrementalism at a time of visionary utopianism, and for openness at a time of profound xenophobia.

In Iran of the mid-1980s, a place where all opposition to the ruling ideology had just been forcibly crushed, Soroush obliquely criticized *velayat-e faqih* and the rigid Islamic moral code its proponents had imposed. Soroush wrote in 1984: "The prophets were not sent to angels, nor did they view humans as imperfect angels [to be transformed into] perfect angels. Man is man and he is not to be transformed into an angel." If humans were perfectible, he reasoned, and politicians charged with their perfection, then those politicians who saw themselves as God's deputies on earth might come to believe they were infallible, and arrogate to themselves special rights and privileges. There was hardly a way to read this but as a direct critique of Khomeini.

Soroush challenged the clerics by writing about religion as though it could be discerned through the work of reason and observation. Such work, like all human endeavors, was always flawed and always subject to improvement. Still, he argued, although faith might be ineffable at its core, the human effort to understand and apply God's truths was one grounded in the limits, the methods, and the temporality of all human studies, whether they took as their subject politics, pharmacology, or the divine. To their benefit, all disciplines of human knowledge were interconnected: an advance in mathematics could produce advances in theology, if only thinkers were open to them. Openness was nothing to fear, in Soroush's view. There was no such thing as a separable, monolithic Western tradition that threatened to impinge upon Islam. Ideas belonged not to any one culture but to human history.

In publishing Soroush's essays, Mostafa raised an eyebrow at the establishment that had embraced him. *Kayhan-e Farhangi* was an organ of the state, and yet the essays it published pushed the official intellectual discourse to its outer boundaries. Mohammad Khatami, Mostafa's boss at *Kayhan*, was nervous. Mostafa knew that he published *Kayhan-e Farhangi* on Khatami's sufferance. If he wanted it to survive, he could not make it only a platform for Soroush but should publish his critics as well.

The most formidable opponent Mostafa found for Soroush was a philosopher named Reza Davari Ardakani, who, along with Jalal Al-e Ahmad,
the author of *Westoxication*, had been a student of Ahmad Fardid, an oral
philosopher who brought the ideas of the German philosopher Martin
Heidegger to Iran in the late 1950s. Fardid and his students took from Heidegger the view that science was merely a philosophy. According to the
Iranian thinkers, it was a Western cosmology in competition with Islam.
The world was primarily composed of either scientifically discoverable
facts or Islamic truths; it could not be both, and so the verities of Islam
must be acknowledged as primary, and protected from the methods and
assertions of science.

Davari extended his view of science to the social contract. The liberal
view of government reduced it to an agreement forged among mortals, each
of whom sought to maximize his rights. But where in this worldview was
there space for a higher truth—moral and social values that existed neither
by law nor by agreement, but because God had ordained them? For Davari,
liberalism was yet another symptom of a civilization gone awry, one that
prized individual freedom over divine truth. A virtuous society should be
governed instead by guardianship and in accordance with revelation. The
alternatives, including democratic governments committed to civil and human
rights, were corrupt and vacuous. Of the freedom of religion articulated in
the Universal Declaration of Human Rights, Davari wrote in 1982: "Modern
man sees his own image in the mirror of Truth and instead of entering into a
Covenant with the Truth, he has entered into a covenant with himself."

Davari believed that the political problem with the West was the product
of its metaphysical problem. The very foundation of the Western tradition,
its core insight, was the belief that humankind, rather than God, occupied
the center of the universe. This humanism had led the West to subordinate
religion and philosophy to science and technology—to choose popular
sovereignty over guardianship—and then to export its own affliction glob-
ally. The Western intellectual tradition was singular and indivisible, in his
view. Outsiders could not pick and choose among its thinkers or its prod-
ucts; all of them ultimately led to, or fed from, humanism. Even Islamic

philosophy, with its ancient Greek influences, was impure. Davari turned to Sufi mysticism to argue for the annihilation of the self, the renunciation of worldly attachments, and submission to God, which ultimately became submission to the state, governed as it was by God's vice-regent on earth.

THROUGHOUT THE MID-1980s, Soroush and Davari's mentor, Fardid, waged a vociferous public battle. Because both philosophers were associated with the ruling regime, their debates were fully aired before the public, neither side beyond the pale of acceptable thought. It would be the last such open contestation over political philosophy under the Islamic Republic.

Iranian intellectuals, perhaps thrilling to the aura of purpose, often describe the battle as a war by proxy between Popper and Heidegger. Soroush had introduced his readers to Popper's thought, which became so faddish that around 1985 three different translations of *The Open Society* appeared in Persian. Thanks to Soroush, Popper attained a celebrity in Iran that undoubtedly exceeded his renown in Britain or Austria, where he was mainly regarded as a philosopher of science and a proximate critic of Viennese positivism. In Iran, Popper's was a household name.

As for Heidegger, his history in Iran was a curious one, as entangled with the idiosyncrasies of Fardid's life and mind as Popper's was with Soroush. Fardid was known as an oral philosopher because he produced nearly no written work. And yet, long before Heidegger's abstruse and difficult philosophy was ever translated into Persian, Fardid transmitted a version of it to students who would gravitate to Iran's hardline Islamism. Whether this version was faithful to the original was ultimately beside the point.

Fardid, who studied continental philosophy in France and Germany in the 1940s, was not a practicing Muslim. But he saw the West as a nearly unmitigated evil, and he believed Islam was a useful antidote to its darkness. From Heidegger he took the notion that "truth" and "being" had once been accessible to men, but that Western metaphysics since Plato had cast them into obscurity, at last leaving the West empty of religiosity and spiritualism, enamored instead of its technology, which was nothing but a tool for domination. Fardid heralded the rise of an authentic East where "truth" and "being" remained uncorrupted. In Iran's Islamic Revolution, he saw what Hegel famously saw in Napoleon: history on horseback.

After the revolution, Fardid's hatred of the West grew virulent, his thinking conspiratorial, and he saw everywhere the villainous pushers of Westoxication lying in wait to roll back Iran's revolutionary gains. Although the German philosopher's masterwork, *Being and Time*, would not be translated fully into Persian until 2007, Fardid and his acolytes offered Heidegger as an antidote to the forces of Westoxication. The atheistic Heidegger, the atheistic Fardid claimed, was "the only thinker whose ideas are consistent with the Islamic Republic."

Fardid was charismatic, learned, ebullient, and persuasive; a former student recalls that Fardid would hold classes at his home, his acolytes emerging blinking into nightfall, unaware of time or space, hunger or fatigue. Like Shariati, he loved to provoke, to contradict himself and say things he didn't believe; but more than Shariati, from the depths of a boundless intellectual arrogance, Fardid styled himself the wise fool, prone to mischief, sarcasm, and feigned ingenuousness. He delighted in insulting people of influence but extended himself generously to freshman students who had nothing to offer him. Although many Iranian intellectuals would claim him for their mentor, Fardid distanced himself from all of them. When a young writer dedicated an essay in a newspaper to Fardid, claiming the old man had taught him all he knew, Fardid remarked, "Every spring I buy grass seed from the store across the street and cast it in my lawn, but what grows there is just quaint and curious weeds and not what I have put in the ground. The same is true of those who claim my legacy or oppose it. They bear no resemblance to what I have sown."

At the behest of a mutual friend, Soroush paid a brief visit to Fardid shortly after the revolution. The encounter was pleasant enough, but afterward, according to Soroush, Fardid spread the rumor that Soroush was a social democrat, which at the time was a term of abuse in Iran. It would turn out to be the least of the epithets the two men slung at each other for the remainder of Fardid's life. Soroush's embrace of Western science and analytic philosophy was a direct challenge to Fardid's demonic view of the West. It was a challenge to the spirit of the revolution, too, to the extent that spirit was defined by nativism. And so the two philosophers and their allies believed they were struggling over the very soul of the revolutionary state.

According to Soroush, Fardid became an unapologetic proponent of the use of violence against all he saw as enemies of the state, of Islam, of the rising East. As Soroush put it, Fardid taught that everything said outside Iran about justice, human rights, democracy, tolerance, and freedom was a lie, and all the world's cultural and political organizations were conspirators. Therefore Iranians shouldn't concern themselves with these pretty words and should instead advance their aims with violence. Even Fardid's former student describes some of his postrevolutionary lectures, collected in a book called *Premonitions from the End of Times*, as nightmarish and rambling.

Just as, in the West, a debate has long raged over whether Heidegger's active membership in the Nazi Party was the inevitable consequence of his philosophical views, Fardid's postrevolutionary embrace of extreme Islamic fundamentalism has raised similar questions in Iran. Soroush never endorsed the efforts of Heideggerians, Eastern or Western, to dissociate their hero from Nazism, and he believed that Fardid's philosophy, too, was fascistic at its core. He would tell an interviewer of Fardid and his circle: "If these people attack liberalism, it's from the position of fascism, not Islam or socialism or anything else. . . . In other words, it's the negative and reviled part of Heidegger's philosophy that has become the lot of us Iranians."

Fardid and his circle took a correspondingly dark view of Popper and Soroush. In his lectures in the 1980s, Fardid argued that Popper propagated a degenerately permissive liberalism; he was an enemy of Islam and a purveyor of ignorance. In 1984, Fardid attacked both Soroush and Popper, writing: "What is this rubbish they advocate as philosophy, these are insults to the history of humanity. . . . These people are managed by the international Jewish organizations and I shall inform Imam Khomeini of their conspiracies. . . . I, Ahmad Fardid, have a short message to Imam Kho-meini: Abdolkarim Soroush will destroy this revolution."

Fardid's admirers took up the battle in essays they wrote for publication, with the most prominent of these being Reza Davari Ardakani's contribu-tions to *Kayhan-e Farhangi*. Davari, who had studied philosophy in Tehran and theology in Qom, also styled himself a Heideggerian and considered analytic philosophy "antiphilosophy" compared to the true tradition of the continent. In a 1985 *Kayhan-e Farhangi* review of a Popper translation, Davari scoffed, "Who is Popper? Our enemies abroad use him to oppose the revolution, and there are people within the ranks of the Islamic Repub-lic who sanctify him and regard any attack on his ideas as sacrilegious." Pop-per, Davari wrote, only pretended to champion freedom and knowledge, in the hope of seducing the people of the Third World into accepting their subservience. In reality, Popper's pseudophilosophy served the march of sci-ence and technology, and the eclipse of religion, Third World emancipation, and social justice. This critique of Popper gained currency in conservative religious circles, where the denunciation of the Viennese philosopher rose to a drumbeat in state-run newspapers and Friday prayer sermons.

PERHAPS THERE WAS NOTHING quite like direct and vocal oppo-sition to concentrate the philosophical mind; perhaps the intellectual stakes were simply where clarity dwelt for Soroush. For it was in these years, the mid-1980s, just after his departure from the Cultural Revolution Institute, that Soroush came out of the closet as a liberal and as a critic of *velayat-e faqih*.

Bazargan's provisional government was long gone. "Liberal" had become a term of abuse attached to it, and Soroush, six years after the fact, felt com-pelled to rehabilitate the term and perhaps the man. Although he had never supported the seizure of the American embassy, he had not spoken out in Bazargan's defense during his tenure as prime minister. Still, over the course of the 1980s, Soroush became increasingly convinced that the Fardid circle had a hand in demonizing the liberal prime minister and that this needed to be rectified.

Soroush gave three speeches at the University of Tehran in 1986, two on fascism and one on liberalism. His lecture on liberalism he titled "Dare to Know," a phrase from Kant's essay "What Is Enlightenment?" He used it to argue that at the vital crux not only of enlightenment but of liberalism were scrutiny and criticism, the absence of secrets, the absence of certainty. Iranians, he suggested at a time of opacity and repression, should aspire to such a liberalism. In another of his 1986 lectures, Soroush argued that to devise and attempt to execute a blueprint for society, especially a heavenly one, would lead ineluctably to fascism.

Soroush expected that not everyone would approve of his arguments, but disapproval came from one particularly disappointing quarter. Mohammad Khatami, now the culture minister, relayed his displeasure to Soroush in a harshly worded message.

Soroush believed that Khatami had come partway under Fardid's influence. At least, he saw that Khatami oscillated, sometimes embracing the ecumenical rationalism of Soroush's circle and other times the anti-Western binarism of Fardid's. When Khatami believed that Fardid was right—that the West was infected by an intrinsic and contagious evil—then he concluded that Western rationality, which Soroush embraced, must be corrupt. Soroush saw in Khatami's lack of clear philosophical loyalties a wavering spirit that would undermine his political effectiveness as well. It was, to Soroush, a source of sadness, for while he saw Fardid as a twisted and devilish soul, a proponent of violence and an opponent of human rights, he believed that Khatami had a good mind and heart that were clouded by equivocation.

Mostafa Rokhsefat was less sympathetic. His relationship with Khatami had grown testy over the cleric's timorousness about publishing Soroush's essays. Khatami was, in Mostafa's estimation, a timid, conventional man. During his years at *Kayhan*, Khatami once said that the role of the press was to voice the views of the people, and the views of the people "are identical to those of Khomeini."

Toward the end of the 1980s, Khatami was asked to put forward the name of an individual to be considered the license holder, publisher, and editor in chief of *Kayhan-e Farhangi*. Mostafa was the obvious candidate, but Khatami did not submit his name. Mostafa resigned, taking his circle of intellectuals with him.

Kayhan-e Farhangi swiftly deflated. Mostafa went to work briefly as a cultural consultant to the government. But his work as a cultural impresario was not yet finished. Neither was the excitement he had stirred with *Kayhan-e Farhangi* or the demand for a continued forum for the discussion it had begun.

And so Mostafa started a journal and intellectual salon of his own, called *Kiyan*, which meant "foundation." *Kiyan* was independent from the state and associated strongly with Soroush. It would become, ironically enough, and against Mostafa's instincts, the vehicle for a political movement that would one day fasten its hopes to Mohammad Khatami.

FOUR

BAPTISM OF BLOOD

THE 1980S WERE A SPIRAL INTO DARKNESS. The revolution that was supposed to yield a just and self-governing Iran gave way first to war, want, and profound isolation. Open contestation in politics had ended with the expulsion of Bani-Sadr; so had the propaganda war that accompanied those political fights, the leaks and appeals to public opinion. Now the country's politics disappeared behind an opaque curtain.

Iran was an international pariah, suffering under blockade and leeching the blood of its young men at the Iraqi front. Years later, many Iranian decision makers would claim to have opposed continuing the war with Iraq after Iran regained its territory in the battle of Khorramshahr. But official Iranian policy was "war, war until victory," or until Saddam Hussein's unconditional surrender. The Basij militia made up fully 84 percent of Iran's fighting forces and 43 percent of the country's 190,000 combat dead by decade's end, according to official Iranian statistics. The Basijis were mainly teenage boys. Their graves populated a vast necropolis called Behesht-e Zahra in southern Tehran, glass cases above the plots displaying photographs of boys too young to shave, in row upon row as in a ghostly high school yearbook.

Starting in 1984, Iraqi Scud-type missiles periodically rained down on

Tehran and other Iranian cities. A young Tehrani woman who lived near a day care would never forget leaving her home one day to find her sidewalk littered with tiny hands. Some seventeen thousand Iranian civilians perished in eight years of episodic war. But this figure does not include the tens of thousands of lives that would be extinguished over decades by the lingering effects of mustard gas, which the Iraqis deployed against civilian as well as military targets while the world looked away and the United States supplied the Iraqi regime with crucial military intelligence.

Iran's economy was in free fall. It was never worse before, nor has it been since. War, inflation, political instability, and foreign sanctions conspired in its unraveling. So did the fact that economic planning was a bone of contention among competing political factions, pulled this way and that to the point of incoherence; and that the country depended heavily on oil revenues at a time when a worldwide oil glut caused oil prices to plummet. By 1988, Iran's gross domestic product per capita was half of what it had been in 1976. Poverty spiked. Decline on this scale was not only new to Iran but, as a leading scholar of the Iranian economy points out, rare in modern history.

Under a cloud of tension and violence, the October 2, 1981, presidential election brought Ali Khamenei to power, and with him the consolidation of single-party rule. Of the Islamic Republican Party's best-known founding fathers—Beheshti, Rafsanjani, and Khamenei—now Khamenei was president, Rafsanjani was speaker of the parliament, and Mir Hossein Mousavi, Ayatollah Beheshti's thirty-nine-year-old protégé, was prime minister. This was the most unified and stable government in many years. The only politics that mattered now were those that divided the Islamic Republican Party from itself, even if only by shades of gray.

Factions coalesced behind each of the three major political figures of the 1980s. President Ali Khamenei was associated with what would be called the Islamic Right. This traditional, conservative wing of the party supported private property rights and opposed the centralization of the economy. Prime Minister Mir Hossein Mousavi's faction was known as the Islamic Left, allied with the students who had seized the American embassy and the club-wielding men of Iranian Hezbollah. This radical faction advocated state control of the economy and a hardline foreign policy of exporting the Iranian Revolution abroad. Ali Akbar Hashemi Rafsanjani's faction was pragmatic. Whether it leaned left or right was a matter of perception, for Rafsanjani was a canny triangulator who knew how to play rivals off one another, and he swung his considerable political weight from one faction to another, often without warning and sometimes playing both ends simultaneously in secrecy. These three protagonists, and the alliances and resentments they forged, would shape the Iranian political drama for the foreseeable future.

ALI KHAMENEI, the Mashhadi cleric with the poetry circle, was a literary man who adored John Steinbeck and Victor Hugo and had ties to lay intellectuals before the revolution. He was also close to Ayatollah Khomeini, having studied with him in Qom in the early 1960s. Khamenei absorbed the anti-imperialism of the left and the Islamism of the Egyptian Muslim Brotherhood, the work of whose ideologue, Sayyid Qutb, Khamenei translated into Persian.

Houshang Asadi, then a member of the communist Tudeh Party, claims to have been Khamenei's cellmate in prison under the shah. His account has been called into question, but if true, it offers a humanizing glimpse of the cleric as a young man. Asadi remembers Khamenei as a mild and genuinely pious person, passionate about literature and tolerant of political differences. When Asadi grew depressed, he writes, Khamenei would invite him to go walking. The two men would supposedly pace around their cell, pretending they were hiking through the landscapes of their childhoods, exchanging thoughts on literature and politics. Together, Khamenei and Asadi conspired to keep a third cellmate alive: a teenage Marxist guerrilla fighter who had been badly beaten and was close to death of starvation but would not unclench his mouth except when threatened. Asadi contrived to threaten the young man so that Khamenei could slip bits of meat between his teeth. After some months of strange camaraderie, when Asadi was about to be moved to a different cell, he saw that Khamenei was shivering and gave the cleric his sweater in parting. The two men embraced; Khamenei, in tears, allegedly told Asadi, "Under an Islamic government, not a single tear would be shed by the innocent."

In scant years, the 1979 revolution propelled Khamenei's group to power and drove Asadi's to the brink of annihilation. Khamenei served, variously, as minister of defense, supervisor of the Revolutionary Guards, and leader of Friday prayers for the city of Tehran. Though Khamenei belonged to the revolutionary inner circle, he did not carry nearly the political weight that Rafsanjani or Beheshti did.

The presidency to which Khamenei ascended in 1981 was shorn of many powers. The clerics had deliberately weakened the position when Bani-Sadr was president, tipping the weight of authority to the prime minister instead. And Khamenei did not care for his prime minister. Economic differences were the main source of dissension, but Mousavi also antagonized Khamenei with public statements to the effect that he, Mousavi, was the real head of government, and the president was merely a figurehead. Twice, Khamenei appealed to Ayatollah Khomeini to replace Mousavi with someone more pliable. Twice, the Leader refused. With some reason, Mousavi would come to be seen as Ayatollah Khomeini's favored son and a rival to Khamenei.

MOUSAVI WAS a young lay intellectual who had been an architect and a newspaper editor. His wife, Zahra Rahnavard, was a well-known artist with ties to Shariati. Mousavi, too, was a regular presence at Hosseiniyeh Ershad in the 1970s, but he did not follow the anticlerical strain in Shariati's thought that led the Mojahedin and its sympathizers to their doom. Instead, Mousavi became an ally and deputy to Beheshti, the ayatollah who spearheaded the assault on liberals after the revolution and helped write *velayat-e faqih* into the constitution. Many times the clerics tried to force Mousavi on Bani-Sadr as foreign minister, but Bani-Sadr rejected him as a radical and a party man for the other side. After Bani-Sadr fled,

Mousavi briefly helmed the foreign ministry, where he was best known for introducing the clerics' ascetic style and removing the handmade carpets, conference tables, and chairs.

Mousavi was a populist who called for a more equitable distribution of goods and services, including education and health care. He supported nationalizing all foreign trade over the objections of the bazaar merchants whose interests Khamenei represented. Those who worked with him during his premiership remember him as an effective if colorless bureaucrat dedicated to pushing policies through the logjammed system that was part parliamentary, part theocratic, and riven with intrigue.

Mousavi's public persona was rather more vivid. He was the external face of Ayatollah Khomeini's radical foreign policy, rejecting every cease-fire the United Nations tried to broker with Iraq and threatening neighboring Arab states that, if they continued to cast their lot against Iran, "the flames of this fire would spread to them." Israel, Mousavi averred, was a "cancerous tumor." In 1985, Suleiman Khater, a border police sergeant in Egypt, shot up a family of Jewish tourists in the Sinai, killing four children, two women, and an elderly man. When Khater hung himself in prison, Iranian state radio quoted Mousavi declaring that "to honor the brave resistance of this great man, a street in Tehran will be named after him." On the fourth anniversary of the students' takeover of the American embassy, Mousavi spoke from the roof of a guardhouse at the embassy wall, lauding the students for publishing documents exposing the "liberal" enemies of the revolution, by which surely he meant Abbas Amirentezam.

None of this much distinguished Mousavi from his political peers at the time. These were ordinary positions and in some cases hackneyed slogans that originated with Ayatollah Khomeini. Still, the notion that Mousavi would one day become the symbol not only of vanquished revolutionary hopes but of a movement for democratic reform was inconceivable during his premiership. His transformation would say less about Mir Hossein Mousavi than about the fast-moving current of Iran's history, which not once but twice would seize him as its vessel.

. . .

AMONG MOUSAVI, KHAMENEI, and the spoiler Rafsanjani, Ayatollah Khomeini played a role much like Marshal Tito's in the former Yugoslavia: not impartial arbiter but nimble balancer. If his view was Olympian, that stemmed less from moral sagacity or political neutrality than from an overwhelming interest in the perseverance and stability of the form of government he had created. No faction could achieve a victory without Khomeini's handing one to its rival as well. On the economy, he veered from left to right and back again, seemingly less concerned with its ultimate structure than with assuring the political survival of all three power brokers and the triumph of none of them.

In the end, for the faction leaders no less than for Khomeini, the eighties were a decade of reversals and compromises. The revolutionaries were inexperienced in matters of governance. They had come to their task armed with ideological commitments that ultimately offered few solutions to urgent practical problems. Politics won out over ideology; but the politicians struggled to dress their pragmatism in revolutionary colors, to reassure a mobilized populace and keep its fervor from turning on the regime itself.

Perhaps the clearest indication of the Islamic Republic's creeping pragmatism was the Iran-Contra affair, in which Iran, hard up for spare parts and newer models for its American-made armaments, conducted secret dealings with the United States and Israel. The Americans were to supply Iran with arms via the Israelis in exchange for Iran's help in securing the release of American hostages held by Iranian proxies in Lebanon. When word of the clandestine arrangement got out, Mousavi and Rafsanjani were at pains to deny the story's details and assert their implacable enmity toward the country's two sworn adversaries.

What had been the de facto drift of the Islamic Republic became its policy in 1988, when Ayatollah Khomeini issued a fatwa that unambiguously placed politics above ideology, and even above religion. The survival of *velayat-e faqih* was the Islamic Republic's highest priority, Khomeini declared. At the ruler's discretion, the regime's interest could even override the injunctions of Islam, like fasting, prayer, and the yearly pilgrimage to Mecca. The fatwa was a breathtaking assertion of power.

Khomeini must have understood that a precarious moment was upon him. The country's resources had been strained to the limit—Mousavi was estimating the military budget at zero—and Iran would need seven times the number of men it already had on the ground in order to defeat Iraq's Western-equipped forces, military leaders told Khomeini in private. Moreover, an American warship in the Persian Gulf had just shot down an Iranian civilian airliner with 290 passengers on board. The United States claimed that the shooting was an accident, but from Tehran that hardly seemed possible—more likely, Iranian politicians surmised, the incident was a harbinger of direct American intervention in the war, which would render the fighting all the more costly and unwinnable. Whether the Iranian regime actually believed this or simply used this line for internal propaganda purposes is still open to debate. For Khomeini had now to talk the public down from a war he had sanctified. To do this, he would need not only sweeping powers but the ability to persuade the people that there was such a thing as national interest that could trump divine command.

On July 20, 1988, Khomeini accepted the United Nations Security Council's call for a cease-fire with Iraq. Explaining his decision to the public, the Leader intoned that death and martyrdom would have been more bearable, but political and military experts had concluded that the war was no longer supportable. "I know it is hard on you," he pleaded with his "revolutionary sons," "but isn't it hard on your old father?" Khomeini was standing down, he emphasized, in the name of Iran's national interest, but also because it was his religious duty: "Taking this decision was more deadly than taking poison," Khomeini said. "I submitted myself to God's will and drank this drink for his satisfaction."

Ayatollah Khomeini could not have known that June 1988 marked the first month of the last year of his life. But at eighty-five, with advancing cancer, surely he did know that his time could not extend forever and that with his passing would come the end of what some would call postrevolutionary Iran's First Republic.

The war's exigencies, and the bathos of its martyrs, could no longer inflame the public or call it to sacrifice. The Revolutionary Guard and Basij would return to the home front, where they would have to be reintegrated into ordinary life. The economy needed drastic reconstruction, which might even call for foreign investment. In all of this, radicalism was no longer helpful. Khomeini needed the society, and the Islamic Left, to stand down. But he had somehow to appease these forces, for the Islamic Republic rested on their unity with the state.

And so his last year was the year of two of Khomeini's most floridly extreme acts. The public one was the February 1989 fatwa calling for the execution of the novelist Salman Rushdie on the grounds that he had written a blasphemous novel. The fatwa kicked up a storm of Western denunciations and it satisfied Mousavi's faction, which pushed legislation through the parliament calling for an end to diplomatic relations with Britain, where the novel was first published. But in the context of Iran's domestic politics, the Rushdie affair was less an affirmation of revolutionary steadfastness than a colorful and distracting sideshow as the state prepared for the transition to a technocratic era of reconstruction.

Khomeini's other, ultimately more consequential act of extremism took place behind the high barbed-wired walls of Iran's prisons. The timing and extremity of this action would leave a puzzle for historians and a trauma on the national psyche.

IN THE FARTHEST NORTHWEST REACHES of Tehran, in a pleasant middle-class neighborhood of steep residential alleys and winding roads, Evin Prison is an optical illusion. Where the vast prison complex should be, there is a mean-looking no-man's-land in shades of brown, uninvitingly but thickly vegetated, remote even from its perimeter. The occasional fence or guard tower winks through the branches, but these could also pass for other things. Before long, the road climbs into a mountainside park bisected by a stream, its banks lined with glistening fruit stands and carpeted outdoor teahouses.

The shah built Evin to house 320 prisoners in 1971, when he understood that his regime was fighting for its life. Throughout the country, the monarchy held as many as 7,500 political prisoners in the early 1970s. Among them were many of the men who would become the Islamic Republic's leaders. The shah's prisons were brutal and brutalizing, and Evin was particularly notorious. Interrogators lashed the soles of prisoners' feet with a knotted electrical cable known as a bastinado. The nerve shock could travel from the feet all the way to the brain, permanently damaging the kidneys and the nervous system. Few victims of torture imagined that Iran's prisons could grow immeasurably worse.

By 1983, under the Islamic Republic, a somewhat expanded Evin held 15,000 prisoners. Rooms built for fifteen housed seventy-five; even the corridors were packed with blindfolded prisoners. Bazargan's former deputy prime minister, Abbas Amirentezam, spent two and a half years in a cell so crowded that the inmates took turns sleeping on the floor, each of them getting just three hours of sleep every twenty-four hours.

The denizens of these fortresses of misery were there for new reasons. The Islamic Republic had criminalized and even instituted the death penalty for things like apostasy, alcohol consumption, "insulting the prophet," and "crimes against chastity," which included extramarital sex and homosexuality, among other things. Prisoners accused of "sowing corruption on earth" or "waging war against God" faced execution as well. The latter crime was defined by Islamic law as taking up arms to cause civil unrest, but under the Iranian penal code its definition expanded to include membership in any armed dissident group, even if the accused never touched a weapon. Members of the country's largest and most severely persecuted religious minority, the Bahai, served lengthy prison terms on trumped-up charges. Many were executed.

The chief warden of Evin, and Tehran's prosecutor, was a former drapery merchant named Asadollah Lajevardi. He'd done prison time himself under the shah for attempting to blow up the offices of the Israeli airline, El Al. Lajevardi had giant, arching black eyebrows behind oversized plastic-rimmed glasses; he wore the stubbled beard of the Hezbollah faithful, and his features crowded themselves in the direction of his chin. He moved his family into the prison, avowedly because he was proud of the institution he ran, but later as protection from would-be assassins, as Lajevardi's name became synonymous with the worst abuses of an abusive decade.

Unlike the ancien régime, the Islamic Republic prohibited torture and forced confessions—but it allowed corporal punishment and "voluntary" confessions, which amounted, in the end, to the same thing. Evin's jailers were Revolutionary Guardsmen, the interrogators young clerics and seminary students. Their job was to extract a self-incriminating "interview" from each political prisoner. Until prisoners agreed to grant the interviews, interrogators would whip the soles of their feet, deprive them of sleep, submerge them in water, burn them with cigarettes, force them into stress positions, and put them through mock executions. They would twist and crush prisoners' forearms and hands, insert sharp instruments under their fingernails, and threaten their family members. Amirentezam, who served 555 days in solitary confinement, was taken blindfolded to the execution chamber three times. Once he sat there for two days. In 1994 he estimated that he had seen hundreds of prisoners die or be driven insane. Another former prisoner recalls being suspended from the ceiling by his ankles and forced to submerge his nose and mouth in a bucket of his own feces. He could smell and taste nothing else for weeks; he vomited continuously and starved nearly to death. More than 7,900 Iranian political prisoners were executed between 1981 and 1985—at least seventy-nine times the number killed between 1971 and 1979.

More even than the executions, the confessions, at least in the early 1980s, appeared to be the point of it all. They were elaborately staged and filmed in Evin's two-story auditorium before an audience of prisoners and aired on two-hour prime-time programs through the fall of 1983. Those who missed them on television or radio could read the transcripts, which were issued in pamphlets called Black Report Cards. Most of the recanters were Mojahedin or leftists. They were forced to denounce even their closest intimates: husbands, children, parents, friends. Some of those onstage had clearly gone insane, adopting split personalities, breaking into hysterical tears or laughter, or begging the wardens to kill them.

The confessions were not meant to be convincing. They were meant to demonstrate the bankruptcy of the opposition and the irresistible power of the regime. The followers of prominent political prisoners found it particularly soul crushing when their leaders repented; one said it was "as painful as observing an actual death." Another wrote that the night the leader of the Marxist wing of the Mojahedin recanted, "something snapped inside of all of us. We never expected someone of his reputation to get down on his knees. Some commented it was as revolting as watching a human being cannibalize himself."

For some repenters, public recantation was only the beginning of their service to the regime they had opposed. Afterward they came under the total control of the wardens, and they lived among the others in the overcrowded cells, spying on their former colleagues and dispatching fellow prisoners to the gallows. Known as *tavob*s, these repenters were morally disfigured by torture and complicity. The *tavob*s enjoyed better and more plentiful food than other prisoners, lighter sentencing, and access to prison workshops; the wardens set up a special Repenters' Society and a newspaper called *Repenters' Message*. But the *tavob*s paid for these small privileges in a currency that was unrecoverable. He became an iconic figure in the Iranian imagination, a totem of shattered humanity, hated for what he did no less than he was feared for what had been done to him to make him do it.

At least two clerics within Khomeini's inner circle had occasion to witness prison life and found what they saw so troubling that they brought their complaints to the Leader. One was the chief justice and head of the judiciary, who brought torture victims to see Ayatollah Khomeini and describe what they had undergone. The other was the man who had been designated to succeed Khomeini as Supreme Leader.

. . .

HOSSEIN ALI MONTAZERI WAS PERHAPS the only living ayatollah of rank and learning comparable to Khomeini's. He, too, had elaborated the theory of *velayat-e faqih* and lobbied for its inclusion in the Iranian constitution. But he could not have been more different from Khomeini in affect or character. Montazeri grew up rural and poor, and he retained the accent of his youth, such that educated men sometimes thought him a buffoon. He wore owlish glasses on his squat nose, and his resting expression was a half smile. He was a radical in matters of foreign policy, pressing Iranian involvement in Lebanon and Afghanistan. He was also a staunch defender of human rights as a matter of simple decency.

For a time in the mid-1980s, Khomeini removed Lajevardi from Evin and placed Montazeri in charge of Iran's prison system. The wardens Montazeri appointed were disgusted by what they inherited from Lajevardi's crew. One referred to his predecessor as having been "truly crazy." On Montazeri's watch, observers from the United Nations and the Iranian parliament were admitted to the prisons, where inmates were at last permitted family visits, warm showers with soap, courtyard time, cigarettes, language classes, writing materials, political discussions, and nonreligious books. The forced public recantations and prayer sessions were replaced by short "letters of regret," and to ease the overcrowding, Montazeri's associates released many *tavob*s as well as prisoners who had completed their sentences but were being held until they recanted. By mid-1986, political prisoners at Evin had shaken off the lassitude of terror long enough to organize a hunger strike, successfully demanding the removal of more *tavob*s and common criminals from their wards.

It was not that Montazeri's condemnation of the Mojahedin, whose members overwhelmingly populated the political wards, was equivocal. His own son had died in the blast that killed Beheshti. But Montazeri did not see the Islamic Republic the way Khomeini and the ruling party, with all three of its factions, apparently did: as fragile as it was righteous, besieged from within, married to a war it could not win and utopian hopes that could either sustain or destroy the all-too-human state they had built. The dawning pragmatism of the principals, including Khomeini, may have been a moderating influence on foreign policy, but on the domestic side it militated against many of the revolution's finest aspirations, suggesting that, toward the end of sustaining the Islamic Republic, the means needed to be neither Islamic nor Republican. Montazeri was of a different cast of mind.

Montazeri had been Khomeini's heir designate for just a year when Khomeini wrote him a letter in 1986 expressing disapproval of what he saw as leniency in the prisons. Montazeri, the Leader lamented, was excessively influenced by the regime's internal critics, and his inclination to discuss their negative views publicly was inappropriate. Moreover, Khomeini implied that Montazeri had been soft on the Mojahedin, and he alleged that the release of Mojahedin prisoners had already resulted in "explosions, terrors and thefts."

In late 1987, Khomeini began to transfer the prisons back into Lajevardi's control. The old masters reentered with a spirit of revenge nurtured during their period of absence. Lajevardi declared that under Montazeri, the Mojahedin—the hard-liners referred to them by the rhyming term *monafiqin*, meaning "hypocrites"—had been treated softly, in a manner "contrary to the expediency of Islam."

In reality, the Mojahedin had all but vanished from Iran's domestic scene by this time. The regime boasted that 90 percent of the group's members were in prison. The group's leaders, including Massoud Rajavi, had fled with Bani-Sadr to Paris in 1981. They were not very effective from that distance, and many of the rank-and-file members had given up the movement and expected to return, on their release, to quiet and ordinary lives.

But in 1986, Massoud Rajavi took a fateful decision. He moved to Iraq, where he set up a base of operation for something he called the National Liberation Army of Iran, a ragtag force of exiles supported by Saddam Hussein. On July 22, 1988—two days after Khomeini announced the ceasefire—the Iraqi army crossed into northern, southern, and central Iran, supposedly in a last effort to topple the Islamic Republic. The National Liberation Army participated in this operation, contributing a reported force of seven thousand fighters under Iraqi air cover and with the code name Eternal Light.

The Mojahedin had at one time stirred passive support among Iranians who saw it as the likeliest alternative to clerical rule. Teenagers, in particular, had gravitated toward the group as the only opposition force that harnessed the radical utopianism of the revolution and was willing to confront the theocrats by force. But it was one thing to disagree with the course the revolution had taken, and even to fight hezbollahis behind barricades in Tehran. It was quite another to join forces with a merciless external enemy in a bid to overthrow one's own government. By allying itself with Saddam Hussein's Iraq, in a war that had terrorized Iran for nearly a decade, the Mojahedin forfeited forever the sympathy of the Iranian people. (In the course of time, under the unrelenting desert sun, the Mojahedin would wither into a sinister and dangerous cult.)

Cutting supply lines and attacking with gunships, the Iranians defeated the invaders handily. But Khomeini was not done with the Mojahedin. He would exact his revenge not only on those captured on the battlefield but on the group's sympathizers from days gone by: the ones who clogged the prisons and who most likely heard about the incursion from Iraq only afterward, on the prison radio. On July 28, 1988, the ailing ayatollah issued a fatwa that would seal one of the great crimes of the twentieth century, although it passed nearly unremarked in the fearful gloom of Iran's isolation.

In his order, Khomeini decreed that "those who remain steadfast in their position of hypocrisy in prisons throughout the country are considered to be waging war against God and are condemned to execution." The "enemies of God" were to be given a cursory examination by trusted officers of the state and condemned to death. Khomeini appointed a three-man commission to undertake this work in Tehran and detailed the composition of similar commissions for the provinces. Of the commissioners, Khomeini wrote, "I hope that you satisfy the almighty God with your revolutionary rage and rancor as regards to the enemies of Islam. The gentlemen who are responsible for making the decisions must not hesitate, show any doubt or concerns, and [should] try to be 'most ferocious against infidels.'" In response to questions from the head of the judiciary—did the fatwa cover prisoners who had not been tried and those whose sentences were already partially served?—Khomeini clarified: "In all the above cases, if the person at any stage or at any time maintains his position of hypocrisy, the sentence is execution. Annihilate the enemies of Islam immediately. With regard to the case files, use whichever criterion speeds up the implementation of the verdict."

ON THE MORNING OF JULY 19, 1988, prisoners' relatives thronged the gates just as they did every other morning, to demand visits or news of their loved ones. But the gates were sealed, the relatives forced to leave without a word of explanation. For the prisoners on the other side of those gates, there would be no phone calls, letters, packages, television, or radio—not even medicines or trips to the infirmary for the sick. The cell blocks were sealed off from one another, communal spaces closed. The prisoners had dropped, it seemed, from the face of the earth.

One by one, the prisoners, starting with the Mojahedin, were called before the three-man death commissions and asked their affiliations. If the prisoner said "Mojahedin," he went straight to the gallows. If he or she said *"monafiqin,"* or "hypocrites," there would be further questions: Was he willing to denounce his colleagues on camera? To put the noose himself around the neck of an active Mojahed? To unmask false repenters? To walk through minefields for the Islamic Republic? If he answered no to any of these questions, the victim would be forced to write a will and forfeit any personal belongings, like rings, watches, and glasses. He would then be blindfolded and escorted to his death.

For the leftists, whose inquisition closely followed that of the Mojahedin, the questions were designed to determine whether or not the prisoners were apostates. Was the prisoner a Muslim? Was he willing to publicly recant historical materialism? Did he fast for Ramadan? Did his father pray, fast, and read the Quran? A Muslim, after all, could be considered an apostate only if his or her father had practiced Islam, implying that the child had rejected the teachings of his upbringing. Those raised in ignorance were largely spared and offered a chance at redemption if they submitted to lashings and forced prayers. So were the women leftists, because they were not considered autonomous adults who could be held responsible for their actions. In later years the eyewitness accounts of these survivors would bore like penlights into the calculated obscurity of those summer weeks.

At Evin, according to one former prison official, every half hour from seven-thirty in the morning until five o'clock in the evening, prisoners were loaded onto forklifts and lifted onto six cranes from which they were hanged. This continued through the months of July and August 1988. The executioners complained of overwork and asked to use firing squads instead, but silence and secrecy were of the essence. Some former inmates at Gohardasht Prison in Karaj, near Tehran, would later recall the arrival of freezer trucks in the lead-up to the killings, and the wordless gestures of an Afghan prison worker who tried to warn them that they would be hanged. According to Saeed Amirkhizi, a survivor from Evin, the inhumanity of the executions even traumatized some of the prison's hardened torturers: "Hajj Amjad, a guard . . . famous for his short temper and brutality, became unbelievably quiet and introverted after the carnage. . . . Another torturer, named Mohammad Allahbakhshi, was in a similar situation."

Nobody knows how many prisoners were executed in the summer of 1988, but popular estimates tend to converge around the four to five thousand mark. Only the city of Isfahan, where Ayatollah Montazeri still controlled the prison system, was spared. Montazeri would later estimate the number of Mojahedin killed nationwide between 2,800 and 3,800 and the number of leftists at 500. Added to the thousands already executed since 1979, the numbers—and the efficiency and senselessness of the killings of longtime captives—were enough to send a cold terror through the populace.

Families of the deceased, informed in batches starting in November, were forbidden to observe the traditional forty days of mourning. Many of the victims were buried in unmarked graves, in the sections of graveyards reserved for the damned. In Tehran the authorities dug huge ditches and filled them with bodies, which rose so close to the surface that one witness recalls seeing bones and personal effects littering the soil. The site was heavily patrolled by security forces, who forbade family members to touch the ground or to sit.

WHY, IN THE WANING DAYS OF HIS LIFE, the very week of the war's end, and seven years after he overpowered all significant opposition to clerical rule, did Ayatollah Khomeini personally order a crime against humanity that would forever blight his Islamic Republic? The historian Ervand Abrahamian speculates that the prison massacre was a "baptism of blood and a self-administered purge": it would weed out the faint of heart and leave behind a ruling elite that had made a blood oath to the system Khomeini had devised. No one has yet come up with a better explanation.

Khomeini and his lieutenants had prolonged the revolutionary moment to the greatest possible extent, first by mobilizing their supporters against the regime's internal enemies—the liberals, the left, and the Mojahedin— and their ideological foe, the United States; later by mobilizing Iranians in a war of martyrdom and sacrifice against Iraq. If fervor, fear, and Khomeini's personal charisma had mingled to charge the country's atmosphere with divine purpose, their dissipation threatened to leave a charred landscape disenchanted and exposed. Perhaps Khomeini feared a demobilized Iran and felt that drastic measures were necessary to shore up the survival of the Islamic state, to make clear beyond the shadow of a doubt the permanence and totality of *velayat-e faqih*.

With the prison massacres, he enclosed the supporters of his regime in a circle of complicity. According to Ayatollah Montazeri, Khomeini's heir designate, the decision had been closely held; neither the president nor the prime minister was privy to it. But the regime's inner circle defended its actions after the fact. Speaker Rafsanjani claimed that only one thousand political prisoners had been executed, which was neither true nor exonerating. In December 1988, President Khamenei alleged that the executed prisoners had "links" with the National Liberation Army: "Do you think we should hand out sweets to an individual who, from inside prison, is in contact with the *monafiqin* who launched an armed attack within the borders of the Islamic Republic? If his contacts with such an organization have been established, what should we do about him? He will be sentenced to death, and we will execute him. We do not take such matters lightly." Prime Minister Mousavi, too, suggested that the prisoners were legitimately executed because they were engaged in a conspiracy.

Only Montazeri himself refused to toe the line. His distaste for prisoner abuse was rooted in moral instincts for which he fought without political calculation. On July 31, 1988, Montazeri wrote Ayatollah Khomeini a letter arguing that while there was nothing wrong with executing the Mojahedin who had been captured on the battlefield, those who had languished in the prisons for years were clearly innocent in the matter of the invasion. He listed nine reasons for Khomeini to reconsider his decision, including that "to execute people who have been sentenced by our courts to punishments other than execution, without any process or new activities, is a complete disregard for all judicial standards and rulings and will not reflect well on the regime."

When this letter failed to stop the executions, Montazeri tried again in a missive dated August 4. A provincial religious magistrate who served on the death commission at a provincial prison had come to see Montazeri, the heir designate wrote to Khomeini. The magistrate was upset because one of the prisoners who appeared before his commission had renounced the Mojahedin in every way, but when he was asked if he would walk across minefields, he had replied, "Not all people are willing to walk over mines! Moreover, you must not have such high expectations from a new Muslim such as me." The intelligence officer on the commission sentenced the man to death over the objections of the religious magistrate. The intelligence ministry's men, Montazeri observed, were in control of the whole operation, overriding the religious judgments of their colleagues. Wrote Montazeri, "Your Eminence can see what types of people are implementing your important decree that affects the lives of thousands of prisoners."

Finally, on August 15, 1988, Montazeri took his complaints directly to the members of the death commission for Tehran.

"I have received more blows from the *monafiqin* than all of you," Montazeri wrote, "both in prison and outside. My son was martyred by them. If it was a question of revenge, I should pursue it more than you. But I seek the expediency and interests of the revolution, Islam, the Supreme Leader, and the Islamic state. I am worried about the judgment that posterity and history will pass upon us."

Many prisoners had professed steadfastness in their opposition to the regime precisely because of how they had been mistreated in prison, Montazeri noted. Their beliefs were not a crime, and the apostasy of their leaders did not make them apostates. Montazeri worried about the rule of law in the country he was to take over: "All the studies we did in Islamic jurisprudence about taking caution when dealing with people's blood and properties, were they all wrong?" He demanded: "By which standard are you executing a prisoner who was not sentenced to execution prior to this? You have cut off prison visits and telephone calls now, but how will you answer the families tomorrow?"

In a devastating final paragraph, the radical ayatollah and coauthor of *velayat-e faqih* made a case for freedom of expression. "The Mojahedin-e Khalq are not individuals," he wrote; "they are an ideology, a world outlook, a form of logic. To answer wrong logic one must use right logic. With killings it will not be solved but spread."

Although his plaints fell on deaf ears, Montazeri did not give up. In October he wrote to Prime Minister Mousavi, arguing that arrests and executions would only alienate people who could be assets to the revolution. He laid the problem at the prime minister's feet because the intelligence minister, Mohammad Reyshahri, popularly known as "the scary ayatollah," was technically Mousavi's subordinate: "We will cause irreparable injustice to many people because of the narrow-minded, draconian and uncaring officials in charge of the ministry of security and information," Montazeri wrote.

But these objections led to the sparing of no lives, so much as they sealed Montazeri's political irrelevance. Ayatollah Khomeini accused Montazeri of sympathy with Bazargan's defeated liberals, into whose hands, he proclaimed, he would never allow the government to fall. He disinherited Montazeri of leadership with a letter observing that "the responsibility [of being Supreme Leader] requires more endurance than you have shown."

The once future Leader retreated from politics, but he preserved his copy of Khomeini's fatwa ordering the executions, with the Leader's personal seal, along with his own letters of objection, for the records of future historians. In the decades that followed, through all that Montazeri was still to suffer, his example would acquire a profound and lasting luster, and his letters would endure as talismans of enlightened humanity under siege.

TWO MONTHS BEFORE HIS DEATH, Ayatollah Khomeini convened a committee to revise the constitution. Although the radicals put up a spirited fight, the conservatives succeeded in eliminating the position of prime minister and centralizing executive power in the hands of the president. The revised constitution also stipulated that the next Supreme Leader after all need not be a grand ayatollah, as Khomeini and Montazeri were, but should be an expert in Islamic jurisprudence who had "the appropriate political and managerial skills." Rafsanjani saluted this decision, pointing out that to become a grand ayatollah took nearly a lifetime, leaving a pool of potential leaders who were too old to lead the country with the necessary energy. And so the institution of *velayat-e faqih* itself descended from the realm of spiritual leadership into that of political management, raising the question of exactly how the Leader's far-reaching powers and lack of accountability could be justified. But that was a question for another day.

The next decision before the assembly was whether the leadership would be assumed by a single man or by a council of three. Either was permissible under the constitution, but as a cleric had once explained, "We need a focus for people's emotions. . . . How can the people shout slogans like, 'We are your soldiers, oh Leadership Council'?" When it was decided that one man would follow Khomeini as Leader, the radicals of Mousavi's faction lobbied for Khomeini's son, Ahmad, to inherit his father's mantle. But they lost this battle as well, and President Khamenei emerged as a compromise candidate among clerics sympathetic to both factions. Because he was not a grand *marja* thronged with acolytes—he had attained only the middle rank of *hojjat ol-eslam*—political actors on all sides may have mistakenly imagined that Khamenei would be pliable.

Khamenei had vast shoes to fill. Hundreds of thousands of Iranians, some pounding their chests and slashing their cheeks, poured into Tehran's streets to mourn Khomeini's death on June 3, 1989. Eight people died in the crush to touch the body; many more were injured. "We are orphaned," chanted the crowd. At one point the crowd knocked the Leader's body from the casket and fell upon the shroud for scraps, mementos. Men leapt into the open grave. Ahmad Khomeini was knocked to the ground. On the spot where Ayatollah Khomeini's body was at last laid to rest, a vast mausoleum would be erected, a cavernous modern shrine that would become a glittering, minaret-laden landmark off the airport highway outside Tehran.

Khamenei assumed Khomeini's mantle with the humility that was required of him by both culture and circumstance. "I am an individual with many faults and shortcomings and truly a minor seminarian," he said in his inaugural address. "However, a responsibility has been placed on my shoulders, and I will use all my capabilities and all my faith in the almighty in order to be able to bear this heavy responsibility."

Bigger men might buckle under such weight. Khamenei would turn out to be smaller than many imagined. He would also prove brittle and stubborn—insecure, many analysts would speculate, in the role that had been thrust upon him.

Just two months after Khomeini's death, Rafsanjani was elected president. There was no longer an executive position for Mousavi, and Khamenei and Rafsanjani closed ranks against the remaining radicals in the parliament. For the next eight years, supporters of the Islamic Left would wander the political wilderness of journals, universities, and newspapers. What happened to them there is the rest of the story.

II

REBIRTH

FIVE

EXPANSION AND CONTRACTION

AKBAR GANJI REMEMBERS THE REVOLUTION as a love affair that blinded him to everything but the paradise on his mind's horizon, an Islamic republic where all men would be brothers. He believed, during the revolutionary caesura that was his late adolescence, that he possessed the singular truth. In later years he would define fundamentalism as exactly that belief. By 1989 the Islamic Republic of Iran was no paradise, and Ganji was not a fundamentalist anymore. Along with many former members of the Islamic Left, he was a man on a journey.

Cast out of the inner circle of power, the militants of the Islamic Left turned to philosophy, sociology, and political theory for new answers to the questions they'd once relied on Shariati and Khomeini to resolve. They gathered at a think tank and a journal where they started, dizzyingly, diligently, nearly from scratch. What was the state? Why did it exist? How could they distinguish the work of God from its reflection in their own eyes? For men like Akbar Ganji, the revolution was a work in progress, susceptible to revision and even fundamental challenge. Ganji did not yet know that this outlook would transform him from loyal Islamic Republican foot soldier to national icon of resistance.

Small and lithe, with mirthful dark eyes and a mobile mouth, Ganji was born in 1960 to a traditional religious family and grew up poor in South Tehran. His mother brought him to mosque and to religious festivals. Islam was the Ganjis' community. South Tehran was dilapidated and crowded; to the city's north, the prosperous classes lived on hills that rose above the choking smog. Tehran was a city of just over two million in the 1960s, less than a third the size it would reach by century's end, and its profound social rifts were difficult to conceal. Ganji came to political consciousness through his resentment of the inequalities that had broken against him, and his attraction to Shariati's notion that a truly just, egalitarian Islamic society had once existed and could be regained. At a place called the Institute for the Intellectual Development of Children and Young Adults, there was a library where Ganji, like so many others of his generation, discovered Samad Behrangi and *The Little Black Fish* as well as the work of Jalal Al-e Ahmad. Ganji and his peers left their parents' traditional mosques for a political mosque of their own, alive with talk of Shariati's Islam of Ali and with leftist currents that reached Iran from as far away as Albania and Latin America.

In the late 1970s, Ganji became one of the leaders of the youth in his neighborhood, organizing school strikes and demonstrations, distributing Shariati's books as well as tapes and pamphlets of Khomeini's speeches. Ganji and other young militants organized strikes in the bazaar, threatening merchants into closing their shops if they didn't do so of their own accord. When the revolutionaries succeeded in toppling the shah, and committees of the faithful raided the soldiers' barracks for arms, establishing the Revolutionary Guard, which was loyal to Khomeini, nineteen-year-old Ganji was one of its first recruits.

Ganji met Mostafa Rokhsefat when Howzeh, Mostafa's artistic army, offered a cultural seminar to Revolutionary Guardsmen. The two men forged a friendship that linked the young guardsman to the revolution's intellectual vanguard. Ganji's agile and mischievous intellect distinguished him, then and always, from the movement whose orthodoxy he still embraced. More even than Mostafa, Ganji was a man who burned the bridges he built. In what would become a storied career as a writer and activist,

Ganji remained neutral toward no one, and no one remained neutral toward him. To his admirers he was a fearless freethinker; his detractors found him reckless and polarizing. His friendship with Mostafa would outlast nearly every other affiliation in his life.

Even within the Revolutionary Guard there were factions, with potentially fatal differences of opinion. Ganji belonged to a group that considered itself leftist as well as Islamist, and this group clashed with the Guard Corps commander as well as with the clerics. Much later Ganji would say that he had begun to distance himself from the revolutionary mainstream at that time because he was reading Hannah Arendt's *On Revolution*, translated into Persian shortly after the overthrow of the shah. He saw shades of the Iranian present in Arendt's account of the French and Russian pasts, and he was beginning to worry for revolutionary Iran's future.

Writing in 1963, Arendt argued that the French Revolution, and the subsequent revolutions it inspired, had failed because they unleashed the force of class rage, allowing the demand for social justice to supersede the demand for freedom. The revolutionaries, fueled by the urgent needs of the poor, and the poor, inflamed by the exposed corruption of the ancien régime, resorted to terror. The American Revolution, by contrast, never proposed to settle the "social question" or to mobilize an underclass, and its protagonists did not lose sight of the liberties of man. In the end, the American Revolution, so often discounted in the study of revolutions, was the one that produced a new form of government, under a constitution that endured. Arendt wrote that "the whole record of past revolutions demonstrates beyond doubt that every attempt to solve the social question with political means leads into terror, and that it is terror which sends revolutions to their doom"; and yet, to mobilize the poor against the rich was always more urgent and effective than to stir the politically oppressed against their oppressors.

If Ganji absorbed this argument as a Revolutionary Guardsman in the early 1980s, it did not yet drive him into open dissent from the course that Iran's revolution, and its Islamic Republican Party, had taken during the years of terror, populism, and single-party rule. But he did pick political fights, mainly with the Revolutionary Guard Corps commander, Mohsen Rezaie. By his later explanation, Ganji and his allies differed with Rezaie over the war policy after the Iranian victory at Khorramshahr, and they held that the Revolutionary Guard should remain aloof from politics, which it was increasingly entering. They likely worried that Rezaie was using his clout to bolster conservative forces against the Islamic Left. When they petitioned Khomeini for Rezaie's ouster, they earned a sharp rebuke from the Leader instead.

After that, Ganji traded his military career for an intellectual one. It was a better fit. Writing for Mostafa's *Kayhan-e Farhangi*, Ganji assailed Iranian Heideggerians for embracing a view indistinguishable from European fascism. Iranian philosophers did not really know Heidegger, Ganji was convinced; what they'd learned from him was simply how to hate the West.

From *Kayhan*, Ganji knew Mohammad Khatami, who became the Minister of Culture and Islamic Guidance first in 1982 and then again in 1989. Khatami's ministry, usually called by the shorthand Ershad, or "guidance," was a curious institution. To the extent that it oversaw media and culture in a repressive state, it was an organ of censorship, surveillance, and control. But by the same token, Ershad was also the ministry that held open what narrow window existed for free expression. If anyone within the Iranian government understood and defended the legitimate functions of journalists and poets, filmmakers and playwrights, it was Ershad, the ministry assigned to encircle and contain them. Particularly under Khatami, Ershad's officials were cultural figures themselves.

Khatami hired Ganji to work in Ershad's international press department. Although Ganji belonged to the ruling establishment, he always imagined himself somehow free within it, a sprite in the revolution's psyche, both loyal and provoking. He was eventually assigned to the Iranian cultural center in Ankara, Turkey. There he promoted his own vision of Iran's revolutionary culture. It was not far removed from the official one in those days of militancy and factionalism, but Ganji invited Abdolkarim Soroush to Ankara twice and had Soroush's work translated into Turkish.

When Khomeini stripped Montazeri of the succession, Ganji made no secret of his disapproval, on the grounds that it cast a shadow on the doctrine of *velayat-e faqih*. Ganji would later recall that he had his doubts about the doctrine before that, too. But in 1988 he made his objections public, and Iranian intelligence agents in Turkey made the symbolic literal: they reported to Tehran headquarters that Ganji had torn up a picture of Ayatollah Khomeini. Ershad recalled Ganji to Tehran, where he was investigated and forbidden to return to Ankara in 1989.

By then, the atmosphere at Ershad had grown more restrictive. The new Supreme Leader, Ali Khamenei, was insecure in his power and placed proxies, usually clerics, throughout the bureaucracy: men whose loyalty was beyond question and who would serve as his eyes and ears. These representatives were linked to one another and to the Office of the Supreme Leader in ways that allowed them to accrue power disproportionate to the positions they legally occupied. Even in Ershad, Ganji felt that he and his colleagues were under watch. He grew less invested in his governmental work and more invested in an intellectual quest that had assumed new urgency for a growing group of seekers.

Throughout the Rafsanjani years, Ganji read sociology. He read Marx, Weber, Tocqueville, Habermas, and Durkheim; through them, and through scattered readings in anthropology, he grew interested in a welter of different ideas, philosophies, cultures. Soroush's emphasis on religious pluralism resonated with Ganji during these years. He envisioned truth as a mountain he was trying to summit: one encircled in pathways, all of which led to the top.

On the crucial question of the period—the relationship of mosque and state—Ganji cast his lot with Soroush. In a religious state, he saw, religion became vulnerable to politics. To criticize the state was to criticize Islam. If the critics of the state were right, religion itself would turn out to be flawed, even endangered; if religion could not be flawed, critics of the state must then be apostates who could not be tolerated. Iran's Islamic Republic took the latter view, defining itself as the guardian of the one true religion. And so Ganji, as an incipient critic of that state, came to view politics as the fruit not of God but of man. If Iran's government was an earthly thing built by human hands, *velayat-e faqih* was nonsense. The country's leader should be chosen by its people and dismissed by them. And the clerics should have no special political role.

UNDER PRESIDENT RAFSANJANI, Mostafa Rokhsefat's new journal, *Kiyan*, flourished. Mostafa was no longer obligated to bookend Soroush's essays with ripostes from Ahmad Fardid and Reza Davari. *Kiyan* became the late realization of that pre-revolutionary dream—the birthplace of something its writers called "religious intellectualism," a thoroughly modern, thoroughly Iranian laboratory of ideas.

A growing circle of thinkers, nearly all of them former revolutionaries or regime loyalists, gathered at *Kiyan*'s offices each Wednesday to work toward a new vision of religious liberalism. Akbar Ganji was influential among them. The discussions centered on Popper and Soroush, and the participants, who numbered as many as thirty or forty, appealed to Soroush as the final arbiter of many questions. For each meeting, different members of the *Kiyan* Circle, as it was known, were assigned to give presentations explicating particular aspects of Soroush's philosophy. Collectively, through the discussions that followed, the *Kiyan* Circle worked toward understanding those ideas and translating them into a more explicitly political vision of pluralism, citizenship, and the role of civil society in an Islamic Republic.

The *Kiyan* Circle was a myth in its own time, a distant object of excitement for religious young people ill at ease with the course the revolution had taken. The journal's essays were heady, its concerns abstract, its frame of reference erudite; and yet, no one would describe it as obscure or as an object of interest only to academics. Rather, *Kiyan* was widely understood to embody the new wave of religious political thought, a corrective to the despotism and violence of the eighties and a solution to the problems of democracy and tolerance, one all the more serious because it emanated from thinkers who had themselves been close to Khomeini's regime.

Kiyan's readership survey revealed that the journal's readers were largely young men, with the average age of thirty. More than a third weren't college-educated, and almost half resided outside Tehran. Close to 80 percent described themselves as believers, ranging from somewhat religious to devout. It was a profile that matched that of the radical revolutionary students of the previous decade: young men, including college students and functionaries, from the society's traditional quarters. By some accounts, it was *Kiyan*'s appeal to the revolutionary rank and file that led the government, at length, to view it as a particular threat to its legitimacy.

SOROUSH PUBLISHED A COLLECTION of his essays as a book called *The Contraction and Expansion of Religious Knowledge* in 1991. Anyplace else in the world, such a treatise on epistemology and metaphysics might be left to molder in academic libraries. In Iran, the language of abstraction, whether poetic or philosophical, was a native one. Soroush's book offered tantalizing possibilities. Through it, one could at last debate the merits of secularism without ever calling it that. One could question the power of the clergy without disappearing to the gallows. And so the book and its author became a very serious challenge to the forces of reaction in the Islamic Republic.

Soroush's core insight was simple, revelatory, and part Popperian, part mystical, in its skepticism. The gleaming inner core of religion—the thing itself—did not belong to us and was unsullied by our hands. Like scientific truth, religious truth was known to us only through the mediation of our minds, our systems of knowledge. And so it was our minds and our systems of knowledge we really knew, and these were neither sacred nor infallible. That which was sacred and infallible—religion itself—was that brilliant gem at the bottom of the well, from which we spent our lives clearing away the obstructions.

Religion could not speak; humans spoke on its behalf, and what humans said was only human. Religious knowledge, like all human knowledge, was subjective, contestable, and shaped by historical context. It was an effort and not an end. Moreover, from the American logician and philosopher Willard Van Orman Quine, Soroush took the insight that all realms of human knowledge were interconnected; he extrapolated that religious knowledge, too, altered and shifted—expanded and contracted—with the circumstances of history and the development of science and other fields of understanding, and that it was susceptible to the techniques and insights of other fields. And so religious men should not fear the advance of human endeavor, including science, so much as embrace it as part of the pulsing organism to which theology, too, belonged.

Popper had called it "critical rationalism": the belief that human knowledge was limited and fallible, and that therefore any search for truth required the exercise of reason in an open-minded, collective effort without end. Soroush noted that to believe the opposite—that there was such a thing as certain truth known to particular men—was to render some questions unanswerable, even unaskable. Why had different schools of philosophical thought survived over the course of time? Why had theologians reached irreconcilable verdicts on matters of ethics and law? Moreover, such certainty cheapened faith, making its convictions a thing believers simply inherited, or received with frightened minds. Faith that came from open disputation and reason, Soroush believed, was far superior. Critical debate would make theology stronger and truer, while dogmatism would encourage demagoguery, opportunism, and greed.

Soroush believed that to be a critical rationalist was to be a pluralist, in matters of religion as well as philosophy. He argued that a true religion was one that pointed out the right path, but the same path was not right for every seeker; therefore, one religion might be true for one person, while a different religion was true for another. Soroush likened the prophets of the three monotheisms to trees in an orchard, each bearing its own fruit.

For those who thrilled to his theories, Soroush liberated religion from the clergy, politics from religion, faith from prejudice, rational debate and criticism from theological dogmatism. If no one could claim to speak for God, there could be no religious grounds for silencing one another. Religious thought, like everything else, should be open to discussion, criticism, debate, revision. Moreover, it could not subsume politics and all other human affairs, as Shariati had wanted it to, for religious knowledge was merely one other human affair and not in itself divine. As Soroush would later put it, where Shariati had sought to make religion corpulent, he, Soroush, sought to make it slim. He suggested that the theological basis for *velayat-e faqih* was weak and so it should be judged by its consequences. Moreover, Westoxication, by Soroush's lights, was dangerous nonsense that mistook blind emulation and total rejection for the only possible responses to a monolithic West. In Soroush's pluralistic view, a self-confident culture was a dynamic and open one capable of recognizing the dazzling variety of its influences.

ALTHOUGH SOROUSH'S CARDINAL WORK of the late 1980s and early 1990s seemed to owe more to Popper and Quine than to Mulla Sadra and Motahhari, he had not abandoned Islamic sources. In fact, there were some he drew on almost as extensively as he drew on Popper, and that matched his sensibility at least as closely. These were the Mutazilites, rationalist Islamic philosophers of the eighth through twelfth centuries, defenders of free will who held reason to be prior to revelation. God, in their view, had purposefully created a rational universe so that humans might discern it by use of their independent faculties. Soroush reflected this view when he scoffed at theologians who offered "Because it is God's will" in answer to the questions of supplicants. A rational God did not will things that couldn't be explained on their own merits. Because Soroush understood God's will to be rational, rather than arbitrary, he believed that theological explanations should owe more to logic than to flat assertions of divine authority.

The Mutazilites—and Soroush—applied the same view to morality. An action was not good or bad because God commanded or forbade it. Rather, God commanded or forbade the action because it was good or bad. Morality stood independent of God and inhered in the actions themselves, so that even someone ignorant of God's injunctions could use reason to discern good from evil. Soroush called this vision of justice "moral secularism" and himself a "Neo-Mutazilite." Among the Mutazilites themselves, moral secularism had led to an internal dispute, with some thinkers concluding that eternal salvation was therefore in reach even for people who had never read the Quran, so long as reason led them to discern and act on the good. Other Mutazilites found this conclusion unacceptable, as it rendered revelation ultimately unnecessary.

On the question of revelation and its provenance, the Mutazilites were radical. They argued that the Quran was a created text, rather than an eternal one, which meant that it was partly the product of its historical moment and could conceivably have been different had external circumstances been different. Soroush concurred with this view and took it even further in a book he would publish much later, in 1999. Soroush took an analogy from Rumi: If we wish to bring the sea into our home, we must provide a container. The sea does not stop being the sea when we pour its waters into a jug, but it does assume the dimensions and capacities of the jug. The same is true when we wish to bring the supernatural into the physical world: it takes on the temperament of its containers, namely, the prophet and the scriptures. But these containers are worldly and temporal. We must not imagine that their contours form the boundaries of the supernatural itself.

Personalities, even those of the prophets, Soroush argued, were incidental in religion. He mused that perhaps the physical gestures and motions of prayer were actually personal idiosyncrasies of the prophets. Maybe these gestures and motions were the effects, and not the causes, of the prophets' communion with God. The rest of us imitate those postures in the possibly vain hope that they will transport us where the prophets have been. Soroush's insight in this later book owed much to both Mutazilism and Islamic mysticism. And yet, it led some clerics in Qom to accuse Soroush of apostasy. "We say that the cherry is the fruit of the cherry tree," Soroush told an interviewer during this controversy. "Do we have to say that the cherry is the fruit of God in order to be a monotheist?"

Based in Basra, Baghdad, Yemen, and in later years the town of Shahr-e Rey, near Tehran, the Mutazilites belonged to a vibrant medieval culture of Islamic disputation, penning treatises that defended their principles against those not only of more orthodox Islamic philosophers but of atheists and freethinkers as well. At the time of the Sunni–Shiite schism over the succession to the caliphate, the Mutazilites had divided loyalties: those in Basra were sympathetic to the Sunni position, those in Baghdad to the Shiite one. Although the Mutazilites produced the official doctrine of the Baghdad caliphate from 765 through 848, their views were elite ones, eventually displaced by those of the orthodox Asharites, whose view that reason was subservient to revelation more closely reflected popular sentiments.

The Mutazilites went into near permanent eclipse. In time, Sunni Muslims came to embrace the Asharite view and to see Mutazilite ideas as heretical. But the often subterranean Mutazilite influence wove itself into the theology of the Persian Shiites and particularly the Yemeni Shiite sect known as the Zaydis. Soroush sought to resuscitate the best of the Mutazilite tradition and to remind Iranians that there was a basis for critical rationality within Shiism.

BY THE TIME OF KHOMEINI'S DEATH, Soroush had found a vast and growing audience, mainly of religious readers who found in his theory a way out of the revolution's moral and political impasses. It was possible, in Soroush's Islam, to be a believer but not a follower; it was possible, even necessary, to be a good Muslim and still engage in open, critical debate, even with the clergy, and to engage the ideas of political philosophers from all over the world.

In Soroush's view, there was no reason Muslim societies should not draw on secular political theories in order to design the best possible state. Politics and ideology were forms of human knowledge, after all, and none could really be said to be closer to the ineffable core of religion than any other. For that reason, Soroush held, to try to derive a political system, even a democratic one, from Islam was nonsensical. What mattered was that those who entered politics in a Muslim state have good Muslim values. From there, everything could be debated and contested, on rational merits, in the open air.

Soroush's critique cut to the quick of the Islamic Republic's legitimacy, and the new Supreme Leader, Ali Khamenei, was intent on refuting it. After Khomeini's death, the new Leader's office declared that "the spread of thoughts which consider religion to be a dependent variable of other human sciences is dangerous and it negates the legitimacy of the Islamic state." Perhaps Khamenei saw in the Fardid circle a like-minded repudiation of occidental liberalism and a convenient defense of the institution of his power. For, over the course of his leadership, those who considered themselves Fardid's acolytes (Fardid himself died of an intestinal illness in 1994) became something like the official philosophers of the Islamic Republic, influential beyond their numbers inside the Iranian political establishment. Its members would rise to control many of the Islamic Republic's cultural and intellectual institutions, including the Academy of Sciences, from which they expelled Soroush. After Fardid's death, many of his followers turned to Foucault and the postmodernists to further their critique of the West.

Soroush countered that postmodernist theories were meaningless in a country still struggling to reach modernity, and that in any case, as he put it, the postmodernists erred in wishing to see reason dead rather than see it humble. In later years, Soroush would compare Fardid's posthumous influence on the Iranian state to the political philosopher Leo Strauss's on the American administration of President George W. Bush. But Soroush's own sway could not be underestimated, nor, despite the fondest wishes of the political establishment, could *Contraction and Expansion* be unwritten. The book sold more than twenty thousand copies and provoked ten book-length responses. It was the beginning of a renaissance in Iranian religious thought.

THE THINKERS at the *Kiyan* Circle did not read only Soroush. Under his influence, they engaged the unlikely field of Anglo-American analytic philosophy, absorbing its insights, and the precision of its language, into the new Islamic thought. The very fact of its nearly mathematical abstraction, its lack of reference to European history or culture, made it transferable to

Iran to a degree that continental philosophy, with its always slightly alienat-
ing embeddedness in the European context, had never been.

Kiyan published a great deal on Popper: translations of his work, essays
expounding on his views, even a 1992 interview with the man himself, conducted at Popper's home in Surrey by a young Iranian scholar named Hossein Kamaly, who had translated some of Popper's work into Persian under
Soroush's supervision. Kamaly would long remember that although he was
close to ninety years old, Popper answered the door himself and showed
the young Iranian student around his home. Kamaly had booked Popper
for a forty-five-minute interview, but Popper gave him two and a half hours.
An early order of business was the lengthy introduction Kamaly had written to his translation of one of Popper's books. At a glance, Popper declared
it too ambitious. Kamaly should publish it elsewhere, and Popper would
supply him with a two-page introduction of his own.

If Popper had not been aware of his stature in Iran before meeting
Kamaly, he certainly was afterward. When an Iranian philosopher criticized
Popper on the grounds that not all of Marx's works supported historical
determinism, Popper wrote him two letters in response, defending his view.
And when Popper died in 1994, a private Iranian cultural institute held a
daylong seminar in his honor, with speaker after speaker propounding on
his work.

And yet, by the time of his death, Popper was barely even read in the
West. He was overshadowed by Thomas Kuhn in the philosophy of science
and secured little space in either analytic or continental philosophy curricula. Kamaly, years hence, would tell an American colleague he was working on a paper called "After Popper," only to have the colleague respond
with utter bewilderment, as though he had bestowed mythical status on a
figure of the most minor importance.

KIYAN WAS NOT THE ONLY intellectual journal of its era, nor the most
daring. *Adineh* published the brave remnants of the secular left. *Zanan*,

founded by another displaced editor from the *Kayhan* group, Shahla Sher-kat, addressed feminist concerns, and had a close relationship with *Kiyan*, with which it shared office space. The journal *Goftogu*, founded by the philosopher Ramin Jahanbegloo and several other secular intellectuals, took up the discussion of democracy, pluralism, and civil society from a nonreligious perspective. Where *Goftogu*'s editors were well-traveled, secular intellectuals from the educated elite, *Kiyan*'s were traditional-minded, religious men from the bazaar class and the lower middle class, most of them the first in their families to pursue a life of the mind. And yet the two journals established a rapport. They traded authors, engaged in discussions, worked common themes.

There were subjects on which more secular thinkers would fault *Kiyan* for its reticence. *Kiyan* published a smattering of essays by women, for example, but it did not contend seriously with the pressing matter of women's rights under the Islamic Republic. Soroush gave just two lectures and two interviews on the "woman question" in the postrevolutionary period, and they might have been lost had an independent scholar not documented them in a book. In those lectures, Soroush stressed that even if the holy texts described women as existing entirely to serve the purposes of men, and even if the Prophet and the imams concluded that women should therefore be regarded as less fully human than men, modern Muslims were not obligated to accept their reasoning. Rather, they had the right to question it both logically and based on contemporary wisdom.

Soroush ducked the debate, then raging in Iranian feminist circles, over the rights of women in Islamic jurisprudence, saying in an October 1996 interview that he believed it was necessary to start with philosophical principles and end with legal rights, rather than vice versa. This position was largely consistent with Soroush's general outlook. He was a philosopher, not a political strategist. The first question should be whether it was possible to argue, as an Islamic philosopher, for the full humanity of women. The jurisprudence would follow the philosophical logic. But this philosophical discussion was not a priority for *Kiyan*, and *Zanan* focused instead on the struggle for women's legal rights. Soroush, for his part, emphasized his belief that there were profound differences between the sexes, which would be unnatural to efface. He seemed to hear talk of "equal rights" or "gender equality" as a denial of difference rather than as a call for universal rights to be shared among rational human beings.

It was on these and related questions that Soroush's distance from secular liberalism was most pronounced. He argued that in the West the notion of rights had been taken too far. A Muslim democracy, in Soroush's view, could not conceivably accord rights to homosexuals, for instance. Although an Islamic democracy, as he described it, would not be ruled by clerics or based on Islamic law, it would be guided—bounded—by the Islamic morality embedded in the hearts of its citizens and elected officials.

The religious intellectuals of *Kiyan* and the secular thinkers around *Goftogu* had substantive differences, if they cared to explore them. But the Rafsanjani years were a time more of unity than of division among these various strains of dissident Iranian thought, all of which would soon find themselves under a violent and unrelenting pressure. For the reformists came to understand, by the mid-1990s, that they had serious enemies— determined and even violent elements within the regime who saw the intel- lectual movement percolating through *Kiyan* as an intolerable challenge to the ruling ideology.

The *Kiyan* Circle was largely caught by surprise. Most of its members saw themselves as a dissident strain within the establishment, their devel- oping creed as an adaptation of the revolutionary ideology to changed circumstances, to trial and error, and not as a counterrevolutionary trend. Moreover, in the far more repressive 1980s, the Islamic Republic had toler- ated Soroush and his supporters. Under Khomeini, the largest and most organized opposition groups—the Mojahedin and the secular left above all—were treated as frank enemies of the state and violently persecuted to extinction. But Khomeini had abided factional differences among those he considered loyal followers, perhaps because he did not have a strong prefer- ence among them, or perhaps because until the Mojahedin and the left were vanquished, he had bigger fish to fry. Rumor had it that when asked about the essays that would come to form *Contraction and Expansion*,

Khomeini said he had no problem with Soroush's thesis. But after Khomeini's death, as Soroush and the *Kiyan* Circle began generating real excitement, the new Leadership revealed a thinner skin.

And so it was that in 1995, shortly after Soroush published an essay arguing that the clergy should not be paid lest it grow corrupt, Khamenei himself wrote an editorial in a state-run newspaper warning Soroush that he should not challenge the authority of the clergy. According to a close associate of Khamenei's, the "Dr. Soroush issue" was a matter of "national harmony" and "Iranian national independence." The speaker of the parliament referred to Soroush when he declared that "enemies of the revolution" were "exploiting naïve people with these complicated theories to undermine their faith in order to defeat the revolution." In Qom, too, Soroush had vociferous critics, not the least of whom was the most violent of hard-liners, Ayatollah Mesbah-Yazdi, who sneered that "we will throw these fashionable ideas into the dustbin of history" and that anyone who spoke of multiple interpretations of Islam should be punched in the mouth.

As early as November 1992, Soroush understood that he was in physical danger. A group of militiamen from a pressure group that called itself Ansar-e Hezbollah threatened Soroush's life when he gave a talk in Isfahan that year. It would come out much later that Ansar was almost certainly affiliated with the power structure, if not directly with the Office of the Supreme Leader, and that it tended to act on Ayatollah Mesbah-Yazdi's bloodthirsty fatwas. Three years after this first incident, in 1995, a group of Isfahani students invited Soroush to come give a talk about Shariati's legacy. When again the threats streamed in, the university administration canceled the talk. Not to be dissuaded, the students found an off-campus venue, where an audience of more than a thousand convened to hear Soroush speak. But no sooner had Soroush opened his remarks than the militiamen surged from the audience, pummeling the philosopher in the face and head and tearing his shirt from his chest. A student rescued Soroush and hid him in the building's basement until the Hezbollahis dispersed.

In those days it was still possible to imagine that the authorities did not endorse such thuggery, particularly against someone so closely associated with the Islamic Republic in its early years. President Rafsanjani himself was thought to be largely sympathetic to the reformers. Soroush wrote Rafsanjani an impassioned letter, imploring him, "I have come to you in humility to seek justice, not for myself, but on behalf of our cultural pride and our dignity that have been subjected to these atrocities." More than a hundred intellectuals also petitioned Rafsanjani on Soroush's behalf. But Rafsanjani was silent, the hard-line newspapers continued to vilify Soroush, and Ansar-e Hezbollah announced its intention to silence the philosopher anywhere he tried to speak.

That October, Soroush attempted to lecture on Rumi at the University of Tehran. Ansar-e Hezbollah stormed the auditorium, throwing chairs onto the stage where Soroush stood, blocking the doors, and claiming they had come to debate Soroush. Soroush retorted that he could not debate under duress. Still, the following spring, when Soroush was invited to speak at an event commemorating Ayatollah Motahhari's death, Ansar showed up in force, wielding clubs and daggers and demanding a debate at knifepoint. Soroush wrote again to Rafsanjani: "The triumph of worshippers of darkness conveys the defeat of our culture, the depletion of our hopes, and the decline of our thoughts. Remaining silent is not permissible, do not allow them to win."

But if the president had the power to halt the attacks, he did not use it. Soroush found no safe quarter during Rafsanjani's era or after it. In 2000 he was invited to speak in the eastern provincial capital of Khorramabad alongside Mohsen Kadivar, a dissident cleric who had been a student of Ayatollah Montazeri and who criticized *velayat-e faqih* from the standpoint of Islamic jurisprudence. As soon as Soroush, Kadivar, and Soroush's adult son disembarked in the two-room airport, they realized that the building was surrounded by members of Ansar-e Hezbollah, who threw stones and brandished knives. For seven hours the militiamen held out, and the reformist intellectuals remained inside the building, unable to move in any direction. At long last, Khorramabad's police chief entered the airport. He suggested that he procure army uniforms for Soroush and Kadivar so that they could steal away from the airport in disguise.

Kadivar erupted. What was the police chief suggesting? Wasn't it the job of the police to save their lives—to protect them from the mob of hooligans?

The police chief, by Soroush's recollection, calmly replied: "We have the names of the people whose lives we are responsible to save, and yours are not among them."

Kadivar refused the uniforms. In that case, the police chief told the men, they could leave the building at their own risk, passing through the armed mob to a bus. Once on the bus, the police chief said, they should not sit by the windows, because he could guarantee nothing: the militiamen might be all along the road, throwing stones or even firing guns. The bus took the intellectuals to an army barracks, where Soroush and Kadivar passed two tense hours before they were ushered into cars and driven back to Tehran, their lecture never given.

During that period, the intelligence ministry called Soroush in three times for lengthy interrogations. Years later, he'd remember the blank sheets of paper on which he was made to write out answers to question after question, and the classic routine of alternating interrogators, one polite and one spitting obscenities at Soroush as he wrote. But there was one incident above all that stayed in Soroush's mind, a parable of his country's recent history and a sign of the growing divisions within the Islamic Republic itself.

Soroush had been arrested on the street, forced into a car, and taken to the intelligence ministry. The man who arrested him and the driver of the car sat with him in a small room where he awaited his interrogator. After a long silence, the man who had arrested him spoke. "I will leave this room soon, and the interrogator will come to you. But there is one thing I would like to tell you before I leave you alone."

In the 1980s, the agent explained, he and his colleagues were quite happy working with the intelligence ministry. They felt they were confronting real evils: "Saddam's people," as he put it, along with the Mojahedin and the leftists. The agent and his colleagues were content even to kill or be killed in the line of these duties. They knew how to do their jobs and they understood the philosophy behind it all. But something now, the agent said, "has broken our backs. And that is arresting people like you. Because we know you."

"How do you know me?" Soroush asked.

"Oh, I have been to many of your lectures and talks," said the man ruefully. "This is something indigestible to us."

SIX

THERMIDOR

IT IS EASY TO IMAGINE WHY, in the aftermath of its revolution, France adopted an entirely new calendar—one in which the week lasted ten days and the months had pseudo-Latinate names, like "Pluviôse" and "Ventôse" in winter, "Germinal" and "Floréal" in spring. History, the revolutionaries surely felt, ruptured at the end of the eighteenth century. For once, it moved not in increments, seconds upon seconds of infinitesimal change, but in a single propulsive heave. Even the past was new, now that it no longer sat cheek by jowl with the present. British onlookers mocked the ponderous novelty of the revolutionary French calendar as though its months named twelve dwarves in a pretentious fairy tale: Wheezy, Sneezy, Freezy, Flowery, Showery, Bowery. The calendar's use lasted just twelve years. How long the revolution lasted is another matter. But it is perhaps fitting that one calendrical coinage from that era has since become a term of art among those who have studied or lived through revolutions.

Named for the heat of the summer, Thermidor began in late July and ended late in August. Maximilien Robespierre, the Jacobin leader of the Reign of Terror, met his end by guillotine on the ninth of Thermidor, year two, elsewhere known as 1794. His death marked the beginning of a period of reaction, one that followed revolution as surely as summer followed spring, and which came to be called Thermidor as far away as Russia and eventually Iran. In Thermidor, the fever of revolution broke and the extremists were executed or driven from power; utopianism was abandoned, order restored, and a technocratic new elite gathered up the pieces of the old bureaucracy. From the chaos and violence of rupture, a new dictatorship was born, promising stability. In 1938 a Harvard professor named Crane Brinton devoted a chapter of his book *The Anatomy of Revolution* to Thermidor, limned as a kind of convalescence from the fever of crisis and a precursor to the restoration of something like the old order.

Brinton was a scholar of the Jacobins and of Talleyrand, and he would go on to serve as chief analyst for the CIA's predecessor, the Office of Strategic Services, in Britain during World War II. In *The Anatomy of Revolution*, which he revised and updated in 1965 (three years before his death, and just two years after Hannah Arendt published *On Revolution*), Brinton compared the French, British, American, and Russian revolutions, looking for parallels that might explain how such upheavals progressed. He wrote with a sort of Hobbesian detachment; he was not so much moved by the bathos of human striving, its euphoria and wreckage, as he was interested in understanding revolution's underlying mechanism. Perhaps not surprisingly, his book found a hungry readership in post-utopian Iran during the Rafsanjani presidency, when intellectuals began to apply its model to the revolution they'd effected.

Up to the point of Thermidor, Brinton's narrative fit Iran's revolution with uncanny precision. Revolutionaries, Brinton noted, tended not to be miserably oppressed people in desperate places, where the wealthy lived in excess unimaginable to the wasting, wanting poor. Rather, they tended to be uncomfortable people in countries whose economies were improving— people who felt they had a right to expect more. "These revolutions are not worms turning," he wrote, "not children of despair. These revolutions are born of hope, and their philosophies are formally optimistic." They tended to occur in societies where the social classes were relatively close together but in which the divisions among them were nonetheless bitter; countries whose governments reacted with laxity or ineptitude to rapid modernization, and where the elites began to distrust themselves, losing faith in the "traditions and habits of their class."

Brinton pointed with particular emphasis to the role of intellectuals in the pre-revolutionary state. In a stable society, like the post-1960s United States, alienated intellectuals might decry, say, modern capitalism, but they lacked a positive agenda and were in no way serious about upending the routines and privileges of their own daily lives. In pre-revolutionary states, however, intellectuals went so far as to transfer their allegiance to another, better world: "What differentiates this ideal world of our revolutionaries from the better world as conceived by more pedestrian persons is a flaming sense of the immediacy of the ideal, a feeling that there is something in all men better than their present fate, and a conviction that what is, not only ought not, but need not, be. And, one must add, a gut-deep hatred for the way things are."

The revolutionary state, once achieved, seemed to follow a predictable calendar of its own. Its first political leaders, according to Brinton, would be moderates—like Iran's Bazargan or even Bani-Sadr—but these men would soon be executed or driven into exile by the rising extremists of the left. The extremists would then centralize power, suspend civil liberties, and crush dissent, using extraordinary courts and revolutionary police. Then, in the grip of moral zeal and the conviction that the world and its inhabitants could truly be made new, they would use their police power to pry into citizens' everyday lives, punishing ordinary vices and extolling an ascetic notion of virtue that came naturally to no one. Brinton called this the Reign of Terror and Virtue. When its dark, fanatic energy was spent—when it had at last arrived at the logical point of executing the extremists who once led it—Thermidor began.

The anatomy of Iran's revolution may not have matched Brinton's sketch in every particular, but the parallels were striking. Thermidor, it could be said, began with the death of Khomeini. True to Brinton's prediction, the original cast of extremists—like the Bolsheviks in Russia and the Jacobins in France—were expelled from power with the remnants of the Islamic Left. But they were not hounded to execution or exile as their European analogs had been, and their colleagues who remained in office were every bit as culpable for the Terror as the Left had been—probably more so. Iran did not pretend to repent for its Reign of Terror and Virtue, nor to sacrifice any Robespierre of its own; rather, the bloodshed of the 1980s would not be spoken of again. Like all repressed traumas, it would exert a force of irresolution and guilt from a place no one could see.

AFTER THE REVOLUTION, a certain look prevailed in Iranian government circles. In men, as proof of faith, it required facial hair: a full beard, or better still, the shadowy insinuation of one. Even thirty years later, young men could not get government jobs without that stubble. But President Rafsanjani, a portly man with small, intelligent eyes and a nearly identical, mirthless expression in every photo, was a conspicuous exception. He disdained the rumpled Basiji look, saying, "If it becomes a cultural phenomenon that being a Hezbollahi means looking unbearable, this is a sin and Islam has fought this." Rafsanjani was famous for his wide, doughy, hairless face; he was fair-skinned and even a little shiny. The public nicknamed him "the Shark," not after the vicious sea creature, but because in Persian the same term neutrally denoted a man who could not grow a beard. As it happened, the name would adhere to the president for reasons beyond the visual.

Just as Brinton might have predicted, Rafsanjani signaled the new era by renouncing the harsh abstemiousness of the Reign of Terror and Virtue. He urged Iranians to stimulate the economy by consuming more goods, and he cautioned that ostentatious shows of piety invited hypocrisy: "Asceticism is necessary only under emergency situations," the president said; otherwise, "pretension to piety and poverty will become pretentious." He admonished Friday prayer imams to ease up on young people, because "through suppression, pressure and threat we can only partially preserve the outer façade of our society."

President Rafsanjani's task was not an easy one. Through the turbulence of the 1980s, Khomeini's charisma, the war effort, and the mass mobilization of the revolution itself had held Iran together in spite of everything. With none of these tools at their disposal, Rafsanjani and the new Supreme Leader, Khamenei, had now to substitute functional competence for ideology, like Thermidorian leaders everywhere.

At first the new Supreme Leader, Ali Khamenei, receded behind the scenes, allowing the shrewd, pragmatic president to set the course of policy. His reticence was understandable. Khomeini's was surely a hard act to follow; President Rafsanjani had a commanding presence and a formidable political apparatus of his own; and anyway, the new administration had inherited a lot of problems. The economy was in tatters. The war had cost Iran some $200 billion and brought millions of refugees over its borders, even as the gross domestic product shrank. Advised by technocrats, Rafsanjani decided to reverse the statist economic policies of the Mousavi cabinet, which he suspected had contributed to the country's malaise.

Rafsanjani's course correction would look to his critics very much like the structural adjustment programs foisted on Third World countries by the International Monetary Fund: the new president proposed to substitute exports for imports and to grow a market economy, even a private sector. He'd rebuild facilities damaged in the war, privatize the agricultural sector, and expand the petrochemicals industry. To do all this, he felt certain that Iran would need allies, even foreign investment. He would start by normalizing the country's relations with its neighbors in the Persian Gulf region. At the same time, Rafsanjani invited a loosening of Iran's censorship regime, giving his Ershad minister, Mohammad Khatami, a green light to issue publishing licenses for newspapers and books. In Rafsanjani's first three years in office, Ershad allowed the publication of eight thousand books, and by 1992, Khatami had more than tripled the number of newspapers and journals. It was not exactly a free press, but it was closer than Iran had come in some time.

Rafsanjani's critics feared that this was Thermidor writ large—that Iran, like France before it, was sacrificing nearly all its revolution stood for and restoring a familiar old order in the name of stability. The conservative right was willing to give the new president a conditional benefit of the doubt on foreign and economic policy, but it saw the cultural loosening as a sign of ideological deviation and religious impurity. The Islamic Left, meanwhile, supported the cultural relaxation but objected strenuously both to Rafsanjani's foreign and economic policies and to its own exclusion from his inner circle.

When Saddam Hussein invaded Kuwait, Iran's internal tensions bubbled to the surface. As the last country Iraq had invaded, Iran could not greet this latest aggression with equanimity, Rafsanjani reasoned; nor, however, could it openly condone an American troop presence on its border. And so, Rafsanjani concluded, Iran would "shed no blood for the United States to accomplish its goals or for Iraq to remain in Kuwait." Iran would remain neutral. But some members of the Islamic Left in the parliament continued to believe that the Islamic Republic stood for nothing if it did not stand against America. The Americans must be expelled from the region, they insisted. Some even felt that Iran should side with Iraq against the United States. Rafsanjani refused.

If Rafsanjani hoped to steer Iran toward a less confrontational foreign policy, the Islamic Left, with its public speechifying on Palestinian suffering and American iniquity, must have seemed to him an embarrassment and an impediment. The president was a bare-knuckled, ferocious factional player when he wanted to be. In his first term, eager to silence the radicals' keening against America and against structural adjustment, he apparently judged the common interest he shared with them on the matter of culture and censorship expendable. So were the niceties of electoral politics, such as they still existed under the Islamic Republic. To secure his short-term victory over the Islamic Left, he made a Faustian bargain: he supported an elections law making "absolute loyalty" to the Supreme Leader a condition for candidacy in Iranian elections. The Guardian Council would determine who did or did not possess this loyalty. It was a law that would effectively allow the clerics arbitrary power over the electoral process. The Guardian Council belonged—in perpetuity, for it was largely appointed by the Supreme Leader—not to Rafsanjani's centrist faction but to the conservative clerics to his right. In 1992 these clerics were Rafsanjani's temporary tactical allies; in years to come, they would be his adversaries. The elections law would remain in force, having dealt a permanent blow to what little popular sovereignty existed under *velayat-e faqih*.

The Guardian Council stacked the rolls for the conservatives in the 1992 parliamentary elections. And conservative hard-liners, to the president's right, took the legislative body in a landslide. Once there, they doubled down on their revolutionary orthodoxy. In books, newspapers, theater, films, and women's dress—all areas that had started to loosen up at the beginning of Thermidor, with Rafsanjani's blessing—the hard-liners hoped to see greater conformity to revolutionary Islamic values. When it came to the economy, the hard-liners defended the prerogatives of the bazaar against the more modern, industrial priorities Rafsanjani favored. So it was that Rafsanjani, who had ensured the hard-liners' victory in the election in order to relieve the pressure from his left, began to feel an even tighter squeeze from the other direction.

Khamenei increasingly took the side of the hardline right against the centrist president. In doing so, he permanently altered the very position of the Supreme Leader. There could be no further pretense that the *faqih* was a wise man on high, balancing power among rival factions. Khamenei was a factional player, the heaviest hand on the scale in favor of the hardline right. When the hard-liners in the parliament took up a relentless campaign against the new freedoms of expression Khatami had allowed, Khamenei spoke out on their behalf. After the Leader's intervention, Rafsanjani had little choice but to replace Khatami with a hard-liner—which he did, in July 1992. Khatami took a quieter post as the head of the national library. The momentary cultural opening was over. The new Ershad would issue publishing permits only to those with the "appropriate" religious and nationalist qualifications, whatever that meant.

At the same time, the hard-liners and the Office of the Supreme Leader cracked down on young people on university campuses and on the streets. The student population had tripled between 1987 and 1992, making campuses potentially troublesome hives of activism. The Supreme Leader's office called for more representatives of its own at universities and for a mobilization against moral and religious laxity among the students. A 1992 Law of Legal Protection for the Basij allowed the youth militia to act as an arm of law enforcement, with the power even to arrest. Basijis manned checkpoints on city streets, exercising their newfound power to search cars for illegal Western music, magazines, and videotapes. The Basij could stop and question young men and women they saw together, arresting those who could not prove they were related to each other. In 1994, the parliament would pass a law allowing law enforcement, which now included the Basij, to shoot and kill demonstrators.

For all that, Iranian campuses at the time bristled with opposition less to the clerics than to President Rafsanjani. The Islamic Students Associations had been formed as organs of the Islamic Left. Now they opposed the president's market reforms on ideological grounds, and in doing so they tapped into a reservoir of popular discontent. Iran's economy was nothing if not volatile, reacting at once to the losses of the war period and the shocks of reform. Iran's nouveau riche—suddenly visible after the war, now that foreign goods, from cars to clothes, were once more available for conspicuous consumption—included formerly traditional families that had come into wealth through connections to the revolutionary state. Rafsanjani's allies, including many Iranian economists, would argue that the Thermidorean president took nothing from the poor, and that poverty in fact steadily decreased over the life of the Islamic Republic, even if the rich did get briefly richer under Rafsanjani. But the obvious presence of this new class created a climate of resentment. The pre-revolutionary elite mocked the nouveau riche for its provincial manners and crass tastes, while to less privileged Iranians, the presence of the new class suggested a culture of corruption, cronyism, and ill-gotten wealth.

The truth was that neither the liberals nor the left had succeeded in shaping Iran's economy. Rather, in the midst of the factional tug-of-war over the country's economic orientation, real control had fallen to a third party that silently consolidated wealth and power. By 1994, fully 40 percent of the economy belonged to what would be called the "para-statal" sector, which consisted of a few giant, semiprivate foundations whose heads, generally clerics, were responsible only to the Supreme Leader. These massive, opaque conglomerates, called *bonyads*, controlled funds seized from the shah's regime and spanned the entire economy, from industry to agriculture to the service sector, sweeping what would have been hundreds of businesses under a few large umbrellas. No small business could effectively compete. Where wealth pooled, whether through the *bonyads* or the oil business, the government was never far from view, and suspicion naturally followed. Once again, the reference to Brinton was irresistible: revolutionary states in the convalescence of Thermidor nearly always turned a blind eye to corruption. In the case of Iran, this development would become associated with the person of the president. It did not help that Rafsanjani and his family had recently made a fortune in the pistachio business.

Around 1992, when inflation reached 50 percent, Rafsanjani tacked left. He began to propose a kind of statism of his own that would challenge the bazaar by shifting capital to the government and the banks. He emphasized industrial production, as though Iran's government could take the economy in hand and force it down the road of modernization that would make it a player in the global economy. To soften the blow and silence his critics, he doubled the consumer subsidies on which ordinary Iranians depended. But his agenda was still deeply distasteful and threatening to the right. In January of 1993, the parliament approved only a much-watered-down version of Rafsanjani's budget. In the year that followed, Iran weathered a major drop in oil prices and a devaluation of its currency. Because it was politically impossible to raise energy prices or cut subsidies, Iranians overconsumed oil; exports plummeted. Rafsanjani had triangulated himself into a corner. From there, little choice remained: he would have to reach out to the banished Islamic Left.

HOSSEIN BASHIRIYEH'S STORY begins with his father, a Sufi seeker and poet. To be a Sufi in Iran was to belong to a minority sect that was alternately suppressed and adored. No literature was more venerated in Iran than poetry, particularly the work of the Sufi lyricists Hafez and Rumi. But Sufism was a faith free of certainty, a quest and not a destiny, a sort of eccentricity in the context of a rigidifying Islam. Bashiriyeh's father meditated, took up mysticism, sought God in all of life and in all religions. So earnest was his search for divinity that he was willing not to find it. In the end he renounced religion altogether, informing his family, "I have found no truth in any religion."

Born in the northwestern city of Hamadan in 1953, Bashiriyeh was one of six siblings. His father was the central influence of his life, the person who taught him the alphabet long before his first school days. He also introduced Bashiriyeh, as a small child, to the classics of Persian literature, particularly the poets Hafez and Ferdowsi. Bashiriyeh was taciturn by temperament, a person of few, carefully chosen words. Although he would devote his life to ideas intimately linked to the history he witnessed, he often appeared to evince more scholarly concern than passion for the ideas, the history, and his own fortunes. This placidity was partly native to him but perhaps also partly willed—a fortress from whose safety he might observe the dangers and disappointments of a political life that mattered all too much.

From his earliest youth, Bashiriyeh studied literature, poetry, and history. He was particularly drawn to the novels of Sadegh Hedayat, a Western-educated, aristocratic modernist whose work implicitly criticized both the clergy and the shah. Bashiriyeh read all of Hedayat's work, but the one that was most influential in Persian letters was his 1937 novella *The Blind Owl*, a dark and dizzying prose poem that shuffles and reshuffles a handful of portentous images: an antique vase, a possibly poisoned bottle of wine, a lush-haired woman with slanted eyes, a hunchbacked old man, a murder weapon, a river, the dusty earth in the ancient town of Shahr-e Rey. The narrator, fevered or mad, imprisoned or dying, wrecked by grief or merely high, has murdered or not murdered the woman, who is an angel, a whore, possibly his mother. *The Blind Owl* was a classic of literary modernism and a riveting portrait of a society at once suffocated and mesmerized by its traditions, among them erotic repression, misogyny, and the dissociation of sin from the better self. A brooding and alienated man, Hedayat committed suicide in 1951, when he was forty-eight years old.

For Bashiriyeh, Hedayat's appeal lay in his nationalism, his love of the pre-Islamic Persian past, and his willingness to ridicule Islam, with its corrupt clergy, its greedy religious businessmen, and the blinkered traditional culture it supposedly fostered. In just the years his slightly younger contemporaries would spend discovering political Islam, Bashiriyeh came to identify soundness of thought with opposition to religion. His father had always urged independence of mind, and in his youth Bashiriyeh understood the poets he admired—Omar Khayyám, Hafez, Saadi—to be arguing for critical thought and against the conventional interpretation of religion. To the extent any religion influenced his thinking, it was the moral outlook of Sufism, with its emphasis on tolerance, individuality, and the inner experience of religion over its external duties and obligations.

Nonetheless, at nineteen, Bashiriyeh started attending Hosseiniyeh Ershad with his friends. Like them, he was looking for illumination; but unlike many of them, he felt that Shariati purveyed an ominous new obscurity instead. One night Bashiriyeh saw Shariati hold forth for six hours, exhausting everybody but himself. He took up very modern ideas, including existentialism, but he used them, Bashiriyeh understood, to call for a return to tradition. That was a call lost on Bashiriyeh, who was looking for release from religion, not its return. A new bigotry, he suspected, was being born.

Bashiriyeh was uninterested in the mundane political affairs of the country, and he would remain so, by his telling, all his life. The politics he loved, which would win him an epoch-making influence he never desired, was a theoretical affair, a matter of philosophy, whose roots and sympathies lay within the secular left. As a university student, Bashiriyeh studied states and political systems from a comparative perspective and a sociological perspective. Not only was he not an activist, but despite his leftist sympathies, Bashiriyeh believed that the monarchy's attempt to secularize and modernize Iran was basically a sound project.

In the late 1970s, as the temperature in Iran slowly rose, Bashiriyeh went to Britain, where he earned his master's in political behavior at the University of Essex and his PhD in political theory at the University of Liverpool. He read Thomas Hobbes and John Locke, Marx and Hegel, and a great deal of British political theory. His great intellectual affinity, however, was for Hobbes. The seventeenth-century British philosopher was the opposite of a utopian thinker. He concerned himself not with producing justice or a vision of an ideal state so much as with observing the state as it existed in order to explain what it did and why it was necessary. In Hobbes's view, submission to a sovereign power was all that stood between humankind and a grim "state of nature" in which human life—"solitary, poor, nasty, brutish and short"—would be a war of "all against all." Hobbes's state was a Leviathan, unbounded by civil liberties, divided government, or an independent judiciary, all of which Hobbes suspected of undermining the central authority's unifying and pacifying power. Rather, the sovereign protected men from one another, and for that mercy, men paid with their liberty. Nations flourished according not to their prosperity but to the obedience of their subjects. "And though of so unlimited a power, men may fancy many evil consequences," Hobbes wrote, "yet the consequences of the want of it, which is perpetual war of every man against his neighbor, are much worse."

Hobbes's view was surely authoritarian. (He even made a brief for censorship on the grounds that it would prevent "discord and civil war.") But the fundamental question he posed—why was the state necessary?—implied that, far from being ordained by God, the state was a contract among men, who willingly made certain sacrifices for the greater good of peace. To that extent, Hobbes was an early exponent of social contract theory, the adumbration of a liberalism later realized by Locke and Jean-Jacques Rousseau.

To Bashiriyeh, Hobbes's pessimistic understanding of human nature, of sinister interests and the function of the state, rang true. Bashiriyeh translated secondary work on Hobbes and, years later, *Leviathan* itself into Persian. It would find an audience that was not only receptive but fascinated. In the first place, here was a foundational work of Western political thought that had never before been introduced to Persian speakers. But the timing was also auspicious. For as Iranians—none more, perhaps, than the disillusioned cadres of the Islamic Left—began to question religious government, they faced the same question Hobbes had raised. If the state was not the vice-regent of God, what was it? Why was it necessary, and what were its obligations? Bashiriyeh specialized in such questions, supplying tools of analytic detachment to the revolutionaries, who now cast about, in some anguish, for a new and deeper understanding of political life. Some saw in Hobbes's *Leviathan* an apt description of the system they had wrought, with *velayat-e faqih* Iran's Leviathan. Some, disabused of utopian hopes, appreciated the British philosopher's cold-eyed appraisal of what was.

During his years in England, Bashiriyeh also discovered Crane Brinton. At the same time, he became enamored of a post-Marxist strain of thought he found in the work of Antonio Gramsci and Nicos Poulantzas—one that viewed the state not as a crude instrument in the hands of a single capitalist class but as host to a dynamic interplay of interests and alliances, which in the end enlisted even the working classes in defending bourgeois privilege. Drawing on Brinton, Gramsci, Poulantzas, and others, Bashiriyeh wrote his dissertation on the Iranian revolution and the unrest that followed it even as the events unfolded in real time.

It was a project oddly suited to the detachment of his temperament. In his home country, militants rose, the monarchy fell, a power struggle ensued, thousands died, and an extreme theocratic ideology triumphed not only over rival dogmas but also over a congeries of inchoate yearnings. In London, Bashiriyeh rooted through the Persian collections of the University of London's School of Oriental and African Studies. He visited Iran in 1979 for a month and again almost a year later, each time filling two very large suitcases with newspapers, pamphlets, and books to bring back to England. Meticulously, he documented the power struggle among the radical clerics led by Khomeini and the moderate Islamic liberals of the Freedom Movement, the radical Muslims of the Mojahedin-e Khalq, and the left. His history of the consolidation of the revolution, from 1979 through 1982, would become a classic after the dissertation's publication in 1984 as

The State and Revolution in Iran. No account of the early postrevolutionary period would fail to cite it. In it, Bashiriyeh argued that the Islamic Revolution was a petit bourgeois, reactionary movement that rose from the resentment of the old social classes against modernism.

Writing at the start of the Mousavi era, when the government was at last consolidated in the hands of the Islamic Republican Party, Bashiriyeh believed Thermidor had already begun. But it was during that period, in 1982, that he returned to a country and a university he scarcely recognized. The Islamic Students Association had more power than the university faculty or administration. Revolutionary Guards manned the gates to campus and searched all who entered. The older professors—the ones Bashiriyeh remembered from his own student days—had retreated into unhappy isolation. Many of the newer faculty members had been hastily trained in religious institutions and dispatched to the universities to reproduce the government's ideology. Bashiriyeh quickly realized that there could be no open discussion in the classroom, because nearly all the students were handpicked, screened for fealty to the new regime. Two of his classes—one took a Marxist approach to Islamic political theory, the other examined theories of modernization—aroused the suspicions of the censors and were canceled after less than a month. He switched to teaching Western political theory and political sociology. These subjects had been taught in the past; they did not deal directly in Iranian realities, and it would be some years before the regime came to see them as threatening.

So it was that at the start of the Rafsanjani era Bashiriyeh taught political sociology, theories of revolution, and twentieth-century political thought at the University of Tehran. When he looked out from the lectern, he did not exactly know who his students were. He knew that the university admissions had given preference to relatives of "martyrs" from the Iran-Iraq War, to veterans, and to families close to the new regime. He knew, too, that right-wing religious groups abounded on the campus. Perhaps he suspected that the better part of wisdom would be to maintain a certain distance from his students, that the less he knew, the better. He told them that it was his object to introduce them to thinkers as persuasively as possible: when he taught Marx, the students would believe he was a Marxist, and when he taught Hobbes, they would think him Hobbesian. He did not exactly know, or choose to know, that his classes had filled up with deputy ministers and other figures of some importance from the disempowered Islamic Left.

EVER ONE TO KEEP his friends close and his enemies closer, Rafsanjani had orchestrated the left's purge from government, but he also set up a reservation to house its thinkers. He called it the Center for Strategic Research. It was a think tank attached to the president's office, although the president never consulted it. As one of its officers later explained, this was not meant to be a dynamic center of intellectual activity so much as a place to warehouse the left and keep it silent and well fed. The government went about its business, taking little notice while the thinkers at the Center for Strategic Research busied themselves debating and building on one another's ideas.

Mohammad Mousavi Khoeiniha was the first director of the Center for Strategic Research. Like so many of his allies on the Islamic Left, he had a checkered history. As the country's prosecutor general in the early 1980s, he was incontestably associated with the country's early reign of terror. He was also the spiritual leader of the radical students who seized the American embassy in 1979. But his acolytes spoke of him as a man with a particularly open mind and unorthodox religious views. Khoeiniha insisted that the Center for Strategic Research engage with conservative ideas and thinkers as well as with the liberal technocrats of Rafsanjani's budget office. The center's thinkers should invite such people in and engage them in constructive dialogue, he seemed to suggest, if for nothing else for the opportunity to measure its thinkers' ideas against those of their adversaries. Moreover, by doing this, the center would model tolerance and civility, mainstays of the democratic school of thought the center would eventually propagate. For inside the center, the Islamic Left began to remake itself as a movement for participatory democracy within Iran's Islamic Republic. That movement would come to be called reform, its exponents reformists.

The Center for Strategic Research had two branches in central Tehran. The social and cultural program had offices a little to the north of the city's center. Among its best-known thinkers were a former hostage taker who now held a secular view of politics, and a former military intelligence man from the Revolutionary Guard who had since come to admire Soroush and the disinherited Ayatollah Montazeri.

Perhaps the more famous branch of the Center for Strategic Research was the one closer to the heart of the government, in central Tehran on Marjan Street. This office included the center's foreign policy and economic departments, and it housed the thinker whose name would be most associated not only with the Center for Strategic Research but with the reform movement itself. Saeed Hajjarian was a heavyset young radical from South Tehran who had worked for Prime Minister Mousavi. Because the revolutionaries had stormed and dismantled the despised SAVAK, the revolutionary regime found itself without a spy agency at the start of the Iran-Iraq War. Hajjarian was the man the Mousavi administration detailed to establish a new intelligence service, first within the prime minister's office and later for the Islamic Republic. Hajjarian drafted its establishing law and went to work for the new ministry when the parliament gave it the go-ahead. By the time he left the Ministry of Intelligence and Security for the Center for Strategic Research, Hajjarian had deep knowledge of and a gnawing foreboding about the direction his revolution had taken. Exactly what he had seen inside the intelligence apparatus to occasion this foreboding was the subject of dim speculation even among his friends.

Like their colleagues at *Kiyan*, the scholars at the Center for Strategic Research suspected that the Islamic Republic required a serious rethinking—that the revolutionary Islamism of Shariati and Khomeini had led Iran to a new despotism from which both Islam and the political establishment needed to be extricated. Hajjarian and two of his colleagues made two trips to Qom. There they prevailed on an iconoclastic young cleric named Mohsen Kadivar to come to the center as the head of a department of Islamic studies.

Kadivar had an open face and an easy laugh, a gap between his front teeth, and a voice that jumped whole registers when he was excited. He had studied philosophy and sociology at university and had been a student of Montazeri's at a seminary in Qom. During the Iran-Iraq War, Kadivar spent one month of every year at the front in Khuzestan as a sort of chaplain to the soldiers. During those visits he had come to question the policy of continuing the war after Khorramshahr. These doubts led to other doubts. After Khomeini's death, he set to work on a book questioning *velayat-e faqih*. Kadivar believed that the doctrine was little more than an Islamized theory of monarchy, which owed more to Plato and the follies of Persian history than to Shiism. Kadivar believed clerics should have authority in society but not power within the political structure. He favored a representative democracy with neither a king nor a supreme guide. When the censors did not allow him to publish his book, he grew depressed. But he discharged his frustration as a crucial member of the brain trust at the Center for Strategic Research.

Because Kadivar's critique of the Islamic Republic was more legal than theological, the thinkers of the Islamic Left embraced Kadivar earlier than they embraced Soroush, who seemed to be arguing for a radical revision not only of Khomeini's theory of the state but of the domain of Islam more generally. Hajjarian and his colleagues at the Center for Strategic Research were familiar with Soroush and even attended the occasional meeting at *Kiyan* (Hajjarian more than the others), but this was not at first their native territory. They were influenced more by Marx than Popper, and they first associated Soroush with his anti-Marxist screeds and the right wing of the Islamist movement, whereas they had originated from the left. Some members of the intellectual circle around the Center for Strategic Research were particularly concerned that Soroush's minimal interpretation of Islam left too little to religion and ascribed too much to the worldly realm. Soroush's view was broadly modernizing, even secularizing, they feared. But they took Soroush seriously. It was Soroush, one of these thinkers would later note, who exposed the roots of totalitarianism in Iran and who offered religious pluralism and philosophical moderation as antidotes. Gradually, the Islamic Left would come to abandon its reservations and embrace Soroush. For his part, Soroush grew ever more radical; he led the Islamic Leftists inch by inch, over a period of years, into a terra incognita.

The role that Popper and Anglo-American analytic philosophy played in *Kiyan* had a parallel in the field of political sociology at the Center for Strategic Research. Like so many of his colleagues on the Islamic Left, Saeed Hajjarian had fallen under Shariati's spell before the revolution. But the business of actually governing had raised questions that Shariati's wild poetry could not answer—precise, pragmatic questions about politics and the function of the state. Even Marx, who had been particularly important to Hajjarian's cohort, seemed to offer only the bluntest of instruments for the resolution of complex problems. Hajjarian, who had been studying mechanical engineering at the time of the revolution, returned to the University of Tehran for a political science PhD even while he ran his division of the new think tank. At the university, he fell under the sway of the urbane young political sociologist Hossein Bashiriyeh.

Saeed Hajjarian, two officials from Khatami's Ershad, a future deputy interior minister, and a future deputy foreign minister were just a few of the emerging politicians who flocked to Bashiriyeh's classes to slake a thirst. They were religious men, many of them more conservative in their religious outlook and more committed to the Islamic state than the circle surrounding Soroush; but they forgave Bashiriyeh his secular background because, unlike Soroush, he was friendly to the Marxism that made up the other half of their political outlook. They knew that the Marxism that had animated them as revolutionaries required revision. It lacked subtlety. From Bashiriyeh they gleaned a line of thought that was influenced by Marx without being exactly Marxist, that was analytical rather than ideological, and that homed in on the diversity of social forces, classes, interests, and ideologies that made the state a site of struggle and conflict. Their revolution achieved, they could see that the state was not a finished affair. To better understand its continuing dynamism, Bashiriyeh brought them Poulantzas and Gramsci as well as the concept of a civil society that was both a part of the state and a valve for constructive opposition. Those, like Hajjarian and his colleagues at the Center for Strategic Research, who were not inclined to take on board Popper's wholesale rejection of Marx turned to the tradition of political sociology Bashiriyeh imported, interpreted, and implicitly applied to the Iranian context.

Within the first three decades of the Islamic Republic, Bashiriyeh authored sixteen books and translated seven others. Among his own works was a treatise on theories of revolution, applying them to a number of actual revolutions, including the French and the Chinese. The book he regarded as his major work, which went to fifteen printings, was called *Political Sociology*, and it examined the role of social forces in political life. He wrote *Lessons on Democracy for Everyone* for a general readership; also, a book on the sociology of modernity, under the influence of Foucault. He translated Barrington Moore's *Social Origins of Dictatorship and Democracy* into Persian, along with works on Hobbes, Habermas, and Foucault. One of his most controversial works was an essay on tolerance, in which he argued that forcing religious beliefs and practices on people ultimately undermined faith by making it an obligation. In another essay—much discussed at the Center for Strategic Research—Bashiriyeh defended the need for a healthy opposition.

The Islamic Leftists, soon to be reborn as the reformists, claimed Bashiriyeh as their mentor. But Bashiriyeh, somewhat like Fardid before him, all but disowned them. To his cool sociologist's eye, these men were players in the factional struggle within the state, elites who had been marginalized and sought to reassert themselves within the power structure. To that end—to enhance, as he would later put it, their own objectives and strengthen their own positions—they used theories of democracy as a political tool. "And perhaps everywhere," Bashiriyeh mused in later years, "democracy as an abstract idea has come into real existence as the result of a real material, political need, to be utilized." The reformists, he suggested,

"found themselves in a position that from among the various interpretations of Islamic government, or from among the various ideologies, it was a
theory of competition that would suit them best. So they understood
democracy in terms of competition. Participation and competition, both of
which are tools, not the ends of democracy."

Still, when Hajjarian invited him to deliver a series of lectures at the
Center for Strategic Research, Bashiriyeh accepted, using the opportunity
to analyze aloud the course the revolution had taken. Bashiriyeh was even
then advising Hajjarian's dissertation on messianism in Russia's Bolshevik
revolution. He did not know that Hajjarian had just then emerged from the
intelligence ministry, and he did not look on these lectures as political
interventions so much as classes delivered outside the university confines.
To the attendees, they were something more, a scaffolding from which to
erect a new façade for the Islamic Republic.

The idea of democracy, once a term of abuse among the ideologues of
the Islamic Republican Party, became nearly faddish in the early 1990s.
Combined with Soroush's argument that religion could be understood in
multiple ways—that it changed with history and was susceptible to no single authentic interpretation—it suggested that the regime, even the *faqih*
himself, held no monopoly on truth, nor any legitimate monopoly on power.

THE THINKERS AND POLITICIANS who would become known as the
reformists emanated from three institutions: *Kiyan*, the Center for Strategic
Research, and Ershad under Khatami's leadership. But the circles were
concentric: the men all knew one another, and when *Kiyan* hosted dinners,
all three groups came. They came to debate the most urgent question of
their time and place, which was the role of religion in the administration of
the state. To be a reformist was to seek to strengthen the republican dimensions of the state against the clerical ones. It was to argue for a dynamic
understanding of religion, one responsive to the needs and realities of
modern people in a modern state. It was to question, however obliquely,
the authoritarian paternalism of *velayat-e faqih*. But, true to the name they

chose for their project, the reformists saw themselves not in frank opposition to the Islamic Republic but as a faction within its inner circle. They would preserve the revolutionary state through reform, and reform would be achieved through dialogue and negotiation among the reasonable people in charge.

In all of this, it was never wholly clear, then or later, whether President Rafsanjani was friend or foe to the reformists. Rafsanjani's economic liberalism met mainly with criticism among the reformists associated with the Center for Strategic Research. But with the decline of the left worldwide after 1989, these thinkers found themselves drawn more and more to social democracy or welfare-state liberalism—visions not wholly incompatible even with that of the most liberal of Rafsanjani's technocrats. By 1996, with the eclipse of the Cold War and their own turn to a more democratic vision of the state, the former Islamic Left stepped back from its anti-Americanism as well. The reformists now seemed likelier allies for the embattled president than the hard-liners he'd helped to power in the parliament.

Nonetheless, Rafsanjani had to answer to the Leader and the right. In 1992 he was obliged to fire Khoeiniha from the Center for Strategic Research. He replaced the radical cleric with a figure from the security establishment. Hassan Rouhani was close to Rafsanjani but far friendlier to the right than to the reformists. He served as the Supreme Leader's representative on the country's National Security Council. Rouhani made it his mission to shut the center down as a hive of reformist thought. "If you think we will fall for your pretty words on democracy," one of the center's thinkers remembers Rouhani saying, "you are wrong. We know you are seeking to topple the regime, but we will not let you, because we will not make the same mistake the Shah made." Rouhani forbade the center's thinkers from doing further research on poverty, injustice, political development, or opposition; Kadivar was to halt his study of Shiite theories of governance. Moreover, Rouhani banned Bashiriyeh from the premises, declaring that he should not even be paid for the work he had already done. When the new director had an informer infiltrate Kadivar's meetings in Qom, the informer accidentally faxed his report to the office of one of

Kadivar's allies. The think tank's members were incensed. They demanded to know why they were being spied on. One morning they showed up at work and were refused entry at the door.

Four years had passed since Rafsanjani helped the conservatives to power in the fourth parliamentary election. In 1996, with so many of his projects stymied or even reversed, Rafsanjani knew he had to tip the next parliament in a different direction. It was time for him to reach back out to the former Islamic Left. He found its moderate wing receptive, in its new guise as the movement for reform. Called Kargozaran, or the Executives of Construction Party, the coalition between Rafsanjani's moderate right and the nascent reform movement emphasized the rule of law, economic reconstruction, and development based on science and technology. In its 1996 parliamentary campaign, the coalition's reformist wing pressed for political liberalism, which included freedoms of speech and association. Student groups, until recently so critical of Rafsanjani, embraced Kargozaran as a vehicle for democratic reform. The new coalition picked up eighty seats.

The intellectuals recently ousted from the Center for Strategic Research found new homes in the nongovernmental space they called civil society. One group decamped for a newspaper called *Salam*, under the editorship of Mohammad Mousavi Khoeiniha, the former director of the Center for Strategic Research. Three former Center for Strategic Research thinkers founded a polling agency called Ayandeh, which allowed them to pursue their sociological study of postrevolutionary Iran independent of state funding or interference. Others, like Hajjarian, drew closer to politics after the parliamentary election. It was Hajjarian who came to define the goals and strategies of the reform movement, which would work within the legal structure of the constitution to enlarge the role of popular participation.

With Kargozaran, Rafsanjani had at last formed an effective alliance that had the political muscle to get things done. But he had done so just as he reached the end of the second term of his presidency. Emboldened by the parliamentary sweep, a spokesman for the president suggested amending the constitution to allow Rafsanjani a third term. The hard-liners were loudly outraged, and Khamenei vetoed the suggestion outright. Rafsanjani could not hold on to the presidency. He determined that the right would not seize it, either. But Kargozaran lacked a galvanizing candidate.

In July of 1996, the part of the Islamic Left that had not been subsumed into Kargozaran announced Mir Hossein Mousavi as its candidate for the 1997 presidential election. Mousavi was the Islamic Left's most distinguished figure: he was a former prime minister, a favorite of Khomeini's who had steered the country through war and privation. But he was also a divisive figure to those who supported the current Supreme Leader, Khamenei; nor did he and Rafsanjani see eye to eye on the important matter of the economy. Moreover, it was very early in Iran's electoral cycle for such an announcement. But the announcement forced the right to follow suit. The hard-liners put forward the speaker of the parliament, Ali Akbar Nategh-Nouri, as their candidate, and they suggested that there would be no need for anyone to run against him, as he was clearly the most appropriate choice.

Three months later, in October, Mousavi announced that he would not run. Perhaps he was intimidated by his old rival who now sat in the catbird seat. Years later, rumor had it that Khamenei, who felt he had at last vanquished an old competitor when he was named Leader, forbade Mousavi from entering or even speaking of politics after Khomeini's death. If this was true, it would certainly explain Mousavi's curious silence. For even while his former advisers, ministers, colleagues, and friends energetically debated social contract theory, Gramsci, Popper, and Islam, Mousavi disappeared into the architecture faculty at Shahid Beheshti University, becoming a political enigma and a screen for various projections.

Rafsanjani could not support Nategh-Nouri, especially after the debacle with his own bid for a third term. He would swing his weight against the hard-liners: he would prove to them that they needed him. But there was no place for him to go. Finally, in January of 1997, an unlikely candidate emerged on the scene.

Mohammad Khatami, the smiling, approachable former head of Ershad, announced that he would run for president. Although he'd become associated with Rafsanjani's controversial cultural policies, he was far from being a firebrand. He was moderate by temperament, cautious, and conciliatory; and on the pressing philosophical debates of his time—Soroush or Fardid, republic or theocracy—it was not totally clear where he stood. The reformists who supported him did not expect him to win. They thought they would use the campaign to raise the profile of a new journal. But in April, Kargozaran endorsed Khatami as its candidate of choice.

SEVEN

THE SECOND OF KHORDAD

MOHAMMAD KHATAMI'S single greatest asset was his face. That was not to say that he lacked other attributes: he was learned, affable, moderate. His affect was gentle and open to compromise. Born in 1943, he was the son of a grand ayatollah from the Yazdi town of Ardakan. As a young man, he had studied Islamic jurisprudence in the seminaries of Qom as well as Western philosophy at the University of Isfahan. In Hamburg, Germany, in 1978, he helmed an Islamic institute where expatriate revolutionaries gathered. For the better part of ten years, from 1982 until 1992, he was minister of culture and Islamic guidance. He held the clerical rank of *hojjat ol-eslam*, and his robes were always warm-hued and well cut. But it was Khatami's face that would be described in newspaper story after newspaper story, for all the years he remained in public life, as though all that mattered about that moment in Iranian history were expressed in its folds.

It was not that he was handsome, although it could be said that he was, in an avuncular way. Ayatollah Ruhollah Khomeini was handsome, too. At least, some Iranians described him that way. In the United States Khomeini's face—gaunt by the end of his life and lengthened by the trailing point of his white beard, his eyes deeply set beneath arching, furry eyebrows that remained black long after the rest of his hair had whitened—would become an icon of Muslim fury and severity. But the young Khomeini had a heart-shaped face with broad, planed cheeks, a sensuously curved mouth, and molten eyes; in his old age, he had the formidable face of a man who had truly lived, a visage inscribed with soulful intelligence and force of character that symbolized the reassertion of a national dignity long denied. Moham-mad Khatami had a different kind of face, and with it he presented a differ-ent face for Iran. Khatami's was open and good-humored, quick with a smile so spontaneous, it seemed to erupt for every occasion. He had the appear-ance of a favorite professor—the sort of face that looked familiar, even if you had never seen it before. Where Khomeini's imposed, Khatami's invited.

To judge from Khatami's writings, however, that invitation did not come without ambivalence. While his colleagues at the Center for Strategic Research, at *Kiyan*, and even within his own ministry, Ershad, seemed to borrow confidently and at will from Western and Islamic canons, Khatami retained a concern that was central to the pre-revolutionary thinkers. He did not want Iranians to suffer the "diluted identity" of Westoxication: "neither ourselves, nor Western." Like Reza Davari, he saw a toxic seed at the core of all Western thought. In the West, Khatami noted, Enlighten-ment ideas had led to imperialism, violence, and godlessness. They served, among other things, as tools for the enrichment and empowerment of a new bourgeois class. Moreover, today the West faced internal crises in its economy and culture. Iranians should observe the whole of the Western experience, look deeply into it, and seek to understand it so that they might better extract what was worth extracting and leave the rest behind.

Still, the very notions of modernity, of development, were Western ones; to strive to become a developed country, Khatami believed, meant adopting Western values. And Iranians had reason to yearn in this direction. Their country lagged behind Western countries in science, economics, and politi-cal power. Its political and intellectual culture had been stunted by a long history of despotism, which had produced quietism among Iranian reli-gious thinkers and an emphasis on metaphysics rather than politics.

The trouble was that the very thing that was most corrupt about West-ern values was also compelling. The West valued freedom: the liberty to eat, drink, dress, think, and speak as one pleased. Human beings were naturally attracted to such freedom. Islam, by contrast, called on believers to exercise restraint—to strive for abstinence, honesty, and rectitude, none of which were inborn, all of which required effort and self-mastery. And so the Islamic system was bound to impinge on individual liberties, and young Iranians were bound to ask why they did not enjoy the freedoms they saw their counterparts enjoying in the West. True freedom, Khatami argued, stemmed from moral and spiritual growth. But people required guidance in order to understand this. Khatami wrote, "To make our society stable and strong we must teach the young a more worthy path than hedonism, such that they gain pleasure out of abstinence."

Khatami believed that the future of Iran lay in the embrace of Islamic civilization. But this embrace should not be an embrace of the past. Muslims should recognize that although their religion was itself eternal, its interpretation was a dynamic thing that could be renewed and made consonant with the modern world. Iranians could reinterpret and refresh Islamic civilization. But this was necessarily an internal endeavor, and it required self-knowledge: "We can only critique tradition if we have a firm sense of our own identity; a traditionless people are invariably devoid of serious thought."

If Iranian intellectuals were to mine the West for its most useful modern ideas while discarding its toxic core—if they were to look deeply into Iranian and Islamic traditions and circumstances, in order to critique and update the indigenous civilization—they would need latitude, fresh air, something like a free press. And so, although Khatami cautioned that some restrictions would be necessary, he favored freedom of information and dialogue with the West: "The cultural strategy of a dynamic and vibrant Islamic society cannot be isolation," he wrote. Later he would emphasize the role of popular participation in politics, calling on the public to supervise, evaluate, and critique the government's performance. "The legitimacy of government stems from people's vote," he declared. "And a powerful government, elected by the people, is representative, participatory, and accountable. The Islamic government is the servant of the people and not their master, and it is accountable to the nation under all circumstances."

The Khatami of these writings was not nearly as liberal as the most liberal of the reformists. And while his vision of a bifurcated religion—immutable at its core, dynamic in its interpretation and jurisprudence—surely owed something to Soroush, it did not approach the vertiginous upper reaches of Soroush's register. Khatami remained a creature of the revolutionary milieu, and perhaps this was appropriate. He was a presidential candidate in a country less than twenty years past its Islamic Revolution, not a representative of the intellectual avant-garde.

Nonetheless, in that sometimes rueful, humble smile and in the quiet sincerity of his words, Khatami seemed to proffer other hopes. Khatami's could not be the face of a regime that ruled by the clubs and fists of street militias or that silenced critics at the gallows. It could not become the symbol of a nation willfully isolated from the world. Khatami believed above all, and perhaps to his ultimate detriment, in the power and the necessity of dialogue.

MOSTAFA ROKHSEFAT HAD ACHIEVED, with *Kiyan*, more even than he had dreamt of in his poster-printing days. Here at last was the vehicle for a cultural renaissance that was vibrant and innovative but authentically Islamic and Iranian. And yet, shortly after founding *Kiyan*, Mostafa left the country. He had always wanted to spend some time studying in the West. He thought it would help him to better understand his own society. And so, in the early Rafsanjani period, he went to Montreal, Canada, where he studied for a PhD in Islamic philosophy at McGill University. He was not there long when news began to reach him of a conflict simmering within the *Kiyan* Circle he had left behind.

In the months between Mousavi's withdrawal and Khatami's entry into the 1997 presidential election, Khatami had met quietly with colleagues and acquaintances to sound them out about a potential run. Akbar Ganji attended at least one such meeting. Khatami told his confidants that he didn't imagine he'd become president. Rather, he expected to get just three or four million votes. With that support behind them, they could publish an exciting intellectual journal that the regime would hesitate to close. For this, Ganji was game.

Other members of the *Kiyan* Circle believed there was a more consequential political moment to be seized, and that *Kiyan's* purpose was not only intellectual but political. Chief among these thinkers was a young technocrat named Mohsen Sazegara, who had served as a head of industry under Rafsanjani until his association with Soroush became a political liability. Sazegara believed that the reformism percolating through *Kiyan* and the Center for Strategic Research was something more than a new trend in Iranian thought. It was, at least potentially, the nucleus of a larger mobilization. As Khatami's campaign gathered steam in 1997, Sazegara pressed the members of the *Kiyan* Circle to organize. Even—especially—if they ascended to power, the reformists would surely face struggles with Khamenei. They needed a political party and a newspaper: infrastructure to sustain them through the coming storm.

Saeed Hajjarian, of the Center for Strategic Research, agreed with this approach. Others, including Ganji, favored remaining more aloof—perhaps publishing a weekly magazine, announcing themselves more as a pressure group within civil society than as a political party with ambitions of its own. They were wary of linking their project's fate too closely to the Khatami campaign.

Mostafa's friends recalled him to Tehran to mediate the dispute. But by the time he got there, it was too late. *Kiyan* had divided—fatefully, permanently. Although the journal would survive the dispute, the intellectual circle that had coalesced around it was rent by new rivalries.

There would not be much mystery about where Mostafa stood. Even Ganji's approach was too worldly: for Mostafa, the reformist project had always been an intellectual one, and that work was far from finished. Done right, it would encompass more and endure longer than politics. As philosophers, sociologists, theologians, and theoreticians, the reformist intellectuals might split open the rigid shell of their society—its traditions, its authoritarian politics—in such a way that it could never again clamp shut. But if they entered politics now, they would confront a regime at the height of its power before they had amassed enough power of their own. Why press for progressive change before the society was fully ready for it, and before the hard-liners had come to see it as inevitable? A party could be banned, a newspaper closed. But a reformation, an awakening, a renaissance, could not so easily be stopped. Mostafa believed that this was what was even then unfolding and that entering the 1997 presidential election, far from touching off reform, would render it stillborn.

Moreover, Khatami was not the man for the job. To stand up to Khamenei required strength, know-how, and, above all, conviction. Mostafa did not see these qualities in Khatami. He believed that Khatami had at times favored Fardid over Soroush, Heidegger over Popper; he had not been a consistent friend to the intellectual movement that had first coalesced at *Kayhan-e Farhangi* under his uneasy watch. Khatami was not, Mostafa argued, a reformist. He was intellectually confused; he vacillated in politics because he vacillated in his heart.

Mostafa would not hesitate to admit that for him the matter was personal. He was the black sheep in a conservative family of carpet merchants; at least one of his brothers belonged to Motalefeh, a secretive association of bazaar merchants close to the most hardline elements of the clerical establishment. Mostafa alone had abandoned the family business for intellectual endeavors. He alone held forth in heated family debates about the promise of reform. He felt himself at once scorned and held dear, loved for all that his brothers saw in him as exceptional, even as he stood for the negation of all they believed. With dread, he watched his friends, colleagues, and allies cast themselves into a political system that he knew would only humiliate and expel them. It was his own dignity as much as their movement that he felt at stake; it was everything he had worked for and the enlightenment he had found in Soroush. For Soroush, to Mostafa's anguish, cast his lot with Hajjarian and Sazegara. He was, Mostafa railed privately, their prisoner. But Soroush, years later, would coolly recall choosing the path of politics of his own free will, with animus toward no one, and he would wonder if the acid discord within the *Kiyan* Circle at that time was the work of hardline provocateurs.

Mostafa withdrew to Canada, to the little apartment where for years life had consisted of nothing but his family, the library, his course work, drills in French and Arabic, his master's thesis. Only his dissertation remained. But when he returned from Iran, his studies no longer meant anything to him. He abandoned the dissertation and turned where he never thought he would: to carpets, which from his student days he had shunned. The Rokhsefat brothers had long pressed cerebral Mostafa to bring the family's business to Canadian shores. He had neither their experience, nor, perhaps, their acumen, but nobody figured on his fury.

In Iran, Mostafa Rokhsefat was a cultural figure of considerable if quiet renown. In Canada he was an inflamed businessman who sold carpets with a demonic determination, a mad competitive energy that he had never before discharged. His family's prestige translated into credit; at one point he had twenty-five containers of Persian carpets sitting in Canadian customs. He distributed them, he would later recall, viciously, wildly, like no one had ever distributed Persian carpets before. He worked his way into debt and out of it, and the experience consumed him. But none of it assuaged the feeling that his true project had been hijacked, that it had come to carry a meaning he never intended and to defy his good judgment at what he knew would be an incalculable cost to history.

KHATAMI HAD NOTHING TO LOSE. His main opponent, Nategh-Nouri, had been handpicked by the Leader. Nategh-Nouri was so favored that he was already making state visits before the campaign had even concluded. The other candidates on the field included Reza Zavarei, deputy head of the judiciary and a member of the Guardian Council, and Mohammad Reyshahri, "the scary ayatollah" who had been Mousavi's intelligence minister. Neither would attract even 3 percent of the vote. The roster was designed to usher Nategh-Nouri into office with little ado.

In every way the establishment candidate, Nategh-Nouri, ran on familiar revolutionary themes. He railed against the "cultural onslaught" from the West, which he believed would saturate Iran with "corruption, decadence and idleness." Only by strengthening its indigenous Islamic culture could Iran become immune from this stealth invasion. Nategh-Nouri stressed the defense of Palestine and an enduring enmity with the United States. His campaign operated through government offices, which functioned normally during the business day. Its operatives little noticed, at first, that the Khatami camp had student activists painting and hanging banners into the wee hours, throwing campaign postcards into the windows of cars, singing in the streets.

Khatami, until recently the head of the national library and a retiring intellectual figure, campaigned in the American style, touring the provinces by bus and glad-handing in a way that was never before a part of Iranian electioneering. He was an unexpectedly charming political candidate. He was open and friendly with voters and, despite the elegance of his robes, he displayed a humility that fit the populist sensibility of postrevolutionary Iran. His ideas—rule of law, civil society, political development—came directly from the intellectual hothouses of *Kiyan* and the Center for Strategic Research. But he rendered them accessible to ordinary people, whose hunger for them exceeded the fondest hopes of his advisers.

What Khatami promised was an Iran where the government's voice would not ring out in silence. Civil society was a catchphrase for all the recourse Iranian citizens lacked: an independent press, grassroots associations, political parties, checks and balances on power—even, for those who dared to hope for it, an independent judiciary that might enforce equality before the law and safeguard the rights and freedoms of individuals. He suggested such a future while wearing clerical robes and a black turban that marked him as a *seyyed*, or a descendant of the Prophet. He was not a radical figure. To vote for Khatami was to express the hope that the Islamic Republic had better days ahead of it, that the 1979 Islamic Revolution might yet be one of liberation.

Still, the weight of the establishment and the authority of the Leader were arrayed against him. For a long time Khatami had only his hard work and native appeal to marshal. Then, just two months before the election, an enormous tactical advantage fell into his lap. In March 1997, Rafsanjani and his Kargozaran Party unleashed Tehran mayor Gholamhossein Karbaschi to endorse Khatami and place the entire machinery of the Tehran municipality at his disposal. Now Khatami had flush coffers and billboards all over the capital, where one in five Iranians lived. By the beginning of May, the month of the election, it was increasingly obvious not only that Khatami was winning but that more Iranians would turn out for this election than for any since 1979.

The reformists watched in amazement, but they were too skeptical even to prepare a victory speech for Khatami in advance. Surely the balloting would be rigged. As Khatami's brother, Mohammad Reza Khatami, told a foreign reporter, "Less than a week before the election, we were certain of Mr. Khatami's victory, although as I say we were not certain it would ever be announced." The Khatami campaign appealed to Rafsanjani, who was still the president after all, and who wielded enormous personal influence behind the scenes. At Friday prayers on May 16, Rafsanjani announced that no sin was worse than vote rigging. Khamenei had to say something. He paid lip service to the same principle. "I shall not allow anyone to give himself the right to cheat in the election, which is contrary to religion and contrary to political and social ethics," he said.

Two nights before the election, the members of the *Kiyan* Circle gathered for dinner. One suggested that Khatami was still lagging behind Nategh-Nouri but drawing closer. The social scientists from the Center for Strategic Research who'd formed a polling institute had surveyed the public, and they chose that moment to unveil that, according to their latest figures, Khatami was about to win by an overwhelming majority. Sure enough, on May 23, 1997, some 80 percent of Iranian voters turned out at the polls, 69 percent of them for Khatami.

Temperate, conciliatory, lacking conviction—years later, Khatami's closest allies and advisers would claim to have seen tragic flaws in him all along. But in 1997, in the wake of an election that would become known as "The Epic of the Second of Khordad," after its date on the Persian calendar, Iran was the site of as-yet-untrammeled hope. No one spoke of it more plainly or at greater cost than Ayatollah Hossein Ali Montazeri, the disinherited successor to Khomeini who had raised his voice against the prison massacres not ten years before.

. . .

AYATOLLAH MONTAZERI HAD GUARDED a tense political silence for nearly a decade. Now, in November 1997, he delivered a rare lecture in Qom, unleashing his anger and outlining a vision he had nurtured for all the intervening years. Maybe he knew these remarks would cost him everything he had not already lost. Maybe he didn't care.

Montazeri, one of the original authors of the doctrine of *velayat-e faqih*, said now that he had envisioned the Leader as a safeguard against despotism in the wake of the shah's abuses. The *faqih*, who was in the first instance the nearly universally adored and respected Khomeini, was to check the power of the prime minister and president, assuring that neither of these assumed absolute rule. But that was not how things had worked out. Instead the Leader had become an absolute ruler. And while the people held the president and the parliament responsible for enacting their will, these elected leaders lacked power. The Leader held all the power, Montazeri lamented, but was responsible to no one.

Only the twelve imams of Shiite tradition were infallible, Montazeri reminded his listeners. Although his followers had dubbed him "imam," even Khomeini was human and never claimed to be anything more. And yet, among the conservative clerics, his words and deeds had assumed the petrified quality of scripture. Montazeri decried the worship of Khomeini as a kind of idolatry. He returned, always, to the Quran, the sayings of the Prophet, and the lives of the imams. Montazeri believed in a kind of dynamic *ijtihad*, the interpretation of the sacred texts in light of contemporary concerns. When he spoke of Imam Ali, founder of the Shiite order—and Montazeri spoke of him often—he depicted him as warm, flexible, and confident, a model and a foil for the brittle Supreme Leader Ali Khamenei.

Montazeri stood out among the political clergy for his fearless and respectful engagement with opposing ideas. He was not afraid of the tumult and tussle implied by free expression and a free press. He could not understand why Khamenei and his lieutenants felt threatened by criticism. Nor did he worry that the people would fall into error if clerics did not preselect their candidates for office. Iranians were good Muslims; surely they would not be mistaken about more than a few parliamentary deputies, who would be rendered ineffectual by the majority. Montazeri believed in the wisdom and goodwill of the public. Verses in the Quran called for rulers to engage in "consultation." Some Islamic scholars, Khomeini among them, interpreted this to mean that consultation was permitted but not required, and that in any case leaders should consult qualified Islamic scholars, not the public. Montazeri took a populist view of these ambiguous verses. At least by 1997 he saw consultation—with the people—not only as required but as the fundamental source of a government's legitimacy.

In his 1997 speech, Montazeri scolded the armed militias that patrolled Iranian universities. "Hezbollah" meant "party of God." No party of God mindlessly chanted slogans and beat political opponents with clubs, he insisted. The Iranian people could not be governed by brute force. Rather, Montazeri said, they deserved a system with political parties, separated powers, free elections, and free expression. The Guardian Council, in his view, had no business selecting the candidates for office. The president and the parliament should be elected directly by the people.

The man who would have been Leader but for the fateful developments of 1988 decried what he saw as the expansion and abuse of the system's supreme office. The Leader was there not to make laws, to play favorites, to crush dissent, or to assure the victory of any particular political faction. He should not command police or military forces or run his own special, extrajudicial court for keeping the clergy in line, as he now did. Rather, he was to "supervise" the affairs of state within the realm of religious law, essentially acting as the government's spiritual adviser. Even in so doing, he should not be insensitive to the will of the people or place himself above the law. In later writings Montazeri would clarify that the Leader should himself be elected and popularly accountable.

Montazeri made no secret of his disdain for the man who had assumed the office of Leader in his stead. Khamenei did not have and would never have the jurisprudential authority of a Khomeini or a Montazeri. But shortly after assuming the Leadership, Khamenei had tried to get himself swiftly ordained with higher clerical authority than his training, publications, and standing in the scholarly community suggested. Montazeri let the Leader know that he found these efforts objectionable. They "degraded" traditional Shiite lines of authority and rendered them "infantile."

Khamenei's interpretation of *velayat-e faqih* had effectively evacuated the elected offices of their power. The president, Montazeri would soon note, could not enforce the rule of law. The instruments were not under his control. The police answered to the Supreme Leader, who also claimed control over the judiciary. Moreover, the Leader could summon the Special Court of the Clergy, whose purpose was to purge the clergy of contrary elements but which had recently extended its jurisdiction even to laypeople who "insulted" the clergy. This ad hoc revolutionary tribunal corresponded to no provision in the constitution, but neither Khomeini nor Khamenei had seen fit to disband it. In fact, Khamenei had expanded it when he assumed leadership, so that it now had branches throughout the country and commanded its own security network, complete with its own prisons. Its judges, prosecutors, and even defense lawyers were directly answerable not to the judiciary or any elected branch of government but to the Leader himself, who was inclined to draw the court's jurists from the intelligence ministry and a network of particularly hardline clerics. Even its budget was overseen by the Leader rather than by the parliament.

Perhaps, then, it should have been no surprise when the Special Court of the Clergy came for Montazeri. His 1997 speech offended Khamenei to the very core. The Special Court sentenced Montazeri to house arrest. The Revolutionary Guard, Basij, and intelligence ministry sent a mob to ransack Montazeri's home, his office, and the *hosseiniyeh* in Qom where he lectured and taught. According to the ayatollah's memoirs, these security forces, all of them answerable to the Office of the Supreme Leader, destroyed the *hosseiniyeh*, sealing it off and leaving it in ruins. Montazeri was barricaded on the second floor of his home and all but one of the doors to the outside were welded shut; inside the remaining door, the security forces built a small room to house armed guards. For five years, this was how Montazeri lived, isolated from all but his immediate family.

His words, however, had already breached the barricaded doors and taken wing. Khamenei, Montazeri declared in that November speech, had made the Islamic Republic into an autocracy hardly distinct from the shah's. There was nothing Islamic about oppression. "If I were you," he advised Khatami, "I would go to the leader and tell him that, with all due respect, 22 million people voted for me while everyone knew that you preferred another candidate. It means, therefore, that the people have rejected the existing order."

III

REFORM

EIGHT

THE CHAIN MURDERS

and the sights that rush in suddenly
turn seeing into a horrid thing,
even as they increase the temptation to look
over the expanse of this landscape dotted by
  white oaks,
or mummies
or faces of crystalline ice
or bodies of crystal salt,
all tugging at your eye to transform them.

—MOHAMMAD MOKHTARI,
"From the Other Half"

WHEN SHAHRAM RAFIZADEH WAS NINE, his mother died, the revolution came, and he discovered poetry. Heavyset, mournful, with tight
brown curls and warm, weary eyes, Shahram was the sixth of seven children born to a rice huller in a village called Shaft, in the northern Iranian
province of Gilan. He shared sleeping quarters with his father and all his
siblings, under a roof made of galvanized iron; at the crack of dawn, he got
up to practice sports and recite poetry while his family begged him for a
moment's sleep.

Shahram was not sure he believed in God. His mother, while she lived, had prayed, but like many working-class people in their part of the country, the family leaned to the secular left. His father was poor but proud and law-abiding. Shahram wanted a bicycle. His father found a man willing to sell one for a price he could afford. But as he and Shahram wheeled the bike away, Shahram's father remembered that he hadn't collected a receipt. They went back to the seller, who said he couldn't provide one. So, to Shahram's distress, his father gave the man back the bicycle.

He spent his mornings alone. His older siblings were in school, his father at work, his younger brother Bahram at his grandmother's. His fourth-grade class met only in the afternoons. One of his older brothers, cleaning the attic, found two things he thought Shahram might use. One was an old space heater, the other a moldering volume of poetry that included selections from, and essays about, each of the great Persian poets, including Khayyám, Hafez, Mowlana, and Saadi. The binding was disintegrating. Shahram's brother stitched it together by hand and gave the volume to Shahram.

The space heater was missing a plug. Shahram connected its naked wires to the 220-volt wall supply the next morning. A fierce electrical shock knocked him to the ground. One of his sisters found him unconscious when she came home from school in the afternoon. He thought he was lucky he hadn't died.

The brother who gave him the heater and the poetry book was an active Marxist and an avid reader. When Shahram was younger, this brother had insisted that he read and write book reports before he could go out to play. Shahram, desperate to play, had read *The Little Black Fish* and other stories by Samad Behrangi. A teacher had given him a book he loved more, an obscure and haunting little story called *Where Are You, Hasanak?*

Published in 1970 and written in verse by one Mohammad Parnian, the story opened with a heavy snow falling on a prosperous village. The village people were frightened and retreated to their homes. But a little boy named Hasanak was determined to bring the sun back from behind the clouds. He led an army of children to the mountains, over the protests of their parents. There are wolves in the mountains, the adults objected, and snow. You will freeze to death up there. But Hasanak led the children on.

Halfway up the mountain, the wolves attacked. Hasanak knew that he and the other children had only so much time before the cold would set into their very bones. So he told the others to stay and fight the wolves while he continued upward to retrieve the sun.

Alone now and undaunted, Hasanak ascended into ever thinner, ever more frigid air, his young body wracked with cold and surely dying. Nevertheless he reached the summit. There he found the sun, sleeping.

"Sun!" he called. "Sun! Wake up!"

The sun awoke to the sound of Hasanak's voice. It rose, casting warmth and light again over the village, and over the other villages, near and far, and over the icy mountain. But when the sun looked down, far below, on the mountain's peak, it could see the frozen, lifeless body of young Hasanak.

Forever after, in the ears of the other children and in the rocks of the mountain, Hasanak's voice still sounded.

"I will go and I will remove the snow," it said.

"I will go and I will sweep the clouds.

"I will open the way in the dark clouds.

"And in the end I will find the sun.

"Whoever wants the sun

"Get up and follow me!"

AFTER THE ELECTRICAL SHOCK that didn't kill him, Shahram left the heater aside for the poetry book, where for the first time he discovered the masters of Persian literature. He read the book to himself and he read it aloud, at the top of his voice. The poems issued from a place of emotion that was never totally submerged from Shahram's conscious life. He began to write. He showed the poems to his older brother, who told him they were extraordinary and that Shahram might become a poet.

When Shahram was eleven, in 1981, Bani-Sadr was president and the

Revolutionary Guard fought the Mojahedin-e Khalq in city streets. Shahram knew a boy in Shaft who had joined the Mojahedin. The boy was fatherless, very tall, and very poor, and he read a great many books. He'd survived the street clashes and fled for a time, but then he returned to Shaft to see his mother. Shahram was sitting at home when he heard a gunshot. He and his family ran toward the young Mojahed's home, which they found surrounded by Revolutionary Guardsmen. Shahram recognized one guardsman, another neighborhood boy. That boy turned his gun on Shahram and his family. "If anyone steps forward," he said, "I will shoot."

The tall, poor young Mojahed had been praying in his mother's home when a guardsman lurking at his window shot him in the forehead. The assailants then entered the house and decapitated the corpse. Shahram saw them drag his neighbor's headless body into a car. It was a ghastly thing to see. He opposed the Islamic Republic because his brother and his brother's friends were Marxists. But from that moment he opposed it from his gut.

Shahram lost his teen years in teen fashion. After finishing his first two years of high school in one, he grew lax in his studies and even forgot poetry to prowl the streets of Rasht, the capital of his province, with friends, eyes fixed to the distant and intermittent glimmer of passing excitement. One day something unexpected came. It was the spring of 1988, and Shahram, seventeen years old, had moved to Rasht. He was walking with his friends when he saw a woman on the street who stirred in him something he had not felt for any girl he had known. Her name was Bita, and she lived just a few blocks from him.

Shahram got her phone number. But Iranian tradition required introductions to be made by families and engagements arranged among parents. Dating was neither legal under the Islamic Republic nor acceptable to traditional families who prized female honor. So Shahram would dial Bita's number from a pay phone, hanging up when her aunt, her mother, or her other family members answered. Finally, Bita picked up. Shahram told her that he loved her. After that they had secret phone conversations. Sometimes they arranged to meet at the movies. They couldn't walk down the street together for fear of being apprehended by the Basij for immoral behavior, and equally for fear of Bita's family. It was 1991 when at last they married. Shahram felt something inside him spring to life. He began to write poetry again, and to read.

Shahram's older brother had settled in Tehran, where his work as a typesetter brought him into contact with poets and writers. He showed Shahram's poems to some of those writers, who began corresponding with him, offering him their views on his work. Shahram exchanged letters with Ali Babachahi, the craggy-faced, wild-haired editor of *Adineh*, Iran's most prominent secular literary magazine. Newly married, his confidence rolling high, Shahram moved with his wife to Tehran in 1992.

A friend in Rasht, the editor of a cultural magazine there, asked Shahram a favor. Since he was in Tehran, could he approach the secular poet and writer Mohammad Mokhtari for an article? the friend inquired. Shahram had never met Mokhtari, who was a well-known figure in Iranian letters. But he did as his friend asked, securing the article from the famous writer with a phone call.

Mokhtari invited Shahram to join him at a gathering at a friend's house. It was a generous gesture from a literary eminence to a striving poet of twenty-two. Shahram felt his age acutely at the gathering. But when Mokhtari heard Shahram speak, he must have sensed in the portly, soft-eyed young man from Shaft a quality of mind kindred to his own. In front of all his friends, Mokhtari walked up to Shahram and planted a kiss on his forehead.

MOHAMMAD MOKHTARI was not a person to chew bubble gum at a gathering. But the last time Shahram saw him, on Monday, November 30, 1998, at a gathering of writers, Mokhtari was chewing gum. Now Shahram was stuck with that detail, insignificant and unforgettable.

The writers at the gathering mulled over their shock at terrible news. Nine days earlier Dariush Forouhar and his wife, Parvaneh, had been murdered and dismembered in their home. The Forouhars were secular nationalists. Dariush, seventy at the time of his death, had been a minister in

Bazargan's government, an activist for more than forty years. He and Parvaneh had criticized the Islamic Republic's human rights record. On November 22, 1998, their bodies were found riddled with stab wounds. The killers had reportedly stabbed Dariush eleven times and Parvaneh, twenty-four, twisting the knife 180 degrees at each entry. They turned Dariush's mutilated body to face Mecca. At the time of the murders, the Farouhar home was under surveillance by the intelligence ministry. No criminal could have entered unseen. The couple had entertained dinner guests that night, and the family's lawyer would recount with some certainty that these guests committed the crime, tying Dariush to the chair where he sat talking with them in his study and surprising Parvaneh as she got ready for bed.

Two days earlier, another writer and critic of the regime had gone for a jog and never returned. Majid Sharif was an acolyte of Shariati's and an editor of his posthumous books. He had also translated Nietzsche and Derrida into Persian. Tehran police found his body by the side of the road on November 24. Pirouz Davani, a leftist activist, had disappeared back in August. His body was never found.

Didn't Mokhtari feel something was wrong with the Forouhar story? Shahram asked him. The train of death, Shahram said, had begun to roll.

That Saturday was a holiday. But Shahram, who wrote for the cultural section of a newspaper, was at work putting together Sunday's edition when a friend called to tell him that Mokhtari had vanished. The friend, an editor, had assigned Mokhtari an article, and when he'd gone to pick it up from him at the appointed time, Mokhtari was nowhere to be found.

He'd been missing since he left home on Thursday evening at five o'clock to buy lightbulbs and milk, Mokhtari's wife told Shahram when he called. The family was waiting until after the holiday to alert the media. But Shahram urged them to move faster. His brother Bahram swiftly placed a newspaper story under the headline "Where Is Mohammad Mokhtari?" So began a fearful week in Shahram's life.

Shahram worked at the newspaper and at a publishing house called Tarh-e No, associated with the reformists, particularly Akbar Ganji. The religious intellectuals who gathered around Tarh-e No were afraid. Shahram could feel it. There was, as he would later put it, no feeling or smell that Mokhtari had been arrested. His disappearance was quiet and, for that reason, more ominous. In three or four days' time, Mokhtari's son identified the poet's body at the morgue.

That very night, Mohammad Jafar Pouyandeh went missing. Pouyandeh was a friend of Mokhtari's, a writer and translator who was just then finishing a Persian translation of the Universal Declaration of Human Rights. He was found strangled in Shahriar, to the south and west of Tehran.

FROM THE TESTIMONY OF MOKHTARI'S KILLERS, Shahram would later reconstruct the final hours of his friend and mentor's life. He committed this chronology to memory, as though its painful recitation could project Shahram's presence backward, so that Mokhtari would have died in loving company instead of terror and solitude.

Mokhtari had gone to a store on Jordan Boulevard, near his home in North Tehran, to buy milk and lightbulbs. He did not know that as many as eight assailants followed him there in two cars, one a Peugeot and the other a taxi. When he started home, some men emerged from one of the cars and showed him a summons. They told him he was under arrest and to get in the car. For hours they drove him in circles around the north of Tehran. The plan was to murder him in the office the intelligence ministry maintained in Behesht-e Zahra, the enormous graveyard south of Tehran; but the operation was a secret one, and while the head of intelligence at Behesht-e Zahra knew about it, his underlings did not. The assassins were to wait until the building was empty.

Under cover of night, they ferried Mohammad Mokhtari through the necropolis, into the intelligence building, to a room where terrible things were known to happen. They laid him on his stomach and looped a length of rope around his neck. Men sat on his back and held his feet. One put a foot on his neck and pulled the rope. They put a cloth under his mouth to catch the blood. From experience, they knew how to tell when a man was dead by the change in color under his fingernails. When Mokhtari no longer struggled or breathed, when his nail beds were gray, they put him in the trunk of the Peugeot and drove to the back of the Rey Cement Factory in southeastern Tehran. There they emptied Mokhtari's pockets and dumped his body.

Mohammad Mokhtari's wife watched, with a group of friends and family members, as her husband's coffin was loaded into a hearse. Then she stepped forward. She placed a pen in his coffin. She said, "I see him off with his weapon."

BEFORE THE REVOLUTION, Iran's literary elite issued largely from the secular left. After the revolution, when the secular left was hunted and silenced where it was not exterminated, Iranian poets and writers retreated into private life. To write in the old literary style was to invite censorship, imprisonment, exile. Mohammad Mokhtari, secretary of the Iranian Writers Association in 1981, served a two-year prison sentence in 1982. The Writers Association was banned. A new literature, coaxed from the revolution's doctrinaire cadres, praised the imams and retold religious narratives. The secular writers spent a decade in deep and perilous estrangement. Mahmoud Dowlatabadi, a novelist and playwright who had risen from poverty into the old elite, would later say that he lived permanently with the sense of a dagger at his back. No mainstream political figure or institution existed to defend the secular writer. The strictures of the constitution did not protect him.

Then came the Rafsanjani years, and with them *Kiyan* and the Center for Strategic Research. The religious intellectuals, including Soroush, Kadivar, Ganji, Hajjarian, and many others, had not been nurtured within the country's old intellectual milieu. They were lower-middle-class, traditional people whose intellectual prominence came, sui generis, with the revolution. They spoke the language of religion and revolution. It was a language riven with contradictions, Shahram felt, starting even with Shariati: religious intellectuals could never quite reconcile Islam with the revolutionary drive for self-determination and free will. But because the reformists were insiders—so it seemed—they could issue bold, provocative calls for political freedom at far less cost than the secular intellectuals. The religious intellectuals were closer to the system. Some were even among its architects. They imagined they would be tolerated.

Some of these new religious intellectuals believed they could go so far as to declaim the injustice, even the impiety, of the theocracy and call for the separation of mosque and state. In a 1992 lecture, the former premier, Mehdi Bazargan, made what looked for all the world like a plea for secularism. *Kiyan* printed an elaboration of that lecture a year later. "Wherever religion and government (even ideology and state) are merged and put in the hands of one ruler," Bazargan wrote in the *Kiyan* piece, "people are deprived of freedom of opinion and the will to manage their affairs. It is always religion that loses, not government." Indeed, he wrote, Iranians "have seen such a face of Islam and Muslimness, of those who claim to act in the name of religion and government . . . that they have come to doubt their own religious beliefs and knowledge." *Kiyan*'s editors prefaced Bazargan's contribution with an apology to the former prime minister for his mistreatment at the hands of Islamic radicals, among whom were some of the *Kiyan* Circle's own number: "Now that the fervor has subsided and fiery radicalism is over, and also the direction of social developments has become evident, many are now trying to ask for his forgiveness, especially the young generation who attacked his policies."

The secular intellectuals observed with cautious excitement the slow shift of the reformist intellectuals toward a nearly secular vision of the state. Their situation was infinitely more precarious than that of the reformists. Still, the religious dissidents had helped create breathing room for their secular peers. Taking advantage of the more liberal issuance of publishing licenses in the first years of Rafsanjani's presidency, secular-minded editors began founding magazines, including *Adineh*. There the secular writers began to publish again. And they began to reencounter one another at clandestine gatherings they called "consensus meetings." When Shahram Rafizadeh moved to Tehran, this was the circle of writers he entered.

For their part, the religious intellectuals extended a tentative hand to their secular peers. The gesture was not without self-interest. The inclusion of the old literary elite in the reformists' circles would prove the sincerity of their call for tolerance and free speech while also burnishing their literary bona fides, since the secular writers were still the culture's standard-bearers of taste. The secular intellectuals, meanwhile, understood that the country had changed and that they could no longer speak for its high culture without recognizing and including some of their religious peers. They opened their consensus meetings to a handful of human rights and women's rights activists from the religious reformist camp.

The intellectuals shared one agenda above all, and that was to widen the space for free speech under the Islamic Republic. In October of 1994, 134 Iranian intellectuals issued an open letter. They called it "We Are the Writers!" It was a call for reactivating the defunct Iranian Writers Association and for an end to censorship. The signatories declared:

> We are the writers! This means that we express and publish our emotions, imagination, ideas, and research in different forms. It is our natural, social, and civil right that our written work—be it poetry or novel, play or scenario, research or critique—as well as our translations of other writers of the world, reach our audiences without any interference and impediment. No individual or institution, under any circumstance, has the right to hinder this process. . . .

The rest of the petition underscored the signatories' benign intent. Their purpose was not political, they asserted, whatever the government or any other political force wished to project onto them. They wanted only to establish a collective presence as writers in order to secure a space for free expression. If political forces inside or outside the country endorsed their call, the writers could not be held responsible. Still, "defending the human and civil rights of any writer, whatever the circumstances, is the duty and obligation of all writers."

Among the letter's signatories were Mohammad Mokhtari, Mohammad

Jafar Pouyandeh, and other victims of what would come to be known as the chain murders, or serial killings.

THE PHRASE "SERIAL KILLINGS" was apt. Like a serial killer, the assassins had a type. They mostly bypassed the religious intellectuals, targeting secular writers, translators, and intellectuals, many of them not even all that well known. Like serial killers, they had signature methods: strangulation, heart attacks brought on by potassium injection, the occasional florid slaughter as in the case of the Forouhars. The victims disappeared on their way to work, appointments, errands. Their corpses were found days later. The murders were cold-blooded and systematic, and they had gone on for nearly a decade before Mohammad Mokhtari was killed. The 1998 killings incurred a crisis because there were so many of them in such a short time; because their similarities were obvious; and because they happened in the first year of Khatami's presidency, when Iranians had reason to expect that the state was growing more tolerant rather than less.

From the Islamic Republic's very inception, powerful forces existed beneath the surface of the state, beyond the reach of the elected government and its ministers. Now they issued from the intelligence ministry, which was the most secretive arm of a security apparatus linked to the Supreme Leader. By some later accounts, the violence could be traced past its executors in the intelligence ministry to its ideological progenitors, a circle of hardline clerics who had footholds in the Guardian Council, intelligence ministry, and judiciary. These clerics were called the Haghani Circle, after the seminary where they'd been trained under the tutelage of Ayatollah Mohammad-Taghi Mesbah-Yazdi, who believed it was the duty of the righteous to physically eliminate those with whom they disagreed. "Killing hypocrites does not require a court order, as it is a duty imposed by the sharia on all genuine Muslims," Mesbah-Yazdi would declare in 1999, in the midst of the controversy over the serial killings. "The order of Islam is to throw them down from a high mountain and kill them outright."

Something about "We Are the Writers!" must have touched a nerve in the most violent defenders of *velayat-e faqih*. The resurfacing of the secular literary elite after its long banishment was a threat to the new cultural order. And the specter of an alliance among religious and secular intellectuals was intolerable, particularly as the religious intellectuals began ever more explicitly to question *velayat-e faqih*. An appeal to the authority and charisma of Ayatollah Khomeini used to suffice to end such discussions. But with the advent of religious intellectualism in the 1990s and the increasing popularity of Western-style social science, reasoned debate faced off against calls for obedience or revolutionary rectitude. An unbridgeable divide had opened within Iran's intellectual and power elite—between those, like Mesbah-Yazdi and the Haghani Circle, who believed that the authority of the Leader was absolute and infallible, and those who expected it to be conditioned upon logical consistency and some degree of popular sovereignty.

By killing off the secular intellectuals, who had no foothold within the power structure and no legal recourse, perhaps the shadowy forces in the security establishment believed they were simply doing their divine duty. Maybe they thought they could liquidate the country's pre-revolutionary literary culture in all its wrongheadedness. Maybe they also understood that their political adversaries, the reformists, were, for now, beyond their reach, as they had not explicitly breached the constitution; but that by targeting the secular thinkers, they could draw a sharp red line and send the reformists a warning that there they, too, should fear to tread.

The religious intellectuals did not edge away. To the contrary, Soroush joined his voice with Bazargan's in the same issue of *Kiyan* and elsewhere, arguing that theocracy did violence not only to the rights of man but to the dignity of religion. When Bazargan died in 1995, his memorial service was held at Hosseiniyeh Ershad, the birthplace of Iran's revolutionary Islamism. There, at the very lectern Shariati once inflamed, Soroush declared: "[A] society in which religion becomes the tool of oppression and humans are crushed and deprived is more sinister than a society without religion, where the oppressor does not commit his criminal acts in the name of God and does not attribute them to religion."

Iran's secular intellectual elite had become the quarry of a merciless apparatus of death. By some tallies, from 1990 to 1998, more than eighty secular Iranian writers and intellectuals died in like fashion: abducted, disappeared, found dead. A former aide to Shariati, Hossein Barazandeh, was suffocated in Mashhad in January 1995. Ahmad Mir Alaei, a writer and translator in Isfahan, died under suspicious circumstances in October 1995. Ahmad Tafazzoli, a writer and translator, was found dead with his skull smashed in Tehran in January 1996. Ebrahim Zalzadeh, an editor and publisher whose fax machine was used to distribute "We Are the Writers!" was abducted in February 1997 and found stabbed to death in March. Six former political prisoners were separately abducted and found dead in Mashhad in 1996. Former prime minister Mossadegh's granddaughter was stabbed to death in April 1998. In September 1998, in the city of Kerman, Hamid Hajizadeh, a teacher and poet, was stabbed to death in his bed, along with his nine-year-old son.

In August 1996, a group of about twenty secular writers, many of them signatories to "We Are the Writers!" chartered a bus to a literary festival in neighboring Armenia. In the middle of the night, they awoke to find the bus hurtling toward a cliff. The driver had released the hand brake, thrown himself out his door, and fled. A passenger lunged for the brakes and managed to stop the bus with its nose over the precipice, one of its tires about to churn the air. The writers were warned never to speak of the incident.

That same summer, security forces raided a dinner party at the home of the German cultural attaché. The writers and intellectuals in attendance were detained and interrogated. One of them was Faraj Sarkouhi, then the editor of *Adineh* and a signatory to "We Are the Writers!" In the two years that followed, Sarkouhi was repeatedly imprisoned and forced to confess to his part in a Western plot to undermine the Islamic Republic. *Adineh*, he was forced to say, was following an ideological script from the German government.

Throughout these years, Shahram's friends in the Writers Association spoke often of a man, identified only as Hashemi, who summoned them for questioning at the ministry of intelligence or stopped them at the airport when they tried to go abroad. Later, Shahram would learn that Hashemi's real name was Mehrdad Alikhani and that he was the intelligence official assigned to the poets and writers of the secular left. The purpose of this program was evidently liquidation.

Then came the late fall of 1998, when the Forouhars, Majid Sharif, Mohammad Mokhtari, and Mohammad Jafar Pouyandeh all disappeared within three weeks of one another. Iranian writers and intellectuals understood that they were living under siege. Lists surfaced: columns of names that purported to enumerate the intellectuals who would now disappear. Hossein Bashiriyeh, the sociologist who had attracted a following at the Center for Strategic Research, turned up on some versions of that list. Although he fit and even exceeded the profile—a secular leftist intellectual with real influence on the thinking of Islamic reformists—he did not believe anyone would harm him. He considered himself too private a figure, a scholar disengaged from politics. Still, his wife put two locks on their door, and friends advised them to sleep elsewhere. Haunted writers roamed Iranian cities looking for couches to sleep on, startling at the sound of footsteps, packing their families off to provincial homesteads for safety's sake. Some cut off contact with all but their closest friends and family. Others left the country to wait out the storm. The reformist press, which had just begun to flower under Khatami, clamored for resolution and justice, suggesting that the intelligence minister, Ghorbanali Dorri-Najafabadi, resign if he could not guarantee the safety of Iran's intellectuals.

PRESIDENT KHATAMI faced a stark challenge. If he could not credibly answer the outcry against the murder of Iranian dissidents, his pledge to expand freedom of speech and the rule of law would prove empty from the start. On the other hand, if he could shine a light into the darkest recesses of the security establishment, not only would he prove to his constituency that deep reform was possible, but he would demonstrate to the hard-liners that the reformists were a force to be reckoned with.

In December 1998, Khatami announced that he had formed a commission to investigate the murders. Hardly anyone expected results. The Islamic Republic was not known for policing its own abuses. But defectors came forward from within the intelligence ministry, and they linked their former colleagues to the Forouhar murders. Khatami used this evidence to force the intelligence ministry to announce its culpability. To the shock and amazement of Iranians, intelligence minister Dorri-Najafabadi, who had been forced on Khatami by the Supreme Leader, resigned in disgrace, to be replaced by the head of Khatami's commission.

The intelligence ministry announced that a band of about thirty rogue agents, under the leadership of a former deputy intelligence minister named Saeed Emami, were responsible for the extrajudicial killings of Iranian dissidents both within Iran and abroad. Emami and his agents were carted off to prison in February 1999. Four months later, Emami allegedly committed suicide in prison by swallowing hair removal powder.

Khatami rode high on the success of his investigation. Never before had the state taken responsibility for the killing of dissidents. Never had anyone been disciplined for such actions. Never had a president exercised power over the security apparatus, using little more than the weight of public opinion and of a comparatively free press. President Khatami showed what a muscular movement for reform was capable of.

But he also demonstrated its limits. The purging of "rogue elements" from the intelligence ministry, followed by the convenient suicide of the man in charge of those elements, left many questions unanswered. Was a deputy intelligence minister really able to carry out such a far-reaching international assassination program—claiming more than one hundred victims—without orders to do so from above? From how high up the chain of command would such a program have been authorized? By Ali Fallahian, the intelligence minister under President Rafsanjani? By Rafsanjani himself? By the Supreme Leader, Khamenei? Were there clerics, like those in the Haghani Circle, who gave this project their blessing—who maybe even issued fatwas condemning the victims to their deaths? Some hardline officials now claimed that Emami and his henchmen were acting at the behest of foreign malefactors. They released a videotape in which Emami's wife confirmed this under torture so severe that one of her kidneys had failed.

WRITING IN THE NEWSPAPER *Sobh-e Emrouz*, Akbar Ganji pressed these questions relentlessly on the president and his reformist government. *Sobh-e Emrouz* was not just any newspaper. It belonged to Saeed Hajjarian, the reformist strategist from the Center for Strategic Research who had once been an intelligence ministry official. Hajjarian had reportedly tried to block Emami's hire during the Mousavi era. Surely he knew a thing or two about the ministry's inner workings.

As for Ganji, he was not just any writer. He was a born gadfly, intellectually spry, physically courageous, and irremediably radical, whether as a Revolutionary Guardsman in the 1980s or as a liberal agitator now. To the reformists, Ganji would prove a potent but exasperating ally. He could not be counted on to play for the team; he was one of its most daring thinkers and most uncompromising critics.

When Saeed Emami was arrested, Ganji applauded Khatami but did not let up. "Directing everyone's eyes toward the intelligence ministry is an optical illusion," he wrote. "The ill-minded bloodsuckers in the field of thought and politics must be identified regardless of their guise or position."

This was not just a matter of exacting vengeance on the perpetrators of crime. There was, Ganji insisted, an "ideology of violence" at large in the country, and it was the government's moral duty to uproot it. Iranian religious leaders, he added, could not keep silent lest they imply their own complicity. Rather, right-minded clerics must not allow the assassins "to set up the market stall of murder and crime in the realm of religiousness or to raise the flag of terror on religion's dome."

When Saeed Emami died in prison, it was Ganji who publicly questioned the official line that the death was a suicide. Ganji wrote in *Sobh-e Emrouz* of his own experience in solitary confinement. A guard looked in on him every half hour; he was allowed to bathe just once a week, for only five minutes, in full view of a guard. How, he asked, could so important a prisoner as Saeed Emami have been left alone with a poisonous substance for long enough to kill himself? Would someone be charged with negligence for allowing this to happen, or would the government launch an investigation into the circumstances of Emami's death?

Ganji's articles found a hungry readership. They would be collected in a bestselling volume titled *The Dungeon of Ghosts*. In it, he traced the links among the members of the Haghani Circle and showed that these clerics, Fallahian and Dorri-Najafabadi among them, had controlled the intelligence ministry from the start. He alleged that a death squad convened secret meetings where its "gray eminence" issued fatwas calling for the murder of specific enemies. Ansar-e Hezbollah, Ganji claimed, answered to these same clerics. Some of what Ganji wrote was speculation infused with high drama and the language of a B movie. His cast of characters included a "red-robed eminence" and someone called "Master Key." But his argument was also ruthlessly logical, and he did not desist from pressing responsibility past Saeed Emami up the chain. He fingered Fallahian, Mesbah-Yazdi, and finally Rafsanjani.

Later, Ganji would say he knew exactly what he was doing. He was shaking the foundation of the regime by exposing its hidden projects, its deepest corruption. Khamenei, he understood, had moved to contain the damage by conceding only four murders—the Forouhars, Mokhtari, and Pouyandeh—and limiting responsibility to Emami and his henchmen. But responsibility, he knew, was far more widely shared, both horizontally and vertically, as well as further back in time. Ganji was clearly angling for Rafsanjani. Later he would say he thought he could trace responsibility all the way up to Khamenei. But for that he would have needed Khatami to endorse his effort—not to purge the intelligence ministry, as he had done, effectively declaring victory and closing the file.

Khatami warned Ganji that he was pushing too far, too fast. Soon enough, other sorts of warnings reached Ganji, from less sympathetic lips.

His articles were heavily censored, cut down by as much as two-thirds before publication. "We had ten editors, not one," he'd later remark. He started getting death threats by phone and fax.

During this time, Ganji was called once to the intelligence ministry and once to the military court. There he was told that if he continued writing, he would serve a minimum of fifteen years in prison. He knew his adventure would end there when he wrote an article called "Playing with Death." He wrote that he felt himself engaged in a duel, likely at any moment to be killed. To interview sources, he had to go to unfamiliar places and meet with strangers. Any one of those meetings could have been a trap. But he continued to survive them and to publish his articles, each more censored than the last.

He was at last arrested in 2000. In 2001 he would be sentenced to ten years in prison and five years of internal exile. He was to become one of the Islamic Republic's most formidable political prisoners, penning a radical manifesto against the theocracy and going on a fifty-day hunger strike that ended only when his doctors told him he was on the brink of irreversibly damaging his brain.

SHAHRAM RAFIZADEH WAS NOT as famous as Ganji, but he, too, tirelessly probed the chain murders in his writings. He suspected that reformist analysts traced the assassination program only as far back as the Rafsanjani administration, because before that, they and their friends in the Islamic Left were close to the center of power. But Shahram—twenty-eight years old and a part of no political faction—believed the program was as old as the Islamic Republic. He would link more than thirty killings, committed over a period of decades, with the ones in 1998. In a book called *Power Play: Ruhollah Hosseinian*, about the deputy minister of intelligence, Shahram also analyzed the public statements of those close to Saeed Emami to show how the Islamic Republic deliberately set forth conflicting narratives in order to obfuscate the truth.

As a result of his writings, Shahram became unemployable. He lost his job at the newspaper, where he'd edited culture pages dedicated to reintroducing Iranian readers to the secular poets and writers, and he lost his job at the publishing house, where he'd gotten to know some of the major reformist intellectuals. At times he couldn't pay his rent. He sold his television and sent his wife and children to Rasht, to live with Bita's father during the violent and tumultuous period between the chain murders and their prosecution. "They're killing all my friends," he told his wife's family bleakly.

Mokhtari had believed in dialogue. He had been one of those who reached out to the reformists within the regime, even though he did not share their religious agenda. He had believed in peaceful coexistence, peaceful struggle. His murder had been a terrible mistake. Just ten days after his friend's body was found, Shahram published an open letter. He called it "The Share of Poets: Solitude, Love, and Death." He wrote that, in Iran, hope itself suffocated poets and writers.

After that, he began writing books, and he did not stop. He owed this to Mokhtari's memory. But his life in Tehran had come loose. He was financially ruined, his family far away, his circle of writers scarred by violent loss. For four years he wrote books. Only one of three of them passed the censors to be published. In 2001 a friend told him that preparations were under way to launch a new reformist newspaper, called *Etemad*. Maybe there would be a job there for Shahram. The newspaper's editor was more conservative than Shahram, but on their mutual friend's advice, he took a chance on the young poet already known in journalism circles for his intelligent and fearless reporting. Shahram became the editor of *Etemad*'s literary page.

One day Shahram wandered over to where the political editors worked. A young deputy editor sat at a table strewn with papers. He could not have been more than twenty-two years old, slender and fine-featured, with his short black hair meticulously side-combed. He had delicate fingers and lucid brown eyes that seemed fixed to something clearer or more beautiful than what lay before him. He appeared to be hard at work, his head down. But when Shahram came near, the young editor said, "Hello, Mr. Rafizadeh."

Shahram was startled.

"I know you," the young editor explained. He introduced himself as Roozbeh Mirebrahimi, also from Rasht. Would Shahram care to write some political commentary for his section?

"How do you know I write political commentary?" Shahram asked warily.

"I have read your book," said the young editor, "and I like the way you look at things."

It would be some time before Shahram accepted the offer. By then, he and Roozbeh were friends. A shared melancholy brought them close, and soon financial hardship made them roommates. After work they would start for home, but mostly they walked together for the sake of walking, traversing the city in conversation or in a communion of silence, past the hour when traffic finally stilled. Sometimes on those walks Roozbeh would sing traditional folk songs for Shahram, his bright tenor ringing out through dusky streets.

The prospect of his arrest was never far from Shahram's mind. He tried to make light of it. "I hope that if I'm ever arrested, they will arrest you as well," he teased Roozbeh one night as they walked to Mellat Park in northeastern Tehran. "For just this one reason: You could sing for me in prison."

NINE

THE EIGHTEENTH OF TIR

IF THE ISLAMIC REPUBLIC was made for anybody, it was made for Ali Afshari. His family was loyal to the new regime and its charismatic leader, shielded from the violence of the revolutionary epoch in every particular. He was not affected by the restrictions on drinking, women's dress, and mixing between the sexes, because he would have adhered to these rules in any case. Born in 1973, husky and bearded even in his twenties, he was devout in exactly the way the ruling clerics approved.

Ali Afshari's father, Naghi, was a lay religious teacher and the publisher of a weekly magazine in the small city of Qazvin, just to the northwest of Tehran. As a boy, Ali nourished and shaped himself in his father's extensive library, a cove of books that extended beyond the imaginations of his schoolteachers. Naghi and his wife were religious people, traditional and middle-class, loyal to Ayatollah Khomeini even when they had minor doubts about the actions of the revolutionary state.

For Ali, the revolution came to Qazvin one night in late fall. The shah's army had battened down the streets in a kind of martial law, but his father disobeyed curfew to attend to Ali's grandfather, who was very sick. Naghi returned home badly beaten, his eyeglasses broken. Ali was six years old. Two months later, the shah fell. Ali felt a tremor of something between excitement

and fear. Within the larger clan of his family, there were Khomeini supporters and also critics; the debates among them were electric. But Ali did not
know anyone so far outside the political mainstream as to be affected by the
purges of that first turbulent decade. From time to time Iraqi warplanes
passed overhead, anxiety on great black wings, headed someplace just beyond.

Ali would remember the wartime rationing, the long lines for basic
household goods. In those years of political upheaval and economic collapse, Naghi's salary from teaching was barely adequate to the needs of his
wife and three children. The atmosphere of repression was an uneasy one,
even to those disinclined to press its boundaries. Ali's classmates wanted to
go to parties and to dress as they pleased. Ali didn't want these things for
himself, but he didn't understand why others should be denied them.

Shariati once waxed lyrical in the cause of social justice, although he
was not himself abjectly poor. For Ali Afshari, the cause was liberty,
although he was not himself oppressed. Liberty was a kind of justice, too.
He bridled against a system that used intimidation, force, and favoritism to
impose its values. He was a creature unimaginable to the revolutionary generation just behind him: one who came to political activism—a ruinous
vocation in postrevolutionary Iran—not to defend his own rights but to
defend those of others.

In his father's library in Qazvin, young Ali Afshari read history, particularly from the time of Mossadegh. He read literature, both foreign and
Iranian—Dostoyevsky, Dickens, Balzac, but also Hedayat, Saadi, Al-e
Ahmad. He read poetry. He read about Islam, and about Persia before and
after its advent. Above all, he read Shariati. In Shariati he found an Islam
that was modern and invigorating, one that furnished a call to political
action. But, next to Shariati, Ali also read *Iran's Revolution in Two Steps* by
Mehdi Bazargan, the Islamic Republic's expelled and disdained first prime
minister. Ali tried to reconcile Bazargan's brand of liberal rationality with
Shariati's exhortation to action. When *Kayhan-e Farhangi* began to publish
Abdolkarim Soroush's essays, Ali was fifteen. He devoured the new publication, and after it, *Kiyan*. Soroush supplanted Shariati in his esteem, and he
determined to follow the exciting new thinker when he reached university.

Ali went to Amirkabir University, formerly Tehran Polytechnic, to study industrial engineering in 1992. One of Iran's most prestigious technical schools, Amirkabir served some ten thousand students in the flat, congested center of Iran's sprawling capital, where the sky hung close and acrid with exhaust but the streets pulsed with restless energy. With its low-slung, poorly maintained concrete buildings, its deep, littered gutters for mountain runoff perilously sluicing between curb and street, its nearly unbreathable air, Tehran was not a beautiful city. But its color and vital force, its ferocious daily momentum, marked it as one of those cities that did more than host millions of lives but somehow channeled their promise and menace through arteries of its own.

Ali Afshari went to Tehran knowing he would become an activist. No one else knew it. His high school teachers remembered him as a mild, traditional young man who had every reason to be satisfied. He was not an angry person. But he was a solid one, physically and mentally. Once he was planted in your path, you could hardly expect to push him aside.

INDEPENDENT STUDENT ACTIVISM had all but died after the Iranian revolution. The Islamic Students Associations on university campuses were arms of the leadership under Khomeini. They were powerful, but only insofar as they were obedient. Each university's Islamic Students Association sent a representative to the national coordinating board that oversaw all the associations, in an effort to keep them in line with Khomeini's views. That board had the awkward, off-putting name of Daftar-e Tahkim-e Vahdat, or the Office of Consolidating Unity. Students knew it as Daftar Tahkim. Until Khomeini's death, it was a pillar of the then powerful Islamic Left.

By the time Ali Afshari entered university, at the start of Rafsanjani's presidency, Daftar Tahkim, and the Islamic Students Associations it represented, had begun to assert their independence from the state. Khomeini was gone, and with him the object of "consolidating unity." The Islamic Left was gone, and with it the student movement's purchase on power.

The Soviet Union and Eastern Bloc were gone, and with them the gravitational polarity of the Cold War.

Moreover, President Rafsanjani was a troublesome figure, as much for the student movement as he had been for the Islamic Left. Daftar Tahkim welcomed his overtures toward political and cultural liberalism, but resented his exclusion of the Islamic Left from power and adamantly rejected what it feared was a free market agenda. In the first three years after Khomeini's death, the Islamic Students Associations felt their way toward an ambivalent new role, from cheerleader to cautious critic of the Islamic Republic. The Islamic Republic responded by establishing its own organizations that would serve as reliable instruments of control over the universities. These included special campus Basij details, as well as Ansar-e Hezbollah and the Office of the Supreme Leader in the Universities.

Ali Afshari might have joined the Basij. Nothing in his background would have led to his exclusion. He was popular, a leader in sports—he was the head of the climbing club—as well as in culture and politics. But Ali's agenda was—quietly, modestly at first—subversive. He felt that the students at Amirkabir did not all enjoy the same rights. Those who supported the regime had privileges. They went on school-sponsored field trips to other cities, to the mountains, to visit shrines. The less-favored students were not permitted to go. The atmosphere that Ansar, the Basij, and the Office of the Supreme Leader enforced was abstemious, punitive: male students were not permitted to listen to music with women singers, nor Western music or any music from the shah's time, even in the privacy of their dorm rooms, and the library was censored beyond what was required by the state. Male and female students could not speak to each other on campus, even to discuss their studies or to share notes or books. On some days students from the Office of the Supreme Leader in the Universities would block the doors of buildings, refusing entry to boys who dared to wear short sleeves. Sometimes they took those students' names and punished them with two semesters' suspension.

Ali Afshari made these inequities and restrictions the first objects of his activism. He got involved in his dormitory's cultural office, within which he formed an organization that offered field trips for all comers, and he used his clout as a religious student to persuade the head of the dormitory not to punish students for the music they listened to or the books they read, but rather to welcome a spirit of debate among the students. The hezbolla-his, he knew—because he knew them well—could ignore a secular liberal malcontent, or a child of the defeated, frightened secular left; but they could not ignore Ali Afshari. He could as easily be one of theirs.

Ali was elected first to his department's student union and then, in 1994, to the university-wide Islamic Students Association. He was thrilled. Among his colleagues in the Islamic Students Association were veterans of the Iran-Iraq War and very religious, traditional young people from fami-lies close to the regime. But, like Ali, they were looking for a new political model, an idea that might free them from the sterile factional bickering between the right and left wings of the ruling establishment. They found Abdolkarim Soroush.

Soroush spoke to them within the idiom of Islam, with respect for its commitments. But he was modern, democratic, and, the students felt, non-ideological. "We wanted to distribute the ideas of Dr. Soroush, to move from Islamic jurisprudence to Islamic modernism, liberty rather than jus-tice, civil society rather than government," Ali would later reflect.

Amirkabir University was a trendsetter. Some universities' Islamic Stu-dents Associations embraced the hardline policies of Khamenei; others pressed for a return to the Islamic Left orthodoxies of the 1980s; and at first only Amirkabir promoted the new ideas emanating from *Kiyan* and the Center for Strategic Research. Within three years, however, Amirkabir's reformism would be embraced by the majority.

NOTHING COULD HAVE MARKED a clearer break with the recent past than the students' rehabilitation of Mehdi Bazargan, the embattled liberal prime minister forced from office by radical students, among oth-ers, in the revolutionary tumult. It was, after all, the forerunner of Daftar Tahkim that took over the American embassy, humiliating Bazargan's provisional government and demonstrating the overweening power of the radical clerics after 1979.

When Bazargan died in early 1995, Ali helped organize a memorial at Amirkabir. It was, he felt, his duty to show Bazargan the respect he had been denied by students in his time. But the campus Basij disrupted the program, threatening the speakers and forbidding them from taking the podium. Ali would later identify the memorial as the event that turned him into an activist for the opposition. From that moment on, he was a person of interest to the Ministry of Intelligence.

When Ansar-e Hezbollah assaulted Soroush at a lecture at the University of Tehran, Amirkabir's Islamic Students Association issued a statement urging the interior ministry to step up: "What need is there to guard the country by night when the law is breached in daylight?" the students demanded. "What meaning do claims of power have when the cultural realm of a university is violated by some while the law enforcement forces act as mere spectators?" Ali Afshari and his fellow student activists determined that Soroush should speak at Amirkabir and that the students there would defend him. They organized the lecture for May 12, 1996.

Some five thousand students were to attend. Ali was in charge of security, and he organized two hundred liberal students into a fighting force that blocked Ansar-e Hezbollah from entering the amphitheater. The students had control of the sound system of the campus mosque, and they used it to broadcast revolutionary songs. But the militias interpreted the songs as an incitement against the Islamic Republic, and they cut the power to the mosque. They seized Soroush and prevented him from entering to speak at the event. Ali Afshari and his fellow student activists were determined to carry on with their program, even if they had only their introductory speaker. They found an alternative source of electricity from a neighboring university building. The state security forces cut the power to the whole campus in response. The students had a generator but no gas; they used their motorcycles to fire up the generator, and this allowed them to turn on the lights and the microphones. The speaker finished his remarks. Soroush never took the podium, but the Islamic Students Association of Amirkabir University had announced itself as an oppositional force to be reckoned with.

The activists who'd organized the Soroush speech started to disappear two months later, whisked one by one to prison or interrogation. Ali Afshari knew his turn was coming. A representative of the intelligence ministry showed up at the Islamic Students Association's office and asked to speak with him. Ali and the agent walked as they talked. Little by little, Ali found himself surrounded by men who quietly escorted him through a back door and into a car, where he was blindfolded and driven to Towhid Prison, a detention center associated with the intelligence ministry.

Ali had a solitary cell. His interrogators didn't touch him. Instead they screamed insults and curses: he was stupid, retarded, an imbecile. He had created turmoil among the masses and acted against national security. President Rafsanjani had a railroad project he'd hoped to unveil, with great fanfare, on the very day of Amirkabir's Soroush debacle. Ali had orchestrated a distraction from the government's great achievement, his interrogators admonished. Surely he'd done so under the direction of the Mojahedin-e Khalq. Surely the student activists were under the control of the reform movement that was then emerging from the defunct Islamic Left. Ali confessed to nothing. After ten days he was brought before a judge. Shariati and Bazargan had founded a deviant religion, the judge sneered. He ordered Ali to spend the night in Evin Prison. In the morning Ali was released on bail.

THAT FALL, a heavy security atmosphere pervaded Amirkabir University. But the Islamic Students Association drew energy from its embattlement. It nominated Ali Afshari as its representative to Daftar Tahkim. At the national level, Ali now represented the students who considered themselves Islamic modernists—the ones who read and admired Soroush. Moreover, it was an election year. Ali and the reformists in Daftar Tahkim supported Khatami over the conservative candidate, parliamentary speaker Ali Akbar

Nategh-Nouri. Students drove the Khatami campaign, and as the campaign's student coordinator, Ali Afshari drove the students.

Daftar Tahkim had a car with government plates, a vestige of the Khomeini era. Ali was not supposed to use the car for campaign purposes, but he did. He drove through the city to check in with the student campaigners. In Islamshahr, a poor community to the south of Tehran, he saw volunteers working all night long on a hundred-meter-long banner of Khatami's name. In the north he saw students tossing Khatami postcards into the windows of moving cars late at night. Ansar-e Hezbollah sometimes broke the windows of cars displaying Khatami's photo, and so Ali helped organize what he called "antipressure groups," which would physically defend Khatami supporters against Ansar. In the final days of the campaign, Daftar Tahkim had four buses of students circling the city, campaigning for Khatami. Eventually, all four busloads were arrested and accused of creating a "carnival of propaganda."

One night, Ali drove the government-tagged car to Fatemi Square, in central Tehran. In the car he had three other student activists and a big poster of Khatami they planned to hang. The police pulled them over and arrested them for misuse of the vehicle. The students spent two days in the basement of the judiciary building, where many other campaigners for Khatami were already being held.

But they were out in time for the day that would become legendary as the Second of Khordad—election day, 1997. There was a huge celebration for Khatami's victory at Amirkabir. As Ali would later remember, "All the students thought that every single problem they had was going to be solved."

IF ALI AFSHARI nurtured such illusions, they were punctured very early when President Khatami appointed ultraconservative university presidents rather than tussle with hard-liners to secure more liberal appointments. Khatami could not afford to duck confrontation, Ali felt. The hardline right would certainly do no such thing, and it still controlled the parliament, the judiciary, the intelligence ministry, the Guardian Council, and the militias. Then came Khatami's bold handling of the chain murders, which allayed Ali's fears. Khatami had some fight in him after all.

Saeed Hajjarian had defined the reformist strategy as "Pressure from below, negotiation at the top." Ali Afshari and his fellow activists understood that their role was to mount the popular pressure that would allow the politicians bargaining room. This was a delicate business. They should push, but not too hard or too far. They were to strengthen Khatami's hand without overplaying it. Students campaigned for reformist candidates for the parliament and the city council. They protested the impeachment of Khatami's most liberal ministers, which parliamentary hard-liners doggedly pursued. The students were avid readers and defenders of the newly vibrant press, which now teemed with publications unafraid to challenge the ruling establishment.

Reform, Ali imagined, was like a bird. One wing was the student movement, and the other was the independent media. Together they could beat the air away and press Khatami's project forward, lift it higher, demonstrate to its adversaries that momentum, and the public itself, was on Khatami's side. And so the student activists were particularly ardent in protesting the hard-liners' harsh treatment of the press. The Special Court of the Clergy opened a branch for press offenses, bringing the prosecution of clerics who held publishing licenses under the jurisdiction of the Supreme Leader's office. Newspapers vanished as quickly as they appeared; editors faced prison sentences; publishers lost their licenses; and young writers bounced between jobs, forever scrambling to chase that last paycheck from a publication that no longer existed. Daftar Tahkim answered all of these affronts with protests. And Ansar-e Hezbollah, the hardline militia, answered the students' protests with violent clashes.

IN JULY OF 1999, the parliament debated a sweeping new law formalizing the hardline assault on the press. The law would greatly restrict the number of publications in the country. It would also eliminate the statute of limitations on press offenses, which could then be prosecuted at any time and not only against editors in chief, as in the past, but against individual writers and reporters as well. Reporters could be forced to divulge their sources, and the supervision of the press would fall partly to clerics in Qom.

Khatami and his ministers urged the parliament to reject the press law. "We have to create laws in accordance with freedom, not freedom according to our laws," protested Khatami's Ershad minister. But the conservative speaker of the parliament had a different view: "The press is a gateway for cultural invasion, so let us take measures," he admonished.

On the eve of the vote, the reformist newspaper *Salam* published an explosive story. The press law, it suggested, was the brainchild of Saeed Emami, the notorious mastermind behind the serial murders. *Salam* published excerpts from an internal intelligence ministry memo Emami had penned, urging the state not only to restrict the issuance of publishing licenses but to use the security apparatus to confront writers "individually, using the law, in order to ban them from writing or publishing."

If the document was authentic, it suggested that the mainstream conservatives in the parliament were doing the bidding of a disgraced intelligence thug who also endorsed strangulation as a means of censorship. The intelligence ministry quickly disavowed the memo, claiming it was a fake. But curiously, when the publisher of *Salam* was called before the Special Court of the Clergy later that month, he was charged with publishing a classified document, among other offenses. *Salam* was shut down, its editors arrested, on the afternoon of July 7, the very day the parliament approved the press law.

It was summer vacation, the study period before exams, and most students had gone home. But this news could not be ignored. Those students who remained at the University of Tehran called friends to come and join them on campus in protest. As the crowd swelled, it grew bolder, chanting slogans against the judiciary and venturing off campus. When the students reentered the university, they found Ansar-e Hezbollah waiting for them with rocks and clubs. Activists fought back, hurling rocks at the militiamen. By Thursday evening there was a confusion of arrests and injuries.

The next day was Friday, the eighteenth of Tir by the solar calendar, and things took a turn for the far worse.

ALI AFSHARI WAS IN QAZVIN. He'd stopped there to see his family before going on Hajj, the annual pilgrimage to Mecca. A late-night phone call led him to abandon his plans and rush back to the capital, arriving early Saturday afternoon on a campus that looked to him as if it had just been sacked by an invading army.

Revolutionary Guards had stormed the students' dormitory in the dead of night, dragging students from their beds to beat them, breaking windows, and setting rooms on fire. Students covered their faces and defended themselves with rocks and Molotov cocktails. Police swarmed a passageway by the dormitory, where they beat students down with clubs. One student would recall seeing his friend dragged by his long hair down that passage, which was studded with broken glass. The friend would spend twenty days in the hospital afterward. A student named Ezzat Ibrahim Nejad was killed in the melee that night. By the time the battle ceased, the dormitory was a burned husk.

Police had sealed the campus gates, but Ali and other student leaders knew the clandestine routes of entry. The university teemed with jangled, maddened students and their supporters. Daftar Tahkim called an urgent meeting. The students would organize a sit-in, they decided, to peacefully protest the dormitory attack. They would call for exams to be postponed until the matter was properly addressed. But even as the activist leaders met and strategized, students flocked to the campus. The police could no longer hold back the crowds, nor could Daftar Tahkim control them as some demonstrators started chanting slogans against the Supreme Leader. The crowd surged through the campus gates and headed for the interior ministry.

The interior ministry, technically, controlled the police. But that ministry was in the hands of reformists, who adamantly denied any role in the dormitory attack. Ali was convinced not only that the students had the wrong address for their complaint but that they were being conscripted into a larger plan. Maybe the leader and his hardline allies were baiting the students into a big street confrontation. Then they would unleash the Revolutionary Guards on the students while impeaching Khatami on law-and-order grounds—for being unable to keep the streets calm and the country secure. Ali's reformist contacts in government circles suspected this scenario as well.

Ali rushed to the front of the crowd that had amassed in front of the interior ministry. He urged the students to turn back. "I understand your concern and your pain," he said, "and I believe that those who committed these crimes should be identified and brought to justice." But the interior ministry was not the culprit, he insisted. By coming to the streets disorganized and angry, the students would only undermine their goals. They should continue their protest on campus.

He began to lead the crowd—he would later estimate it to be between sixty thousand and seventy thousand people, but most news sources suggest it was closer to twenty-five thousand—back to the university. Along the way, a group of students started agitating to bring the crowd to the president's office instead. Again Ali Afshari objected. Khatami wasn't responsible. "Let's go and demonstrate in front of Khamenei's house," said another activist. "He's responsible!"

This might have been closer to the truth, but to Ali it was the worst idea of all. The students would accomplish nothing and meet with violence. But the crowd was deaf to verbal entreaties. Ali and the members of Daftar Tahkim lay down in the street to stop the students from going to the Supreme Leader's house.

At long last, the student leaders wrangled the crowd back to campus. There they had, Ali reflected, a "magnificent" demonstration. Students chanted slogans, including, "The murderers of the Forouhars are hiding inside Khamenei's robes." Ordinary people came to the campus to bring the students food. When Ansar-e Hezbollah attacked again, student vigilantes seized the militiamen and confiscated their weapons, including guns and knives. They turned the militiamen over to the interior ministry together with a list of the weapons they'd carried. The next day the demonstration became a sit-in organized around Daftar Tahkim's clear list of demands: that the chief of police be fired; that those behind the dormitory attack be identified and prosecuted; that the press law be killed; that *Salam* be allowed to publish; and that the public learn the complete truth about what had happened to the victims of the chain murders.

But Ali could see that the crowd was slipping from his grasp. Not everyone endorsed Daftar Tahkim's reformist strategy. More radical students believed that the demonstrators should leave campus and take over national institutions like state television and police headquarters. Another part of the crowd consisted not even of students but of people with a disorganized array of grievances, who were eager to turn the sit-in into an uprising. By Monday, as the Tehran demonstration grew and as demonstrations spread to other cities across the country, Supreme Leader Khamenei was at last compelled to speak.

Khamenei condemned the attack on the University of Tehran dormitory. "This bitter incident hurt my heart," he said. "In the Islamic system, it is not acceptable to attack the house and shelter of a group, particularly overnight or at the time of congregation prayers. The youth of this country, whether students or not, are my children, and it is very difficult and bitter for me to see them embarrassed and upset."

He said that he forgave even the demonstrators' insults to his person, and he urged calm, telling hard-liners to "keep quiet even if they burn or rip my photographs." At the same time, however, Khamenei insinuated that a foreign hand was at work on those fevered streets and that a victory should not be handed there to the Americans. "I want to tell students to watch out for enemies, strangers who come among you disguised as friends," he admonished.

NONE OF THIS ASSUAGED the students' anguish or answered their demands. Several hundred activists brushed aside Daftar Tahkim's objections. They left the campus and took their protest to the streets. There the demonstration quickly spiraled into violence and confusion, with shop windows smashed, vehicles burned, and more students injured and arrested. The Revolutionary Guards doused the campus in tear gas. Showing scenes of mayhem in central Tehran, state television accused the students of attacking mosques, robbing banks, and burning buses.

After the undeniably brutal attack on the sleeping students just a few nights earlier—after the Leader's televised contrition and sadness—the hard-liners now succeeded in taking control of the public narrative. The state media characterized the students as violent, anarchic, and counterrevolutionary. As Ali Afshari had feared, some of the demonstrators' actions had helped reinforce that impression.

On Wednesday, July 14, 1999, hard-liners packed the University of Tehran campus and the surrounding streets with counterdemonstrators in strict Islamic dress, holding banners of Khamenei's face and chanting "Death to America." Reformists charged that these were ringers bused in from the provinces or the suburbs. Whoever they were, most foreign media estimated their number at one hundred thousand, but Iranian state-run media reported a crowd a million strong. Thousands of hardline militiamen thundered through the city on motorcycles that day, policing streets now plunged into an uneasy silence.

On the university campus, a succession of turbaned clerics addressed the hardline crowd. One among them stood out for the ferocity of his condemnation of the reformist students. He was a conservative cleric with deep ties to the security apparatus, to Rafsanjani, and to the Supreme Leader. He all but called for student protesters to be executed. His name was Hassan Rouhani.

"We will resolutely and decisively quell any attempt to rebel," Rouhani declared. "Those involved in the last days' riots will be tried and punished for fighting God and sowing corruption on earth." Those were charges that carried the death penalty.

Some two thousand students were arrested that day, including Ali Afshari's brother. Most were released about a month later, but some— particularly those without major organizations behind them—served long and terrible prison terms.

"That was the day they almost buried the heart and soul of the peaceful university student movement," one student leader later mourned. "No one asked us what happened. The people were so happy that the government had stood against anarchism."

MANOUCHEHR AND AKBAR MOHAMMADI, brothers from a village near Amol in the southern Caspian province of Mazandaran, were among the unlucky ones. They led a nationalist student group that, because it was secular, could not shelter even among the reformists. Manouchehr, whose great arching brow lent him a sorrowful look, impressed foreign journalists at times as grandiose, at other times as fragile; when his ordeal came to an end, he would be described by one of his fellow exiles in the shared ship-wreck of Washington, D.C., as "a child reporting a tragedy."

Manouchehr's father, a rice farmer, was one of very few men in his village who could read and write. His wife, thirteen at the time of their marriage, bore six children, including Akbar and Manouchehr. Villagers came to the Mohammadi home to present their disputes for resolution, or when they needed help writing a letter. The Mohammadis were the first in their village to own a refrigerator that ran on gasoline. Most families stored their perishables in ditches. Manouchehr's mother made ice in her refrigerator and gave pieces to neighbors, who would line up outside her home.

Manouchehr grew up with anxiety and prayer—prayer that he might wind up in paradise, anxiety that he might fail to avert his eyes from women, that he might stumble into sin. He washed his hands and face in the ritual way before praying. He tried to train his mind away from temptation. The village school went no further than fourth grade, so after that he walked an hour each way to lessons in a neighboring town. His father wanted him to be a doctor.

Manouchehr adored his younger brother, Akbar, and like younger brothers everywhere, Akbar looked up to Manouchehr. Akbar was compassionate, principled, humane. He was proud and obstinate as well. In later years Manouchehr would speak of his brother as of a sainted alter ego.

His Akbar sought to help children, the handicapped, beggars, the injured. As boys, the brothers peered together into a grown-up world that often repelled and frightened them. State television in the 1980s seemed to celebrate killing and violence in the name of Islam. The Mohammadi brothers were ashamed to see their religion marshaled to such ends. In time they became not only secular but nonbelievers.

When Manouchehr registered for his studies in economics at the University of Tehran, he refused to join the Islamic Students Association, which he distrusted as an arm of the government. He and Akbar decided instead to form an organization of their own. It was independent of the state, nationalist and secular, and they held meetings and recruited members in secret. Their frank opposition to theocratic rule rendered them marginal to the politics of the era, but Manouchehr talked himself up to whoever would listen, to the point that a *New York Times* reporter described him as a "fast-talking self-promoter."

Manouchehr's youthful grandstanding may not have convinced Iranian students of his importance, but it provided the regime with a useful scapegoat after the Eighteenth of Tir, as the campus crisis in July 1999 came to be known. Hard-liners in the regime could accomplish many things at once by arresting the Mohammadis. The brothers were at once well-known and isolated; like the victims of the serial killings, they had little recourse inside the system because they were secular. By making an example of these young men who had often claimed to speak for the student movement, but whose role was in reality very limited, the security apparatus could declare victory after the unrest but without waging war on student groups with deeper social and institutional roots. And so state television pronounced Akbar and Manouchehr the ringleaders of the student uprising; it also pronounced them foreign agents who sought to overthrow the Islamic Republic under the guidance of the United States and European powers.

The Revolutionary Court found Manouchehr and Akbar Mohammadi guilty of waging war against God. First they were sentenced to death; then the sentence was commuted to fifteen years in prison. In the end, the brothers served seven years and two months, but there was no mercy in this. The

Mohammadi brothers were tortured with the special savagery reserved for the condemned. Their interrogators lashed them with cables, suspended them from the ceiling in stress positions, dunked their heads in toilet bowls, ruptured their eardrums with deafening noises, and deprived them of sleep twenty-three hours a day for days on end. They tortured Akbar in front of Manouchehr and Manouchehr in front of Akbar. They put the brothers through mock executions and convinced each in turn that the other was dead. They beat the sides of Manouchehr's body with an iron rod until some of his vertebrae fractured.

Manouchehr gave a forced televised confession early on. He copped to being the leader of the student demonstrations and to inciting unrest on behalf of the United States and other foreign powers. Other students, under similar duress, implicated Manouchehr in confessions of their own. The official narrative took shape through this theater of coercion. It remained only for Akbar to fulfill his role. Day after day, interrogators demanded that Akbar implicate his brother in a foreign plot against the state. Akbar refused. In the end Manouchehr could have suffered no worse torture than his brother's resistance.

Their mother did not recognize Akbar the first time she visited him in prison. He weighed less than a hundred pounds. He bled internally, from his kidneys and stomach; his feet were purple from the lashings, and some of his toenails had fallen off. A disk in his spine had ruptured. He had lost much of his hearing and some of his eyesight from blows to his head. One surgeon who operated on the injuries to his head and face discovered blood clots moving swiftly toward his brain. Akbar mounted his last hunger strike as a plea for access to medical care in July of 2006. According to Amnesty International, he "was administered an unspecified 'medicine'" on July 30. His condition worsened. By one of the family's accounts, Akbar was taken not to the intensive care unit, where he belonged, but to a general prison ward, where he was left on a stretcher to die.

Under pressure from the media and international human rights groups, the judiciary granted Manouchehr a twenty-day furlough to attend a memorial for his brother. On the eighteenth night, with the help of Iran's Kurdish

Democratic Party, he slipped over the Iraqi border. Kurds ferried him through the mountains into Turkey, from where he fled to the United States.

Manouchehr, with his bruised vertebrae, his haunted psyche, would become his brother's evangelist. Together with his sisters, he would make a secular martyr of Akbar, in Shiite fashion. The Islamic Republic, perhaps the world, had never been equal to Akbar's presence. Manouchehr would have his brother's prison memoirs translated into English, he would start a foundation in Akbar's name. He would escape Evin Prison but never again see the forests of Mazandaran.

He came to report a tragedy—to the vast, indifferent American West, where he settled in Las Vegas, because it was cheap, and to an Iran that grew more ghostly to him than Akbar ever would.

IN THE DAYS THAT FOLLOWED the student unrest, Khatami was quiet. He gave no special remarks and made no public appearance for two weeks. The students and their supporters were dumbstruck, then angry. They were the president's constituency. Surely he could spare a word of support for them, a word of condemnation for those who had arrested and beaten them, those who would sentence the Mohammadis and two others to die.

Ayatollah Montazeri, barricaded in his home, had shown no hesitation. Montazeri called the students "the true children of the revolution" and "the eyes and the light of the nation." The hardline forces that beat them back, said Montazeri, had "betrayed the religion and the nation" by yoking violence to Islam. Akbar Ganji voiced his support for the students as well. But it was Khatami the students longed to hear from, and Khatami who eluded them.

The president did have a long-scheduled speaking engagement in the western city of Hamadan on Tuesday, July 27. As that date approached—a full two weeks after the hardline counterdemonstration at the University of Tehran—what would have been a routine provincial appearance became a test of Khatami's mettle. Tens of thousands of spectators crowded into Hamadan's soccer stadium.

The president praised students and faculty as "among the best support-ers for the progress and advancement of our nation," and he criticized the police and militias involved in the dormitory attack. That nastiness, he sug-gested, was hardline payback for his prosecution of the serial killings. But he also stressed his support for the revolutionary state and asserted that there was no daylight between him and the establishment's conservatives. "There is no split between the government, the presidency and the Supreme Leader," he said; any appearance to the contrary was an "illusion."

Alas, Khatami lamented, the student demonstrations had devolved into rioting, which Khatami condemned as "an ugly and offensive incident." He blamed the violence on evil outsiders intent on making trouble, but he left ambiguous whether these were hardline provocateurs or foreign conspira-tors. "All persons and elements responsible for the recent riots in Tehran will get tough punishment no matter who they are," he declared. And he praised the restraint of the security forces: "My dear ones, today in order to put down the riots and in order to put out the flames of violence for the nation, others use tanks, armored cars, and heavy weapons. Our forces did not use firearms to tackle the rioting. The disturbance was put down calmly and without resorting to firearms."

The speech seemed written to placate two audiences, and it was only partially effective. The more radical students came away convinced that, between the students and the Supreme Leader, Khatami had chosen the Leader and could never be trusted again. How foolish the students had been to expect that Khatami would act as anything other than an official of the regime he served. But the reformist student activists, like Ali Afshari, had not yet run out of patience for political maneuvers, and they continued to extend Khatami the benefit of the doubt. Khatami, Ali believed, had shifted his focus to two achievable ends, both of which deserved the students' sup-port. The president was determined to commute the death sentences of the Mohammadi brothers and the others. And he was looking ahead to the par-liamentary elections, which the reformists were poised to win.

Ali and his friends pressed Khatami on the matter of the imprisoned students. They wrote letters and attended a meeting of the National

Security Council. They could see that the reformist government was locked in battle with the Revolutionary Guards, the police, and the judiciary, all of which believed that the demonstrators should not be treated as students but as the agents of foreign countries determined to overthrow the Islamic Republic. That the Mohammadis were not hanged that summer was a victory, but it was not enough.

With the help of student campaigners, the reformists carried the February 2000 parliamentary election by a landslide. Khatami could not be better empowered than he was now. His faction commanded both elected arms of government—executive and legislative—as well as the support of the populace, twice proven through elections. But within the system the reformist faction stood alone. Akbar Ganji, in the essays that had landed him in prison, fingered Rafsanjani as a key node in the network responsible for the serial killings, and in retaliation Rafsanjani had withdrawn his support for Khatami and his colleagues. Ali Afshari and his fellow student activists were pleased. They had always distrusted Rafsanjani as an opportunist with no enduring interest in political liberalization, and they opposed him on principle on economic matters. They were happy to support a reformist faction positioned solidly on the economic left. But Rafsanjani, never one to linger in the cold, swung his weight behind the clerical conservatives on the Expediency Council, which he ran, and the Guardian Council, which had veto power over parliamentary legislation.

The reformist deputies drafted legislation reversing the press law that had inspired the student riots, and they had the numbers to pass it. But the Leader ordered the new speaker of the parliament, the reformist cleric Mehdi Karroubi, to withdraw the new press bill without a vote. Revolutionary Guards surrounded the parliament and threatened to storm the building and arrest the deputies if they disobeyed. Karroubi withdrew the bill, and the campaign of arrest, intimidation, and closure continued against the reformist press. Most of the bills the parliament passed after that, the Guardian Council struck down.

Ali Afshari and his friends asked Khatami to call them to the streets. They wanted to stage demonstrations in front of the parliament, demanding that the Guardian Council stand down before the people's representatives. But Khatami declined. He did not want a showdown.

By now Ali Afshari understood that electing reformists was not enough—not when the elected representatives were accountable to the Leader rather than to the people. At an activist conference in Gurgan, in the north of Iran, Ali proposed a new strategy that he called "Beyond Khatami." The students should come to the streets and press, without violence, for fundamental institutional change. Daftar Tahkim suddenly looked less like a Soviet youth group than like Polish Solidarity. Ali Afshari became the spokesman for the group's new strategy, declaiming the need for what he called "encompassing criticism," a posture of dissent that did not exempt Khatami from its sights.

SHORTLY BEFORE THE MEETING in Gurgan, Ali had spent nearly two months in prison, nineteen days of it in solitary confinement. He was one of several activists arrested for participating in a conference of Iranian opposition activists in Berlin, organized by the German Green Party. His interrogators insulted and threatened him for eight hours at a stretch, then sometimes sent him to swelter in a glass room that overheated in the sun. He was released on bail. When his trial concluded with a five-year suspended prison sentence, the students at Amirkabir held a protest. Ali Afshari would exemplify the stance of encompassing criticism: he gave a speech criticizing Khamenei and the reformists who'd caved in to him. Two weeks later he was summoned back to court, this time accused of trying to overthrow the regime.

Nothing had prepared Ali for the ordeal he was about to suffer. For all that he'd called for setting activist sights "Beyond Khatami," he was still a member of the loyal opposition, until recently a supporter of the political faction that held both the presidency and the parliament. Within the student movement, he had been a force for moderation and cooperation. Now he stood accused of insulting the Supreme Leader and propagandizing against the regime. He could have dealt with those charges. But he quickly understood that his interrogators wanted him to confess to something more: to planning an armed insurrection against the Islamic Republic, to holding a secret arms cache in the office of Daftar Tahkim, and other treasonous crimes.

Unlike the Mohammadi brothers, Ali was not a scapegoat so much as a prize target. His arrest signaled that the hard-liners had come to view the student movement as a genuine threat. By imprisoning a student leader with national stature and friends in government, by breaking and debasing him, the hard-liners could hope to demoralize the movement that looked to him as a leader. Ali would not be left to die in prison or run off a provincial highway in darkness. Whatever happened to him, it was meant to be public and to demonstrate the irresistibility of his captors' might.

Ali Afshari's detention began in a part of Evin Prison he would later understand to be associated with the Revolutionary Guards. Interrogators came for him at sundown and questioned him all night, every night. There were as many as ten of them, though usually no more than three or four in the room at a time. They relieved one another in shifts all night long. He stood blindfolded facing a wall while one interrogator bombarded him with threats and insults and another soothed him with blandishments. If he'd only cooperate, said one, a fine position awaited him with the state television station. If he didn't, said the other, he would find himself in Ganji's dungeon of ghosts, from which no one returned alive. For a week Ali was not permitted to sleep at night and barely slept during the day. Then one morning the guards wrapped him in a blanket and put him in a car. Sleep deprivation had made him sick. He vomited in the car. By the time he arrived at a Revolutionary Guard prison known as Prison 59, he was very ill. He remained blindfolded until he was in his solitary cell, where the air pressed hot and close.

"Prison 59 isn't like the other prisons you have been to," his interrogator announced that night. "You will not be pampered here. Do as you're told or die."

Ali's interrogators punched and kicked him, mainly in the head and on his sides. One interrogator wanted to talk about philosophy. Did good and evil inhere in actions? the interrogator asked. Or did a person's perceptions and intentions determine whether his acts were good or bad? Ali might have noted echoes of Soroush and the Mutazilites. But these discussions ended in beatings. The interrogators wanted Ali to confess to treason, but they also wanted him to parrot their beliefs—about current events, about the chain murders, about the reformists. Ali had two options, an interrogator told him: surrender or the grave. Stronger men than he had broken here.

Ali was too hot in his cell and too cold in the interrogation room. He ate little and slept less, as he was forced to stand for days on end. If he nodded off, his interrogators would jerk him to his feet by his hair. Once he was awake for four consecutive days. He was dizzy, disoriented, entirely alone. An interrogator whispered in his ear continuously, suggesting more and worse tortures to come. He would rape Ali if he didn't surrender. He would sodomize him with a bottle. He would suspend him from the ceiling by his head and whip him to the edge of death. He'd pull the nails from his fingers and toes. He would keep Ali in prison for twenty years.

Ali spent a month in Prison 59 before returning to Evin. There he had a freezing underground cell, thin pajamas, and just one blanket. At mealtimes he had to stand facing the wall with his hands behind his neck until the guard had delivered his food and departed. He should have slept by day—the exhaustion had shredded his psyche—but his shivering kept him awake. At night he returned to the interrogation room. Sometimes there were as many as four interrogators there with him; he could feel two or three of them punching and kicking his head from behind. Once Ali was sitting in a chair when an interrogator kicked his side so hard that he fell to the ground. The interrogator lifted him by his hair to force him back into the chair. If Ali didn't confess, they told him, he'd be consigning his father, his sister, and his friends to torture like his own.

One night an interrogator told Ali to prepare to be executed. He dragged Ali blindfolded into the prison yard. Another interrogator was talking on his cell phone, apparently begging a judge to show mercy. But a third voice rang out: "No. That's not possible. The execution has to be carried out." The man on the phone begged for clemency. "No," said the first interrogator. "This guy is a lost cause." The man with the phone begged Ali to think of his parents and confess, rather than go before the firing squad that awaited him. For thirty minutes the interrogators bandied Ali's fate among them. For the first time Ali felt his will collapsing. Maybe they didn't really mean to kill him. But maybe they did.

He would confess, he imagined, against himself. But that was not what his tormentors had in mind. They wanted him to confess to things that would implicate other people and that would surely result in his own execution. He was to say that Daftar Tahkim had a weapons stockpile and that he'd intended to assassinate a provincial governor. He was to testify against specific people, implicating them in crimes they hadn't committed. His torturers bound him to a bed like the one where they'd whipped the Mohammadi brothers, and they showed him the cable wires they would use to lash his flesh.

"I felt like a lonely and vulnerable child who had lost his parents and was left among a group of strangers," Ali would later say in a deposition to a human rights organization. For 140 days he had resisted. He feared that if he tried to hold out longer, the tortures would grow so severe that in the end he would confess to even worse things than he was being asked to confess to now. "As a result," he told the human rights group, "I accepted some of their allegations regarding the smuggling of Molotov cocktails into the university dormitories. They then untied me from the bed."

So BEGAN THE SECOND and worst phase of Ali's imprisonment. His captors returned him to Prison 59. In the interrogation room, Ali negotiated the wording of his confession. He'd agreed to deliver it on videotape, provided his interrogators allowed him to incriminate only himself. There was a script from which he could deviate but little. He was to confess that, under orders from the reformists, the student movement was acting illegally and destructively against the regime. He was to portray himself as a naïve, inexperienced dupe who now knew right from wrong and was ready to apologize to the Supreme Leader. Ali and his interrogators drew up a document and submitted it to something identified to Ali as the "experts" committee. The committee marked up the confession and returned it to him with orders to incorporate changes.

The editing process seemed interminable: back and forth, from Ali to his interrogators to the "experts." Then there was the taping. Seven or eight times, by Ali's later recollection, he was forced to rehearse the script, so that he would sound natural when at last he delivered it on camera. After that, they taped him four times. He began to feel as if he really were making a movie. Sometimes there were lines he refused to read, like one that claimed the students sought to overthrow the regime. He was transferred to solitary confinement, or threatened with beatings, until he accepted them. Altogether, the writing, the editing, the rehearsing and taping, took around two months. While the camera rolled, Ali's interrogator stood behind it, out of the frame but directly in Ali's line of sight.

One morning in May 2001, Ali awoke to a flurry of grooming. He was given a shave and a haircut; he was permitted a shower and given a change of clothes. Then came the blindfold and a disorienting drive to a Revolutionary Guard air force base that was a part of the Prison 59 complex. State television was there with a reporter and cameraman. So were Ali's interrogators. He was to be interviewed, they told him, but it was not for public broadcast; they just wanted higher-quality footage than before. For one session an interrogator assumed the interviewer's chair while the camera focused solely on Ali; for the other, the interviewer from the television station asked the questions while the interrogators stood just outside the frame. Ali was to answer according to the script he'd memorized.

The two sessions from that day were spliced into a single interview that was broadcast on national television. Ali sat in an office chair across a glass coffee table from an interviewer. He explained how the student movement had used tactics like civil disobedience in an effort to replace the Islamic Republic with a secular regime. Swallowing uncomfortably, Ali apologized to the Leader, the Iranian people, and above all to the Islamic Republic's war martyrs and their families. He wore a gray plaid shirt and charcoal slacks. He was clean-shaven but for a dour-looking mustache, and his shoulders sloped. He sat next to a plastic plant and a television set in a featureless, beige room. From time to time, the camera caught Ali's eyes. Their expression was unfathomable.

Ali Afshari had been obliterated. He did not know himself. The person who uttered fluent falsehoods on national television was a malicious imposter. Years later he would read the accounts of Auschwitz survivors and learn that in the Nazi camps, people who were forced to act against their beliefs died earlier. They described feelings Ali had felt. He'd betrayed everyone; he'd evacuated his own character. Alone in his cell, he pounded his head into walls, hoping to die. He had no appetite. The impulse to kill himself was almost mad; it was frantic, devoid of any plan. Up on the ceiling were some exposed electrical wires. He grasped and strained and obsessively plotted, but he could not reach them. Then he had an idea.

He would let his interrogators torture him to death. They had every means to end his misery. Sure, it would be better to go by his own hand, but he was never going to reach those wires. All he had to do was to recant his confession and resist. His captors would take care of the rest. By doing so, they would also expose their own brutality.

Ali wrote to the judge in his case explaining that his confession was obtained under duress, the interview staged, and the statement dictated by his interrogators. The judiciary pressed him not to recant, but now Ali stuck by his story. Soon enough, he was back in the interrogation room. His father, in Qazvin, was summoned to court, allegedly over a satirical cartoon published in the magazine he ran. What Ali was about to endure, one captor told him, would make him forget all the other tortures. This did not impress Ali as it might have once. His cell was next to an airport runway, where the din of planes taking off kept him awake night and day. But something curious had happened to Ali Afshari.

To begin with, he was starving. He was served the same prison food, but now he ate voraciously. He saw the same interrogators and lived in the same isolation—he would spend the next six months in solitary confinement—but from the abyss of self-negation he had emerged beyond torture's reach. He'd given up on life, and so his torturers no longer had anything to hold over him. True resistance looked like this. He did not confess and he did not die. Instead he recovered himself. And he felt sublimely powerful. He understood that his torturers were not omnipotent— that it was up to him to submit or to refuse. After six months they gave up trying to get anything from him. The beatings stopped. He had seen power siphon from his own spirit into the system that imprisoned him, and he saw himself siphon it back.

When Ali Afshari was released from prison in December of 2001, he gave a press conference explaining that his May confession had been false and obtained under duress. He wanted the world to know what happened inside Iran's prisons. He apologized again to the Iranian people, this time for having broken. He still had a sentence to serve, so he returned to Evin two months later and served two years in a general ward. This was nothing like what he'd already endured. He could study and play volleyball. He had visits from his parents. He wrote articles and letters that were smuggled back to campus.

Ali came out again in 2003. Daftar Tahkim had not forgotten him. The students all but drafted him, as a graduate student now, back to the organization's central board. He'd come a great distance from the young man who'd organized field trips and advocated leniency for boys in short sleeves. He'd gone far beyond Khatami as well. He argued that Iran needed a new constitution. Nothing would come of elections. Iran should hold a referendum on the form its government should take. Where Ali Afshari went, so did the formerly reformist, now liberal wing of Daftar Tahkim.

But Ali did not stay to fight for the referendum. In 2005 the court handed him a six-year prison sentence on one of his still-open cases. If he served it, he would emerge at age thirty-eight, having given the Iranian penal system almost a quarter of his life. Getting to Dubai was easy, and from there to Dublin was not so hard. He wound up living in exile in Reston, Virginia, still a graduate student, now in systems engineering at George Washington University. If the Islamic Republic was made for anyone, it was made for Ali Afshari. But there was no place there for him.

TEN

MASTER PLANS

THE WORLD'S FIRST INDOOR SHOPPING MALL—the sort anchored by two department stores with a soaring atrium in between, lit from skylights, traversed by escalators, graced by indoor gardens and dozens or hundreds of shops—opened its doors in Edina, Minnesota, in 1956. The mall was called Southdale. It was an architectural innovation and a marvel in its day. Unlike the strip malls that had begun to line America's suburban highways, the mall turned blank and windowless exterior walls onto a vast moat of parked cars. All of its vitality faced inward, in what its groundbreaking architect, Victor Gruen, imagined as a vibrant, interior downtown for communities that otherwise threatened to shoot apart into centrifugal space.

Gruen, a Viennese Jew, arrived on American shores after the Anschluss. From the ruin of exile, in the city of New York, Gruen built a legendary career as a retail architect. It was a crass and lowly field at the time. Gruen changed it forever. He believed that the design of stores—their façades, their window displays, even the immediate environment outside them—could compel shoppers or repel them, and that the key to retail success lay in generating an atmosphere that seduced customers and even distracted them, at first, from the business of consumption. This would become known as the Gruen effect. Its unlikely author was a socialist who hated cars, strip malls, and suburbs with a passion equaled only by his contribution to their advance across the American landscape.

Gruen was a peculiar, yet strangely apt, urban planner for the sprawling, car-bound city of Tehran. More peculiar still was the effect his work would have on the fortunes of the men who made Iranian politics—particularly those who erected an edifice they called reform astride his urban reverie. For the reformists would make city politics the theater for their deepest and most ambitious plans. Like Gruen before them, they would come to learn that half the power in plans lay in their subversion.

Gruen first imagined shopping malls as an antidote to the evils of American ribbon development. They would furnish town centers to the bedroom communities that ringed American cities; around Southdale, Gruen planned for Edina to put up apartment houses, a hospital, a park, a lake, highways, schools. The shopping center itself would draw suburbanites into contact with one another as in a European town square. They would do their retail business, then sit over coffee in the atrium garden, making conversation with neighbors as they paused to admire the giant giraffe sculptures.

None of that ever happened. Instead, land values skyrocketed and speculators moved in, lining the pockets of the retail giants that had been Gruen's clients. The shopping mall, isolated behind its parking lots, anchored nothing so much as it contributed to unplanned and unchecked "scatteration," as Gruen and the social critic Jane Jacobs called it in their contentious exchange at the time.

Frank Lloyd Wright foresaw much when he traveled to Southdale upon its opening, hoping to understand what the fuss was about. Of the mall's celebrated atrium, Wright said, "Who wants to sit in that desolate looking spot? You've got a garden court that has all the evils of the village street and none of its charm."

Yet the shopping mall was a runaway commercial success. Gruen's design became so commonplace that no one would think to associate it with any architect at all. Gruen, ambivalent but unrepentant, moved on.

By the end of the 1950s he had turned from designing stores to redesigning entire cities. At the behest of the president of the Texas Electric Company, Gruen reimagined Fort Worth, Texas, as a city of pedestrian malls and sidewalk cafés, where cars entered by a belt road only to be fed off into parking garages, and pedestrians traversed an untrafficked town by electric trams. Even Jane Jacobs thought the plan was a marvel. But it ran aground in the Texas state legislature, which worried that its execution would infringe on private property and make way for "graft and corruption."

By the mid-1960s, Gruen had indelibly marked the American landscape, from Fresno, California, to Rochester, New York; but he hated the American built environment so intensely that he returned to his native Vienna, whose cohesion he found threatened by a nearby shopping mall. Around that time, he heard from Shah Mohammad Reza Pahlavi.

The Iranian monarch offered Gruen everything Texas Electric could not: bottomless funds, unlimited authority, and a world capital that was a vast canvas, with a rapidly growing population and little history of urban planning. Gruen partnered with a highborn Iranian master architect, Abdolaziz Farmanfarmaian, to draw up the first Comprehensive Plan for Tehran.

As Gruen's biographer would later write, "The world of postwar America [Gruen] so lamented was, in part, his own creation. He better than anyone should have realized that the choices between planned development and unplanned sprawl were never so simple." Unintended consequences were the story of Gruen's career. That was true in America, and never truer than in Iran, where Gruen's Comprehensive Plan for Tehran would determine everything, precisely by determining nothing.

TEHRAN BEGAN ITS LIFE as a suburb to the north of the ancient city of Rey, and it would come of age as the sum of its suburbs well after Gruen and the shah were gone. But these were not suburbs in the First World sense. They were spontaneous communities that had arisen out of necessity and seismic social change, and they posed a nearly insoluble puzzle to both the monarchy and the revolutionary regime that followed it.

Bound by the Alborz Mountains to the north and the Kavir Desert to the south, Tehran sloped sharply, its northern boundary more than six hundred meters higher than its southeastern one. The unevenness of the land inscribed itself on the city's soul. The northern heights had clean water, sweeping views, and breathable air. The southern flatland had industrial plants and shantytowns, toxic smog and an occluded view of the northern slopes that looked down upon it. The landscape was also a source of drama and beauty. Within the city limits were winding creeks and villages that climbed hills. The understated grace of Tehran's low, symmetrical architecture set off the spectacular verticality of the Alborz. Valiasr, as the city's majestic central artery would be called after the revolution, was the longest thoroughfare in the Middle East, lined end to end with some sixty thousand towering sycamore trees.

Since the demolition of the city walls in the 1930s, Tehran's population had grown first, at mid-century, through planned middle-class neighborhoods in the city's east, and then—as the Pahlavis' modernization policies sent landless rural Iranians flocking to the capital—through illegal settlements in the city's south. Between 1905 and 1979, Tehran's population grew from 160,000 to 5 million. (It would top 12 million in 2004.) Many of the new migrants crowded with their extended families into small apartments in the city's slums, where open sewer ducts bisected muddy alleys and whole households occupied single rooms. Others erected makeshift dwellings on the city's outskirts. There were shantytowns built of mud brick and even tin cans. At the time of the revolution, fully 35 percent of Tehran's population lived in slums or shanties. The squatter communities were not, technically, part of Tehran, and so they did not qualify for city services, like sewers and garbage collection, which the city claimed it could in any case ill afford; but the need was vast, and to fulfill it would become a matter of humanity, public health, and social peace.

Gruen and Farmanfarmaian imagined Tehran as a giant flower stretched on an east-west axis along the Alborz foothills. Like a rose, the city would comprise circles within circles. Ten subcities would each have a center, around which there would be ten towns; the towns would each have centers, around which would bloom four communities; each community would have a center, from which blossomed five neighborhoods. Green valleys would cut across the map, highways and public transport routes sluicing through the valleys. For all its grace and greenery, the plan reproduced the city's north-south divide in explicit terms: the north was designed for higher-income residences and lower density, the south, for lower incomes and higher density as well as for industry.

Density—the number of people presumed to inhabit the city's square acreage—was destiny for Tehran. Gruen and Farmanfarmaian assumed that overall it would remain very low. They envisioned a sprawling, low-rise city like Los Angeles, one that would extend across relatively unspoiled space, preserving traditional Iranian courtyard dwellings, with ample room for parks and gardens. Gruen and Farmanfarmaian set city boundaries that could be extended every five years in predetermined increments until they reached the edge of a twenty-five-year expansion area. The city was obliged to provide services, such as water, garbage collection, and electricity, only to the area within its boundaries.

The Comprehensive Plan for Tehran was approved in 1968. According to one architectural historian, "There are few examples of a megacity being tamed by a single idealistic planning vision like Tehran; and there are few American cities where the planning ideas being developed in the universities and offices were carried out to such an extent as in Tehran." But big swaths of the city lay outside the city, beyond the scope of its services or the grace of its Comprehensive Plan.

Around the same time that Gruen's plan was adopted, a new municipal law allowed the monarchy to respond to the proliferation of squatter settlements with a brutal and unpopular campaign of demolition. From 1974 until the eve of the revolution, the imperial regime razed squatter communities at will, often arriving with paramilitary soldiers and bulldozers in the dead of night. When it was too late—in September of 1978, just five months before Khomeini's flight home from France—the monarchy shifted course, enlarging the city limits beyond the Gruen plan's stated boundary for that year and promising to provide the squatters in the enlarged area with piped water and electric power. Then the shah was gone.

The Comprehensive Plan for Tehran, with all its insufficiencies and its received elitism, was but one piece of imperial baggage the Islamic Republic inherited. Everything about its provenance sat ill with the new regime. Its authors were not even Tehran natives. But it was the only plan the city had. Like a Roman garrison town overwritten by medieval chaos or a colonial outpost overtaken by the megacity, writes the Dutch architectural historian Wouter Vanstiphout, Tehran's story became the story of its master plan's subversion. But in Paris and Jakarta, Vanstiphout writes, "centuries went by and generations followed each other before the original source code of the city was forgotten and all traces seemed to have disappeared beneath the new layers of the urban palimpsest. . . . In Tehran, however, this process happened in the space of ten to fifteen years, and the forgetting of the source code was an ideological decision."

TEHRAN AND OTHER BIG IRANIAN CITIES had been the seats of the monarchy's power, showcases for its cosmopolitan pretensions and its dubious modernism. The Islamic Republic made an about-face, deliberately shunning the cities, particularly Tehran, and anchoring its identity and its nationalism to the Iranian countryside. The Tehran subway system, the construction of which had begun under the Pahlavis, lost its funding. City planning was a thing of the past. Resources were scarce, especially when oil prices plummeted in the mid-1980s, and what the Iranian state had, it channeled into making staggering improvements to village life, extending the benefits of modernization to the country's long-marginalized rural population.

The Islamic Republic brought electricity, clean water, modern appliances, and an impressive network of medical clinics, complete with family planning, to the villages. Under the shah, rural women bore an average of eight children each; under the Islamic Republic, only two. Rural women stayed in school twice as long under the Islamic Republic as they did under the monarchy. The Rafsanjani administration would extend a network of new universities into the hinterland. By 2015 rural and urban Iranians would reach a rough parity in education and standard of living. These would rank among the signature achievements of the Islamic regime.

And yet, for all its emphasis on rural culture, the Islamic Republic governed a more urban country than the shah had ruled. Between 1976 and 1986, Iran's urban population grew by 72 percent. By 1983, more Iranians lived in cities than in the country. And the new migrants needed decent places to live, with basic urban amenities. "Neither east nor west!" ran one anti-imperialist revolutionary slogan. In 1985, squatters lined a highway outside Tehran, mockingly chanting, "Neither east nor west, neither water nor electricity!"

Outside Tehran, the migrant settlements quietly expanded. Squatters were not just building shanties now. They were building towns. To the west of Tehran, along the road to the neighboring city of Karaj, these towns quadrupled in population over a span of ten years. With the revolutionary regime preoccupied by domestic upheaval and a foreign war, the squatters created facts on the ground. They diverted electricity and water from the city mains, effectively stealing city services when they weren't supplied. The land they seized was public land; the dwellings they built were private ones.

The Islamic Republic responded much the way the shah had done: with demolition, particularly starting in 1984. But it was a war of attrition. By 1989 the regime changed tack, working to integrate the new settlements so that it could control them, collecting payment for city services and even rent for the land. The Islamic Republic extended Tehran's boundaries all the way to Victor Gruen's final twenty-five-year expansion line, about a decade early. Then the regime infiltrated or replaced neighborhood associations in the new settlements with associations controlled by the clergy.

Neglect had not starved Tehran of residents or centrality. On the contrary, throughout the 1980s, Tehran was swelling, unchecked and unplanned, a convection of density and sprawl. Tehran choked on its own pollution, gridlocked traffic isolated its neighborhoods from one another, and green space all but vanished. Forced Islamization had produced an angry and alienated middle class that sat cheek by jowl with the politically empowered but economically deprived. The streets were impassable, the atmosphere grim, the air filthy. Nothing worked. And the city was nearly bankrupt. Iranian property taxes were traditionally very low, and with oil revenues down, the municipality had few resource streams to tap. The scale of Tehran's need—for fresh planning as well as public transportation and basic services—dwarfed its budget. In 1987 and 1988 the Islamic Republic commissioned a study on the feasibility of relocating the nation's capital someplace more manageable. But economists concluded that it would make no difference. Even if the government left, the city would continue to suffocate. That was when President Rafsanjani decided to appoint a new mayor.

GHOLAMHOSSEIN KARBASCHI called for flowers. For Tehran had not only a budget shortfall: it had a beauty shortfall. Flowers would not house the homeless or purify the air, but they would remind Tehranis of what their city could be. In the spring of 1990, shortly after assuming office, Karbaschi asked Tehranis to put flowerpots at their doorsteps, at home and at work. Outside homes and shops, offices and hotels, the city's residents obliged the new mayor with displays of color and greenery. This would be the least of all the things Karbaschi did—the least permanent, the least controversial, the least expensive. But it was symbolic.

Before Karbaschi, hardly anyone inside or outside Tehran knew or cared who the city's mayor was. Thirty-five, slender, and square-jawed, with wire-rimmed glasses and a penetrating gaze, Karbaschi was to transform the Iranian capital so profoundly, for better or worse, that even his critics would call him the Iranian Robert Moses. He was a celebrity, with public fans and detractors. People instantly knew him on the street. Part cleric and part technocrat—the son of an ayatollah from Qom, he'd cut his seminary studies short to become governor of Isfahan in 1984—he was a manager, a businessman, and a powerful politician who attended presidential cabinet meetings.

The new mayor had a mission that his predecessors had not shouldered. A 1988 law required Iranian cities to become financially self-supporting. In a country with only minimal taxation, this law meant that the cities had either to make a new compact with their residents by raising taxes or to find something valuable they could sell.

If Karbaschi had raised property taxes in Tehran, he might have supplied the city with a stable economic foundation for the foreseeable future. He would also have taken a bold step toward democratizing Iran. To raise taxes, Karbaschi would have needed to negotiate with the public, to explain his plans, garner support, and be accountable to taxpayers for how that money was spent. These were steps the central government had never taken. Iran was a classic rentier state (the term was coined by an Iranian scholar in 1970): oil provided the central government with a stream of revenue that did not depend on the productivity or cooperation of its citizenry. Karbaschi did not alter this arrangement. Instead, he replicated it. Tehran might not have had its own oil supply, but Karbaschi saw that it had a more ingenious resource at hand: density.

The Gruen plan was a dead letter. It imagined an impossible city by the lights of the early 1990s, with buildings no more than two stories high. But precisely for this reason the plan, which was still on the books, was a treasure chest.

Karbaschi sold developers the right to exceed, sometimes by as much as 400 percent, the density limits set by the Gruen plan and revised slightly upward since. The municipality—the very authority charged with enforcing the Comprehensive Plan—raised its revenue by selling the right to violate that plan. When a firm presented Karbaschi with a new comprehensive plan for the city, he rejected it. He was better off keeping the old plan, which no one expected him to enforce, and exempting developers from it for a fee.

Karbaschi started with the city's north. New high-rises transformed Tehran's skyline without regard for earthquake safety codes—Tehran sits astride major fault lines—or neighborhood cohesion. Modern, featureless, built, like everything in Tehran, of pale brown concrete or pale brown brick, they crowded into narrow alleyways and jostled one another loomingly close, creating dense, narrow warrens of steel-framed towers, each built on its developer's volition, without regulation or plan, without open vistas or relief. At times the municipality even partnered with private developers and profited from the sale of luxury apartments in these new buildings. The construction sector boomed, becoming a major employer and economic engine for the city. And real estate speculation followed. The city faced a housing crisis—hundreds of thousands of families still needed adequate shelter—and yet, as many as 10 percent of Tehran's housing units stood vacant, priced out of the market, built and purchased only for resale.

These were bonanza years for people who already owned their homes and could sell the vertical space above their dwellings. But for renters, life only grew more difficult. Speculation tripled housing costs, including rents, even while the average apartment size declined by half. Working people struggled to afford life in the capital. Many fled for the unregulated developments that fringed the city's outer boundaries. Inside Tehran, there weren't enough parking spaces, sewer lines, or garbage trucks. People complained. But in just two years Karbaschi quintupled the city's budget. Altogether, from 1990 to 1998, he raised $6 billion, three quarters of it from the sale of density. What he did with that money again made Tehran a showcase for the country.

Karbaschi invested in parks, freeways, billboards, malls, cultural centers, forest plantations, sports centers, and a glossy four-color newspaper. The pale brown city burst into color. Karbaschi created six hundred new parks, three times the number there had been before; he turned thirteen thousand vacant lots into recreation areas; and he removed the fences from around the parks that already existed. Karbaschi's parks had benches and playgrounds, basins and fountains, kiosks and food stalls, and they accommodated everyone from old men playing backgammon to teenagers surreptitiously exchanging love notes.

Karbaschi did not redress the city's polarities—on the contrary, he was often accused of privileging the north with more green space and luxury development—but he linked the city's north and south with fast-moving

freeways and renewed progress on its metro system. The neighborhood of
Naziabad, in the slum-ridden south of Tehran, housed the city's slaughter-
house. The area around it, fetid with animal parts, had long been a petri
dish for urban blight, including crime and prostitution. Karbaschi closed
the abattoir and turned its grounds into a magnificent cultural center, with
theaters, cafés, galleries, classrooms, a library, gymnasia, an ice-skating rink,
and a swimming pool set around grassy lawns. The Bahman Cultural Center became a destination, not only for South Tehrani youth, but for North
Tehrani elites, who flocked there for film screenings and weekly concerts.

More even than the highways that physically united the city's hemi-
spheres, the migration of concert- and filmgoers across neighborhoods
once stigmatized as impassable suggested that Tehran could yet be a single
city. The Bahman Cultural Center was just the first of 138 such centers the
municipality founded under Karbaschi. Some hard-liners disapproved of
the Tehran mayor's incursion into the country's cultural life. Ayatollah
Khamenei warned Karbaschi against the erosion of Tehran's "Islamic identity." But the city's cultural centers and parks also relieved pressures that
were building on the Islamic Republic. For, by accident or design, the revolutionary regime had cultivated a garden it was ill-equipped to tend: young
people, educated women, and new members of the middle class all challenged the Islamic Republic that had nurtured their growth. Karbaschi had
found ways to embrace these demographics, even to harness their
vital energy to the city he ran.

After Karbaschi, Iran's urban life would never be the same. Iranians
who left their country at the time of the revolution would pepper the world
literary market with memoirs of life in a Tehran that no longer existed—
one where alleys of low-rise dwellings were like shared compounds, with
neighbors entwined in one another's daily lives and rooftops where families slept on summer nights. The growing sea of poverty to the city's south
also had its place in that exile literature—an ill omen of social unrest, the
tale of revolution foretold. By the end of the Karbaschi era, Tehran had
become something at once more familiar outside and less familiar within,
a megacity with teetering high-rises helter-skelter and pollution to rival

Jakarta's and Beijing's. The new circumstances called not only for a new literature but for a new approach to the very structures of city governance.

Everything had its price. At the bottom of Karbaschi's achievement was the Comprehensive Plan he had reviled. Tehran's economy was built on a commodity that was all but imaginary: the density Gruen had not foreseen, delivered with deliberate opacity into unaccountable hands. The city appeared to be working—better, perhaps, than it ever had. But to keep working, it had to keep on climbing into vertical space, haphazard and unregulated, in partnership with speculators and in excess of its plans.

THE REFORMISTS WHO ACCOMPANIED Mohammad Khatami to power set their sights on city government. Here was an open field, they surmised, where they could seed new democratic institutions—flowers within flowers, crosscut by the green valleys of federal government.

Among President Mohammad Khatami's advisers, Saeed Hajjarian carried special weight. A touch of humor in his eyes set off the stern gravity of his jowls. His large gold-rimmed glasses rested on gray-stubbled cheeks even back when his mustache and closely cropped hair were still black. He was an intellectual who spoke of political theory like a science that could be applied—as though democratic reform were a series of chemical reactions Iran could fastidiously produce.

The term of art that he and his fellow reformists used was "political development." Iran had experienced only authoritarian government. It needed accountable political institutions, but it also needed constructively engaged citizens. "Political development" referred to the cultivation of both. And so Hajjarian's reform was not a matter merely of replacing authoritarian personalities with democratic ones. He envisioned building a vast political infrastructure that would begin with something Iran had never had: local politics.

Hajjarian pointed to a provision in Iran's constitution that allowed for directly elected, autonomous city councils. Since the revolution, this provision had sat on the books much as the Gruen plan had, unrealized and unenforced. Now Hajjarian insisted that holding city council elections would push the entire country down the path of political development. The campaigns would furnish a training ground for more than a hundred thousand new politicians who would otherwise never find their way onto the scene. They would also give Iranians a taste of competitive democracy and self-government.

Karbaschi had been a technocrat bent on getting his city working again, even if his policies were implemented through opaque and authoritarian channels. Khatami and his allies were cut from a decidedly different cloth. They sought to transform less the physical space around them than the very institutions of power. When Hajjarian looked upon the teeming, vibrant capital city, his eye fell not on the mechanics of running or planning a city of Tehran's size but on the inadequate and antiquated structure of its government. Accountability and transparency were afterthoughts to Karbaschi; for Hajjarian, they were the whole game.

Iranian society, Hajjarian observed, crackled with activity, energy, and amorphous discontent. Elected council members could absorb some of that energy and channel it into a constructive relationship with the state. The Iranian public would begin to organize into interest groups, civic organizations, and eventually political parties. To start with, Hajjarian theorized, you really needed only two. People would decide which party came closer to representing them, and then press and shape it to their needs. More parties would follow.

None of this had much to do with the way Iranian cities had ever been run. But Hajjarian was nothing if not visionary. Karbaschi, he told an interviewer, had managed Tehran in a corporate fashion that favored elites and viewed the citizenry "primarily as sources of revenue." Hajjarian envisioned a city that taxed its residents instead and, in return, included them in its governance.

Thanks to Hajjarian, Khatami made holding city council elections a campaign promise, and he began to prepare the ground for them when he took office in 1997. The reformists set up a party, called Mosharekat-e Iran-e Islami, or the Islamic Iran Participation Front, to field candidates.

Mosharekat would become Iran's national party of reform. But it began as a local initiative with a strikingly vague identity. Mosharekat's members did not take a united position on the matter of selling density or articulate a better solution to city financing; it did not have a program for earthquake-proofing the precarious, overpopulated capital or for better regulating the construction that had become the city's economic engine. These and other issues would come to divide and embitter the reformists in local government, leading to embarrassment and failure. For when they came to the Tehran City Council, having staked so many of their political hopes upon it, they seemed for all the world like a philosophy department that had been placed in charge of a foundry.

BEFORE THE ELECTION WAS EVEN HELD, in April 1998, Mayor Karbaschi was arrested on charges of embezzlement, misconduct, and mismanagement. His real crime, many reformists speculated, was supporting Khatami's presidential campaign, in which Karbaschi's final push had made all the difference. For a few days the mayor conducted the city's official business from behind bars. Demonstrations erupted on his behalf. The charges were byzantine and hardly incredible, but Karbaschi was wildly popular, and his arrest smacked of politics.

Karbaschi's trial opened in June. The judge was also the prosecutor. The entire proceeding was televised. "The Karbaschi Show," as it became known, was one of the most popular television programs in Iranian history. For the sake of viewers at home, the mayor requested that the trial be aired at times when it wouldn't conflict with morning prayers or World Cup soccer matches. When a trial date conflicted with Iran's match with the United States, the court agreed to reschedule it.

At the Imam Khomeini Judicial Complex, in a brown-paneled room with auditorium-style seats, the judge sat onstage, at a grand desk, while Karbaschi and his lawyers squeezed into wooden chairs below the proscenium. Karbaschi, gaunt and angry with a lock of lank hair falling over his forehead, was not easily cowed. He sparred directly with the judge, his characteristic expression dour and intense, chin lowered, head tilted, a hard, skeptical gaze directed upward and sidelong at his interlocutor. "I don't accept any of the charges," he said on the trial's opening day. "They are all lies." The courtroom was packed, with several hundred more onlookers watching the trial on screens outside.

Karbaschi's unregulated dealings in the shadow economy of speculative development gave him little cover from the charges he faced. Accused of embezzling millions of dollars, receiving bribes, mishandling public property, illegally possessing public property, illegally conducting government transactions, and engaging in "despotic and dictatorial behavior," Karbaschi maintained that not one rial of city money had gone into his pocket. "All that I have done is turn a stagnant city into one that is modern and livable with hundreds of kilometers of highways, green spaces and cultural centers," he told the judge.

On the merits, Karbaschi's defense at times seemed weak and disorganized, not least because many of the charges took the mayor and his legal team by surprise. But Karbaschi had a larger strategy. With the whole country watching, the mayor brought the discussion back, again and again, to the judiciary's strong-arm tactics and the question of procedural legitimacy. Karbaschi reminded viewers that he was learning of many charges against him only in court, and that police had stormed his office and confiscated his confidential documents. When the judge presented confessions from city officials who had been interrogated in prison, Karbaschi retorted, "You've set up a group of 70 men, most of whom have little more than a high school education, and put them in charge of this investigation. They take each person into a basement and emerge with a confession. What is the meaning of this?"

On July 11, at the court's seventh and final session, Karbaschi presented his concluding arguments. He spoke for four hours. He wept. He spoke of his revolutionary past. He noted ruefully that this investigation had cost the municipality time, money, and jobs. After eight and a half years of fifteen-hour workdays, the mayor lamented, here he stood. The judge sentenced Karbaschi to five years in prison (reduced to two on appeal), sixty lashes, $530,000 in fines, and a twenty-year ban on political activity.

．　．　．

WITH THE MAYOR OF TEHRAN just a few months from the start of his prison sentence, Iran held its first municipal elections in February 1999. It was the most open political field the Islamic Republic had ever known, with some 330,000 candidates competing. And the reformists swept it. They dominated the councils nationwide, but nowhere was their showing more definitive than in Tehran, where they took fourteen of fifteen seats.

They spanned the gamut of their faction's views and pedigrees. Some were technocrats close to Karbaschi and the old city management. Others, like Ebrahim Asgharzadeh, the organizer of the U.S. embassy takeover in 1979, were more radical populists. Still others, like Saeed Hajjarian, came from Khatami's forward-thinking brain trust. As mayor, the Tehran City Council appointed a centrist technocrat.

Once in power, the reformists faced the same options Karbaschi had. To raise taxes, the municipality would have to build trust with the citizenry—something the central government, with its oil rents and authoritarian history, had never done. And it would mean reconfiguring the finances and political arrangements of a city that appeared to be working—even to be a symbol of recent managerial success.

And so Tehran continued along the path Karbaschi had blazed. The municipality commissioned a new Comprehensive Plan for Tehran in 2000. But it would not be approved, let alone implemented, for another six years. Tehran's urban planners came to suspect that the reformist city council was stalling just as Karbaschi had. To adopt a city plan meant regulating density—and looking for a new way to raise money.

Moreover, Tehran's city council members were distracted. Quite a few of them were determined to keep one foot on the national playing field. One city councilman ran for president; others ran for the parliament in a campaign for which Saeed Hajjarian was the chief reformist strategist and adviser.

Hajjarian had no more ambitious vision than the one that launched the city councils in the first place. But with the city of Tehran standing by, the parliamentary campaign he spearheaded (he told reporters that he'd learned how to put together coalitions and campaign strategies from reading American political journals) won by a landslide, with the reformists carrying close to 77 percent of the legislative body's 290 seats. The moment was an exhilarating one for a movement on the ascent—enough so, perhaps, to offset the frustrations of urban management.

SAEED HAJJARIAN BEGAN FIELDING death threats in the spring of 2000. An anonymous cassette tape informed him of his impending execution. He was a particular bête noir to the hard-liners, who not only presumed him to be the reformists' mastermind but also suspected him of being the Deep Throat behind Akbar Ganji's reporting on the chain murders. Hajjarian had once worked for the intelligence ministry, after all, and he held the license for the newspaper in which Ganji published.

At 8:35 one Sunday morning, Hajjarian parked his car near the white stone-and-glass tower that housed Tehran's city hall. He strode toward the building with a colleague, and as he mounted the few shallow steps at the building's entry, a group of men approached him. One handed Hajjarian a letter while others detained him to ask questions. A high-powered red motorcycle, of a sort reserved for use by the Revolutionary Guard and Basij, pulled up curbside. A young man leapt off the back of it.

His name was Saeed Asgar, and what he did next he would later say he was told to do by associates from his mosque—a circle around an extremist cleric in Shahr-e Rey. He claimed he had nothing against Saeed Hajjarian. He had read some of his articles and even voted for him for city council. But he'd been told it was his "religious duty" to assassinate the man known as the brain of the reform movement.

Because he did not know what Hajjarian looked like, Asgar hesitated, awaiting a signal from an accomplice to tell him which man was his target. Then he approached Hajjarian and shot him point-blank. He aimed for the city councilman's temple, but because his hand shook, he shot Hajjarian in the face.

Asgar leapt back on the motorcycle and, together with an accomplice, sped away. He shed an extra pair of pants he'd worn so witnesses wouldn't recognize him, went to the movies, paid his water bill at the bank, and then headed home, weaving through the capital's gridlocked streets.

WHEN SAEED HAJJARIAN AWOKE from his coma, a bullet was still lodged at the base of his neck. His legs were paralyzed and his speech was painstaking. He had survived his assassination, but he would never be the same. Nor would the reform movement. Nor would City Hall.

Reformists decried the attempt on Hajjarian's life as a political act ordered by hard-liners. President Khatami declared, "The enemies of freedom wrongly believe that they can attain their goals by assassinating a pious intellectual who was serving the nation." Supreme Leader Khamenei called for calm and restraint. Nothing was known about the assassins, he told the public, and to leap to political conclusions was inflammatory and unhelpful. True, the assassins used a type of motorcycle issued only to the state-run militias. But conservative spokesmen argued that this indicated only that one of the conspirators was a guardsman, not that the plot originated from any authority within the system.

Eight men were arraigned and tried. Five were convicted, their sentences ranging from three to fifteen years. Even the judge seemed perplexed by the accused men's casual demeanor, their lack of malice toward their target. He ordered psychiatric evaluations, which found the conspirators mentally competent. But at the trial the men were not linked to any chain of command.

Perhaps it had all along been Hajjarian, with his long view of politics, his visionary patience, his refusal to relinquish the historic opportunity he'd felt within his grasp, who had kept the Tehran City Council from descending into the mire of personal rivalry and political intrigue. Or perhaps that future was already inscribed—in the conundrum of political development, which called for starting somewhere but seemed always to require one or another condition not yet met; in the history and mechanics of running the city of Tehran, which yielded only unpopular choices, and whose managers had never before had to answer to its citizens, let alone promised to make their city the springboard for democratic reform.

In November 2000, eight months after he was shot, Hajjarian returned to work. Damage to the base of his brain left him able to stand only momentarily but not to sustain his balance; when he tried to walk, he felt as though he were moving through a swimming pool. The very air opposed him. His left hand was paralyzed and his right hand shook, so that he could not write. His speech was halting, his face slack, although his mind remained alight.

The Tehran City Council had disintegrated into rancorous factions. Its members battled one another, the mayor, and the interior ministry over who held sway over what domain and who would decide how the city would finance itself. Disputes between one councilman and the mayor went to arbitration. Another councilman was briefly charged with complicity in the plot to kill Hajjarian (he was acquitted); another was jailed on charges of defaming a police official involved in the Karbaschi trial; two councilmen resigned, allegedly because of "certain internal organizational problems." Hajjarian tried to resign in order to seek medical care abroad, but the council did not accept. Bowing to pressure, the mayor eventually stepped down, to be replaced by a new one who almost immediately fell out with the same councilman as his predecessor.

The fundamental urban issues remained. Tehran was still overbuilt and polluted, and density sales were still underwriting its economy while undermining its stability. Seismologists were still issuing dire warnings about the likelihood of urban collapse. Rumors abounded that some city council members were profiting from the sale of vertical space to developers.

What had begun as a promising experiment in local governance had devolved into a circus. In January a national arbitration board dissolved the Tehran City Council, on the grounds that it failed to meet regularly or to make decisions regarding the budget. The mayor was fired and sentenced to five months in prison for corruption and abuse of his position. Less than three months before the country's second provincial elections, Tehran's entire management had apparently collapsed.

. . .

THE CITY OF TEHRAN, and the reformists themselves, had done the hard-liners' work for them, showcasing the reform movement's every failing—its vanities and petty rivalries, its managerial inexperience, its predilection toward abstraction.

The hardline press lost no time in writing this failure as large as possible. *Kayhan*'s managing editor wrote of the Tehran City Council: "During the past four years the only thing that did not concern the council or take up too much of its attention was the city's problems and the execution of its legal duties." Another commentator in *Kayhan* crowed that this vaunted civic institution had been "stillborn." A group of "inexperienced politicians" who saw the elections merely as "launching pads" for their national political careers threw the people's trust to the wind. The councilmen "bashed each other on the head every day and threw Tehran's situation into further chaos."

These editorials must have stung the reformists to the quick, in large part because they were true. But the hard-liners' indictments did not mention the arrest and trial of the outgoing mayor, or the attempt on Hajjarian's life—two episodes that served not only to demoralize the reformist politicians but to deprive them of significant sources of advice, support, and expertise. Nor did they account for the reformist vision's daring. When Hajjarian imagined the role city councils could play in the political development of the country, he did not factor in the foibles that plague municipal politics the world over: personal rivalries and power plays, human weakness, systemic corruption, problems that required revenue to fix, revenue streams that created more problems to solve.

The *Kayhan* editorialists did note that, unlike the councils managing Iran's swelling modern cities, the councils in rural areas had been a success. The conservative pundits attributed this to the cohesion of rural communities, which had elected local leaders they had reason to know and trust. They might also have noted that the provincial councils handled issues whose scale and nature were manageable and familiar. Half a century earlier, Iran had only one city with a population over a million; now it had at least six, and about seventy with between one hundred thousand and a million residents. The reformists may have imagined that, by opening direct democracy at the local level, they were starting small. But actually they were beginning with some of the least familiar and least tractable of the country's managerial puzzles.

ALTHOUGH THE REFORMISTS did not succeed in entrenching themselves or their ideas in urban governance, they did create the conditions for others to do exactly that. Not one but two major national political figures would rise to prominence thanks to the urban machinery the reformists set into place. The Tehran City Council would, in the end, incubate powerful new forces in national politics—just not reformist ones.

The 2003 election for city councils carried such a low profile that it practically slunk onto the national stage. Conservatives were well positioned to win, so long as they made little noise. Low voter turnout would work in their favor, as hard-liners were stalwart voters. More liberal-minded Iranians had to be persuaded that elections were worth their while, something the performance of the outgoing city council had done little to suggest. Sure enough, in the provinces, where the local councils had enjoyed a quietly successful four years, some 95 percent of voters turned out. In the cities overall, the turnout was closer to 65 percent. And in Tehran it was a stunningly low 10 percent.

Conservatives took fourteen of Tehran's fifteen seats. They did it by carrying between 85,000 and 190,000 votes in a city with four million eligible voters. The winners were not conservatives of particular national renown. Rather, they came from a previously unknown group that called itself Etelaf-e Abadgaran-e Iran-e Eslami, or the Alliance of Builders of Islamic Iran, and which announced itself dedicated to "safeguarding the achievements of the Islamic Revolution" and preventing "materialistic people" from influencing decisions. Abadgaran claimed to belong to no faction and to disdain partisanship altogether. President Khatami welcomed that stance, urging the new Tehran City Council to steer clear of national politics and to remember that low voter turnout limited its mandate.

While the reformists held meetings and round tables to determine what had gone wrong, the new Tehran City Council set about consolidating conservative control of the capital city. Within a month, it had appointed Tehran's new mayor. He was a former governor of Ardabil, a little-known traffic engineer with ties to the Basij. Upon his confirmation with twelve out of fifteen votes, he vowed to fight corruption and ensure transparency. If the reformists had not established local government, and then flubbed the first Tehran City Council, he might never have emerged into the hard light of Iranian politics. His name was Mahmoud Ahmadinejad.

ELEVEN

THE MIRACLE ROOM

ZAHRA KAZEMI, known as Ziba from the age of two, belonged by middle age to that small and sturdy tribe of international photojournalists who turn up wherever there is conflict. She had loose, unkempt curls and a face both delicate and rugged, with a generous mouth and knowing, guarded eyes. She was Iranian, born in Shiraz, but she'd left to study in France before the revolution and returned only to visit. She became a mother and a Canadian citizen. Her work took her to Africa, Latin America, and the Middle East. Sometimes she lived in refugee camps to draw closer to her subjects. She was fifty-four in 2003, the year she went to Iraq to photograph the consequences of the American invasion. From there she planned to go to Central Asia, but her visas for Uzbekistan and Turkmenistan were slow in coming. She decided to wait for them in neighboring Iran.

Like all dual citizens, Kazemi entered the country using her Iranian passport. Like all visiting journalists, she applied for press credentials from Ershad, which licensed her to photograph ordinary residents of Tehran going about their daily lives. On June 23, 2003, she photographed a scene outside Evin Prison's gates. Family members of people arrested in demonstrations earlier that month were holding a vigil there. A guard at the prison entrance noticed the foreign woman talking with protesters and occasionally snapping photographs. He asked a lieutenant if this was allowed. The lieutenant said it was fine so long as Kazemi was an authorized journalist and causing no unrest.

But someone had alerted the head of prison security, who strode into the crowd with another prison official. The officials accosted Kazemi personally. Couldn't she see the sign on the prison wall stating that photography was prohibited? Witnesses, including the sentry in the guard tower, saw the head of prison security demand Kazemi's bag. When she refused, he pinned her arms and wrested it from her, dealing a blow to her head so violent that Kazemi fell to the ground, where she sat stunned for a prolonged moment, seemingly unable to get up. Then the photojournalist was ushered through the prison gates.

The guards and drivers who handled Kazemi inside the prison complex would later recount that she was barely conscious when she entered. She fainted in a car, could not stand, and had to be carried limply into a cell block. Neither her alarming injury nor her trivial offense—taking photographs where they were prohibited, which was not even a crime—afforded her the slightest clemency. She was taken not to the prison clinic but to a solitary confinement cell. By later accounts, she was hardly ever alone there. Tehran's chief prosecutor, Saeed Mortazavi, together with his deputy, hurried to the prison, where they interrogated Kazemi for four hours in the middle of the night. For four days Kazemi would be traded off between Mortazavi's custody, that of the intelligence unit of the police, and that of the Ministry of Intelligence and Security.

SAEED MORTAZAVI HAD A PROSPEROUS LOOK. His face was full, his dark hair gleaming, his mustache meticulously groomed. He wore rimless glasses and shiny gray three-piece suits. He had colorless lips and a mild, patronizing manner of speech. Before taking over the prosecutor's office, he ran a special court for press offenses, where he'd earned the moniker "the Butcher of the Press" for his role in shutting down newspapers and jailing journalists. Many journalists and editors knew him personally, because he was inclined to deliver his threats firsthand. He had liaisons in every newsroom and could dictate the terms of censorship according to his whim. To those he sought to convince of his rectitude or bend to his will, Mortazavi described a world laced with malevolent conspiracies, one in which journalists, both domestic and foreign, were operatives in an international web of spies determined to bring down the Islamic Republic.

These claims were outsized but not altogether incredible in a country that understood itself to be beset by powerful enemies. The United States under President George W. Bush had invaded two neighboring countries and declared Iran a member of an "Axis of Evil." It had also adopted an explicit policy of "regime change" in Iran and expressed a desire to distribute money to Iranian opposition groups. What preoccupied Iranian hard-liners most of all were the bloodless revolutions in former Soviet satellites, where opposition forces, sometimes overtly or covertly supported by Western foundations and government affiliates, had succeeded in removing repressive regimes unfriendly to American interests. The Islamic Republic was not wrong in imagining itself a potential target of such efforts. But the determination to stave off a "velvet" overthrow would become both paranoid fixation and carte blanche for internal repression.

Mortazavi wasted no time in declaring Kazemi a spy. He could furnish no evidence, because the photojournalist had exposed her film to light upon her arrest, rendering it unreadable. Moreover, although Mortazavi denied it, her papers were in order, approved by both Ershad and the intelligence ministry, which demanded that the accused be relinquished into its custody for questioning by counterintelligence. The prosecutor refused. Rather, Zahra Kazemi was first in the custody of the prison and the prosecutor, then the intelligence unit of the police; then she was given back to Mortazavi and finally, on June 26, to the Ministry of Intelligence. But by then she was in no condition for questioning. She began vomiting blood and was transferred to a military hospital, where she slipped into a coma.

The doctor who examined Kazemi on admission to the hospital noted extensive bruising all over her body, including on the soles of her feet, her breasts, and the backs of her arms. Some of the bruising on her arms may have been defensive, forensic experts later speculated—as though she had sought to ward off blows from a blunt object. Her nose and fingers were broken, several toes and nails crushed; she had "deep parallel linear abrasions" on her neck and stripe-like wounds on her back; a pelvic examination revealed bruising consistent with "a very brutal rape." A scan of her brain showed multiple contusions on different sides of her head that were bleeding internally; one final blow to the jaw, probably administered on June 25, had snapped her head fatally back from her spine, fracturing her skull at its base. She was brain-dead. On July 10 she was removed from life support.

THE MURDER OF ZAHRA KAZEMI, and the political circus that was to follow it, revealed with terrible clarity the limitations of Khatami's reform of the security apparatus. The intelligence ministry was at long last under the control of the elected government; but, through parts of the judiciary, the Leader's office sustained networks of intelligence and enforcement that were ultra-hardline and accountable to no one. Incredible documents would emerge from the Kazemi episode: reports pitting the intelligence ministry against the prosecutor's office, letters from otherwise apolitical figures alleging pressure to participate in a cover-up. But most of these documents would remain unavailable to the Iranian public, thanks to the heavy-handed censorship of Saeed Mortazavi.

Zahra Kazemi had suffered a stroke, Mohammad Hossein Khoshvaght, the head of foreign press at Ershad, told the public in a written statement that July. Later, Khoshvaght would disown this statement, saying that Mortazavi had called him to the prosecutor's office and threatened him personally. After all, his name was on Kazemi's permissions; he was an accomplice to her spying, Mortazavi told him, and could be sent to prison himself. Didn't Khoshvaght understand that all those Anglophone reporters he admitted were actually operatives sent to distribute money to the opposition? Mortazavi dictated the press release, had Khoshvaght type it on ersatz Ershad letterhead Mortazavi had made on his photocopier, and forced Khoshvaght to sign it and distribute it to the press. But Mortazavi had miscalculated. Khoshvaght had a measure of immunity, because his sister was married to the Supreme Leader's son. (His father was an ultra-hardline ayatollah rumored to be among those whose fatwas authorized the serial killings.) He became a key outspoken witness to Mortazavi's cover-up of what was surely a crime.

The doctor who had examined Kazemi upon her admission to the hospital also refused to keep silent. Kazemi's body had been buried in haste, her medical history obfuscated with claims that she'd suffered a stroke, or a head injury occasioned by a single accidental fall. "In view of Ms. Zahra Kazemi's inhumane treatment and considering the efforts of Islamic Republic authorities to swiftly bury her to conceal the evidence of torturing her, and considering that I was the night shift emergency resident physician on June 26, 2003 and that I was her examining physician at the hospital," Dr. Shahram Azam wrote, "I consider it my moral and human duty to give testimony and pronounce my observations to international human rights organizations with regard to injuries inflicted on her through torture, assault and battery and, in this regard, play a small role in exposing the inhuman and brutal nature of the Islamic regime." Having no relation, by marriage or otherwise, to the Supreme Leader, Azam fled the country and found asylum in Canada. His family members issued a statement, almost certainly under duress, claiming that he was mentally ill, had never worked for the hospital in question, and was being used politically by the Canadian government.

President Khatami designated a committee to investigate the Kazemi murder. It consisted of the ministers of intelligence, justice, interior, health, and Ershad. All of these ministries were in one or another way implicated in the events under investigation. The presidential commission met seven times and pieced together records from each member's domain. Its report furnished a timeline of Kazemi's custody and asserted that the fatal blow had to have been struck sometime on June 25 or 26. Anyone who had come into contact with Kazemi during that period, the commission noted, should be investigated. Oddly, the commission did not reference its own timeline to state the obvious, which was that this narrowed the suspects to the prosecutor's office and the Ministry of Intelligence, with the prosecutor and his lieutenants spending the greater share of time interrogating her.

There were oddities about the presidential commission's report. It suggested more than once that Kazemi was a disagreeable person, rude and argumentative, as though this might explain or justify her harsh treatment. It claimed that Kazemi had chosen to stay at Evin rather than be parted from her camera and other belongings. Surely, one prominent Iranian human rights lawyer pointed out, prisons were not like hotels, where one stayed electively. Why hadn't she been told to leave? Moreover, the report neither clarified nor questioned why a woman with no criminal record, picked up for nothing more serious than taking pictures in a restricted area, should have been interrogated for hours on end by the prosecutor's office or anyone else.

Zahra Kazemi's mother viewed the body once before burial and saw plainly that her daughter had been beaten. She was forced to sign papers authorizing a swift burial, but she also brought her concerns to the parliament. Under Article 90 of the Iranian constitution, anyone with a complaint about legislative, executive, or judicial actions could request a parliamentary investigation with publicly reported findings. These requests had availed Iran's citizens little in the past, but now that the parliament was in the hands of reformists who claimed to uphold the rule of law, Article 90 seemed a promising recourse for the Kazemi family. The commission set to work on the most far-reaching inquiry into Kazemi's case. Its report was blunt and disturbing.

There were political overtones. The intelligence ministry, after Khatami's 1999 housecleaning, allied itself with the elected reformist government and claimed to pride itself on abstaining from extrajudicial violence, while the judiciary, which included the prosecutor's office, sustained links to the elements Khatami had purged from the intelligence apparatus. In depositions to the Article 90 commission, intelligence officials fumed about being dragged into Mortazavi's unsavory mess. Their recommendation, they insisted, had been to free Zahra Kazemi on the grounds that no basis existed for charging her with spying; but if Mortazavi had meant to insist that she was a spy, he should have turned her over to them, as their ministry was the proper bureaucratic channel for counterespionage. The notion that she should have been kept at Evin under constant supervision and relentless, violent interrogation ran counter to the ministry's advice. Complained one deputy intelligence minister, "How could it be that the Ministry of Intelligence, which had suggested that the individual should be freed, would later go to the prison and kill her?"

Mortazavi disdained to meet with the Article 90 commission at all, and this inflamed its members against him. He replied to the commission's questions in a high-handed letter suggesting that the parliamentarians were ignorant of the law. In response, the commission members cited chapter and verse to argue that Kazemi's detention had most likely been illegal; that Mortazavi had falsified the reports of prison guards on her medical condition and fabricated a story about her lacking clearance from the intelligence ministry to work as a journalist; and that prison record books had been tampered with and witnesses silenced. The scale of the cover-up, and the commission's relentlessness in detailing it, were staggering. The prosecutor's office was not solely at fault. Some twenty prison guards and sentries who had previously testified as witnesses, the commission noted, were later rounded up by the prison's intelligence staff and instructed to deny their testimonies. But there could be little question of whom the parliamentarians held ultimately responsible for Kazemi's murder, and even less so after one commission member lambasted Mortazavi in a speech and in an open letter to the prosecutor.

By law, the Article 90 commission report was to be read publicly and released to the press. After an unexplained two-and-a-half-month delay, a deputy read the report in the parliament on October 28, and this session was broadcast on state-run radio. But something strange happened the night the print media was to finalize its account of the commission's findings.

. . .

ROOZBEH MIREBRAHIMI, the twenty-four-year-old political editor of *Etemad*, thought the Zahra Kazemi affair was horrifying, but he also hoped it would galvanize the reformists. Their movement seemed nearly moribund, between the failure of the Tehran City Council, the crushing of the student movement, the ineffectuality of the parliament, and the impunity with which major reformist figures were shot, in the case of Saeed Hajjarian; jailed, like Akbar Ganji; or forced into exile, like Abdolkarim Soroush. The Kazemi affair, and the blatant abuse of power it suggested on the part of the judiciary, might light a fire under the reformists, Roozbeh imagined. Like the serial murders, it just might spur them to action to defend the rule of law. After all, what happened to Kazemi, Roozbeh knew, could happen to him or any of his colleagues at any time. By investigating it relentlessly and exposing the perpetrators, the reformists in the parliament and the media could ensure that journalists could not be abused and killed without consequence.

The Article 90 commission report supported Roozbeh's optimism. Reformist members of the parliament had exposed the prosecutor's apparent obstruction of justice. They did it in the interest not of activism but of the law. At its very best, a committed reformist faction was capable of this. *Etemad* dedicated a page to the Article 90 commission report. But sometime between 8:00 and 8:30 on the evening of October 28, 2003, Mortazavi called *Etemad*'s editor in chief and informed him that if the newspaper covered the Article 90 commission report at all, the prosecutor would reopen a pending case against *Etemad*, which would surely result in the paper's closure. Roozbeh's boss informed him that the paper had no choice but to withhold the page its young political editor had helped prepare.

The morning of October 29 was remarkable for its silence. The parliament had just released a scorching report on judicial involvement in a murder, and but for one paper, *Yas-e No*, which was already at the printer by the time Mortazavi called, the story had vanished without a trace. Newspapers did not so much as summarize the commission's findings. It was as though the report, aired on the radio and the floor of the parliament just the day before, had been scrubbed from the public record. A reporter from the American-run Persian-language radio station, Radio Farda, tried to get to the bottom of this. He interviewed Roozbeh, who bluntly informed him that Mortazavi had threatened *Etemad* with closure if it covered the parliamentary commission's findings. The reporter asked if Roozbeh was willing to go on the record with this claim. He was. Mortazavi had acted illegally, Roozbeh added; the parliament had already read the report on live radio, indicating that it was not classified in any way.

He imagined that other editors would fall in behind him, disclosing that Mortazavi had pressured them, too. He would have opened the floodgate for their resistance to censorship by thuggery. Readers would know that their media had not conspired to fail them so much as it had been strong-armed against its will. But no one stepped forward to corroborate his story. Roozbeh, young and slight and refined beyond his years, stood alone. He did not know it yet, but he had just taken the last step off a precipice he had been approaching so slowly, he'd hardly noticed it was there.

FROM THE TIME he was a boy, Roozbeh had been told to avert his eyes from crimes his elders did not wish to explain or describe. The crimes did not touch him; he would have known neither the perpetrators nor the victims. But his generation was steeped in their atmosphere, a sense of menace that lurked somewhere just beyond the frame of a child's vision—the animal smell of one's parents' fears, the suspicion that one's own security might have come at another's cost. The truths one's parents benevolently concealed seeped edgewise into consciousness. Guilt, like a shadow unmoored from the object that cast it, settled where it least belonged.

For Iranians of Roozbeh's generation, violence and secrecy formed the boundaries of the knowable landscape, no less than the Alborz mountain range that separated Gilan province from the province of Tehran. As a boy in the city of Rasht, Roozbeh would visit the graves of relatives with his family. But whenever he neared a particular unmarked tract of the cemetery, his mother watched him shrewdly, calling him back with a peculiar note of tension in her voice. The place took on a mystique for him. He went there on his own sometimes, peering at the unyielding ground as though if he looked hard enough, or stood long enough just breathing the air, he could discern what evil had rendered those plots off-limits to those who would comfort the dead. Much later he came to understand that this was where Rasht's victims of the 1988 prison massacres lay buried—separated, as infidels, from the faithful.

Rasht was a languid, green city of just over half a million. The capital of Gilan, it hugged the Caspian coast and had once been a major silk-trading town. It was the first Iranian city to host a theater, a library, a bank branch; it was a center of liberal activism against the monarchy at the turn of the twentieth century, and it enjoyed a sometimes comical reputation for being temperate in its climate, its politics, even its relations between the sexes. The revolution itself, it was often said, came late to Rasht. Roozbeh was born a month afterward, on March 19, 1979.

His older sister, Rita, was six at the time of the revolution—old enough to form an indelible memory. She was in the town center the day revolutionary militants stormed the SAVAK headquarters, killing nine people. When they were older, passing through town, she would show Roozbeh where—by which tree—she'd seen a slain man's hand, where legs. Later still, when Roozbeh's more hotheaded peers urged revolt against the Islamic system, this recollection, not even his own, would stay him. Political violence had a physical shape, a psychic consequence.

Roozbeh's mother, a seamstress with a high school education, carried herself with an air of refinement. She had married an unlettered taxi driver sixteen years her senior—a remote, dignified man, warm but inexpressive. Their three children all took nicknames beginning with *R*: Rita, Roozbeh, Rasool. For the first five years of Roozbeh's life, the family lived in a single room of his grandmother's home, a traditional courtyard dwelling in one of Rasht's oldest neighborhoods. During the war years, the Mirebrahimis moved into a house of their own in Shalekoo, a neighborhood of dirt roads, unfinished houses, and only the barest utilities.

Roozbeh was even-tempered and reserved, the sort of person who could sustain himself for long periods on scarce stimuli. He would grow into an affect not unlike his father's: calm, abstracted, humane, undemonstrative. This demeanor would set him apart from others around him, he could never quite say whether for better or worse. It made him hard to read and easy to project upon.

His parents were not particularly religious, but Roozbeh was. He read the Quran on his own, observed his daily prayers, and spent the Shiite holy month of Muharram at mosque. Because his father could not read or write, Roozbeh read the sports pages aloud to him from the newspapers and magazines he brought home. Little by little, Roozbeh began to read the other pages of those publications, too, and to imagine that he might one day be a journalist.

Roozbeh lived, then and always, less in the physical world than in the world of books and ideas. In high school he fell in with a circle of older boys who started a sort of salon. They had weekly meetings at each of their homes in turn. There they would discuss religion, movies, novels, and eventually works of political philosophy. Through this group, Roozbeh took an interest in Descartes and then in Machiavelli. He compared the understanding of the West he gleaned from these thinkers with his own perceptions of Iran. He wrote essays on political philosophy for a local magazine. Two of the boys adored Shariati, but Roozbeh found Shariati's Islam too rigid, too encompassing. He preferred Soroush and another, similar thinker, a former cleric named Mohammad Mojtahed Shabestari, who argued that religion was not a complete system and could be complemented by other sources of understanding. Roozbeh and his friends subscribed to *Kiyan*, where they read Soroush and Shabestari at the height of their novelty and influence.

Politics during those years remained distant and opaque to Roozbeh. There were no sympathetic actors. For most of Roozbeh's young life, the

Islamic Left had been an object of fear. Members of that faction patrolled Rasht's city center, making the environs dangerous for young people who ran afoul of stringent codes of behavior and dress. When prominent members of the Islamic Left peeled off into the reform movement, Roozbeh and his friends still feared the reformists' past radicalism and suspected that their commitment to civil liberties would be instrumental and fleeting. But then Khatami ran for president in 1997. Roozbeh had never heard of this mild-mannered librarian. The opposing campaign portrayed him as a liberal who would blast Iran's intellectual space wide open. This was meant to scare voters, but for Roozbeh, it was compelling. If the conservatives feared and hated Khatami this much, Roozbeh reasoned, maybe Khatami really was a force for good.

When Khatami was announced president-elect on the Second of Khordad, Roozbeh felt himself reeling. Anything, everything, good might happen now. He felt as he imagined the revolutionaries must have felt the year of his birth: he was lucky to be young at such a time.

LIKE MANY IRANIAN PARENTS who aspired for their children to enter the middle class, the Mirebrahimis wanted Roozbeh to be an engineer. Only the very best students were accepted into engineering programs at the university level. Roozbeh didn't want to be an engineer. He weeded himself out by passivity and design: he didn't study for the all-important university entry exam, and so he didn't qualify. His parents were disappointed, but Roozbeh felt liberated. He registered instead for military service and shipped off for Iranian Kurdistan.

Sarbazi, or mandatory military service, in Iran as everywhere, was something most young men simply endured if they could find no way to avoid it. But Roozbeh embraced it. He found a quality in himself that he would call on many times in the future: an acceptance of circumstance that made him oddly flexible if not impassive in the face of change, even as he also seemed untouched by experience. He would have been the same Roozbeh in a field of battle as in a room full of books, in a prison cell as in a foreign country. As military service was mandatory, he reasoned, there was no benefit in ruining the experience by resisting it. He welcomed the independence, the novelty, the travel, the opportunity to build his strength. Every day of his conscription, he wrote in a diary. He called it "The Journey Called *Sarbazi*." His fellow conscripts laughed at him. *Sarbazi* was not, to most of them, a journey of self-discovery but a detour, a period of grudging duty and a two-year wait for life to begin. But Roozbeh was proud of his diary. He kept it to give to his brother, Rasool, that he might be better prepared for his own *sarbazi*.

Roozbeh had been liberated—from the dependency of youth by *sarbazi* and from his parents' expectations by his performance on the engineering exam. When he returned to Rasht, he registered to take a different university entrance exam, one considered lesser, in that time and place: the one for the humanities. He qualified to study social science at the public university in Rasht, or to study political science at a private university in Tehran. His family urged him to stay in Rasht, where tuition and housing were free. But by now Roozbeh knew what he wanted. He loved political science, and he would find a way to pay for Islamic Azad University and for housing in Tehran. He took his parents' money only to register. After that he worked. He became a journalist even as a university student, and he got a job at *Etemad*, the newspaper licensed to the parliamentary deputy from Rasht.

The Islamic Azad University was the brainchild of the Rafsanjani administration, which had established a network of campuses across the country, charging tuition and making higher education available to Iranians in more localities than ever before. Unlike the public universities, which were traditional hotbeds of activism with all the attendant dangers, including militia clashes and layers of surveillance, the private university's campuses were run in classic Rafsanjanist fashion: under a heavy hand that rendered them functional and peaceable at the cost of forbidding student associations and political activism. Roozbeh's intellectual hungers were political, so he slaked them with his reading, above all with the work of the secular leftist sociologist Hossein Bashiriyeh.

Roozbeh had read Bashiriyeh since his high school days in Rasht, when a magazine about economics and politics carried some of Bashiriyeh's essays. The essays opened a window on a world of political philosophy that few Iranian teenagers had reason to visit. Roozbeh was particularly intrigued by Bashiriyeh's essay on tolerance. He had begun writing essays of his own, and when he went to Tehran he nurtured a fantasy that he would meet the sociologist who had ignited his intellect. One day he gathered up an essay he had drafted on democratization and ventured onto the University of Tehran campus in search of Bashiriyeh's office. He presented himself to the professor as a student from another university who wished, nevertheless, to learn from Bashiriyeh himself. Would Bashiriyeh read Roozbeh's freshman effort and tell him where he was right and where wrong?

Bashiriyeh accepted. He told Roozbeh to leave the essay and come back in a week's time. He critiqued the essay generously and honestly. And Roozbeh asked for one thing more. Bashiriyeh taught a PhD seminar in comparative political science, and Roozbeh wanted to sit in on it. Bashiriyeh welcomed him, and Roozbeh made him his mentor. He followed the course on Western philosophy with Bashiriyeh's course on Iranian sociology, and he followed that by reading all of Bashiriyeh's books. To Roozbeh, there was more in this literature than in anything he had tasted through *Kiyan*. Soroush, Kadivar, Shabestari—they were scholars of Islam, Roozbeh reasoned, who sought above all to liberate the religion they loved from the political system that was smothering it. Bashiriyeh was a man not of religion but of politics. And for Roozbeh, too, politics and history, far more than religion, were the spades with which he hoped to unearth the deepest truths.

To Roozbeh, growing up in the Islamic Republic sometimes felt like coming of age in a house whose corridors were lined with locked doors. Behind those doors lay rooms whose contours he could see as though through frosted glass: the hostage crisis, the prison massacres, the Iran-Iraq War, the expulsion of Bazargan's government. But to truly enter into those rooms, to understand not only the details of that history but the motives of the men who'd shaped it, required keys.

Ebrahim Asgharzadeh, a pugnacious city councilman who had been the leader of the hostage takers back in 1979, held a key to one forbidden room that Roozbeh longed to explore. Through him, Roozbeh imagined he could reconstruct the logic and atmosphere around the embassy seizure—the rupture of relations with the United States, which had so much set Iran's course in Roozbeh's lifetime. But he also wanted to publish an interview in which Asgharzadeh would admit that the hostage taking had been a terrible and costly mistake. According to Roozbeh, Asgharzadeh came close to such admissions privately, but would not renounce publicly the activities that had catapulted him to prominence.

And so Roozbeh kept worrying the knobs of those locked doors. Once, he and a colleague from the paper went to Qom to interview Sadegh Khalkhali, the hanging judge of the 1980s—a cleric by whose direct order hundreds, perhaps thousands, of dissidents, Kurds, monarchist elites, generals, and others were executed by firing squad during the reign of terror that followed the revolution. Saeed Mortazavi would be no match for the elder cleric, in deeds or in psychopathy. Khalkhali's very face—round and crowded beneath his white turban, with unnaturally small eyes and a cruel twist to his upper lip—was an object of fear for Roozbeh and other ordinary Iranians. But the man Roozbeh encountered in Qom was someone diminished, nearly comical.

Khalkhali would die within the year. He had always been small, but now he seemed shrunken. Instead of his turban he wore a peaked cap that reminded Roozbeh of a baby's hat. He had entered the late stages of Parkinson's disease, and his answers to the reporters' questions were often bizarre and off topic. But his long-term memory seemed intact. Sure, Khalkhali told Roozbeh and his friend, he'd signed more than a thousand execution orders. "Many of the people fled," he recalled. "If I could have gotten them, I'd have executed them, too."

.   .   .

ROOZBEH WAS NOT A REBELLIOUS YOUNG MAN. He yearned for older figures he could unreservedly admire, if not revere. The problem was that they were hard to come by. Roozbeh fastened on to Abbas Amirentezam, the debonair deputy prime minister under Bazargan who had been charged with treason on the basis of documents seized in the American embassy and so had been in prison as long as Roozbeh had been alive. Amirentezam had published two memoirs during a brief furlough in 1997. Roozbeh saw them in a shop window and hastened to buy them before they were banned. He had a lot of books he'd bought like that—in eagerness to squirrel them away before the censors caught on to their existence. But these books were something special. Roozbeh devoured them in just two days.

Roozbeh had heard about Amirentezam since he was a child. Like most ordinary Iranians, he knew of him as a prisoner, not as a thinker or actor on the political stage. But precisely because he was the Islamic Republic's longest-held captive, Amirentezam enjoyed a kind of popular goodwill along with his celebrity. He was often called Iran's Nelson Mandela. Like Mandela, he would serve some twenty-seven years in prison or under house arrest. He had witnessed horrors in that time, including the massacres of 1988. And he had never left prison because he never confessed.

During Amirentezam's 1998 furlough, the former Evin warden from the bloody 1980s, Asadollah Lajevardi, was assassinated in the bazaar, where he had retreated into private life as a merchant of women's underwear. Khatami and other regime officials eulogized the man who had presided over the most abusive era of the modern Iranian penal system. Privately, many Iranians cheered that justice had been done. But Amirentezam gave a remarkable interview to a radio station. "Terror does not solve any problem," he said. "I'm not happy at this news. A man probably exceptional for his ruthlessness, his violence, his vices and his atrocities is made a hero, a martyr, a people's servant." For these and other statements critical of Lajevardi, Amirentezam was sent back to Evin.

Roozbeh seized a rare opportunity to write about Amirentezam in

2002. In one of his books Amirentezam all but identified a reformist intellectual as the hostage taker who had interrogated him shortly after his arrest. That intellectual now wrote an angry screed disputing Amirentezam's recollection. Roozbeh replied with an unsigned article in *Etemad*. In it, he noted that even though many of Amirentezam's former accusers now stood closer to him politically than to the conservative elite, they seemed incapable of admitting past mistakes.

One day not long after this article appeared, *Etemad*'s editor in chief summoned Roozbeh to his office. Amirentezam's wife was on the phone. She wanted to know who had written the piece about her husband. When Roozbeh took the receiver, the woman told him that her husband had asked her to thank him for writing what he did.

Roozbeh was astonished. He hadn't even known that Amirentezam had left prison for medical treatment and was now living under a sort of intermittent house arrest. He asked if he could come and see the former deputy prime minister. Amirentezam lived under lock and key, with a kiosk at his door where guards monitored his visitors. Roozbeh would draw attention to himself by going there; he would come under surveillance and suspicion. But he had an opportunity to meet one of his heroes, someone he'd never dreamt anyone could meet.

Amirentezam agreed to meet weekly with Roozbeh, who compiled their conversations into a book he would publish years later. But the conversations were more than a journalistic exercise for Roozbeh. Amirentezam impressed Roozbeh with his improbable equanimity, his lightness of spirit. How was it possible for a man who had spent most of his life in prison to be happy? And yet, Roozbeh was certain that Amirentezam was not only happy but optimistic, his mind fixed always on better things to come. Moreover, Amirentezam was a patriot. He had spent his time in prison thinking earnestly about his country. He contemplated the revolution and its aftermath; he drew up plans, in his mind, for the future of Iran, down to the Tehran metro system. He had unburdened himself of rage by forgiving his adversaries. Roozbeh admired Amirentezam like a father, and he felt that Amirentezam loved him like a son.

Roozbeh began to interview Amirentezam's critics for *Etemad*. He found public figures who disliked Amirentezam's books or disagreed with his views, and he published them in order that he might then publish Amirentezam's replies. Roozbeh hoped in this way to smuggle Amirentezam's words into the paper and to drive his readers to Amirentezam's books. In the meantime, he helped Amirentezam organize his documents into files. He helped him locate information he needed in books and newspapers. A conservative newspaper took note of their relationship, publishing an article stating that Roozbeh Mirebrahimi, political editor of *Etemad*, had become Amirentezam's manager. Roozbeh's colleagues warned him to be careful. But Roozbeh had never done anything so meaningful, and he was not about to stop.

One day Amirentezam told Roozbeh that he'd gotten a call from student activists at Amirkabir University. They wanted him to come and speak. He was delighted but also suspicious. Did Roozbeh know this student group? Was it a religious one? Roozbeh knew that Amirkabir was the campus under the influence of Ali Afshari, the liberal reformist student leader. Afshari was in prison at the time, but the activists on his campus shared his orientation. Roozbeh urged Amirentezam to go.

On May 5, 2003, Amirentezam and a small entourage were ushered into an amphitheater packed with students Roozbeh's age and younger. When the host uttered Amirentezam's name, the amphitheater erupted into whistles and applause that lasted a good fifteen minutes.

Amirentezam spoke for two hours. He spoke of his arrest and the charges against him, some of which made the students laugh. Amirentezam had been convicted for, among other things, having American officials address him as "dear" in their letters; being a Bahai who was also a Jew; and being extremely rich. He talked of the past but he also spoke about the new generation. It seemed to Roozbeh that everybody loved him. A quarter of a century earlier, student activists had consigned Amirentezam to prison for life. Now student activists had made him a totem of resistance to the state their elders had wrought.

KHATAMI'S PRESIDENCY WAS AT FIRST a springtime for young Iranians who believed in incremental change, in the process Saeed Hajjarian had called political development, and in the capacity of reasonable people to bring moderation to the institutions they served. Khatami's response to the serial murders had demonstrated that reformists in government were far from powerless. Where else in the world had an intelligence agency been forced to take responsibility for killing opposition figures? But at the same time it was clear that Khatami could not restrain the judiciary, parts of which, including the Tehran prosecutor's office and the Special Court of the Clergy, appeared to operate out of the Leader's pocket.

Ayatollah Montazeri remained under house arrest. The Special Court of the Clergy indicted two of Khatami's cabinet ministers on political charges. In February 1999 it arraigned Mohsen Kadivar, the dissident cleric who had argued that *velayat-e faqih* shared more with Iran's tradition of monarchy than with its tradition of Shiism. Kadivar was charged with undermining the Islamic system, insulting Khomeini and Khamenei, misleading the public, supporting Montazeri, and advocating the separation of mosque and state. In April he was sentenced to eighteen months in prison. Students protested, carrying banners that read, "We think like Kadivar, so you can arrest us too."

By the time Khatami's first term was over in 2001, the state had shut down 108 periodicals, and Mohsen Kadivar and Akbar Ganji languished in prison along with numerous student activists and journalists. The reformist coalition strained at its seams. Liberal students called for civil disobedience and a referendum on the entire system of government. Reformist clerics, like parliamentary speaker Mehdi Karroubi and the president himself, called on voters to be patient while they continued negotiating with a conservative faction that appeared increasingly intractable.

A group of lay reformist politicians struck a middle course that was muscular but not inflexible. The deputy interior minister, Mostafa Tajzadeh, was one of its leading figures. He was both an intellectual and an effective political operative. Tajzadeh was Khatami's protégé—they had worked together in Ershad under Rafsanjani—and when the elder cleric became president, he handed Tajzadeh the sensitive portfolio of security and political affairs, which included overseeing elections. It was the election for the parliament in 2000—swept by the reformists, particularly in Tehran, where they took all thirty seats—that made Tajzadeh a lightning rod for conservative fears. The Guardian Council alleged irregularities and annulled some seven hundred thousand votes. Tajzadeh pushed back. These were the "cleanest and freest elections" in the history of the Islamic Republic, he protested. The Guardian Council took Tajzadeh to court, and Tajzadeh responded in kind, filing a largely symbolic lawsuit against the council's powerful secretary general. In 2001 the court handed the deputy interior minister a suspended one-year sentence and barred him from government work for three years.

Tajzadeh had never believed that street protests should figure into reformist strategy. The public was deeply aggrieved and poorly organized. If protests turned radical, the conservatives would crack down. They'd close what little space existed for reformist maneuvering; they'd destroy more young people in the prisons; and nothing would be gained. Tajzadeh and other reformists had long counseled their supporters to resist provocation and their colleagues to persevere in their internal efforts at negotiation and compromise. But after 2001, Tajzadeh tweaked the formula in a more aggressive direction. He still discouraged street mobilization, but now he called for reformists in government to use their positions to battle repression and expose the deep illegal apparatus of political violence. The Article 90 commission report investigating the Zahra Kazemi affair was exactly the sort of thing he had in mind.

IN A NEIGHBORHOOD CALLED ESKANDARI in south-central Tehran, the poet and writer Shahram Rafizadeh shared a not-quite-five-hundred-square-foot one-bedroom apartment with Roozbeh and another colleague from *Etemad*. They lived on the third floor of a four-story building, in a space adorned with little but beds and books.

From the time Shahram accepted Roozbeh's invitation to write for *Etemad*'s political section, the men had become close friends as well as roommates and colleagues. Shahram was older and already becoming known.

His book *Shooting at Reform* had just passed the censors, to be published with only a few words excised. This book was about Saeed Hajjarian, and in it Shahram and a coauthor reconstructed from newspaper archives and legal documents the mechanics and motives behind Hajjarian's attempted murder. The journalists linked the shooting to other state-sponsored assassinations and explored Hajjarian's ideas, showing how they had made him a particular target. Writing about reformists gave Shahram cover that writing about his friends in the Iranian Writers Association never had. So long as the reformists remained in power, the red lines of censorship would be elastic enough to accommodate their ideas. But Shahram never expected that to last forever.

Shahram knew the reformists, although not as well as he knew the writers. He had worked for the reformist publishing house Tarh-e No back in the nineties, and he'd encountered Tajzadeh and some other reformist intellectuals there. Now he and his fellow editors from *Etemad*, including Roozbeh, occasionally met with Tajzadeh and other reformist officials in the course of their work. Shahram respected some and kept a skeptical remove from others, aware that the members of what was once the Islamic Left probably could not tolerate very deep changes to the structures they themselves had helped build. Still, like his old friend Mohammad Mokhtari, Shahram sought out common ground.

During his court-mandated hiatus from politics, Tajzadeh started a bold online publication called *Emrooz*. Shahram and Roozbeh both began writing for it even while they worked at *Etemad*. Iran's online media was relatively new, and it promised a comparatively free space for exploring sensitive subjects. Friends at another newspaper introduced Shahram to weblogs. The technology looked easy to master and difficult to censor. Back at *Etemad*, Shahram began asking around. Could anyone teach him how to post and update such a site? An Internet-savvy colleague built Shahram and Roozbeh each a blog.

Roozbeh, Shahram, and several other journalists from their circle were pioneers in this new medium. Although they published under their own names, their blogs had so few readers—mainly intellectuals, journalists,

and activists—that they were unconcerned about reprisals. But blogging—
much of it not overtly political—would soon explode in Iran as a means of
sharing experience in a country that lacked unmonitored public space. By
2005, Persian would be one of the world's leading languages for blogs.
With blogs, Iranians could outrun the censors, taking sites down and putting them back up elsewhere, technologically always strides ahead of the
old-fashioned intelligence apparatus.

Roozbeh called his blog *shabnameh*, or "night letters," a Persian term for
samizdat. He mainly used it to publish uncut and uncensored versions of his
newspaper stories. Shahram posted about freedom of expression and the
censorship of books and newspapers. He continued writing about the chain
murders. He covered allegations of more recent murders carried out on the
orders of the same ayatollah thought to have masterminded the serial killings. And he wrote about a notorious court case in which a woman accused
of killing a security officer claimed she was defending herself from rape.

If Shahram wasn't already a marked man, an article he published
online—in *Emrooz*—in 2003 certainly marked him. The essay was called
"The Miracle Room," and it was about forced confessions. The Miracle
Room was the interrogation chamber in which political prisoners, seemingly by magic, transformed into repentant lackeys. Shahram analyzed several published confessions, including Ali Afshari's, and he tried to explain
how interrogators went about breaking people. He took special note of a
prominent reformist journalist (and hostage taker) who had recently "confessed" under pressure. This confession signaled a turn, Shahram noted:
Even famous reformists were now fair game. His essay and its title would
enter the lexicon of Iranian politics and help render speakable the psychological power of torture.

IN EARLY NOVEMBER 2003, Roozbeh was summoned to the intelligence ministry's main office. There, in an interrogation room furnished
with a table and chairs, an affable agent informed Roozbeh that Saeed
Mortazavi had complained about him to the Supreme National Security

Council. Just three days had passed since Roozbeh had spoken to Radio Farda, telling the reporter that Mortazavi had silenced the press on the Kazemi affair. In his complaint, Mortazavi had pointed to a circular his office had issued a few months earlier forbidding Iranians to give interviews to foreign media. Moreover, Mortazavi charged, Roozbeh had libeled him by describing his actions as illegal.

Roozbeh's interrogation lasted about three hours, but he did not feel it was unfriendly. He explained that he believed the constitution protected his speech, despite Mortazavi's circular. And he tried to persuade his interrogator that it was good for the public to know that the regime did not stand united behind the violence done to Zahra Kazemi. Mortazavi, he told the intelligence agents, was but one face of the regime; he, Roozbeh, knew this, but much of the public did not. His interrogators told him that they were worried about him. They came from the intelligence ministry, which was part of the reformist government. But Roozbeh might yet hear from a less sympathetic parallel intelligence service that was connected to the Revolutionary Guard and the prosecutor. These people, he was told, knew about his relationship with Amirentezam.

Roozbeh answered questions about Kazemi and Mortazavi, but also about the reform movement and the Supreme Leader. Someone had told the intelligence ministry that Saeed Hajjarian had trained Roozbeh in psychological warfare. Roozbeh laughed. He had seen Hajjarian just once in his life, he replied, and that was after the political strategist was shot. He understood from some of the questions that his cell phone had been monitored for some time, but he had suspected this in any case, as he'd heard beeps on the line when his calls went through.

He was released with nothing more than a verbal warning and an admonition not to speak with the foreign press. The agents, he understood, wanted a relationship with him. They gave him a card and urged him to call them if he had problems. Could they, an interrogator asked him, call him as well if they wanted his opinion on something?

Roozbeh declined. He didn't like to talk with intelligence agencies, he informed them coolly. If his interlocutors were curious about his opinions, they could always refer to his published work.

SHAHRAM, partly by dint of his character and partly on account of his background on the secular left, seemed to float above Iran's filigree of factional rivalries. He moved in a world that was lousy with intrigue—journalism, compounded with politics, compounded with heavy surveillance by a divided state. He brought to this a nearly studied innocence that was also a moral posture: a refusal to live as though it were true. Little else could explain the friendship he cultivated with a haunted young man named Payam Fazlinejad.

The first time Shahram met Payam, it seemed to be by chance, at a movie theater. One of Shahram's poet friends introduced him to the wiry, narrow-faced young man, who could not have been more than twenty-one years old at the time. Shahram had heard of Payam. He'd once been a writer for a weekly cinema magazine. When a senior cultural figure was arrested in 2001, Payam Fazlinejad was one of a number of acquaintances arrested along with him. Payam was young, inexperienced, and apolitical. He was not somebody one might expect to mount a heroic resistance to physical pressure. As a condition for his release, it was widely believed that he had agreed to confess against his friends and then to become an informer—a modern-day *tavob* operating outside the prisons rather than within. There was something mouselike about him, at the same time pitiable and unsettling.

Shahram felt certain that Payam had been sent to get to know him, but he did not resist. Rather, he agreed to meet with him, always in public places. Sometimes Roozbeh joined them. Shahram reasoned that he had nothing to hide. He would treat Payam like anyone else. And anyone who knew Shahram even slightly knew that he was as honest as he was deep. He spoke openly with Payam about the Islamic Republic, about its officials, and even about Islam. Payam insisted that he wanted to see where Shahram worked. At length Shahram agreed to let him stop by *Etemad*, where Payam struck up conversations with the journalists, flattering them and ingratiating himself.

One night, working late at *Etemad*, Shahram took a desperate phone call from Payam.

"I'm calling to say good-bye," Payam told Shahram. "I've betrayed my old friends. I've talked too much." He could not live with it anymore, he said, and he had decided to commit suicide.

Shahram and Roozbeh conferred. They collected Payam and, finding him disheveled and very dirty, as though he had been sleeping on the streets, they took him to their apartment to bathe. While he showered they washed and ironed his clothes. He seemed soothed by their company and he stopped talking about killing himself. Instead, the three young men decided to go to Darband, on the outskirts of Tehran, where a trail lined with traditional restaurants and teahouses climbed the Alborz foothills. Payam, who, despite his appearance, had turned up with a new white Kia Pride, was driving, and he asked if Roozbeh and Shahram would mind stopping by his office first. He wanted to smoke a little hash he had there.

Payam pulled up to a building near Fatemi Square, by the Ministry of Interior. Roozbeh and Shahram sat in an anteroom while Payam disappeared within. Much later, Roozbeh would learn that this office belonged to a special cyberintelligence detail of the parallel intelligence apparatus— not the Ministry of Intelligence, but the spy agency that had formed from the elements purged from that ministry, in coordination with Mortazavi and the Revolutionary Guards.

Payam emerged, and the three young men continued on to Darband, where they sat over chelo kebab and a water pipe. They got to talking about a mutual acquaintance, a defector from Ansar-e Hezbollah who had just fled to Turkey. Did Shahram want to speak to him? Payam asked eagerly. Shahram demurred, but it was too late. Payam had dialed the number and put the phone to Shahram's ear. Shahram greeted the acquaintance. Then Payam thrust the phone at Roozbeh, who also blandly wished their mutual friend well.

SOLMAZ SHARIF WAS WORKING at *Etemad* as a sports reporter when she noticed Roozbeh. He wasn't like other men she knew. He seemed gentle and lucid, walled within a force field of tranquillity that set him apart from the tumult of youth. She wondered if he was unhappy, or distracted by a love affair, or simply putting on an act. She wanted to know him. When a group of colleagues including Roozbeh went to Chitgar Park one Thursday night, Roozbeh invited Solmaz to join them. She accepted readily. She had met Roozbeh before, through a mutual friend at the paper, but this was the first time they really spoke. Two months later, Solmaz asked Roozbeh to marry her.

Solmaz could hardly have found a man more different from herself. Where Roozbeh's intelligence pulled him into a world of ideas, hers fastened her to the concrete. She was street smart without being exactly practical; rather, she was audacious and persistent, and she lived by the belief that even unlikely things might come to those who were not afraid to ask for them. She steered her mother to end her unhappy marriage and find work as a lawyer. She practically raised her younger sister, in the flat the family owned in a concrete development near Mehrabad Airport, in southwestern Tehran. She was seventeen when she got herself her first job in journalism by cold-calling television stations to tell them that they really should hire female sports reporters. Solmaz accepted few constraints, even from her own psyche; depression, when it came, was something to be named, stared down, and defeated. She was aggressive, in her way, undaunted by self-consciousness or fear of error. But she was also girlish, voluble, and high-spirited, and she hated to be alone.

In Roozbeh she'd found a man as solitary as she was social, as static as she was active, as reserved as she was forthright. They complemented each other and also ruffled each other. But they were not without commonalities. They were in different ways idealistic, in different ways worldly, in different ways resourceful in a life that would anchor them to little. They resisted the traditional gender roles assigned to them and sympathized with Iran's underground feminist movement. They agreed in the end to a wedding, but only under pressure from their puzzled families.

Their ceremony was intimate. Solmaz's parents and sister were there, along with a relative of her father's who came as the witness from her side. Roozbeh's parents and siblings attended, too. His witness was Abbas Amirentezam. When the wedding party presented itself to the government office responsible for the paperwork, an official took their documents and requested the identity cards of the witnesses.

"Is this Amirentezam," the official said, indicating the card in his hand, "any relation to, you know, *that* Amirentezam?"

"What do you mean?" Roozbeh asked. "This is Abbas Amirentezam. There is only one."

The official rose from his desk and clasped Amirentezam in his arms, kissing his cheeks. It had always been his dream, he confided, to meet this man. He would not accept the payment the family owed; it was enough, he said, that he would have there in his file the marriage documents with Amirentezam's signature upon them.

Roozbeh and Solmaz were married at the turn of the Persian new year, in March of 2004. It was an unstable time in Roozbeh's life. He'd left *Etemad* and worked now, briefly, at a newspaper called *Jomhuriat*. Solmaz worked for *Jomhuriat* as well, reporting on women's issues and social affairs. Their stint there was truncated because *Jomhuriat* did not last long, publishing only thirteen issues before it was banned on account of its insistence on following the Zahra Kazemi case. Roozbeh and the rest of the staff continued to report to the office, but they were forbidden to publish a newspaper.

PAYAM FAZLINEJAD WANTED TO KNOW all kinds of things: about Shahram's life, his home, the documents and sources he drew on for his work. One day he warned Shahram not to keep any documents in his apartment. Shahram thought Payam was trying to scare him. He didn't take Payam seriously. But his friends did. Payam was a dangerous person, a number of friends warned him when they saw Shahram out with him. He should sever his relations. In due time, he did.

A few months passed quietly. He didn't publish much of anything. Roozbeh, bit by bit, moved out of the Eskandari apartment and into a cramped one-bedroom near the train station with his wife. Shahram planned to go to Rasht to spend a week with his family, move them into a new apartment, and enroll his daughter in first grade. Just before he was to leave, he was at work at *Etemad* when a young man brought him a summons. But the summons was for a date already past. The young man apologized and told him to report to a police station the following morning. Shahram agreed and went back to his work.

Forty minutes later the young man returned. Shahram should leave the building now, he said. A senior officer was waiting for him in the street and would answer all his questions. Shahram argued with the young man. If the senior officer wanted to see Shahram, he should come in. No, the young man insisted; Shahram had to go out. If he refused, he would be arrested.

But as Shahram suspected, the arrest was already happening. Outside the *Etemad* office, where a group of his colleagues kept watch after him at the gate, another man emerged and ordered Shahram to follow. He flashed a gun and handcuffs, and took Shahram by the hand.

Shahram recognized this man. He'd seen him once, talking with Payam Fazlinejad.

"Aren't you Payam's friend?" Shahram asked.

No, the man replied.

The first stop was the apartment in Eskandari, which the men ransacked for documents while Shahram looked on. On his shelf, Shahram spotted copies of the Iranian constitution and criminal code. He asked if he could take them. The men told him he would have no need; he'd be released soon enough. Then they put him in a black car with curtained windows, hit him from behind, and said, "Put your head down."

He was blindfolded, but his senses were on high alert when the car stopped. He was not at any known prison. The site felt quiet, residential. He felt himself guided through a courtyard, down a corridor on its left side, and into a building about the size of an urban house. His captors took his glasses, his belt, and his shoes. He heard a metal door open. He was thrust into a pitch-dark cell with a large vent. For hours Shahram sat, listening to odd noises he could not identify.

At long last, he was dragged into a chair, his hands cuffed behind his back. He heard a low voice.

"Do you know where you are?"

"No," said Shahram.

"You are in the Miracle Room."

Shahram smiled. Then he landed on the floor with the chair still bound to his back. He could not tell how many people punched and kicked him as he lay handcuffed and blindfolded. He did not know how long it lasted. When he came to, he was in a bathroom. The hand he lifted to his face came away covered in blood.

TWELVE

THE SPIDER'S HOUSE

The parable of those who take guardians besides
Allah is as the parable of the spider that makes
for itself a house; and most surely the frailest
of the houses is the spider's house did they
but know.

—THE HOLY QURAN, 29:41

BEFORE HE WAS ARRESTED, Shahram Rafizadeh had a recurring dream. He stood in a beautiful garden, surrounded by all kinds of singing birds. He wanted to leave, but the garden had no exit. Every path was a blind alley. One led to a room. There, Ruhollah Hosseinian, an important intelligence official at the time of the chain murders, stood wearing his turban but not his robes. Hosseinian did not speak. With a gesture, he instructed Shahram to push up his sleeves: like this, like this.

Shahram had never put much stock in dreams. But he became convinced that the courtyard of his prison was the garden from his dream. Sometimes, within his cell, he could hear birds. Much later he would circle that detention center by taxi and study it on Google Earth. Just to the left of Hosseiniyeh Ershad, off Javanan Square, was the house with the gracious courtyard that no one knew concealed six Miracle Rooms, nine solitary cells, off a narrow corridor with a dim green light.

The cells were so small that a person could not turn around without walking backward. Shahram estimated that his measured about three feet by five feet. It was always dark. The green bulb in the hallway cast almost no light. Up near the ceiling was a barred window; in the door there was a narrow slot for delivering food. An air ventilator ran for hours at a time, making a grating and deafening noise.

For the first month Shahram was hardly ever in his cell. He was in the interrogation room where he was beaten, then questioned, then beaten again. The interrogation room had windows covered with white film, so that he could not see out but others could see in. His interrogators switched a video camera on while he was questioned, off while he was beaten.

Shahram's face went numb from the punches and slaps. His interrogators smashed his head into walls. Once they broke a washbowl on his head. They whipped the back of his body from his shoulders to his heels with cable wires. They told him they would arrest his father and torture him in Shahram's presence. They threatened to harm his children. Hundreds of traffic accidents happen in Tehran every day, they reminded him. His family might suffer one. Or maybe they would bring Bita, his wife, to prison: "And you know what will happen to her next."

All his life, Shahram's interrogators told him, he had made mistakes. They wanted to know about his connections and activities from the time he arrived in Tehran. Shahram protested that he was only twenty-two when he came to the capital. He'd forgotten a lot of things.

"If you forgot," an interrogator told him, "you will remember here."

They had seized a Revolutionary Guard document from Shahram's apartment that belonged neither to him nor to Roozbeh but to their third roommate. They wanted Shahram to confess that the document was his. They also wanted him to confess to unlawful sexual relationships. They showed him lists of names of every woman he knew, demanding that he confess to affairs with at least one. They questioned him about the Writers Association, about his writer friends, including Mohammad Mokhtari and

Houshang Golshiri. They wanted him to incriminate Shirin Ebadi, the human rights lawyer who had just won the Nobel Prize for Peace.

From the beginning, Shahram's interrogators told him they would arrest Roozbeh, but they didn't know where to find him. Shahram tried to convince them that Roozbeh was not important. He said he didn't know his friend's new address. One day they put Shahram in a car and demanded that he lead them to Roozbeh's married home. Shahram led them to three buildings in three alleys. He did not know which one was Roozbeh's, he lied. The roads all looked alike. He and Roozbeh had once made a deal that if one of them was arrested, he'd hold out information about the other for twenty days, giving him time to leave the country. Shahram kept his word.

He was given only one set of clothes: pants, an undershirt, and a short-sleeved shirt. He wore this for seventy-two consecutive days, and he was allowed to wash the clothes in his cell only once. He was permitted to use the restroom three times a day, for three minutes at a time, and he was required to perform ablutions during those visits. He believed there were drugs in his food, because he began to hallucinate. He would see himself in the middle of a road or surrounded by people who wanted to kill him.

But no drug was more powerful or more terrifying than solitary confinement itself. His senses starved. In time he saw nothing, heard nothing, tasted nothing. There was nothing to touch, nothing to smell. Only memory bound him to the world of experience and human connection. But memory began to elude him. In the beginning he conjured images of the people he loved, their faces hovering before him during interrogations and when he was alone in his cell. But day by day the nothingness lapped at Bita and the children until, to his anguish, their faces vanished. He strained and railed against the blackness. He could no longer picture his daughter's eyes.

MUTUAL ACQUAINTANCES URGED ROOZBEH to leave the country. Web technicians associated with reformist sites had begun disappearing months before. With Shahram, the crackdown had taken a clear political turn, as he was not a programmer but a writer. Moreover, Roozbeh's life and his work were intertwined with Shahram's. But Roozbeh, in his phlegmatic way, shrugged off the warnings. He let the twenty days lapse. He had committed no crime. In the meantime he worked with Shahram's family to spread the word about his friend's disappearance, giving interviews to newspapers and calling government offices in the attempt to force his release.

Roozbeh and his wife had moved to a southern Tehran neighborhood called Gomrok, famous in pre-revolutionary days as the gateway to the red-light district. Solmaz, who was otherwise busy petitioning Ershad, the Ministry of Culture and Islamic Guidance, for a license to start a women's sports magazine, set about making the apartment a home. She had no domestic instinct or experience, but she gamely began to teach herself to cook. A glass-fronted corner cabinet in the couple's tiny living room displayed a collection of wineglasses and figurines; blue-and-white plates hung on a wall. A large wedding photograph in a gilt frame overlooked the facing wicker-framed couches that crowded the space. In the picture, Roozbeh wore a red flower in his lapel, and Solmaz gripped his shoulder. They looked intelligent, uncomfortable, and young.

"What will you do if I'm arrested?" Roozbeh asked his new bride one evening at home.

"Nothing," Solmaz teased, smiling. "When you're released, they'll make you editor in chief."

She was cracking wise about the way journalists made heroes of political prisoners. But she was also trying to puncture the tension she sensed building in him. Moments later she confronted herself in the bathroom mirror. It was a valid question he had asked. What would she do?

She would give as good as she got, she told herself. It wouldn't be an equal fight, but she would make those responsible suffer.

Solmaz woke Roozbeh early on the morning of September 27, 2004. She'd had a terrible dream, she told him. She'd dreamt that he was arrested in a small café where they sat with Shahram's brother and another colleague. The colleague was covered in blood. Roozbeh rose from sleep and stood at the bedside. The doorbell rang.

Shahram had protected Roozbeh's address, but their former roommate had not managed to hold out. He was at Roozbeh's door now, with the men who had arrested Shahram. They wanted Roozbeh, he told Solmaz through the door. They had forced him to lead them there. Solmaz hesitated only long enough to catch Roozbeh's eye. She girded herself inside, determined to show no emotion. Her composure, she felt somehow certain, was vital, both for Roozbeh's peace of mind and for whatever lay ahead of them. And then she opened the door.

Two men burst through as though expecting a chase. But the apartment hardly left room to walk, let alone run. To reach the bedroom closet required climbing over the bed.

One of the men looked around in amazement and blurted out, "This is the apartment? Where is the money from the CIA?"

They presented a torn piece of paper on which someone had scrawled instructions to search Roozbeh's home and detain him. There was no letterhead, no seal. The handwriting was a mess. The men were in plainclothes. But they said the office of the chief prosecutor, Saeed Mortazavi, had sent them. One told Roozbeh, "I see that you write articles and provide interviews to antirevolutionary radio stations working against the regime."

Roozbeh had never imagined that anyone could search such a small space for two full hours. But Mortazavi's men left nothing to chance. They emptied Roozbeh's folders and studied his photographs, flipped the pages of his books and checked under the furniture; they even searched the refrigerator and freezer in the hope of finding alcohol, possession of which could be entered as a charge against him. They were visibly disappointed not to find an illegal satellite dish.

Solmaz's equanimity seemed to irk them. "It seems the lady hasn't realized what is happening yet," one of the agents remarked to the other while Roozbeh was in the bathroom throwing on his clothes.

"I realize it," she answered coolly. "But my faith will see me through."

"You'd best make breakfast for your husband," the man retorted. "He won't have anything to eat for days."

"I'll make breakfast for you, too," said Solmaz. And she did. But no one ate.

The men lit on some of Roozbeh's CDs: a recording of Soroush's lectures, a couple of movies. They loaded these, together with some of Roozbeh's papers and Roozbeh himself, into a Paykan parked outside.

Before they left, one of the men put a finger in Solmaz's face. "Don't do any interviews with the international media," he commanded her. "If you do, it will be very bad for you."

The Paykan took Roozbeh to a police station on Motahari Street, where he waited about two hours in a basement room. When his captors transferred him into a van with tinted windows, he stole what he knew would be his last look for some time at a normal city thoroughfare, bustling with quotidian activity. Then he was blindfolded with a napkin, his hands zip-cuffed behind his back, his head shoved beneath the driver's seat as the van zigged and zagged at a sickening pace to the secret prison with the garden full of birds.

OMID MEMARIAN HAD NOT PREPARED for adversity the way adversity had prepared for him. He was a golden boy, ambitious, intelligent, hardworking, and charmed with success. Clean-cut, with thick, close-cropped curls and an oblong, open face, he had an ingenuousness about him, a quality frank and expectant. He seemed perpetually delighted to have been invited to the party that was his life. When he spoke, the words tumbled so rapidly that one was hardly finished before the next began; the listener invariably straggled paragraphs behind. His name meant "hope," and it suited him.

Omid came from a lower-middle-class family. His parents were civil servants with high school educations, and they raised him partly in a northeast Tehran neighborhood called Lavizan and partly in the gritty outlying city of Karaj. He read and wrote poetry; he thrilled to Shariati and struggled through Soroush when he was still in high school. He went to university to study metallurgical engineering, but he found his vocation as a community organizer instead.

For the price of an ice cream cone, Omid and a friend offered tutoring sessions in math and physics at a neighborhood mosque. Within six months they had nearly a dozen tutors serving close to a hundred students, many of them abjectly poor. Omid and his friends started publishing a newsletter. They hired a psychologist to man a hotline for marriage and family counseling. Almost by accident, Omid had created a civic group like the ones Hajjarian had envisioned: a neighborhood association that could help organize the public according to its affinities, its needs, its demands.

But the mosque was a contested space. Omid and his friends looked and talked like outsiders: clean-shaven, educated, unabashedly cosmopolitan. Although the imam welcomed them, and although the congregants consumed their offerings hungrily, the local Basij distrusted their influence and lobbied the imam, saying that Omid and his friends had girlfriends, that they were sinners and infidels. The Basij had money, authority, connections Omid's group did not have. Militiamen began to demand copies of Omid's newsletter before publication. Eventually, Omid registered his group as a nongovernmental organization, linked it to similar groups from other parts of the city, and moved it out of the mosque.

If Omid had been less inclined to optimism, he might have understood his experience at the mosque as an ominous one. The talk of civil society, so anodyne to Western ears and so thrilling to Omid's cohort, rang as a threat and even an insult to Iran's religious elements, which already understood themselves as civic actors. What was the mosque if not an institution of civil society? What, even, was the Basij? Who were these arrogant young men, and with what foreign ideas did they hope to supplant the hard-won revolutionary order? The Basij, for its part, little understood the effects of civic disempowerment on the educated middle class: the alienation young people like Omid felt, their hunger to contribute to their country's development.

Under Khatami, the interior ministry licensed hundreds of nongovernmental organizations. Some of these were surely exercises in grant writing and career inflation. But others were sincere efforts to assume responsibility for social welfare, to build the vital bridge that Hajjarian had spoken of between society and state. Omid never imagined that this would be dangerous work. The president himself had made it his signature. Some of the new organizations served the environment and helped the city recycle. Others addressed the rights and welfare of women and children, or helped educate immigrants, or issued microcredit, or addressed the growing and hidden problem of drug addiction. To be a citizen, this new crop of organizers believed, had to mean something more than voting every four years and expecting politicians to change everything. One nongovernmental organization took on Tehran's rat problem, laying poison on blighted boulevards.

Omid converted his NGO into a think tank and resource center for the leaders of other NGOs. He called it Alternative Thinkers of Civil Society and got funding from the Tehran office of the United Nations Development Programme. He was the organization's public face, holding meetings with newspaper editors and reformist members of the parliament and the city council. He published a magazine. When a newspaper brought him on as a columnist, Omid felt that he'd arrived. He adored seeing his name in print, hearing strangers talk about his ideas. Soon he was helping the municipality of Tehran coordinate among the NGOs serving the city. Later the interior ministry took him on as an adviser on social issues. Through this work, Omid had access to privileged information, to official reports and high-ranking politicians. He couldn't publish all the information to which he was privy, but he could steer other journalists to sources and topics he knew were worth excavating.

Gholamhossein Karbaschi, the former mayor of Tehran, tapped Omid to run for city council in 2003. Omid was a logical choice. He had the voracious ambition, the connections in both government and media, and the command of the urban landscape. He was also witty and personable. He campaigned all over Tehran, addressing crowds that reached, at their height, five thousand listeners. He reminded his audiences that he was an ordinary guy, clean-shaven and cologne-wearing, not the son of an ayatollah. This was a kind of reverse populism for a postrevolutionary age. And it was not ineffective. But Omid knew the election was doomed when his mother told him she would not be voting.

"Omid dear," she said, "even if you are elected to city council, what can you do?"

Although this was the municipal election that the reformists lost spectacularly, Omid placed a respectable fifty-fourth out of 1,200 candidates. He was not given to regrets. He was the sort of person who savored even his rejection letters for the attention they suggested someone had paid to his submissions. Now he turned his attention to writing a blog, which he published in Persian and English, and to his work with Alternative Thinkers of Civil Society.

Through his civil society work, Omid started traveling abroad. He went to conferences, mainly in Europe. He visited nine countries in two years. He and his boss at the UNDP raised money from European foundations to publish books and train civil society leaders. He felt privileged to be doing something that he loved and that his elected leaders also desired and rewarded. Only later would Omid understand that he had placed himself in the crosshairs—that he had taken on exactly the project that hard-liners like Mortazavi most feared as the groundwork of a velvet revolution. Then he would imagine himself a soldier who'd advanced with his army only to turn around, too late, to see that everyone had retreated, leaving him in no-man's-land.

ROOZBEH STUDIED THE WALLS of his cell with his fingers. Slowly, systematically, he caressed them from the floor to as high as he could reach. He felt for carvings left by other prisoners; he felt for bumps and divots and bubbles in the paint. He had the uncallused, painstaking fingers of a blind man or a surgeon. There were no books, nor was there light to see or read by. He read the walls instead, and he committed them to memory, centimeter by centimeter.

Roozbeh's cell was on a different hall from Shahram's. He learned this from the prisoner who had been sent from Shahram's block to mop the hall in Roozbeh's. Near Roozbeh were a man from Mashhad, arrested for selling photocopies of law books at the legal bazaar, and the head of the Japanese yakuza organization in Iran, one Haj Ali, whose body was covered in tattoos and who was accused of a major role in trafficking heroin and cocaine. Haj Ali served only a week or so. Massoud Ghoreishi, the young webmaster of one of the reformist sites for which Roozbeh used to write, was also there, and would remain for ninety days because of his refusal to confess. The prisoners could communicate sometimes after two in the morning, when the guards were asleep, through the vents at the tops of their cells.

The interrogations had begun immediately after Roozbeh arrived. At first he faced only one question. The interrogators put a piece of paper before him and told him to disclose all of his illicit sexual relationships. Roozbeh wrote that he'd had none.

"Get up," the interrogator ordered.

Roozbeh stood. The interrogator slapped him.

"Are you lying to me?"

"I have no reason to lie."

The interrogator beat Roozbeh, tore up the paper, and ordered him to sit down and answer the same question again. Roozbeh answered in the same way.

"Are you being hardheaded?" the interrogator demanded.

"But I haven't had any!" Roozbeh exclaimed. "You have brought me here and are accusing me of having illicit relationships. What is the charge? What is the crime?"

The interrogator ordered Roozbeh to his feet, then punched his stomach and chest until he hit the wall. It was the first time anyone had laid a hand on Roozbeh in anger in his life. And the interrogation went on for nine hours that day. Sometimes his captor smashed his head into the table or the wall. Once he threatened Roozbeh with a baton, though he never used it. The second day of questioning and beatings lasted from eight in the morning until after midnight. After that, the schedule mellowed into a six-hour routine, four hours in the morning, two in the afternoon. Roozbeh told the time by his scant bathroom breaks.

On the third day, he accepted the charge, hoping that this would be the end of it. Sure, he said. He'd had a relationship with a woman. The interrogator placed in front of him a list of female journalists: "Which one?"

There was a plan, Roozbeh soon discerned, and the question was not whether he would play his part but when. The interrogator steered him toward a particular woman who had been a reporter at *Etemad* when Roozbeh was there. She, too, had covered the Zahra Kazemi affair. She was Roozbeh's friend. They went for walks sometimes, or out for coffee, to talk about work; once, Roozbeh accompanied her and her boyfriend on a trip to the Caspian, and they had all stayed with Roozbeh's family in Rasht. This woman was not his girlfriend. She was the mutual friend who had introduced him to his wife. But like Roozbeh, and unlike most unmarried Iranians, she lived independent of her parents in an apartment in Tehran. Roozbeh, Solmaz, and their friends often went to gatherings there.

His interrogators knew this. They also knew all kinds of things that weren't true. They presented Roozbeh with statements from other imprisoned journalists, alleging a relationship between him and his former colleague.

The female colleague had recently married and started a new life with her husband, away from journalism. Now Roozbeh might become the instrument of that life's destruction. The interrogators would force him to confess to things that would sow distrust in her marriage and add ammunition to her judicial file. Resistance met with blows. He allowed himself to believe the interrogator who reassured him that this confession would not be used against his friend.

Roozbeh must now describe their sexual acts, the interrogator said. In graphic detail.

"I was alone in a room with her," Roozbeh replied. But when he couldn't supply anything further, the interrogator dictated from his own lurid fantasies. In due time, Roozbeh wrote what he was told.

Of all the things that were done to him in prison, this would be among the most mortifying and the hardest to undo. When that female colleague was arrested, Mortazavi's deputy placed Roozbeh's confession before her, telling her she would most likely be stoned for what she'd done.

. . .

WHAT A MESS THEY'D LEFT. Solmaz sat, stricken, on one of the wicker couches in her ransacked home. She must have sat there for forty-five minutes after Roozbeh was taken away. Sometimes she cried. At other times she just stared and thought. She was not surprised, but she was in shock.

Don't talk to the international media, the man had said. But media attention was the only thing that ever helped. And she was a journalist. All her resources lay there. But then, she told herself, he'd said the international media. He hadn't mentioned the domestic media at all.

She pulled herself together and went to *Etemad.* Her mood was heavy, which puzzled her colleagues on the sports desk, but she didn't say a word to them. She picked up the phone and dialed an editor she knew at ILNA, a news agency close to the reformist government. The line was busy. It took her half an hour to reach the editor. "They took Roozbeh today," she told him when she got through. She felt the room around her go silent.

The minute the news went up online, her phone began to ring. Reporters were calling her for comment. She told a Radio Farda reporter she could not talk to the international media but to track the national news and follow its coverage.

She didn't go back to the apartment. It felt menacing now, claustrophobic and lonely. The first night she stayed with Roozbeh's uncle, who was often by her side; from the second night until she couldn't stand it any longer, she lived with her mother, whose apartment near Mehrabad Airport became a headquarters of sorts for the two families brought together by marriage just five months before and now stewing in a shared anxiety and helplessness that came to separate them more than it bonded them.

Solmaz understood from Shahram's family that the men had been taken to a police outpost on Motahari Street. For the first three days after Roozbeh's abduction, she reported there, demanding to see her husband. She planted herself near the entrance for hours on end so that no one coming or going could escape the sight of her. But no one seemed to know where

Roozbeh was. In the middle of the third day, whether out of pity or annoyance, a man finally spoke to her.

"Your husband isn't here," he said. "Go see the deputy prosecutor for Branch 9, in Mehrabad Airport." And so she did.

"You started very quickly," the deputy prosecutor remarked when Solmaz introduced herself.

She had—quickly and intensely. She'd done at least one interview a day, generating at least one news story with each call. She was determined to keep Roozbeh's name in the papers, to make it clear that he could not be made to quietly disappear. She'd gone to see Mohsen Rezaie, the former head of the Revolutionary Guard; Mehdi Karroubi, until recently the speaker of the parliament; and two reformist political parties. Nobody knew where Roozbeh was or how to shake him loose.

Nothing came of her first meeting with the deputy prosecutor, either. But at the end of the week she got a phone call. She'd relinquished her phone into the care of Roozbeh's uncle, and now he came charging up the stairs at *Etemad*, shouting for her. Roozbeh was on the line.

"Solmaz," Roozbeh told his wife, "you have to stop giving interviews."

Solmaz tried to hold him on the line. "Why do you say that?" she asked.

"I'm coming out soon," he replied blandly. "Don't worry."

"Okay," she said. She tried to keep it noncommittal. She would not say yes, she would not say no. His interrogators, she suspected then and would later learn for sure, were in the room with him, listening on the speakerphone.

For the next week she didn't give any interviews. But every day she compiled news items about Roozbeh, Shahram, and other bloggers who had by now been taken into custody, and she asked her colleagues at every newspaper she could think of to slip those paragraphs into stories that were related in any way at all. She placed three that week. And then she gave an interview.

"Roozbeh called a week ago," she told reporters. "He told me not to give interviews because he was going to be released soon. But he hasn't been released and he hasn't called. I'm worried about his health."

She'd vowed to make a nuisance of herself. She was surprisingly good at it. She had no political background, but some combination of ingenuity and obstinacy matched her to this fight. Still, when she consulted Shirin Ebadi, the human rights lawyer urged her to be cautious. Solmaz was a young journalist herself and could easily become a target. She'd be no good to Roozbeh in prison. Ebadi advised her to lower her profile and put Roozbeh's mother out front instead.

When the Mirebrahimis came down from Rasht, Solmaz brought them to the deputy prosecutor's office at the airport.

"Roozbeh is confessing," the deputy prosecutor informed them.

Roozbeh's parents looked shattered. Everything in Solmaz clenched. They sat before people who would only take pleasure in their pain.

"In that case," she broke in coldly, "you're done with Roozbeh. When will he be released?"

Mr. Mirebrahimi did not last long after that. Like Roozbeh, he was exquisitely sensitive but inexpressive, and he nourished himself on solitude. Solmaz could see from his face that he had withdrawn into a private world of pain. Solmaz and Mrs. Mirebrahimi bade him return to Rasht. He had never been away from home for so long. And so it was with Roozbeh's mother and his brother, Rasool, that Solmaz returned to the deputy prosecutor's office the day they were told they could have a meeting with Roozbeh.

They stood waiting a long time in the yard of the building in the airport complex before a car approached. Men dragged Roozbeh from the backseat with his hands cuffed. He had a full beard and he was very thin. He was wearing his wedding suit—the change of clothes the men who'd arrested him had yanked from his closet—which had been a size too big in the first place. Now he swam in it. Roozbeh's mother gasped.

Solmaz squeezed Mrs. Mirebrahimi's hand. "Don't," she said sharply. "Get ahold of yourself."

For a long moment they all stood awkwardly. Solmaz realized that everyone was waiting for her to embrace her husband. She did, and they sat down in the small room the deputy prosecutor's office reserved for prayer.

Mrs. Mirebrahimi broke the silence. "They say you are confessing," she said.

In an instant Solmaz understood the cruel efficacy of the forced confession. Roozbeh's mother was ashamed. Mortazavi's men wanted it that way. Moreover, the confession was sexual in nature, and Solmaz understood that everyone was worried about how she would take it. But Solmaz didn't care if Roozbeh had had relationships before her. She'd had boyfriends, too.

Roozbeh turned to Solmaz. "Don't pay attention to anything you hear until I come out," he told her.

Her composure was a ferocious thing.

"Do whatever it takes," she replied. "Do what you need to do."

THE INTERROGATOR GAVE HIS NAME as Keshavarz, but Roozbeh also once heard someone call him by another name: Fallah. Both words meant "farmer." He was one of those purged from the intelligence ministry. Now, Roozbeh believed, he was in almost daily communication with Mortazavi. Although he was not much taller than Roozbeh, he was thicker, with heavy, meaty hands. His face, when Roozbeh finally saw it, was unforgettable precisely because it was so ordinary.

All his life, Roozbeh had believed in a benevolent God who would guide him in times of darkness. But he felt no such presence in prison. Here there was only Keshavarz, or Fallah. This man held Roozbeh's very life in his unyielding grip. He could withhold or administer pain, connect or sever Roozbeh from the outside world, grant or deny him food, dignity, even air. He owned the truth and could deliver, extract, distort, or refuse it. He knew everything about Roozbeh, and Roozbeh could not escape his will. The interrogator was God. Roozbeh had come to prison a practicing Muslim. Now that he had seen this God, he resolved never to pray again.

Keshavarz wanted personal information about Roozbeh's friends and colleagues. Under the Islamic Republic's draconian moral code, nearly every Iranian was guilty of something that could carry a prison sentence: extramarital sex, drinking, even shaking hands with members of the opposite sex. What had begun as a religious imperative had become little more than a system of universal blackmail. The right information could afford an interrogator a good deal of leverage over a political prisoner. The interrogator would show it to the person confessed against, in the handwriting of the person from whom it had been obtained. Roozbeh knew because this had happened to him. It had the effect of making the prisoner feel trapped and alone, like there was no point in resisting and no one he could trust. And then, once he had confessed against his own friends and lovers, colleagues and employers, he would have nowhere to turn but to God.

Once he had broken, Roozbeh felt, for a time, at peace. He was doing the only thing there was to do. To relax was to survive, just as it was for a person falling from a great height: the tenser the body, the more likely it would shatter. He cooperated. He would hold the interrogator's trust until he didn't have to anymore, maybe when he went to trial. He gave away secrets he knew, and some he didn't. There were some small dignities he kept in reserve. He never cried. He was always calm. And he would not ask for anything. He would not ask to use the bathroom or to walk in the cramped prison yard. He did not ask to speak to his family. He tried to forget his wife.

Keshavarz put Roozbeh's sexual confession aside. The beatings stopped. But business had only just begun. The interrogator informed Roozbeh that he was likely to spend the next twenty years in prison, given the seriousness of his charges. Roozbeh believed him.

When the interrogators wanted more information about another prisoner, they put him in Roozbeh's cell for the night and questioned Roozbeh in the morning. Roozbeh told them the prisoner was not an important person. When the interrogators had a warrant for the arrest of someone new, they brought the warrant to Roozbeh and asked him: What did he know about, say, Omid Memarian? As it happened, Roozbeh knew very little. But when they came for information about a former colleague named Javad Gholam-Tamimi, and Roozbeh offered an account of Javad's work history, Keshavarz was impatient. He wanted to link Javad to Reza Pahlavi, the exiled son of the deposed shah. When Roozbeh demurred, the interrogator showed him a warrant for Solmaz's arrest. Roozbeh could send either his colleague or his wife to prison. Javad Gholam-Tamimi emerged from his first interrogation screaming curses at Roozbeh.

One day Keshavarz presented Roozbeh with something to read. It was an editorial called "The Spider's House," published in the newspaper *Kayhan*, which was associated with the Supreme Leader. In it, Hossein Shariatmadari, the paper's ultra-hardline managing editor, claimed to have uncovered a network of Iranians working for the CIA. Some twenty-three Iranian expatriates in Europe and North America were in league with the American spy agency, Shariatmadari alleged, naming names. He linked these expats with seven prominent reformists inside Iran, among them Khatami's vice president Mohammad Ali Abtahi; the parliamentary deputy Behzad Nabavi; deputy interior minister Mostafa Tajzadeh; and former hostage taker Mohsen Mirdamadi. But the crucial node connecting the seven to the twenty-three was a web of thirteen young, little-known Internet journalists who were charged with spreading propaganda inside Iran and to the West. Among these pawns of international intrigue were "Roozbeh M.," "Shahram R.," and "Omid M." Shariatmadari recommended rolling up the network by arresting all thirteen of the young people he named.

For days, Roozbeh was instructed to write confessions addressing all the charges against him, but to do so in a manner that would confirm the hypothesis of "The Spider's House." Apart from his nonpolitical charges (engaging in an illicit affair, drinking alcohol, and shaking hands with women), he stood accused of acting against national security, participating in illegal demonstrations, belonging to illegal organizations, insulting the Supreme Leader, disturbing the public mind by conducting interviews with the antirevolutionary media, and disseminating propaganda against the regime. His interrogator supplied him with notes to prompt his writings. One piece of evidence used against him was the call Payam Fazlinejad had made from Darband to the defector in Turkey.

Roozbeh told himself that he would cooperate in prison and then renounce his confessions when he got out, as Ali Afshari had done. Many of the charges were wildly improbable to anyone who knew him. Roozbeh had never attended a demonstration, legal or illegal; he belonged to no organizations; and his published work located him within the reformist camp, which was after all the governing faction. But Roozbeh confessed not only to attending demonstrations but to being their primary organizer.

One day Roozbeh learned, to his pleasure, that Shirin Ebadi had agreed to take his case. But when the retainer agreement arrived in prison for Roozbeh's signature, it came with a note from Mortazavi: Roozbeh was to refuse to sign the agreement, Mortazavi instructed, or five years would be added to his sentence. Ebadi, according to the prosecutor, was an agent of Israel. Roozbeh should declare that he considered her incompetent and would not allow himself to be used by her. He was given a text to copy in his own hand. It was full of spelling errors. Roozbeh copied it letter for letter, hoping that the uncharacteristic illiteracy of his note—so many elementary spelling errors, from a newspaper editor?—would make it an object of interest to the press.

THINGS STARTED TO GO WRONG for Omid Memarian at the very end of September. He was invited to speak at the Woodrow Wilson Center in Washington, D.C., but when he went to board his U.S.-bound flight in Frankfurt, two police officers stopped him cold. His name was on the no-fly list. Omid made an unlikely international terrorist. He flashed his press card. Mistakes happened all the time, the officers told him, but there was no way he could complete his journey.

Omid returned to Tehran. Ten days later, four armed officers came for him at work. They threw him to the floor of a van, covered him with a blanket, and held him down with a foot to his neck. In his cell at the secret prison, the light always blazed and other prisoners' screams reached him through the vent near the ceiling. Sometimes Omid imagined that he was in a grave and that people were walking over him. He felt himself dislocated in time. Once he asked a prison guard the hour, and the guard replied, "Who cares what time it is?" But it was six o'clock, the guard informed him. When Omid thought six or seven hours had passed, he asked again. It was seven. After five days Omid thought he'd been in prison for two months. Time, he understood now, had been a map of mental space. Now he had no map, no bearings, no notion of what the hours even meant.

Prisoners, including the Japanese yakuza boss and other criminals as well as young journalists, used the bathroom in groups of four, but there was no door on the toilet stall. They were forced to defecate in view of one another. There was a camera in the shower. Omid refused to undress before it until he could no longer stand his own smell, sixteen days into his detention. Then he broke down in sobs. He could only imagine who was watching this footage, to what end. For a year even after he was released, he could not bear to touch his own body to wash.

Day and night, Omid could hear the guards screaming and laughing at him and his fellow inmates. "Come out, animal!" they would taunt a prisoner when they opened his cell for a trip to the bathroom or the interrogation chamber. Once Omid saw another prisoner in the bathroom whose pants were caked with blood and his foot broken. He was an ordinary guy from the south of Tehran, imprisoned for getting into a fight with a Basiji.

Interrogators told Omid he was a traitor, that he would never be released. They ordered him to write a list of the "shit" he'd been up to in recent years, then pounded his head into the wall when his list included nothing illegal. Once they kicked his stomach until he vomited. Nausea was his resting state, prison food churning on anxiety. One day the interrogators demanded he confess about his trip to the United States. They knew all about it already, they told him. Others had confessed against him; they had copies of his speeches and photographs of his meetings with royalists in Washington. The file was a hundred pages long.

"I never went there!" Omid protested. "I couldn't! I'm on the no-fly list, like all you gentlemen!"

Keshavarz, or Fallah, was a sick person, Omid sensed, given to ecstasies of violence, periods when he was lost to Omid even as he pummeled him with fists or feet. On one occasion Omid dodged a kick and Keshavarz's foot landed hard on a chair. The interrogator flew into a rage, flattening Omid to the wall. Omid managed to open the interrogation room door. "Leave me alone!" he screamed. "Stop it!" But there were only other prisoners to hear him. Maybe Omid would like to talk to someone who could give him some advice on confessing, Keshavarz said when Omid was on the verge of breaking.

He called on Shahram. Shahram agreed to talk to Omid, but not in the interrogation room. He would see him in the prison yard. Keshavarz agreed.

SHAHRAM HAD NEVER MET OMID before prison, but he'd heard of him. And he could see now that Omid was very upset and shaken. The pressure was always worst in the first two to three weeks, Shahram knew. His own experience had been altogether more intense than he had imagined even from researching "The Miracle Room." He saw an opportunity not only to help Omid but to forge a relationship that could supply a lifeline to both of them.

Shahram understood that the only way to earn trust was to give it. And so he took a chance. He gave Omid advice that Omid would later say changed his life. But it was not only the advice that had this effect. Shahram looked into Omid's eyes like a brother. Omid did not relax into that warmth right away, but once he decided to, he found in Shahram a deep reservoir of decency and strength.

"There are secrets you are keeping, people you want to protect," Shahram told Omid the first time they met in the prison yard. It was true: Omid had seen colleagues go to parties and drink alcohol. He'd had relationships of his own with women, and he knew personal secrets that could be used to hurt people. He didn't want to give any of this away. "You need to hold one story to yourself and make up another story for the interrogators," Shahram advised. "Otherwise, you will tell them everything."

Shahram told Omid to build a wall around the personal secrets he knew, his own and other people's. If he gave those things away, he would never get them back. He should not talk about contacts in foreign countries, lest he be charged with espionage. He should not confess against his friends or colleagues. But he had to give away something, to at least appear to cooperate. To the extent it was possible, he should direct his confessions against people he couldn't hurt, either because they were dead or because they were very famous.

Omid cleaved to this advice. He sealed away what he knew about people's personal lives. To the extent he was able, he would not supply the anvil on which others were broken, and he would not allow his tormentors to sever the relationships that mattered most in his life. Still, he confessed.

For his sexual confession, he made up names of women who did not exist. Keshavarz circled him, caressing his cheek or his arm suggestively as he pressed him for graphic detail. How did the sexual encounters begin? Did he use pornography? Who brought the condom? Did she open her mouth like so? Omid was shaking with fear and disgust, sweating through his clothes. He did not disclose this kind of detail to his closest friends. The fifty-five-year-old bearded, supposedly pious interrogator liked to call Omid "pretty boy," and he seemed quite possibly to be stroking himself through the pocket of his pants.

Omid would never know for sure whether the sexual violation and the lack of physical privacy served his wardens' predilections, or whether they were calculated to humiliate Muslim men raised in a culture that observed strict boundaries around the body and erotic life. Maybe both were true. At one point Keshavarz presented Omid with a picture of Jennifer Lopez he'd found on Omid's computer. Who was she? Had Omid had sexual relations with her?

Omid's political confessions, like Roozbeh's, were to follow the template of "The Spider's House." Omid was told to confess that under the direction of reformists like Mostafa Tajzadeh and Behzad Nabavi, he had written articles and blogposts whose aim was to "blacken the face" of the Islamic regime and to bring about a velvet revolution. For the reformists planned to destroy Islamic society within fifteen years, and they had tasked Omid with increasing the influence of Western culture and reporting back to them about any "revolutionary resistance" that might stand in the way.

In exchange for Omid's cooperation, the reformists paid for his foreign travels.

Omid's objections to this narrative—that he had never met or barely knew the politicians in question, that his writings expressed his own views, that his foreign travels were paid through transparent channels, including the newspapers he worked for and the organizers of the conferences he attended—quickly collapsed. Keshavarz made sure Omid understood that if he did not confess to these charges, he would face much more serious ones, like espionage. The confessions Omid signed contained maddening kernels of truth. He had visited foreign countries, interviewed foreign dignitaries, and spoken with foreign journalists in the course of his work, and he had written about these encounters. Now he was to explain that he'd done these things in order to inflate these foreigners' status in Iranian society in the service of the CIA plot.

Omid came to believe that he and the other bloggers—for by now there were twenty of them in detention—were pawns in a battle between two parts of the Iranian intelligence establishment. Hajjarian's held that to save the regime required reforming it; the late Saeed Emami's believed that opposition had to be violently eliminated. The two groups shared a common origin in the bloody security apparatus of the Khomeini era. Keshavarz claimed to have personally broken the most famous Tudeh leaders in the 1980s. "We smashed Ali Afshari's head in," he boasted as well. But Omid should have no illusion about his allies' past.

"*We* didn't make these secret prisons for you," Keshavarz jeered at him. "This was your friends—your reformist friends have built these places."

Even so, Omid was rarely alone in his mind and never imagined himself alone in the world. The reformists were his friends and colleagues. He was sure they would support him when he got out and told them what he'd endured and what danger they, too, clearly faced.

BRANCH 9 OF THE PROSECUTOR'S OFFICE, at Mehrabad Airport, was a dead end, Solmaz decided. The deputy prosecutor had no real power. She needed to talk to Mortazavi himself. But the chief prosecutor's reputation was monstrous; the Zahra Kazemi affair had sealed it. A fellow journalist told Solmaz that if she met Mortazavi, he would hypnotize her with his eyes and she would give up all the information he desired. No young journalist met the prosecutor if he or she could avoid it. Solmaz didn't think she could avoid it much longer. She screwed up her courage and left Mortazavi a message.

When he called her back, it was evening, and she was walking across an empty expanse near her mother's home. The space was quiet, the air chilled. "I got your message," Mortazavi informed her.

"I called to follow my husband's case," Solmaz explained. "I'd like to know when he will be released."

"How do I know that you're his wife?" Mortazavi countered.

Before she could stop herself, Solmaz snapped at him. "I don't think anyone else would go to this much trouble."

She wished she could rescind the words the moment they escaped her. Her tone was all wrong. She had controlled her temper with everyone else, only to lose it with the most dangerous and powerful figure of all.

She listened fearfully to the dead air that followed. Finally, Mortazavi said, "Meet me tomorrow."

Her stomach dropped. What had she done? She burst into her mother's apartment and told the relatives assembled there about the call.

Roozbeh's uncle laughed. "Why did you say that?"

"I don't know," said Solmaz miserably. "He asked me a stupid question."

The prosecutor's office reminded her of an aquarium. Upstairs, she passed through a security door to a room with a glass wall. On the other side of that wall was the reception area. Solmaz had arrived with her mother, who was determined not to leave her daughter alone in a room with Mortazavi, at 8:30 in the morning. By afternoon they still had not seen the prosecutor. Solmaz began to wonder if Mortazavi had called her there just to keep her idle and waste her day.

She surveyed the reception area. Surely there was a camera somewhere. When she spotted one in a corner near the ceiling, she contorted herself to stare directly into it fixedly. She stared so awkwardly and long that other people in the waiting room were compelled to turn and look where she was looking. After half an hour of this, the receptionist ushered her and her mother in to see the prosecutor.

Mortazavi did not stand up when they entered the room. But he directed them to sit, in a tone of calculated warmth.

"You're an active lady," he told Solmaz.

She studied his face. He was not happy to see her, she understood. But he was curious. She was startled to see how short he was. Across the room from his desk was a small television set that displayed the feed from the waiting room.

"I want my husband back," she replied. "He's innocent."

"You're mistaken," Mortazavi said. "He's not innocent. He hasn't told you everything."

"I don't care what he did before our marriage," Solmaz replied. "I don't believe he has committed any crime."

"I would recommend you go and live your life," Mortazavi told her. "Remarry. You're a young, beautiful woman. Your husband will be in prison for twenty years."

Solmaz understood that she had just one card to play. Her record was clean, and she was a bereft new bride. "We married just five months ago," Solmaz entreated. "If you release Roozbeh, I'll take care of him. I'll make sure he doesn't commit any crime against the system." She had heard of wives playing this role.

But Mortazavi didn't seem interested in anything she had to offer. His manner was confident, almost breezy. "Roozbeh isn't worth anything to us," he told her dismissively at one point. She'd remember that.

She left, seemingly with nothing, but with the feeling that she'd gotten somewhere at last. She had the beginning of a relationship with Mortazavi, and she would thrash it for all it was worth.

She became a fixture in the prosecutor's waiting room. Each time, she'd wait an hour or two, and then she'd turn to face the surveillance camera until he let her in. She felt strangely unafraid.

"You talk back a lot," Mortazavi observed once. "You seem to be hallucinating about where you are. More important people than you break down here. Akbar Ganji's wife comes here to plead with me for her husband's life."

Solmaz saw Ganji's wife in the waiting room on one of her visits. Aware of the surveillance camera, Solmaz kept her distance. Mrs. Ganji was admitted to the prosecutor's chambers first. From within, Solmaz could hear her reading Mortazavi the riot act at the top of her lungs. Solmaz smiled to herself.

Between visits to the prosecutor's office, Solmaz was frantically active. She let Roozbeh's family members talk to the press, while she spent most of every day on the phone to powerful people who might use their weight to press for Roozbeh's release. Roozbeh had come into the crosshairs on account of his association, however tenuous, with reformist figures like Mostafa Tajzadeh and Behzad Nabavi, she reasoned. These people were far more powerful than Roozbeh was. Surely the reformists could keep Mortazavi's phone ringing with requests for Roozbeh's release. Every day, Solmaz would call politicians' offices and request that they call Mortazavi. Then she'd call back, again and again, to inquire if they'd done so. She didn't care if she annoyed them; she was good at that, and it had its uses. But the experience embittered her. Ebrahim Asgharzadeh, for whom Roozbeh had worked, even supporting his brief and ill-fated campaign for president in 2001, would not take Solmaz's calls or return her messages. Mostafa Tajzadeh did not call for weeks, until he heard that Solmaz had been complaining. When he did get in touch, he pointed out that a call from him might not have helped her situation, which was undoubtedly true.

Only two politicians were helpful, and she would never forget them. Mehdi Karroubi, the onetime radical cleric who was now a centrist reformist in the parliament, took her calls and responded promptly through his son, who also updated her regularly on Karroubi's actions on Roozbeh's behalf. And Khatami's vice president Mohammad Ali Abtahi, who wrote a popular blog and was himself named in "The Spider's House," was sympathetic enough to check in with her from time to time, even texting her jokes at night to cheer her up.

On her second or third visit to Mortazavi, the prosecutor asked something of Solmaz. She could help Roozbeh, he told her, if she would just sign a little confession of her own. She'd need to write a letter about Mostafa Tajzadeh, Behzad Nabavi, and Emadeddin Baghi, a sociologist who was the editor of *Jomhuriat* and who had been active in exposing the serial killings. Solmaz should allege that these three men had misused young, naïve journalists in the pursuit of their own ambitions and that they had forced Roozbeh to spread lies about the regime.

"I don't know these people," Solmaz protested. "If you're angry with them, why have you arrested Roozbeh instead?"

"Their time will come," Mortazavi replied darkly.

Solmaz was not sentimental. As she understood it, she and Roozbeh were exposed and alone and in danger, paying the price for the ambitions of more important men who did not rise to their defense. She would sign what she needed to sign to get Roozbeh out of prison. But even when she'd resolved to do it, she could not make the pen move on the paper the prosecutor placed before her.

"I've read your open letters about your husband's case," Mortazavi prompted her. "You're a writer. Write this." In the end he dictated her confession word for word.

ONE DAY IN NOVEMBER, when Roozbeh had been in detention more than forty days, he and Shahram were thrown into a single cell no bigger than their solitary ones. They understood they'd been reunited in the hope that they would incriminate themselves in conversation. Instead they traded stories and recounted memories from better times. At night Roozbeh sang for Shahram, just as he had promised so long before in jest.

After ten days they were transferred, together with Omid and Javad Gholam-Tamimi, to Evin Prison. That day seventeen others associated with their case—now known as "the bloggers' file," although it included civil society activists as well as journalists—were released.

Evin was a vast improvement on the secret prison. The food was incomparably better. The guards were ordinary working people who showed them no malice. And Roozbeh, Omid, and Shahram were no longer in solitary confinement. Instead they shared a suite composed of two solitary cells with a shower and a kitchenette. These suites, on the fourth floor of Evin's Section 9, were the prison's showpieces when international human rights groups came calling. They also happened to sit on death row. The halls echoed with violence, and in the early mornings the cellmates could hear the condemned being led to their executions.

A cell down the hall from theirs belonged to a notorious serial killer named Mohammad Bijeh. Just twenty-four years old, Bijeh had been convicted of murdering and raping some seventeen boys between the ages of eight and fifteen, as well as three adults. He and his accomplice lured their victims to the desert south of Tehran, where they killed them by poisoning them or striking their heads with heavy stones before raping them and burying them in shallow graves.

Omid had an idea. Could he interview Bijeh? he asked a prison guard. He imagined publishing an article after his release, maybe on the occasion of Bijeh's execution. No one would have access to the killer any later than he. His cellmates teased him: even in prison, that was Omid, always looking for his next big chance. Sure, the guard told Omid. Just so long as he didn't mind sharing Bijeh's cell for the night. Omid thought better of it.

In their shared confinement, Roozbeh, Shahram, Javad, and Omid fought bitterly over who had revealed what about whom and why. The first hours were an ugly catharsis. The "Spider's House" editorial, by all appearances, was little more than Shahram's coerced prison confession, twisted, distorted, and layered with additional malign untruths. Omid was uncomfortable sharing a cell with Roozbeh, who he felt had given away too much, too easily, delivering himself into the interrogators' hands. As Roozbeh understood it, they had all agreed to cooperate until their release. There was little point in making a show of struggle as they did so. But when the recriminations were spent, the cellmates could also confer. Their cases, they understood, were linked. Javad had been charged with espionage. They understood that he had been grouped with them to lend gravity to the case file. All of them had the sense that they had been arrested opportunistically, that they had been interrogated as a kind of fishing expedition, and now they were being used to set up known targets, like Tajzadeh and Nabavi.

The weeks they'd spent in the secret prison—Shahram had been there almost three months, Roozbeh two, and Omid a little less—had scarred their psyches, and every day they spent in prison compounded the damage. The most important thing, they agreed, was to get out. Then they could follow Ali Afshari's example and renounce their confessions. For now, they would do what was necessary to be released.

They spent their time in Evin writing and rewriting their confessions for Keshavarz, who was an exacting editor. Omid was to specifically incriminate Nabavi, Tajzadeh, and two other reformist figures as he confessed to taking money and orders from them in order to blacken the image of the Islamic Republic. He was also to smear NGO activists. Shahram was to incriminate poet and writer friends who were already dead and then to confess to having sought to inflate his own reputation by association with such people. Roozbeh assumed responsibility for everything from street demonstrations to secret scheming sessions with reformist conspirators.

They worked slowly and meticulously, for they'd noticed that Keshavarz left them alone as long as they were busy writing. And then there were the rehearsals. Each in turn, but never together, they sat in the office of the prison director, which had been staged with plants and a pitcher of orange juice, and recited their confessions into the camera.

Shahram noted that this process began only after his visible bruises had healed. But for the most part, the bloggers' bruises were not visible to begin with. Theirs had been a classic program of white torture—battery afflicting the body far less than the soul.

THE CHIEF JUSTICE OF IRAN, Ayatollah Mahmoud Hashemi Shahroudi, was an Iraqi-born cleric with a relatively moderate temperament. He had ostensibly appointed Mortazavi to his post, but it would be alleged that he tried several times to fire Mortazavi, only to find that the prosecutor's position was protected by forces he could not challenge. Ayatollah Shahroudi held monthly public meetings where thousands of ordinary people could petition for his ear. They filed past him, making their pitches either to a subordinate or to the chief justice himself. Solmaz decided that she needed to be one of them and that she needed to speak to the ayatollah personally.

She got permission to attend the public meeting the same way she seemed to be getting everything lately: through insistence verging on harassment. She'd gone to the judiciary's spokesman's office with a letter in hand making her request. The spokesman took the letter, tucked it away, and hurried upstairs, saying he'd see to it. Solmaz called to him from the bottom of the stairs: "I'll wait right here until you come back with my permission." It was, she understood, her last shot. She got what she came for.

Solmaz liked Ayatollah Shahroudi instantly. Among the clerics there were some who exuded ambition, severity, even cruelty, but there were others who seemed fully men of the cloth, sincere in their religion and committed to the vision of justice they found there. Shahroudi, Solmaz felt, was among the latter. He was a black-turbaned cleric in his sixties, with a long white beard and an easy smile. Solmaz handed him her letter and pleaded her case as swiftly as she could. She was a young newlywed who wanted her husband, whom she believed innocent, home for Eid. Moreover, she understood that her husband's keepers had broken a law Shahroudi himself had passed, prohibiting blindfolding and handcuffing in the prisons, as well as interrogations lasting more than forty-eight hours. "I'm a journalist," she appealed to him. "I know what it means to break your law."

Ayatollah Shahroudi told her to wait while his people prepared a letter. When she left the public meeting, she clasped a sealed envelope, the seal stamped by the judiciary. She was to bring the letter to Mortazavi. But Solmaz knew better than to bring the prosecutor anything she had not read herself. That night she and a friend took turns holding the envelope to the light, trying to discern what was typed on the folded sheet within. It took them three hours and a world of patience to make out the words and transcribe them to Solmaz's notebook. When they finished, they were ecstatic. It was an order for Roozbeh's release on bail.

Solmaz returned to Mortazavi's office in the morning. "I have my husband's release order," she told the prosecutor's assistant. "Please deliver it to Mr. Mortazavi."

And then she sat and waited. She didn't look at the camera this time. She figured Mortazavi would need a little time to compose himself. She felt well prepared. She knew she'd need bail for Roozbeh, and she'd persuaded a journalist friend to sign over the deed to some property worth eight million tomans. Solmaz had the paperwork in her bag.

"You lied to my assistant," Mortazavi said when she entered. "Mr. Shahroudi didn't order your husband's release. He only asked me to cooperate."

Solmaz took out her notebook and read Mortazavi the transcript of the letter as though she had been given a copy of it herself.

"Sit down," he said at length. "Let's talk about bail."

Solmaz showed him the deed to her friend's property. He repeated the name of her friend slowly, with interest.

"But this will not be enough," he told her. "Roozbeh's bail is fifty million tomans."

"I thought you said Roozbeh wasn't worth anything to you," said Solmaz, furious. Fifty million tomans—more than $20,000—was more than twice the bail on which other bloggers had been released.

"He's not worth anything," Mortazavi affirmed. "But that is his bail."

No one in either Roozbeh's or Solmaz's family had property worth fifty million tomans. Solmaz's parents' homes had been mortgaged; Roozbeh's parents rented theirs. There was not a relative Solmaz could think of with anything close. What was worse, she had already told Roozbeh that she'd secured his release. Now he was waiting in prison, with no way of understanding that she was scrambling to come up with the money.

Solmaz got back on the phone. She left messages for Asgharzadeh, but he didn't return them. When at last she successfully connived to get him on the line, she was in no mood to be polite. Could he help with Roozbeh's bail?

Asgharzadeh said he'd work on it. Solmaz knew he wouldn't. To a reformist newspaper editor, Solmaz was even less deferential. She had gone begging to all her family members, she told him. Was Roozbeh in prison because of her family members? You reformists, she said, are all in one party, advancing one agenda against the conservatives. Surely you should help one another when one of you becomes a target of those conservatives. Young journalists did everything for the reformists and assumed all the risks.

At length she reached out to Roozbeh's mother. Wasn't there a family member, Solmaz recalled, who'd stayed with them for a year before buying her own place? To ask that relative for the bail would not be easy, but at least she owed them something. She was their best and only shot.

Solmaz got the deed to that relative's home, but it was worth only 30 million tomans. This was, she understood, the very best their two families could do. She would have to finesse the rest. And so she went to see Mortazavi with the 30-million-toman deed in hand and a gambit born of desperation and fantasy.

"Something has happened that you should know about," Solmaz informed the prosecutor gravely. She'd promised him that she would look after Roozbeh and keep him away from the pernicious influence of Nabavi, Tajzadeh, and Baghi, she reminded Mortazavi. But now Tajzadeh and Baghi had contacted her. They'd heard she was short on the bail and they were offering to make up the difference.

"I'll have to accept it," Solmaz said, doing her best to play the ingenue. "But it's a big debt, and if they ask us for anything, we'll owe them. I don't see how I can keep Roozbeh away from them after this."

This scheme was so crazy, she figured, it just might work. And it did. With a stroke of his pen, the prosecutor reduced the bail.

That night Solmaz waited outside her mother's apartment. The families of prisoners knew the routine: Evin released prisoners at nine at night. If your loved one was not home by ten, it was not his day. But Solmaz had posted bail. Surely Roozbeh was just briefly delayed. Until midnight she sat outside in the cold. Then she went to bed, feeling truly hopeless for the first time.

. . .

MORTAZAVI AND HIS MEN were scrambling, Roozbeh would later understand. They'd been ordered to release him, but they were determined not to do so without getting what they'd come for. Keshavarz presented the cellmates with a plan. They would be freed on bail under the condition that they publish confession letters *after* their release, bringing their letters personally, as allegedly free men, to their media contacts.

All along, they had imagined that their confessions would be aired while they were still in prison and clearly under duress. Then they would renounce everything upon their release. This expectation had sustained them. But Mortazavi was well ahead of them. Release from prison, Roozbeh understood now, would be something short of freedom. He would emerge less like Ali Afshari than like Payam Fazlinejad.

Roozbeh was to go first. He was freed with the understanding that only when he'd published a confession letter would the second of his cellmates be released. On publication of the second prisoner's letter, the third would be released, and so on. Roozbeh would later describe this as a hostage situation. Shahram, Omid, and Javad were his collateral.

He walked out of Evin Prison the night of November 26. He searched the crowd at the gate for a familiar face. No one had known to come for him. He had only the clothes on his back and a long way to go, from the northern hills near Darakeh to the edge of the southern plain at Mehrabad. He hailed a taxi, hoping someone would be home to pay for it on the other end. It was 9:45 p.m. when he rang the doorbell of the apartment near the airport. Solmaz dashed outside barefoot when she realized who was there. They embraced on the steps. Roozbeh, Solmaz noticed, was clean and groomed, unlike when she'd seen him at the deputy prosecutor's office. She clasped him tightly, jubilant, convinced that at last their ordeal had come to an end.

Friends and relatives started arriving almost immediately. By midnight, twenty or thirty people had come to Solmaz's mother's apartment, including some of the bloggers who'd been released when Roozbeh went to Evin. Roozbeh received a hero's welcome, and he cringed from it inside. He was trapped in a vise that he did not dare mention. The confession letter, when he published it by his own hand, would humiliate and incriminate him; it would point a finger at others and announce him as a collaborator. What would all these people think of him then? He told himself that his friends in prison were on his conscience. If he talked about the confession letter, if he told anyone at that night's gathering that he was still under pressure, someone, he imagined, might go to the prosecutor and reveal his double game. Roozbeh had left prison, but he brought with him his all-seeing God.

The next morning the first phone call came. Roozbeh was to meet Keshavarz in Azadi Square, not far from where he was staying with his in-laws. He took Solmaz into his confidence then, explaining the unfinished business before him. She studied her husband. He had always been remote, but now he seemed lost to her, imprisoned still in some unknowable place, his passivity like the zip cuffs that tightened when he struggled against them. She would have to fortify his will, she saw.

Solmaz went with Roozbeh to Azadi Square. She borrowed a digital voice recorder from a friend and slipped it into Roozbeh's breast pocket. He only had to switch it on and leave it there, she told him. She didn't know how or when or where, but she felt certain this evidence of coercion would be useful one day.

Keshavarz greeted Solmaz as though he'd known her all along. But he needed to talk to Roozbeh alone, he told her, and he took Roozbeh into his car while Solmaz waited on the street.

Had Roozbeh written the letter for publication yet? the interrogator demanded. Roozbeh pleaded for time. He was released only the night before; he hadn't even been to Rasht to see his parents. But Omid, Shahram, and Javad were waiting, Keshavarz objected. He handed Roozbeh a pencil and paper and dictated a list of the subjects Mortazavi wanted him to address. Roozbeh was to write the letter that afternoon, give a copy to Keshavarz, and then publish it before leaving for Rasht.

Roozbeh faxed the letter to ISNA and ILNA, two government news agencies controlled by reformists, just before he and Solmaz left for Rasht.

He knew that neither network would publish a forced confession, but he'd gone through the motions.

Three days later Keshavarz reached Roozbeh on Solmaz's cell phone. The interrogator was furious. Roozbeh hadn't published his confession! His friends were still waiting for him in prison! Roozbeh protested that he'd sent the letter to two agencies. It wasn't his fault they hadn't printed it. Mortazavi was not happy, the interrogator insisted. Roozbeh should come back to Tehran, publish the letter, and report to the prosecutor's office. Roozbeh and Solmaz were on their way back to the capital when a friend called to tell them that a letter had already appeared under Roozbeh's name in Fars News, the media organ of the Revolutionary Guard. Mortazavi had faxed the confession himself.

After that, the prosecutor called the newspapers where Roozbeh had worked and ordered their editors to publish the confession in full, under lurid headlines: "Exposed!," "The Confessions of a Reformist Journalist," and "Roozbeh Mirebrahimi Reveals Secret Group in Reformist Movement." The letter read, in part:

> I, Roozbeh Mirebrahimi, have been one of the accused in connection with the file of internet sites. . . . During the past few years I and others like me had fallen into the hands of those whose only strategy was to vouchsafe their own political interests, and who made use of people like me in order to implement their evil projects. . . . I strongly attacked various pillars of the system, especially the judiciary, by making various allegations against them, and I have portrayed them as being against human rights. . . .
>
> During the past few years, it was an undeniable fact that there existed . . . a frightful network, one end of which was inside the country and the other end existed beyond the borders. . . . Due to my weakness, I also joined that network. . . . The involvement of some organizations and individuals from outside the country for supporting

individuals such as me is shameful, because people like me have trampled upon the laws of this country and have committed an offence. . . .

The claim that I was in solitary confinement is not true about me under any circumstances. Throughout the period of my detention I experienced nothing but kindness and respect from those who were dealing with us. Here, I wish to express my gratitude for the kindness of those individuals and to pray to God Almighty for their success and well-being.

I was detained in Evin prison, and I was released from that prison too and returned to the warm embrace of my family. . . .

With best wishes for the glory and steadfastness of all true servants of the people.

Roozbeh Mirebrahimi,
November 26, 2004

OMID AND SHAHRAM NEVER BELIEVED that their release depended on Roozbeh's confession. The interrogators told lies and made false promises as a matter of course. Omid thought that if Roozbeh recanted and appealed to the reformists for help, all of their confessions would be discredited before they published them, and the pressure might redound to Mortazavi instead. But none of the cellmates trusted Roozbeh enough to offer him this advice. Suppose Roozbeh reported to Keshavarz that the others were not sufficiently repentant? Omid, for one, could hardly see past his cellmate's preternatural calm to know where, if anywhere, Roozbeh's outward compliance ended and inner refusal began.

Omid never doubted that help was forthcoming. The journalists' union was organizing a sit-in on the bloggers' behalf. Even the European Union was pressing for the bloggers' release. Still, the prosecutor's office stalled. For nearly a week after Roozbeh was released, Shahram and Omid fielded new threats. Shahram learned that his younger brother, Bahram, had been arrested. Keshavarz told Omid that his brother would be next.

Finally, Evin's warden came to see Omid, Shahram, and Javad in their cell. "Why are you still here?" he said abruptly when he walked in. Within thirty minutes, Omid and Shahram were released, with orders to publish their confession letters right away. Javad would stay behind.

Keshavarz took the time to communicate one last warning to Shahram. "There are devils waiting for you outside," he said. "And they want you to speak against us again. Be careful. You have three bouquets of flowers." Shahram understood that Keshavarz was talking about his children. "Those three bouquets are your bail."

Shahram never returned to the apartment in Eskandari, even though all his belongings were there. Instead he resolved to go to Rasht as soon as possible. They needed a strategy, Shahram urged Omid. They should make themselves as difficult as possible for their tormentors to reach. Shahram had no cell phone; Omid ignored blocked calls on his. And they should reach out to everyone they trusted, inside or outside the country, to explain what had happened to them in prison. Shahram wrote to Shirin Ebadi, called friends who reported on Iran from outside the country, and alerted his colleagues and higher-ups at *Etemad*. His case, he knew, was linked to the work he'd done on the serial murders. His very life was at risk. He came to Tehran as infrequently as he could, but that was still not infrequent enough.

Omid returned to his family's apartment in Lavizan. He had always been an open person, expressive and forthcoming, given easily to intimacy, not least with his parents. Now he wrestled with memories he couldn't share and anxieties he couldn't explain. He felt humiliated and angry, and he cried a lot. Sometimes when he was alone in his room, crying, he could hear his mother crying just outside his door.

But to reach out was natural to Omid even now. He wrote to two Iranian journalists living abroad, explaining the ordeal he had just endured. He did it in his own name, but Shahram persuaded him to include his and Roozbeh's as well. Then Omid took a deep breath and sought out everyone he could think of whom he'd named in his confessions, warning them and apologizing, even when it meant facing their anger.

Through a colleague in the NGO world, Omid obtained the e-mail address of a researcher at Human Rights Watch in New York. He set up an alternative e-mail account and wrote a long letter to the international watchdog group detailing the bloggers' treatment in prison. Human Rights Watch soon published a report on the incident that stunned Mortazavi with its inside knowledge. On Shahram's advice, the next time Omid communicated with Human Rights Watch, he planted a piece of misinformation to cover his tracks. No, he could tell Mortazavi, he was not the source of the reports—whoever the source was had reported that Shahram was flogged in prison, which he and the other witnesses all knew wasn't true.

And yet, he also did the unthinkable, much as Roozbeh had done. With the threats to his brother and to Shahram's children in mind, Omid approached ISNA and ILNA with his and Shahram's confession letters the day after his release. The letters were inscribed with beautiful penmanship, the product of stalling tactics and boredom. The government-run, reformist-operated news agencies refused to publish them. ISNA even asked that Omid return with a lawyer. Finally, Omid brought the letters to Fars, which turned out already to have copies. Just as he had done with Roozbeh, Mortazavi ordered the reformist papers to follow Fars in publishing Omid's and Shahram's letters on their first or second pages. Editors called Omid to apologize, but they did as they were told.

When the confession letters were all published, Mohammad Ali Abtahi, Khatami's vice president, who had been so kind to Solmaz during Roozbeh's incarceration, wrote a scathing blog post titled "Repentant and Unrepentant Bloggers," unfavorably contrasting Roozbeh, Omid, and Shahram with the others in their case file who'd been released before them, without conditions. Abtahi referred to Roozbeh, Omid, and Shahram as *tavob*s, equating them with the hated collaborators in the prisons of the 1980s.

Omid, enraged, called Abtahi from a taxicab. What Abtahi had written was completely unfair, Omid fulminated. He had no idea what the bloggers had been through. And as a matter of fact, Omid told the vice president, the interrogators had made it very clear that Abtahi would see them in prison soon enough, and that they anticipated a very colorful confession from him then. Abtahi snapped at Omid that his phone was tapped. What did Omid want from him? An apology, Omid demanded. Abtahi published a follow-up article conceding that there might be aspects of the case he did not know.

ROOZBEH DIDN'T HAVE CONTACTS abroad or relationships with reformist politicians. He was little-known, young, and connected only tenuously to political figures, who were unlikely to assume any risk on his behalf. He withdrew in prison and he withdrew now. Even his friends did not take him into their confidence. When Mortazavi or Keshavarz called him, he answered, and what they asked, he mostly did. Javad was still in prison, he reasoned, and he was there because of Roozbeh. The most prudent strategy was to comply and keep quiet until he could make a clean break.

His reputation was ruined. The reformist media and elites were nearly unanimous in their condemnation: the young blogger had broken in prison and sold out his colleagues. He'd betrayed the whole Second of Khordad movement. He should have been stronger than that. Now Mortazavi called him into his office with numbing regularity, demanding one or another self-destructive public statement. Thirteen times, Roozbeh reported to the prosecutor's office. Mortazavi had him sign over his confessions to an Article 90 commission in the parliament as evidence against the reformists. Roozbeh drew the line when the letter he'd signed to the Article 90 commission wound up in the hands of *Kayhan*, which called Roozbeh for comment. If *Kayhan* published one word of that letter, Roozbeh told the caller, he would recant everything.

Roozbeh had always been taciturn; now he was nearly mute. He avoided people, skipping even a relative's wedding in Rasht. Strangers sometimes recognized him on the street and expressed sympathy and understanding, but the elites were obdurate in their disapproval. One day Ebrahim Nabavi, an Iranian political satirist in exile abroad—the recipient of one of Omid's letters, though Roozbeh didn't know it—published an article reprimanding his countrymen for piling onto young men who had clearly been coerced. Anyone who had spent even an hour in prison would see this thing for what it was, he wrote. Lies cast no light. They revealed only darkness. Not these young men but their interrogator should be ashamed before his children of the filthy job he'd done. When Roozbeh read the article, he didn't say a word. He cried soundlessly, unaware that Solmaz saw.

OMID, SHAHRAM, ROOZBEH, AND SOLMAZ kept a tight circle when Shahram was in town. As Shahram saw it, they needed one another, even if they did not all trust one another. They had no one else. The conservatives had already hurt them, and now the reformists feared them because they were potential weapons in Mortazavi's hands. They stood alone, and so they had to stand together. They had a secret meeting place, a nondescript café where they came together at night, taking care to shake off anyone who might be following them, and confiding the location to no one else.

It seemed to Omid that Roozbeh had gone over to the other side and was a liability to the others now. Roozbeh never guessed that Omid felt this way about him. He thought they were in the same boat, paddling against a current that wanted to carry them all toward the same ignoble fate. But Roozbeh's placidity rendered him inscrutable. He did not take Omid into his confidence, and Omid kept Roozbeh at a stiff arm's length. Their persecutors had labored to achieve exactly this: To shatter bonds of trust and forge new ones of mutual destruction. To take three young men, all of them innocents, each in his own way exemplary of his generation's good faith and constructive potential, and turn them radioactive in their own and one another's eyes.

Omid wanted to cut Roozbeh loose. Shahram refused. If Roozbeh went down, he told Omid, they all went down. What they had to do instead was to shore up Roozbeh's strength and prove to him, if he didn't know it, that he could still come in from the cold. Nabavi's article and Abtahi's retraction, both of them the fruits of Omid's tireless advocacy, had helped. Now they would bring Roozbeh to see Rajab Ali Mazrui, the head of the journalists' union, who was annoyed with the young bloggers for publishing their confession letters.

Mazrui scolded them but heard them out. Shahram and Omid thought they were doing Roozbeh a favor. Roozbeh needed to see that if he reached out, these people would forgive him, his friends reasoned—he needed to know that there was a way back. But what Roozbeh would mainly remember about that night was that Mazrui was harsh and ungenerous at a time when others, like his former editor Emadeddin Baghi, had shown sensitivity to his plight. Baghi once told Roozbeh to confess against him all he needed to if he thought it would be of any help.

At the café at night, the three bloggers and Solmaz conferred about each day's news and debated their options. They could break with Mortazavi and speak about everything that had happened to them. But it was not far-fetched to imagine that Mortazavi would have them killed. They could cooperate until the prosecutor was finished with them. But who knew if he ever would be? And to what harmful use might he put them in the meantime? They needed allies in the system if they were to escape this bind. Otherwise they would stand alone, powerless players in a dangerous game. They decided to try to see the president. Omid went to one of Khatami's spokesmen, whom he knew from better times, and he went to Abtahi.

RAJAB ALI MAZRUI wrote an open letter to President Khatami. He described the conditions his son had endured in prison as one of those accused in the bloggers' file, and he suggested that Shahram, Omid, and Roozbeh had confessed under pressure. The president should look into the matter, Mazrui wrote. The prosecutor's office should be investigated with regard to the bloggers' file.

The "repentant" bloggers did not have time to be grateful for this intervention. Mortazavi, furious, summoned them right away. He demanded that they respond with a letter of their own, refuting Mazrui's claims, making the "unrepentant" bloggers out to be liars and lauding the conditions of their imprisonment. Javad Gholam-Tamimi was still in prison, he reminded them, and his fate rested in their hands.

They composed a letter denying that they had been held in solitary confinement, denying that they'd been tortured, and thanking the judiciary for having given them the opportunity to recognize and atone for their many mistakes. They exaggerated to the point of absurdity, claiming that the prison guards had shared their own food with the prisoners out of the kindness of their hearts. Mortazavi was not amused. He was angry. He told them he would not publish the letter. But he did not send them home. He had made other arrangements.

"When you walk out of this room, there will be reporters waiting for you," Mortazavi said. "Tell them the things you were going to talk about in court and in your letter about Mr. Mazrui." Javad had been brought from Evin to join them for this press conference.

"This is the last thing you have to do," Mortazavi told them. "Do not play with your lives. In this country, many people die in car accidents. It's not only journalists who die in car accidents. Merchants, members of the parliament, butchers—all of them die in traffic accidents."

Outside the prosecutor's chambers, a press scrum awaited them. Reporters from ILNA and ISNA were there, along with IRIB, the hardline television network, and Fars News. Omid saw the Fars news reporter greet Keshavarz as though they were old friends. For some reason, Payam Fazlinejad was also there. The reporter from the reformist ILNA sidled up to Roozbeh and assured him that his network would be asking no questions.

The four young men sat in a row of hardbacked chairs in front of a low coffee table. On the far left, Javad Gholam-Tamimi wore a windbreaker and spectacles and looked at the floor. Next to him, Omid glowered, in a posture of closure, his arms folded, his legs crossed, his expression tense. Shahram wore a gray blazer and cocked his chin at the camera; he alone looked more angry than wounded. Roozbeh looked positively haunted. He wore a black jacket and kept his arms folded, his face a presentiment of fear.

There was a long silence while the reporters before them seemed to wait for a cue. Then Shahram pointed to the Fars reporter and the questioning began.

The bloggers denounced Mazrui and denied his claims. Omid's hands shook uncontrollably. He spoke through tears, recounting how he'd sought to blacken the face of the Islamic regime. Later a hardline journalist would jeer that he had cried like a baby, but Omid didn't care. He figured his demeanor had made it clear to anyone watching that he was under duress. Shahram confessed to having become secular under the influence of his writer friends. Roozbeh spoke of being a pawn of the reformists. Mortazavi had instructed Roozbeh to link the Mazrui family to the Mojahedin-e Khalq, but he did not.

One of the television reporters approached the bloggers at the end and tried to console them. "We know what an animal Mortazavi is," the anchor confided.

Omid exploded at his interrogator that day. He'd reached the end of his tether, he said. No more. Pushed one more inch, he would turn on the prosecutor. He'd reveal everything. He could not do a single thing more at Mortazavi's behest.

The press conference aired that night at eight, and then again, again, and again. That it had taken place in the prosecutor's headquarters was never mentioned. Javad went back to Evin. Shahram went to Rasht, but Mortazavi frequently called him back to Tehran.

Keshavarz continued meeting Roozbeh in public squares and on street corners, pulling him into his car for chats—as though they were mafiosi, Roozbeh would later muse. Solmaz had Roozbeh record everything surreptitiously from his pocket. The interrogator had good news, he told Roozbeh once. He'd found an excellent venue for Roozbeh's writings. *Kayhan* would pay him handsomely to write a book about the reform movement and how it was all made up of spies. Keshavarz had set up a meeting for Roozbeh with *Kayhan*'s editor, Hossein Shariatmadari, the author of

"The Spider's House." Roozbeh just needed to sign a paper. Roozbeh might as well join *Kayhan*, Keshavarz urged; he had no friends left among the reformists, after all. Roozbeh rejected the offer.

Earlier Keshavarz had tried to lure all three young bloggers to work at a research institute attached to *Kayhan*. Omid had been livid. He could hang himself, but he could not do this. If they so much as met with Shariat-madari, the game would be over. They would have given Mortazavi their very souls. Keshavarz had once told Omid that sixteen hardline newspapers could not equal the value of one flipped reformist advocating against his own side—one Payam Fazlinejad.

PRESIDENT KHATAMI HAD RESPONDED to the Mazrui letter by asking something called the Constitutional Watch Committee to investigate the bloggers' file. The committee, which included several high-ranking clerics as well as government ministers, professors, and members of the parliament with legal backgrounds, invited several of the "unrepentant bloggers" to testify. Mohammad Ali Abtahi was on the committee and heard the testimony. He wrote a blogpost about the meeting, giving credence to the allegations of solitary confinement and torture.

Mortazavi sprang into action. He called the chair of the Constitutional Watch Committee and berated him for meeting only with the "unrepentant" bloggers. Roozbeh, Omid, and Shahram—the "repentant" bloggers—had complained about this, the prosecutor lied, and they would take their complaint to the parliament, which would be forced to form an Article 90 commission to investigate the matter. The "repentant" bloggers had a very different account of their time in prison, and the committee should meet with them, too, to hear their side, Mortazavi insisted. The committee chairman agreed to this. Without consulting his quarry, Mortazavi scheduled the meeting for the very next day, which was a Saturday.

Roozbeh got the call from Mortazavi's office with only hours to spare. The prosecutor needed him, Omid, and Shahram to report to his office immediately, Roozbeh was told. They were going to the Constitutional Watch

Committee. At once the film unrolled in Roozbeh's mind: Mortazavi and Keshavarz would threaten and intimidate them, then breathe down their necks while they testified, making sure they didn't deviate from the script. Just as in the press conference, the three former prisoners would become instruments in Mortazavi's hands, used to exonerate him of the offenses he'd committed against them and to bludgeon the bloggers who'd told the truth. Roozbeh thought fast. The lack of notice would work in his favor. He told Mortazavi's assistant that he couldn't make the meeting; he had work to do, he wasn't in Tehran, today just wasn't possible. Then he switched off his phone and called Omid from Solmaz's.

"Meet us in Enghelab Square," he told Omid. "I need to talk to you."

Roozbeh told Omid about the phone call and about what he imagined Mortazavi's plan to be. He had a plan of his own. They should avoid Mortazavi and allow him to believe he needed to reschedule their appointment with the committee. But then they should go to the committee by themselves. Without the thugs or the scripts or the threats, they could at last tell their story to people close to the president, who might listen. Roozbeh joked that while God had chosen not to help them through their reformist allies, perhaps he'd done so through Mortazavi himself.

Omid was stunned. He had already agreed to meet with a member of that committee in private, though he had not scheduled an appointment. He'd never expected that Roozbeh would come with him, let alone testify before the whole committee. What Roozbeh proposed now was a breathtaking act of courage—all the more so because his reversal would come, seemingly, from nowhere. Omid readily agreed to it. They talked frankly for what might have been the first time, acknowledging that their lives were about to change forever. At the very least, they would likely be arrested again. But there was no better way to break free and clear their names.

Roozbeh called Abtahi to confirm the meeting's time and place. Abtahi was abrupt and rude. But yes, there would be a meeting at two o'clock at the office of the president, on Pasteur Street.

Omid, Roozbeh, and Solmaz entered the committee's chamber at two.

Shahram could not get down from Rasht in time. Before them sat Abtahi; the minister of justice; a member of the governing committee of the parliament; an elderly ayatollah from the Assembly of Experts; and a number of legal experts.

The minister of justice was puzzled when they walked in. Mortazavi had called to say that the meeting was canceled, he told them. Roozbeh explained that they had shaken off Mortazavi to come on their own.

"We have decided to talk about things that we have never spoken about," he said, "and we put our trust in you."

"Wait a second," said the minister of justice. "If you think that what you're about to say will have negative consequences or cause you trouble, know that we can't guarantee your safety."

Solmaz choked back rage. These powerful men—a vice president, the minister of justice—professed powerlessness even as Roozbeh and Omid risked everything to sit before them. They lacked the courage of the young people whom Abtahi, at least, had dared to call cowards.

"I am really sorry that we are sitting in the presence of three government ministers who say such things and can't guarantee our safety," Roozbeh replied. "But it's not important to us. We realize that as soon as we walk out of this building, there will be trouble."

"Okay, okay," said the committee chairman. "We will listen to what you have to say."

"It's not important to us what happens to us," Roozbeh went on. "The only thing that is important is that you are the president's confidants, and as long as the president knows what happened to us, that is sufficient."

Roozbeh told his story first. Solmaz described her meetings with Mortazavi during Roozbeh's imprisonment. They produced the recordings Solmaz had insisted Roozbeh make, proving that the interrogator had continued to harass and coerce him after he was released.

The justice minister interrupted Roozbeh impatiently. Roozbeh kept speaking of pressure. What did that even mean?

Omid asked Solmaz, the only woman present, to leave the room.

"Why are you asking us to describe the pressure?" Omid, incensed, demanded of the justice minister. "You've been an interrogator! You've been in the intelligence service for years. You're the minister of justice! You've been head of the organization of the prisons. Now you're saying you don't know? You're lying to us!"

He wheeled on a cleric who was falling asleep in his chair, and yelled at him to wake up. He began to reenact one of his interrogations, detailing the sexual abuse he'd suffered, beating himself, throwing papers at the head of the committee. He demanded, "Why should we pay the price because your interrogators are sexually sick? No matter that they fought in the war with Iraq. Why should we pay the price for that?"

After two hours everyone was drained and unsettled. Some of the committee members had even wept while Omid spoke. Abtahi took a picture with his cell phone, capturing Roozbeh and Omid with red-rimmed eyes. Within twenty-four hours Abtahi would publish an account of the meeting on his blog and give an interview to ISNA verifying that the "repentant" bloggers had recanted their confessions. Overnight, the collaborators would become heroes. And they had no greater advocate than Mohammad Ali Abtahi.

But before that happened, Mortazavi, knowing nothing of their visit to the committee, was quoted in yet another interview claiming them for his side. The "repentant" bloggers would set the record straight on the bloggers' file, the prosecutor confidently explained. When Roozbeh saw that, he winced. Maybe Mortazavi really would kill them when he found out what they'd done.

WHEN ROOZBEH, SOLMAZ, AND OMID emerged onto Pasteur Street that afternoon, they understood that there was no place safe for them to go. That week Mortazavi called everyone who knew them, leaving instructions for the three young people to turn themselves in. He sent a summons for Roozbeh to the relative who had posted his bail. He also sent Roozbeh a message reminding him that two more traffic fatalities would hardly be noticed in the city of Tehran. Shahram, in Rasht, got a warning that his children's lives were at risk. For twenty days Roozbeh, Solmaz, and Omid were homeless, wandering city streets by day, showing up at friends' houses unannounced at night, staying in any one place only long enough to sleep. But the bloggers were no longer divided now: they were all unrepentant, and Roozbeh was no longer cut off from his peers.

Thanks to the Constitutional Watch Committee, Khatami had spoken to the country's chief justice, Ayatollah Shahroudi, about the bloggers' case. Shahroudi initially objected that Mortazavi could not possibly have done the things the bloggers alleged. But Khatami insisted that the claims needed to be investigated.

Shahroudi assigned a deputy to debrief the bloggers in secret. Under cover of night, the bloggers met this intermediary at an office not far from Evin Prison. There they spoke for five hours, presenting all the evidence they could muster, including blindfolds that they'd secreted out of prison. After the deputy made his report, Shahroudi said he would meet with the bloggers himself on December 31, 2004.

Shahram came down from Rasht. He was selected to open and close the presentation. The ayatollah had only an hour to give them, they were told, as he had a high-level meeting just after them. There in the justice's chambers, Roozbeh told Shahroudi that until that moment he had presumed that Mortazavi, as his subordinate, acted with the chief justice's knowledge and approval. Now he understood that the prosecutor often acted independently. But Mortazavi's actions reflected badly on the judiciary as a whole, and Shahroudi should not allow his own reputation to be sullied by them. He told Shahroudi about the death threats, and that Mortazavi had once said to him, "I can do whatever I want! I am one quarter of this country."

Shahroudi chuckled. "It's a good thing he's satisfied with just a quarter."

The ayatollah seemed genuinely troubled, muttering *"Allahu Akbar"* from time to time when Omid detailed the sexual aspect of his interrogations. The story of the sexual confessions offended him as a man of religion. Even if the bloggers had sinned, they should not have been questioned about it, Shahroudi explained; to question a sinner about his sins was itself a sin. He was shocked to learn of the threats against Shahram's children. "Oh!" he exclaimed. "Are my subordinates really involved in these kinds of things?" He canceled his later meeting and talked to the bloggers for two hours instead of one. And then he got up to go perform his prayers.

Shahram stopped Shahroudi on his way out. He took the ayatollah's hand.

"What will be the result of this session?" Shahram demanded. "When I walk out this door, there might be another one of those white cars with tinted windows waiting for me. How do I know they won't take me again? How do I know they won't make me write another letter, saying that everything I just told you was a lie?"

Then Shahroudi said something remarkable. "If anyone, from anywhere, calls you and summons you and says they need to discuss something with you, do not obey them or answer them," the ayatollah instructed. "Simply tell them that your case is being handled by Hajj Agha and that they should follow up with me.

"Go live your lives," the chief justice told the frightened young journalists, "and do not worry about these matters."

Roozbeh, Solmaz, and Omid at last returned to their homes. The next day the judiciary announced that the bloggers' file had been removed from the prosecutor's office and remanded to a three-member committee for investigation. In the end, that committee would exonerate everyone but the four who'd been indicted by the prosecutor: Roozbeh, Omid, Shahram, and Javad. They would have to settle their cases in court. During the long interval while their cases remained open, the person to whom Shahroudi had assigned their file, Jamal Karimi-Rad, died in a car accident, and the file reverted to the prosecutor's office.

But to Omid, the glass was assuredly half full. The bloggers had succeeded in removing the stigma of their false confessions from themselves and attaching it to Mortazavi instead. The public learned the truth and was broadly outraged. And for the first time in the history of his country, so far as he knew, the head of the judiciary had been forced to meet with defendants to hear claims of abuse in the prison system.

. . .

ROOZBEH WAS FREE, at least for the moment, but he was unemployable. Mortazavi made sure of that. No newspaper could hire him or Solmaz
even as a freelancer without facing threats of being shut down. Roozbeh's
last opportunity came from a source he would never have expected before
he went to prison. Mehdi Karroubi, the cleric who had been speaker of the
parliament, was starting a newspaper for his moderate wing of the reform
movement. Before his arrest, Roozbeh had been critical of Karroubi and
sympathetic to his rivals within the reformist faction. But Solmaz had told
Roozbeh of Karroubi's help and compassion through his prison months.
Now the editor of Karroubi's forthcoming newspaper, *Etemad Melli*, hired
Roozbeh to a committee that helped conceptualize the paper and build its
editorial staff. *Etemad Melli* gave Roozbeh a place to channel his energies
during tense and difficult months.

By June of 2005, Shahram and Omid had both quietly left Iran. Omid
told Roozbeh he was off to work on a project in a provincial city. Instead, as
the only one of the three with international connections, he made his way
to the United States by way of Istanbul.

Shahram just told Roozbeh he was going away. He didn't have a passport. He placed his life in the hands of smugglers, reaching Canada by way
of Turkey, with its squalid and anxious refugee towns near the Iranian border; by way of the United Nations High Commissioner for Refugees, where
the application process could—did—take years. It was the way out of Iran
for those who had no way out of Iran. In due time, his three children would
come to speak English, maybe even to think of themselves as Canadian.
Shahram and Bita were made of other elements.

On the outskirts of Toronto, Shahram wrote poetry, as he had always
done. He also wrote for his weblog, and for Persian-language websites
based in Europe, about who in Iran had been arrested and who had been
killed; about a university professor who raped a student; about the time the
police killed eighteen women in Khuzestan. There was nothing natural
about this existence. Sometimes Shahram imagined it was the water that

had followed him. When he opened the faucet to fill a glass in Canada, the water that came out was Iranian. He drank of it, secreted it. Other times he imagined himself as a balloon expanding over a fire, the warm air inside him originating abroad. He bobbed through cool Toronto streets where people worked or relaxed or lived simply for themselves, and soon enough he would explode.

Roozbeh remained in Iran for another year, until August 2006. He would later say that the person he'd been before prison was dead: a new Roozbeh had taken his place. Sometimes the new Roozbeh still worried Solmaz. The torturers had dimmed a light in him and ferried his spirit even further from the surface of his skin. But Roozbeh had thought about a lot of things in prison, too. He had learned that the country's judiciary was as complex and factionalized as its other branches of government; that it housed men of conscience cheek by jowl with the psychopaths and power mad. The same was true of the intelligence apparatus. He still believed that the key to Iran's future was an honest reckoning with its past. He took reformists to task for their avoidance of that discussion.

Roozbeh had no illusions about Khatami by the end of the president's second term. He believed that when Khatami had asked Ayatollah Shahroudi to look into the bloggers' file, he'd done so because others around him had forced his hand. Shahroudi, by contrast, had been genuinely troubled by their story and moved to make it right. But if anything, this made the case for reform even stronger. It was not the person of the president who could bring justice to bear. It was the system itself, if only its ranks were populated by people with open minds. That kind of evolution— painstaking, irresistible, psychological as much as political—had to come from the society.

If Roozbeh had been able to work in his chosen field, he might have stayed in Iran, even knowing that sentencing still awaited him. But penury combined with repression drove him and Solmaz first to France and then to the United States. The last person they saw before leaving Tehran was their old friend Abbas Amirentezam.

In February 2009, the Tehran court at last handed down sentences on some of the bloggers' charges. For Shahram, nine months in prison and twenty lashes. For Omid, two years, ninety-one days and ten lashes. For Roozbeh, two years and eighty-four lashes. A couple of years later, an appeals court would drop all the charges against them. But by then it was far too late. Even before they were sentenced, all of them had gone.

THIRTEEN

POSTMORTEM

By criticizing our theories we can let our theories die in our stead.

—KARL POPPER, *The Myth of the Framework*

Apart from our ideas we are flesh, we are like any other animal, any other plant. Isn't it the case?

—ABDOLKARIM SOROUSH, 2008 interview

ON DECEMBER 6, 2004, President Mohammad Khatami and his security detail squeezed through the crowded halls of the Faculty of Technology building at the University of Tehran. The students had long anticipated the president's visit on this day, celebrated annually as Student Day to commemorate a university uprising that the shah violently crushed in the early 1950s. Some students greeted the official entourage by singing the anthem of the student movement; others sang the national anthem of Iran. But the television cameras that followed the official delegation to the ceremonial hall captured a different sentiment. Students held up handwritten placards to the camera lenses:

"Khatami! What happened to freedom of expression?"

"The Iranian nation detests despotism!"

"After eight years, students want a response."

"We will stand like a candle that is not afraid of fire."

The ceremonial hall was too small. Students thronged the corridor outside, yelling and pounding against the door until their hands bled. The president's security squad beat them back. Inside the hall, student leaders rose one after another to denounce the president when he had finished speaking. Khatami had failed to make good on his promised reforms. He'd allowed the regime to shut down newspapers and suppress student protests with violence.

"Mr. Khatami!" exclaimed another student speaker. "Was it necessary for us to endeavor for eight years only to learn that the root of our problems lies in the fact that our spirit has been crushed by despotism?" A young woman rose to protest the exclusion from the room of many students who had waited there since dawn; one of the security guards in the corridor, she added, had "hurled an insult at me that I will never forget for as long as I live."

Khatami would later say that the humiliating scene was simply evidence of how far Iran had come from the violent repression that had followed the Islamic Revolution in 1979: the students at the gathering felt safe criticizing their president to his face, surely something that had not been true under the Rafsanjani administration before him. But that day at the University of Tehran, there was a nearly palpable sense that, for better or for worse, something was coming undone, and the president stood by helplessly, watching and reasoning with chaos.

There, amid the waving placards and the accusatory slogans—"Khatami, you turned your back on us!" and "Khatami, give us back our votes! Khatami, guilty of treason, treason!" the students chanted—the president did what it seemed he always did: too little, too late. He calmly explained that the auditorium was too small. He told the students to "behave, listen, and tolerate." And at long last, as the cries mounted outside the hall and the chanting inside drowned out all other discussion, he called out to his security team.

"Gentlemen!" he admonished weakly. "Please hurry up and stop the beating of students."

Khatami walked the usual reformist tightrope in his speech, but for an audience that had grown less convinced that it would amount to more than spectacle. He affirmed that reforming the Islamic Republic was Iran's only true path to democracy. The regime must be preserved. "I see the defense of the revolution as my individual duty, for the sake of democracy, freedom, and liberation from foreign control," he said. Indeed, no viable alternative existed. And yet, he added, "long-lasting tyranny is our chronic pain, and the cure for this pain is the rule of the people. We demand freedom. There is no escape."

As President Khatami himself once put it, from the time he assumed the presidency, he confronted a crisis every nine days. It was not enough that the elected institutions—the presidency and the parliament— came under the supervision of immensely more powerful clerical ones. There was also a deep network of violence that eluded the president's grasp. By 2003, few could avoid the conclusion that the reform movement, conceived in hope and high abstraction, had run aground on opposition more tenacious and ruthless than any of its theorists had anticipated.

From the hardline clerics of the Haghani Circle, to the purged elements of the intelligence ministry, to the office of Tehran's chief prosecutor, to the vigilante pressure groups like Ansar-e Hezbollah and even mysterious cells like the one dispatched to kill Saeed Hajjarian, the Islamic Republic was riddled with mafia-like grids that operated in secrecy. Those who oversaw these forces, many reformists now observed, enjoyed high favor and believed in the righteousness of physically eliminating their competition. They opposed democratic reform not only opportunistically but deeply and insurmountably, in principle.

When they captured the presidency, the reformists had been united in the belief that the conservatives were amenable to compromise and that elected positions were available and effective levers for change. They were confident—perhaps fatally so—that the people overwhelmingly supported them. But they chose to call on the people only as voters. For the populace, nearly all the reformists believed in 1997, was disorganized, potentially radical, and angry. Eruptions in the streets would only provoke brutal reprisals from the security apparatus. The Eighteenth of Tir reinforced this fear. So the reformists instead labored to hold open the windows of free expression and association just wide enough to allow Iranians to begin building civic institutions. These would eventually help channel the ambitions of the silent majority so that the people's grievances could be heard.

But by 2003 the reformists' consensus on tactics had shattered. The conservatives were not negotiating. Unlike the reformists, they had no ideological investment in a political process of give-and-take. And the people had begun to turn their anger on the reformists, who looked weak and conciliatory in the face of hardline coercion. What were Khatami and his allies to do?

FIVE REFORMIST LUMINARIES convened a seminar. The transcript of their exchange would read like the final act of an existentialist play. Five men navigate a labyrinth, only to find one another in a locked room at its end. Each has an escape plan as noble as it is futile. Even as they speak, the walls grow higher, seal tighter against the mounting uselessness of their plans.

The question before the thinkers was whether Khatami and his allies should remain in government or walk out—and, in either case, to what end. Nearly two years remained in the president's second term, and his brain trust foundered between anguish and paralysis, cynicism and the grim logic of sunk costs.

One speaker—the journalist, activist, and former hostage taker Abbas Abdi—suggested that, as they had no prayer of realizing their goals, the morally responsible thing for the reformists to do was to walk out of government. The other four thinkers leapt on Abdi. Imagine the repression that would surely follow! There would be no one to protect the people, and what little the reformists had achieved would be undone.

Alireza Alavitabar, a reformist social scientist who'd once headed the Center for Strategic Research's cultural division, suggested the reformists go for all or nothing. They should propose a popular referendum on all the fundamental issues they cared about: eliminating the Guardian Council's role in elections, amnestying political prisoners, empowering the parliament, reigning in the judiciary, freeing the press, normalizing relations with all countries but Israel. They should be prepared to resign and mount a campaign of civil disobedience when this referendum was prohibited. Their true allies lay outside the political system, not within it: "The foundation of democracy is a peaceful dialogue," Alavitabar said, "but not with fascists."

But this was warfare, the other theorists protested. They would never succeed with this strategy. They would only alienate their opponents, polarize the society, and empower a strongman to right the chaos.

Mostafa Tajzadeh, the former deputy interior minister, observed that Iranian elites tended to see politics as a zero-sum game: someone won and someone lost, the losers facing total exclusion or worse. Reform was meant to break this deadlock—to allow political rivals to share power and to force the ruling system to tolerate diversity, criticism, and dissent without reprisal. The reform movement, as Tajzadeh saw it, had always been as much about its means as its end: lawfulness, decency, and nonviolence could not be achieved by resorting to their opposites. The trouble, said Tajzadeh, was that Iran's hard-liners did not accept these terms of engagement. They did not persuade when they could coerce, and they were bent on suffocating critics out of the public sphere.

So long as Iran lacked a powerful civil society or private sector, the government was the country's only domain of political action, and those outside it were both ineffectual and vulnerable to violence. Tajzadeh saw no virtue in the reformists' retreating to that wilderness. He said, "Until the time when rule of law is established in our society, until the time when civil institutions are empowered and powers of the government are restricted, and until the time we can develop capable citizens, our presence in the government is obligatory."

And so Tajzadeh recommended that Khatami remain as president. He had a duty to the people who had elected him. The reformists should keep trying to achieve their goals. At the same time, they should use their elected positions as a base from which to expose and obstruct the violent conspiracies of their opponents.

Saeed Hajjarian, not three years after a bullet had lodged at the base of his skull, was at once social scientist and political actor, analyst and partisan. His language at the seminar was ethereally abstract, his ambitions prosaically worldly, as though he were a theoretical physicist explaining how to fix a car engine. At a moment when the movement he'd helped father was questioning the very purpose of its existence, Hajjarian opined that the Islamic Republic of Iran was what Max Weber would have called a patrimonial state, a kind of autocracy that appealed to traditional values and in which the ruler seized the military and even the economy as instruments of his personal will.

Hajjarian acknowledged that his tactic of building pressure from below while bargaining at the top had failed. He had some regrets: "We should have created hope and fear; we should have fought and compromised at the same time; we should have bargained with the heads of these [clerical] institutions. And we did none of these." But he refused to believe, even after all he'd seen and personally suffered, that negotiation was impossible. "I firmly assure you that there are no dogmatist forces among our opponents," he asserted. "And if our presupposition about their rationality is wrong, we have then established the Second of Khordad movement on a misunderstanding."

Khatami had brought Iran something Hajjarian called "dual sovereignty," by which he meant the simultaneous presence of competing political forces within the ruling establishment. Khatami had achieved this much, and the result was a system more dynamic and responsive than in the past. The trouble was that one side of it—the theocratic one—controlled the security forces. To negotiate, the reformists needed power, too.

The reformists' best option now was to stand very firmly for their beliefs and force the conservatives to throw them out. The reformists' honor was at stake, along with their efficacy. To walk out, Hajjarian declared, would be an act of desertion. "In people's opinion, it is associated with incompetence, fear, escape, instability, and abandoning." Expulsion would give the reformists the upper hand: "It would be accompanied by imprisonment, filtration, and house arrest, which would make the reformists more active and organized, whereas walking out would be followed by a passive disengagement."

This strategy, Hajjarian contended, would delegitimize the hardline government by exposing its intolerance: "The state may survive the policy of walking out, but after expelling the state's opposition—through a coup, for example—no state can survive."

PRESIDENT KHATAMI DID NOT RESIGN. He did not introduce a referendum, he did not expose the hard-liners' networks of violence, and he did not force the conservatives to expel him. He served out his second term, toeing a winnowing line, with fewer supporters by the day.

He must have known that his popularity was waning. But with the press censored, political parties all but illegal, and opinion polls marred by surveillance and distrust, the Iranian people were a cipher to those who would rule them. In the years to come, popular discontent at the end of Khatami's presidency would be ascribed to economic malaise or political suffocation, impatience with reform or rejection of it, isolation from the West or domination by it, hostility or yearning. Starting in 2004, election results, too, concealed mysteries, as the candidates were ever more selectively approved and the voters ever more politically self-selected.

The reformist Sixth Parliament staggered to the end of a term during which it was virtually paralyzed by the Guardian Council, which made liberal use of its veto power. In September of 2002, Khatami introduced two sweeping reform bills that together would have empowered the presidency and the elected government at the expense of the judiciary and Guardian Council. The Guardian Council, unsurprisingly, vetoed both. So much, then, for enduring structural change.

The Guardian Council was done fighting with the parliament. Before the seventh parliamentary election rolled around in February 2004, the council disqualified more than two thousand candidates from running. Of 290 seats, reformists—including 87 incumbents—were effectively forbidden to contest 200. The council had never before exercised its supervisory power with quite such heavy-handed partisanship.

The reformists in the parliament did not wait for Khatami to tell them what to do. After a three-week sit-in, 125 of them resigned. Their statement compared Iran's religious government to the Taliban's in neighboring Afghanistan. "We cannot continue to be present in a parliament that is not capable of defending the rights of the people," they proclaimed. Some thirty governors and twelve cabinet ministers submitted their resignations, too. The interior minister proclaimed that he would not hold the election on its scheduled date. Even the cautious Mehdi Karroubi admonished the Guardian Council: "Now we see that a couple of old men want to run the country."

But Khatami could not be persuaded to take a stand. To the disgust and bewilderment of many of his advisers, he rejected the resignations of the ministers and governors, and he insisted on holding the election as scheduled on February 20, 2004.

Khatami, his critics railed, had endorsed the legitimacy of an engineered election that was really a political putsch. The reformists imagined that Iranian voters would stay home, but they did not. Nationwide, the turnout was lower than in the previous parliamentary election, but wholly respectable, and certainly higher than the reformists had imagined possible without their presence in the field. In Tehran, where the turnout was low, the faction that called itself Abadgaran and identified strongly with the mayor, Mahmoud Ahmadinejad, swept all thirty seats. The parliament went to the conservatives, and Khatami was now a lame duck.

. . .

AKBAR GANJI HAD SPENT much of Khatami's presidency in prison. Just one line for his freedom, an interrogator liked to tell him: "I made a mistake." Ganji resolved that if they kept him in prison for fifty years, he would say no such thing. He endured six years without breaking, and he would later reflect that he did it by telling himself that nobody cared. He was alone, responsible for his own actions, and accountable to his own convictions. He was hospitalized more than once on account of his hunger strikes, one of which lasted more than eighty days. His body would never be the same.

"The goal of the system is to break and destroy me," Ganji wrote in one of his "Letters to the Free World," smuggled from Evin in 2005. "This body is on the verge of complete deterioration, but since I believe in the conjectures I have made (all of my opinions), I see no reason to deny their truth." He called on Popper, though not by name: "It is a trivial fact that all these conjectures must be tested with the sword of falsification. Commitment to 'critical rationality' is different from 'giving up our beliefs by force of prison.'"

Ganji's first book-length Republican Manifesto was smuggled from Evin in 2002. In it, he broke radically from the reformists, arguing for a secular liberal republic in which religion would have no official privilege. None of the hedged reformist strategies would produce such a state— certainly not Hajjarian's "dual sovereignty." *Velayat-e faqih* simply could not be reconciled with a republic.

Ganji believed that the trouble with Iranian political thought harked back to the Constitutional Revolution of 1905. That movement forced the Qajar kings to make Iran a constitutional monarchy. But it should have abolished monarchy instead. Perhaps then Iran would have not fallen into this trap of believing that a small measure of power could be wrested from absolute rule. Dual sovereignty, constitutionalism—these were the blandishments of inertia that dissipated Iran's republican energies such that they never truly threatened autocratic rule.

Like Hajjarian, Ganji turned to Weber to classify Iran's current form of government. He settled on sultanism, which was a kind of patrimonialism, but one that sustained itself less on tradition than on the autocrat's personal discretion. Such a regime was not reformable. The reformists, in Ganji's view, should stop collaborating with it by participating in its fig-leaf elections. They should boycott elections, withdraw from government, and use people power, through civil disobedience, to push back against unjust laws and to demand a referendum on Iran's form of government. He pledged to stand "shoulder to shoulder" with the people in this struggle. "If civil disobedience needs leadership and planning, we must go after creating organizing bodies and leadership," Ganji reasoned in 2005, "not shut down the struggle for freedom with the excuse of lack of leadership." To build civil society was itself an act of civil disobedience in a state without legal freedoms of speech and association, Ganji noted. There was no half measure for this.

Ganji wrote as a man who, already in prison, had little left to lose. Even if the people defend tyranny or are indifferent to it, he wrote, "[a] freedom-loving democrat still has the right (nay, the duty) to stand against such a system, alone and by himself." Some would say he was grandstanding, that his writings were a dangerous incitement. He did not have the instinct for nuance—or for political survival—that acted as a weight in other men's shoes. What he did have, often in breathtaking profusion, was courage.

"I do not believe at all in the theory of *velayat-e faqih* and I think it is anti-democratic and violates human rights," he wrote. "I will not stand the master-slave relationship, in which the Leader ascends to the ranks of a god and the people descend to the level of slaves. I apologize in place of Mr. Khamenei to students, journalists, bloggers . . . families of the victims of serial murders, the family of Zahra Kazemi . . . for all they have gone through these years." He added, "I strongly apologize in place of Mr. Khamenei to the families of the executed prisoners of the summer of 1988 all over the country." After meeting with the bloggers during a furlough, Ganji wrote, "Forcing repentance letters on prisoners is the method of Stalin's interrogators inherited by Iranian Stalinists."

Ganji's writings were thick with references: to Hafez, Motahhari, and Socrates; to Freud, Foucault, and Adorno; to Tocqueville, Rawls, and Locke; to Richard Rorty, Milan Kundera, Claude Lefort, and even contemporary European academics, like the Italian literary critic Franco Moretti and the British social theorist David Beetham. He had come a great distance from his revolutionary roots, which he would later describe as having lodged in the soil of his class resentment as a boy in the southern Tehran slums. By 2005, Ganji argued that the conservatives' rhetoric of social justice was a cloak for oppression. How could one claim to stand for social justice while holding that there were unequal classes of humans, whether men and women, clerics and laypeople, or Muslims and non-Muslims? Even if Iran's rulers meant to condone justice only in the distribution of wealth, surely they should allow a free press to expose the corruption that impeded economic fairness in Iran. But they did not.

As for President Khatami, he had always been the wrong man for the job of reform. "He didn't have the mettle," Ganji would later reflect. Khatami hadn't really known what he meant by civil society, or even by democracy. And so it was little wonder he did not persevere. "We need someone like Gandhi, like Havel, like Nelson Mandela," Ganji insisted. "If you ask me, we need mostly Gandhi."

GANJI WAS NOT ALONE in his categorical rejection of the constitutional order. The radical wing of the student movement called for a referendum on the Islamic Republic, to mirror the one that had founded the revolutionary state in 1979. The activists issued an online petition named for its outsized ambition of garnering six million signatures.

Saeed Hajjarian described the referendum campaign as delusional. With what leverage did the radicals imagine they could force their referendum on the conservatives? Moreover, the radicals' strategy rested on the presumption that "the people" both wanted a secular republic and were ready to expose themselves to violence in order to obtain one. But Iranian society was diverse, divided, and traumatized. As Omid Memarian later observed, to be one step ahead of the people was to be a leader; to be five steps ahead was to walk alone.

The things Ganji said, everyone knew, Omid reflected; but not everyone thought that directly articulating them would be helpful. Khatami's equivocation could be taken for fecklessness, but it could also be taken for political acuity. He governed a divided country that seethed with mutual distrust, whose lasting stability depended on assuaging tension, and in which his opponents held all the coercive instruments. People like Omid, who had spent the reform years building fragile new institutions that encouraged Iranian citizens to cooperate and work together, felt they had much to lose by polarizing the political atmosphere and raising conservative hackles. Thousands of nongovernmental organizations operated by the middle of Khatami's second term. Their founders' goal was not to win a war of ideas but to convince all parties to lay down their arms in pursuit of common, constructive aims.

The NGO network, like the reformist media before it, would be decimated by the political warfare within the regime. After the parliamentary election in 2004, the hardline press began a drumbeat against these civic groups as nodes in the foreign-sponsored conspiracy bent on regime change. This was when *Kayhan* published its "Spider's House" editorial and when other media close to the security establishment began suggesting that the NGOs were linked to Western governments and foundations that had pushed for regime change in places like Serbia. Activists protested that they had studiously rejected outside funding, and they entreated American journalists to beg the administration of George W. Bush to stop expressing support for Iranian civil society. But within the Iranian political system, there was no one left to fight for the NGO network. The reformists had vanished from the parliament and the Tehran City Council; the students had set their sights beyond reform; the media was increasingly censored; international pressure was counterproductive; and Khatami was on his way out.

On the eve of the 2005 election, the reformist elite still spoke of reform as "irreversible." After all, the reformist project was not only a political campaign or a policy proposal. It was an intellectual shift, a popular groundswell, a cultural watershed. All that was, arguably, true. But it was also true, as Omid noted ruefully, that many of reform's concrete achievements had indeed been reversed: institutions built and unbuilt, elected offices obtained and lost, newspapers published and censored. Maybe it was a visionary optimism that kept reformist theorists focused on the far horizon. Or maybe it was hubris, or denial—the refusal to take stock of all they'd lost.

KIYAN CONTINUED PUBLISHING almost to the end of Khatami's first term. It remained, as Mostafa Rokhsefat had conceived it, an intellectual wellspring and not a political organ. Two of its founders decamped to found a popular reformist daily, bringing the sensibilities they'd nurtured at *Kiyan* to the popular mediascape that Khatami had briefly transformed. One of Soroush's acolytes, a young man named Ebrahim Soltani, who had come to the *Kiyan* Circle in the Rafsanjani era as a medical student with a passion for philosophy, became the journal's editor in chief.

Soltani's *Kiyan* continued to lead with Soroush's essays and interviews. In subsequent pages, Iranian scholars translated and debated the work of foreign philosophers, wrestled with the vexed interplay of liberalism and Islam, translated and discussed Latin American literature and poetry. As Soroush had once said of science, perhaps *Kiyan*'s editors and contributors believed of their journal's domain: philosophy was wild and had no homeland. The work before them was not to assert a national identity through the provenance of their ideas, but to forge a liberal theory of the state that was true to the parts of that identity they considered most vital.

In the fall of 2000, Soltani and his colleagues received a letter from the judiciary ordering them to cease publishing *Kiyan*. The order took Soltani by surprise. No one had interfered with the journal in the preceding months; Soltani had just published its fifty-fourth issue, dated October–November, with Soroush on scientific and political development, a translation of a John Keane essay on media and democracy, and other essays on Socrates and Hegel. But that was to be the last issue of the reform movement's flagship journal. Now it went the way of the rest of the reformist press, despite its best effort to sail above the political fray.

Kiyan's leading light, Abdolkarim Soroush, was not in exile, or so he said; but he could neither publish nor teach in Iran, nor could he lecture there unmolested. Starting around 2000, he alighted in a succession of bare academic offices without nameplates, where bookends stood marooned on the shelves and the contents of his briefcase of an evening could as easily have packed him off to a new locale. He was, at different times, a visiting scholar at Harvard, Yale, Princeton, Columbia, and Georgetown universities; sometimes he was in Germany, and for a stretch he could be found at the heart of a maze of hallways at the Library of Congress in Washington, D.C. The peripatetic life seemed to suit him. He was tranquil, solitary, and less combative as he aged.

Now he returned to Marx, reading the German giant without the animosity that had fired his intellect as a young man. And he stood for the first time truly in awe of the insight, influence, and explanatory power of a Marxism he once used Popper to deride. "I think I have been a little unfair to it," Soroush confessed. To recognize the importance of social and economic forces, he understood now, was not to take anything away from reason. Rather, such forces behaved as Freud's unconscious behaved. "You are induced, so to speak, to reason in a particular way because of some of the social and economic factors around you, because of some of the interests that drag you along, and put some words on your tongue or some thoughts in your mind," Soroush reflected. Perhaps he had something of his own strange life's journey in mind.

Still, as a formula for political emancipation, Soroush contended, Marxism had failed. Democratic socialism, much longed for, had materialized neither in Iran nor anywhere else. Deep down, Soroush surmised, many of Iran's reformists were disappointed with that. They found socialism attractive, and compatible with Islamic teachings. "But they do not know how to make it compatible with social liberty, democracy and so on."

Soroush was critical of Khatami's performance as president. In July 2003, he'd issued an open letter observing that the president stood at a crossroads. "He either sides with the people or joins hands with the conservatives, and in either situation he would be the loser," Soroush wrote. "He can no longer join the people because they demand not the reform of the present theocracy, as the reformists want, but a fundamental change towards full fledged democracy and secularism. He can't join the conservatives because they consider him as a used handkerchief."

He believed that Khatami should have acknowledged that he couldn't run the country in the presence of hardline vigilante groups. The reformists should have exposed the sources of funding and chains of command that allowed those groups to function, and they should have demanded that the vigilantes be restrained. As for the students, Soroush surmised that they were demoralized because they were never granted their rights and their assailants had never faced justice. These were legitimate complaints.

Soroush believed passionately in the moral and practical force of ideas, and he attributed Khatami's irresoluteness in action to his irresoluteness in thought. He said of the outgoing president, "Lack of vision theoretically leads to lack of courage in action." As a result, Soroush said of Khatami, "he'd sometimes go one way and sometimes the other way. He'd raise an idea and others would follow him and then he'd suddenly slam on the brakes. He'd pull back and come to a grinding halt and startle everyone."

Soroush worried that Khatami's performance would reflect poorly on an intellectual project that he believed was far from dead. "We need theoretical debates just as much as we need institution building and political action," he observed. And the consensus that had emerged from such debates was a striking one. The reformists' ambitions were democratic and politically secular, a secularism Soroush defined as the belief that the state should be neutral toward religion and that the legitimacy of the political system was not divinely given but depended on the system's justice.

Soroush, more than any of his protégés in the reform movement, emphasized that democracy was a matter not only of self-determination or freedoms but of rights. "All the important, modern, political institutions are founded on rights," he argued. "If we want to enter political modernity, this is the route that we have to take. As long as the concept of right has not taken on as much importance as we attach to family and honor, our modern institutions will lack meaning; they'll only be hollow names." And rights began with a powerful, protective, independent judiciary. This was something Soroush had observed as a student in Britain. He argued now that an independent judiciary was more crucial than civil society; it should have been the first and least negotiable of Khatami's aims.

For all that Soroush's vision was bold and uncompromising, he was not a political radical like his close friend and acolyte Ganji. He remained the lower-middle-class boy who demurred when invited to be a guerrilla fighter, arguing that society needed philosophers, too. The Iran he knew, and felt integrally connected to, was a pious and conservative place. The rulers he might have chosen, had he been free to choose, were religious ones, although they would not rule a theocratic state.

Like many Iranian thinkers, Soroush ruminated on the classic dilemma of his country—so classic that it had ossified into cliché: Iran, the country forever torn between tradition and modernity. Soroush reflected that it was not meaningful to speak of tradition as a thing to be preserved or jettisoned, because tradition was not one thing but a thousand things. Nor was it meaningful to speak of modernity as a state to be engineered or rejected: modernity, too, was multifarious and, perhaps more important, it was not planned or chosen so much as it was the unintended consequence of human endeavor.

"We are neither modern nor traditional," Soroush remarked. "We are neither here nor there. We are just feeling our way as if in darkness. Sometimes we see better, sometimes not." This in-betweenness, to Soroush, was not a thing to be lamented. It was an impetus to dynamism. At some time in the past, perhaps, Iranians had lived in a world whose philosophy was consistent with its ethics, science, and politics. "Now we are no longer in that state of equilibrium. We are between two things—the harmony lost to us and the harmony yet to be gained."

By May 2005, former president Ali Akbar Hashemi Rafsanjani looked poised to replace Khatami as president. He was everything the reformists had measured themselves against for years. The reformists associated Rafsanjani with the chain murders, with economic corruption and inequality, and with the more repressive atmosphere that preceded their own rule. And they feared his pragmatism. Unlike a true conservative, he would know to open pressure valves—for example, by allowing the people superficial freedoms, like laxer enforcement of the dress code—and how to present a moderate face to the world. But unlike a true reformist, he had no principled investment in democratizing the regime.

Rafsanjani's campaign was flush with funds of mysterious origin and alight with a slick and giddy optimism. It printed no end of glossy stickers and posters; its headquarters teemed with heavily made-up women in glittery sandals and scanty hijab; and young people eagerly snapped up paid work tossing campaign paraphernalia into the windows of cars idling in traffic, lending the Rafsanjani camp a façade of youthful energy. Campaign posters showed an unaccustomed sight: below his narrowed eyes the beardless, plump-faced ayatollah smiled, a tense and mirthless smile that did not inspire joy.

Near mythical in his backroom influence, Rafsanjani was the candidate of the cynical and the uncommitted. His rallies were filled with supporters of other candidates who had come to take in the festive atmosphere or to ask themselves whether whatever it was they wanted done might be done most effectively by someone who was already very powerful. As the sociologist and newspaperman Emadeddin Baghi explained, "People make judgments like this: Khatami was good but too weak. Rafsanjani isn't good, but he's strong."

The reformists could not agree on whether they should present a candidate, let alone on whom that candidate should be. So in the end they presented three. Mehdi Karroubi, the populist cleric who still believed it was possible to negotiate with the conservatives, was the closest to center. He appealed to traditional voters of modest income who had voted for Khatami. His principal campaign promise was a universal $50 cash handout. Mostafa Moin, a colorless former education minister close to the students, was the candidate for the lay reformist party, Mosharekat. He appealed to the modern, urban, and intellectual wings of the reform movement, and embraced the strategy Tajzadeh had articulated in the 2003 seminar, of using government positions for a kind of internal activism. A third candidate, Mohsen Mehralizadeh, little-known outside the northern provinces, served to further divide the reformist vote.

To Rafsanjani's right, the field was crowded as well. The favored conservative candidate, Mohammad Bagher Ghalibaf, was the country's chief of police, a Revolutionary Guardsman who presented himself as a modern conservative, hip to young people's concerns and savvy with modern technology. Thuggish-looking campaign workers in purple jackets zoomed around Tehran on motorcycles to promote Ali Larijani, a hard-liner in the state media and culture establishments. The little-known mayor of Tehran, Mahmoud Ahmadinejad, was the election's darkest dark horse, presumed to trail the other two conservatives, who trailed the centrist former president. Not a single political association or newspaper endorsed him.

Ganji, the student leaders, and a number of other reformists called for boycotting the presidential election. After what had happened to the parliament, there was no point in lending popular legitimacy to a regime determined to expel its loyal opposition. Even some reformists who publically repudiated the boycott privately confessed that they themselves would not vote. Khatami's presidency had deflated their optimism and unmasked the regime's inner inflexibility. Moreover, neither reformist candidate inspired passion.

In the end, the boycott and apathy would hurt no one more than they did Moin, as it was his constituency that was most likely to tilt toward the radical call for noncooperation. To many reformists' surprise, Soroush endorsed Karroubi, although he was closer to Moin both personally and intellectually. Karroubi, in Soroush's view, was closer to the grain of Iranian society and truer to the mood of his moment in history. Moreover, Soroush liked what he saw of Karroubi's conduct, particularly "the relatively free atmosphere that he brings about for thinkers and scholars."

Rafsanjani easily led the first round of voting on June 17 with 21 percent of the vote. The reformists won about 35 percent even with the boycott. But these votes were divided among three candidates, all of whom were sunk. Karroubi won 17.2 percent, Moin 13.8 percent, and Mehralizadeh 4.4 percent; Mehralizadeh's share alone would have catapulted Karroubi into the second round of voting against Rafsanjani. But Rafsanjani would face an unexpected challenger from the right instead. On the eve of the election, the Supreme Leader had shifted his favor from Ghalibaf to Ahmadinejad, who edged past Karroubi with 19.4 percent of the vote. Within the city of Tehran, where the reformist voter boycott was most pronounced, Ahmadinejad even led Rafsanjani by some 200,000 votes in the first round, with the reformists trailing well behind their national totals.

Mehdi Karroubi cried fraud. When he went to sleep at five in the morning on the eighteenth, he famously proclaimed, he was in second place; when he awoke two hours later, he was in third. In fact, the sequence of events was stranger than this. At one point the interior ministry and Guardian Council simultaneously issued partial returns that differed by a count of 6 million votes. The ministry claimed that 15 million votes were in, with Karroubi polling second; but the Guardian Council claimed that 21 million votes had been tabulated, with Ahmadinejad polling second.

Karroubi issued an open letter claiming that Ahmadinejad's share had been artificially inflated. The newspapers that carried the letter were forbidden to circulate. Karroubi resigned from all his political posts, including one as an adviser to the Supreme Leader, who accused him of "poisoning the atmosphere." More surprising was that Rafsanjani, the undisputed frontrunner, suggested that there had been "an organized interference" and lent credence to claims that the Basij and Revolutionary Guard had used six million unexpired birth certificates of dead people to force Ahmadinejad into the second round.

AS IT HAPPENED, Ahmadinejad was an ingenious foil for Rafsanjani. The older ayatollah was the consummate political insider, spectacularly wealthy, associated with widening economic inequality, and perceived as a schemer and dissembler. Ahmadinejad was an outsider if ever there was one. The Tehran mayor was a plainspoken everyman, the son of lower-middle-class rural migrants and an economic populist who spoke with naïve simplicity of bringing the country's oil revenues to the people's kitchen tables. His social conservatism soothed the anxieties of traditional voters even as the fact that he was not a cleric pleased voters weary of theocratic rule. The mayor's face, homely and weathered, had something comical in its proportions: the goofy grin, the swooping wing of side-combed hair, the eyebrows that could lift almost vertically in certain moments of enthusiasm. The scruffy beard and perennial windbreaker marked him, to the urban elite, as a roughneck, a rube, an impression belied by the canny intelligence in his deep-set eyes.

Like Khatami before him, Ahmadinejad could call on the Tehran municipality's war chest for campaign funds, and also like Khatami he ran a masterful campaign, if not in the election's first round, then in its second. During the week between the first and second rounds, an Ahmadinejad ad with poor production values aired incessantly on television. It showed Ahmadinejad driving his 1977 Peugeot, then lingered long inside his small house in South Tehran, where he had remained even as mayor. The ad counterposed these images with shots of a lavish mayoral palace from the shah's time. A voice-over admonished that greed should be eradicated among government men. "Why do they want so much when so many people have nothing?" To the theme song from the 1960 western *The Magnificent Seven*, the voice-over spoke of Ahmadinejad's childhood. The mayor had no money. He'd had to create his own games and toys. "What is youth?" the voice-over asked. "Youth is purity, courage, sacrifice, and serving others."

One of Ahmadinejad's flyers listed five reasons that his opponents might say he should not be president. First, his clothes were not as expensive as those of his security detail. Second, he never took a government car to use for his sons' friends' birthdays. Third, when he met with the city council, instead of speaking for two hours, he sat for seven hours and listened. Fourth, unlike the previous mayor, he didn't smoke a pipe or have an expensive bulletproof car. Finally, instead of paying out tax money to loyalists, he distributed it to young people to help them get married.

The reformists seemed unprepared for this populist assault from the right. Halfheartedly, some of them lined up behind Rafsanjani and called on their supporters to vote for him. But it was hardly a full-throated endorsement. One poster the night before the second-round vote read, "We supporters of Moin, because we do not want to end up in the hands of the Basij, now vote for Hashemi." Even the Rafsanjani campaign had an ironic quality. Some of its young campaigners needled the Ahmadinejad camp by chanting for their candidate as "DJ Ali Akbar."

The streets of Tehran were electric the night of June 22, but the atmosphere had tilted from festive to volatile by an imperceptible degree. Campaign paraphernalia, from posters and bumper stickers to CDs, rained down on passing traffic from the sides of the roads. Young bearded men, less visible in the first round, now owned large tracts of the city for the Ahmadinejad campaign. They had a sober, earnest quality, especially in comparison to the slightly ironic cast of the Rafsanjani campaign. Revolutionary Guardsmen and Basijis manned the intersections.

Among Ahmadinejad's young voters and volunteers were many who had voted for Khatami just four years before. They were young men and women from the lower middle and working classes, some of whom had embraced Khatami's call for greater political freedom. But they did not feel they'd gotten much out of eight years of reformist rule. They imagined that Ahmadinejad, by virtue of being a common man without a turban, would better understand their economic problems. And to the extent that reform had not produced any freedom that mattered in their lives, they did not fear that Ahmadinejad would cost them anything of value.

MAHMOUD AHMADINEJAD WAS ELECTED president on June 24, 2005. In August he appointed a cabinet that made his intentions unmistakably clear. He drew ministers from the ultra-hardline Haghani Circle of clerics that Ganji had once linked to the serial killings. The judge who had presided over Mayor Karbaschi's trial, Gholam-Hossein Mohseni-Ejei, was made minister of intelligence. The new interior minister, Mostafa Pour-mohammadi, had served on the three-man board that consigned prisoners to execution in the 1988 prison massacre. The Tehran chief prosecutor, Saeed Mortazavi, would swiftly emerge as one of Ahmadinejad's closest associates and political allies.

After the election, Roozbeh Mirebrahimi resembled a bereaved man sorting through the personal effects of a loved one who had unforgivably disappointed him. The reform movement as he knew it was dead. Sometimes it seemed to Roozbeh that it deserved to be.

For Roozbeh, Khatami embodied the movement's promise and its failure, and it was with pained ambivalence that he watched the president leave office on July 30. He wrote on his blog, "I only feel sorrow for Mr. Khatami, that everything he had in the palm of his hand in most regards will disappear into the sky." Later he questioned his own sorrow. Khatami held a ceremony honoring his return to private life. At the event, he was asked about Akbar Ganji. "The problem is more on Ganji's side," Khatami said, blaming Ganji's extended incarceration on his refusal to stop speaking out.

Roozbeh wrote, "Truth be told, a while ago I wanted to get a letter to him somehow, which I wrote upon the end of his presidency, and thank him and let him know how well I appreciate the lasting accomplishments he made during his term. I'd readied the letter a while back, but the position Khatami took about Ganji made me abandon the idea of sending it."

As he reread his letter, Roozbeh wrote, he felt depressed. "But what gains did we make in that time that we screamed: 'Do something!' Only his silence was our answer . . . In any case, now still, we must sit and, with fear and never-ending hope, look to the future together.

"With shame, I must say to those who support the reformists that, even in your dreams, in the next election you won't be allowed to so much as put up posters."

IV

RESISTANCE

FOURTEEN

A COMMON MAN

IRAN NEVER HAD A POLITICIAN like Mahmoud Ahmadinejad. It had suffered the paternal stewardship of monarchs and learned clerics, aristocrats and scholars; even Mohammad Mossadegh was a patrician sort. All were elites, whether they spoke of social justice, national dignity, or civil society. Ahmadinejad was something else. He was a common man, and a demagogue. The body politic reacted as to some new and potent liquor—some parts of it euphoric, others suspicious, as though watching a normally staid loved one stagger from the dinner table.

Ahmadinejad circled the country, visiting some two thousand towns in two years. He all but threw money into the crowds that greeted him. He pledged federal funds on the spot for a town's pet project or most glaring need, to uproarious applause. He was like a game show host or a faith healer. He made miracles; he anointed ordinary people with his largesse. He stayed long enough to feel the shining eyes upon him. The state bureaucracy scrambled behind, frantically squeezing budgets and breaking rules so as not to disappoint the hopes he'd raised.

To make good on the president's impulsive promises required raiding the country's oil stabilization fund, set up by the Khatami administration in order to float the country's economy in years when oil prices dropped.

Sometimes the president just ordered the banks to issue more currency. Ahmadinejad didn't care to look forward or back. Oil was at a premium, and (so he believed) the provincial people loved him.

Ahmadinejad would be associated, particularly in the international press and among the upper classes in Tehran, with the Iranian hinterland. But he was entirely a creature of the capital city. Born in 1956, Ahmadinejad was one of the millions of rural migrants who swelled Tehran under the shah. His family moved there from a village called Aradan when Ahmadinejad was only a baby. His father was a blacksmith, forging iron gates in the economically diverse eastern neighborhood of Narmak. The chip on Ahmadinejad's shoulder must have been a familiar protrusion among men of his background: internal immigrants, Iranians who had never actually known village life but absorbed their parents' alienation from the cities they called home.

Ahmadinejad was small, wiry, and cocky, his chin jutting upward in nearly every youthful photograph, as though waiting to deflect a blow. He discovered Shariati during his university years—he stayed close to home, studying engineering in Narmak at a university called Elm va Sanat—and he would devote his political career to his interpretation of Shariati's radical call for social justice. But unlike many of Shariati's acolytes, Ahmadinejad swung to the Islamic right rather than the left. Like Soroush, he was attracted to the right-wing anti-Bahai group called the Hojjatieh. He was either the founder or an early member of Elm va Sanat's Islamic Society, which, also like Soroush, dedicated itself to combating Marxism with Islam.

After the revolution, Ahmadinejad was active in the Cultural Revolution, serving on the committee that purged his university's faculty and student body. Well before Ali Afshari, he was a member of the national student council, Daftar-e Tahkim-e Vahdat. But when students took over the American embassy, Ahmadinejad balked. The hostage takers hailed from the Islamic Left, and Ahmadinejad from the right: by some accounts he argued that the students should seize the embassy only if they took the Soviet embassy as well. By other accounts he argued that occupying the embassy would lead to lawlessness. In any case, for an ambitious young revolutionary, the embassy seizure was an opportunity missed. The hostage takers vaulted into Iran's permanent political class. Ahmadinejad would have to get there the hard way.

As a young man, Ahmadinejad went west. He was just twenty-four when his revolutionary associates offered him political postings in the provinces along Iran's western borders, where he was charged with helping to put down a Kurdish insurgency and yoke ethnically diverse borderlands to the increasingly repressive central state. In 1993 he was made governor of the sizable, ethnically Azeri province of Ardabil. He was an unpopular governor—a Tehran native whose priorities lay well to the east of Ardabil. He used his post to campaign for Nategh-Nouri, Khatami's conservative rival for the presidency in 1997, and later came under investigation for diverting local funds to the presidential campaign. When Khatami came to power, his deputy interior minister, Mostafa Tajzadeh, cleaned house, sweeping the old governors out of office and replacing them with reformists. Ahmadinejad would remember Tajzadeh for this.

It must have seemed to Ahmadinejad, when he moved back to Tehran, that the reformists had taken everything. He ran for city council in 1999 but lost; for the parliament in 2000 but lost. According to his biographer, he was active in those years against Khatami to the point of being a regular speaker at private gatherings of Ansar-e Hezbollah. But it was the victory of the conservative faction called Abadgaran in the municipal elections of 2003 that would restore Ahmadinejad's ambitions.

Abadgaran was as much a child of the revolution as reform had been. The Basij, the Revolutionary Guard, the hardline seminaries, and other revolutionary institutions had now been around long enough to credential a new class of political hopefuls. These young men and women had marinated in the rhetoric of the early revolutionary period, but not in the complexities of governance. They spoke the language of the past with the zeal of the untried. Now they rebelled as much against the smug paternalism of the right as against the syncretism and perceived impiety of the reformists. They made Ahmadinejad mayor of the vibrant, difficult, teeming city he called home.

. . .

THE CITY OF TEHRAN BECAME, for about two years, Ahmadinejad's problem. Surprisingly or unsurprisingly, the underlying machinery of the city did not change. When Karbaschi had set it all in motion—density sales, overbuilding, the casino of construction and property flipping—it seemed an expression of the Rafsanjani faction's mentality, opaque and even a little ruthless in the name of efficiency and growth. When the reformists, for all their talk of popular participation and political development, failed to replace the Karbaschi machine with something more transparent or fair, it seemed a political failure, a reflection of fecklessness and abstraction. Now came Ahmadinejad, a hardline conservative with a populist bent, a common man who refused to live in the mayoral residence and granted himself only the secretary's cubby of Karbaschi's former penthouse office. Ahmadinejad, too, sustained Tehran on density sales.

As they had done so many times before, city planners beseeched the mayor to stop selling building permits. Tehran's population was about to exceed nine million, which would pose serious problems for earthquake safety and water supply. Ahmadinejad refused. "The city lives because of construction," one city planner remembers Ahmadinejad telling the city council. "Can you imagine Tehran without construction? Would it be a living city?" With a stroke of a pen, at a single meeting Ahmadinejad threw the planners' work into chaos by increasing the city's density by 10 percent beyond what the planners had carefully negotiated over the previous two years.

Ahmadinejad was trained as a traffic engineer, and in the end, arguably, his most lasting achievement as mayor was the construction of turnouts to facilitate U-turns. But he did everything he could to be remembered instead for his devotion to Islam, to the martyrs of the Iran-Iraq War, and to the values of the traditional lower class from which he came. He would bury the remains of Iran-Iraq War dead in the city's public squares, he told the public. The city would become a monument to its martyrs. When city dwellers recoiled from this as morbid and manipulative, he assigned the graves to university campuses and parks instead.

Ahmadinejad restricted the programming at the cultural centers Karbaschi had founded, giving them a more Islamic cast, and he announced his priorities by offering generous grants to neighborhood religious groups, mosques, and the Basij. He repaved the streets in poor neighborhoods but not in rich ones, and he cultivated a close relationship between the city management and the Revolutionary Guards. None of this made Ahmadinejad a hero or a villain to the Iranian public, nor, certainly, did it prepare anyone for his star turn as president. In fact, hardly anyone in Tehran knew his name. Only later would a character affix itself to those two years in Tehran's municipal life—one that was brash and contemptuous of expertise but adept in symbolic politics.

PRESIDENT AHMADINEJAD hated economists. They were penny-pinching killjoys who always found reasons not to make the people happy. "Immediately these people say our decisions raise the people's expectations and that they are not in accordance with the science of economics," Ahmadinejad complained. "If your economics does not help meeting the rightful demands of the people, then we hate your economics!"

When the new Iranian president promised to bring the oil money to the people's tables and to improve the lot of Iran's lower classes, he did not propose to do so through economic planning or any structural change in the country's distribution of wealth. Rather, he meant to hand out money. He disbanded the Management and Planning Organization, which was the one governmental redoubt of economists dedicated to solving the country's deep-seated problems. And he injected billions of dollars in oil revenues directly into the economy. He did it with his rural bequests, his grants to young married couples, his precipitous hikes in wages, and his looting of the country's savings. There would be no economic planning under Ahmadinejad; only damage control, after the fact.

About a year into his presidency, fifty economics professors wrote an open letter to Ahmadinejad, imploring him to reverse course. He risked squandering the oil surplus and stoking inflation, they protested.

"Economics, like any other science," they wrote, in tones at once pedantic and pleading, "is the result of the accumulation of human knowledge, and scientific achievements of economics are used for the advance and prosperity of human societies. For this reason, economics can and must be used in drawing up the government's economic policies." Ahmadinejad gleefully discarded their advice.

Liquidity increased by nearly 40 percent in the space of a year. Iranians used this cash to buy imports, which buried local industries and sent prices soaring. Within a year of Ahmadinejad's election, Iran's inflation rate was the fourth highest in the world, after Zimbabwe, Uzbekistan, and Burma; by the summer of 2008 it topped 28 percent. Meanwhile, Ahmadinejad slashed interest rates, a move that encouraged lending, drove the country's fragile banking sector to the edge of ruin, and contributed to a surreal housing bubble in Iran's cities. In 2007 and then again in 2008, Tehran real estate prices more than doubled.

The analyst Saeed Laylaz said of Iranians who rented their homes, "One night they slept, and they awoke in the morning and they realized that they were under the poverty line." Nearly seven hundred thousand urban Iranians fell into poverty in 2006. Inequality worsened for the first time since the Rafsanjani reforms. But Ahmadinejad fancied himself a man of the people, with his thumb in the eye of the reformist elite.

AHMADINEJAD APPEARED TO MAKE foreign policy the way he made fiscal policy: he smashed things and watched indifferently as others picked up the pieces, moaned over the consequences, or tried to divine his motives and knit them into policy. He shocked world opinion by denying the Holocaust and then inviting fellow Holocaust deniers, anti-Semites, white supremacists, neo-Nazis, and other sinister Westerners to Tehran for a conference celebrating his views. He wrote arrogant, rambling, messianic letters to world leaders. He even invited German chancellor Angela Merkel to cast off the weight of historical guilt and humiliation unfairly heaped on her great country and join Iran in an alliance against the victors of World

War II. He evinced little to no understanding of diplomacy or world history, and he swept aside all the efforts of his predecessors to find revolutionary Iran a place among nations that was respected if not loved.

But foreign policy, unlike economic policy, was not then and never had been administered from the pocket of the president. Ahmadinejad's provocations, his flagrant anti-Semitism, his demagogic style, were surely his own, but Ayatollah Khamenei remained firmly in control of the deep security state, in both its domestic and its international dimensions. If Ahmadinejad's theatrics provided Iran time and cover of darkness under which to pursue nuclear technology, this was not a vicissitude of factional politics but a rational decision on the part of a largely consistent foreign policy establishment that now saw an American military presence on two borders and understood itself targeted, as a member of an "Axis of Evil," for regime change. At home, too, the judiciary, the intelligence apparatus, and the militias, all under the command of the Leader's office, were no more answerable to the president than they had been under Khatami. If the space for free expression constricted, if the reformist parties and media came under pressure, this was not the doing of the president alone. It just so happened that he approved these measures and that there was not much daylight, during Ahmadinejad's first term, between the security apparatus and the elected government.

And yet, if Khamenei had expected Ahmadinejad to act solely as his deputy, he had severely misjudged the man's character. No one as impulsive and grandiose as the little man from Narmak could be held entirely in line. Ahmadinejad undertook the most far-reaching governmental housecleaning since the revolution itself, replacing a reported twenty thousand bureaucrats, including all the bank managers and some forty diplomats. "They were very arrogant," said Nasser Hadian, a childhood friend of the president's, about Ahmadinejad and his camp. "They didn't want to make any compromises. He has stood against the entire political structure in Iran, not inviting any of them, even the conservatives, to be partners. You don't see them in the cabinet, you don't see them in political positions." And for that there was a price to be paid. The conservatives split into two broad camps: one, ultra-hardline and populist, was linked to the president, and another, known as traditional conservatives, were more seasoned, cautious team players who were ultimately loyal to Khamenei.

THE PRESIDENT'S RELIGIOUS PREDILECTIONS were eccentric. He dropped references to his personal relationship with the Mahdi, or the vanished twelfth imam and Shiite messiah. He spoke of seeing himself surrounded by light when he addressed world leaders in New York, and of how none of them, while bathed in his aura, could so much as blink. He claimed that the United States had dispatched spies to Iraq and Iran to hunt the Mahdi because they knew his return was imminent and sought to foreclose Iran's coming state of grace. Traditional Iranian clerics found such talk offensive, self-regarding, and borderline heretical. The ultra-hardline Ayatollah Mohammad-Taghi Mesbah-Yazdi encouraged it.

Mesbah, as the ayatollah was called, had known the president and stoked his spiritual delusions for more than a decade. The authoritarian cleric had an occultist, superstitious streak. He suggested that certain mortals could open direct channels to the Mahdi, who would then speak and act through them. Ahmadinejad was apparently among the anointed. In 2005, Mesbah and his acolytes campaigned for Ahmadinejad and hailed his ascension to the presidency as a divine miracle. For Mesbah, it might as well have been. In the first year of his presidency alone, Ahmadinejad allocated $3.5 million from the federal budget to Mesbah's institute in Qom; by 2011 the allocation would reach $7 million.

Skeptics would note that Ahmadinejad's occult pretensions were as much a political tool as his cash handouts—that they preyed on the ignorant and the desperate, fostering passivity and slavish devotion. As president, Ahmadinejad invested in shrines to the twelfth imam, encouraged the susceptible to see ubiquitous signs of his imminent return, and suggested that his own policies were the work of the exalted hidden world. The country's first elected lay president since Bani-Sadr had sacralized himself more than any of his cleric predecessors had ever dared to do.

Mesbah's political aims were no secret. He sought to purge the reform-ists from power and consolidate religious autocracy. He openly disparaged popular sovereignty, free speech, women's rights, the separation of powers, and Islamic reform. The elected institutions, Mesbah believed, served at the pleasure of the Supreme Leader. Because God ruled Iran through the person of the Leader, to complain of despotism was blasphemy. "We shall wait to see what place these foxes who set claim to be the supporters of reform will occupy in hell," he proclaimed, and, of participatory democ-racy: "It doesn't matter what the people think. The people are ignorant sheep." Mesbah held that the government should regulate the content of speech "just as it checks the distribution of adulterated or contaminated foodstuff." He called for the violent elimination of those who disagreed with him. Ahmadinejad, too, scorned all efforts to establish democracy in Iran as counterrevolutionary. He was as much a tool in Mesbah's hands as Mesbah was a tool in his.

Mesbah had powerful supporters in the establishment, including the elderly ayatollah who presided over the Guardian Council. But other tradi-tional clerics balked. Not only did they reject, as a matter of doctrine, the notion that the Mahdi meddled in this world from his occultation, let alone that he did so through select mortals, but they worried that the president and Mesbah undermined Islam by toying with the people's faith in order to justify Ahmadinejad's policies.

THERE WOULD BE TWO MIDTERM ELECTIONS during Ahmadinejad's first term. The first, in December of 2006, was really two elections in one. Iranians were to elect their city councils on the same day that they elected the Assembly of Experts, the body of high-ranking clerics that would select the next Supreme Leader should anything happen to Khamenei. The Assembly of Experts election was normally a quiet affair, held once every eight years with candidates drawn from preselected lists of elderly ayatol-lahs. Scheduling it the same day as the city council election was meant to drive voters to the polls. Ahmadinejad further enlivened the scene by offering his own slates of candidates. For the city councils, it was a front related to Abadgaran and mystifyingly called the Pleasant Aroma of Service. For the Assembly of Experts, Ahmadinejad endorsed Mesbah and a ticket of ultra-hardline scholars associated with him.

Mesbah had been waiting for this. In the fall of 2006, his group put forward a tidal wave of candidates in a bid to transform the assembly. The Guardian Council disqualified more than half of all proposed candidates for the Assembly of Experts, and this time the rejects included not only most of the proffered reformists, but a large number of Mesbah's students as well. Even so, clerics associated with Mesbah stood a reasonable chance of winning forty of the assembly's eighty-six seats.

But the electorate rejected both the hardline Islamic scholars and the Pleasant Aroma of Service. Reformists won some 40 percent of all city council seats and even dominated in some cities. The conservative city council candidates who did well were not those associated with Ahmadinejad. Most dramatically, for the Assembly of Experts, Rafsanjani's vote dwarfed Mesbah's nearly two to one. This was the first of two midterm elections that would offer clues about Ahmadinejad's public standing.

UNDER PRESIDENT AHMADINEJAD, Iran became a tensely coiled country, as much confused as suppressed. The red lines delineating the boundaries of acceptable behavior and discussion had never been drawn with clarity or consistency; now they seemed to be tightening nooselike around a public sphere that had enlarged, despite its difficulties, under Khatami.

Reform was not irreversible, it turned out. Politically undesirable university professors could be fired, and some two hundred were. Students could be punished for their activism, and they were, via a "star" system that marked them for expulsion on political grounds. Ahmadinejad introduced a "Program for Social Safety" that dispatched police vans to city squares to harass improperly dressed women; he pressed legislation that eroded the status of women in marriage and set quotas limiting the numbers of women accepted to universities in certain fields. By 2008, newspapers associated with Rafsanjani and Karroubi were the last redoubts of the critical press. Karroubi's political front, called Etemad Melli like its newspaper and consisting of cautious clerics, was the only reformist party still active in politics.

When the reformists stopped to ask themselves how they'd reached this pass, they had to concede one thing to Ahmadinejad. It was, as might be said elsewhere, the economy, stupid. Iran's economic problems were structural, and they predated both Ahmadinejad and the reformists. The government depended on oil for 65 percent of its revenues. So long as Iranians understood that their country was rich in resources, the have-nots would look in suspicion on the haves. The money was there. It was the people's birthright. Why, then, did some Iranians live well and others poorly? The very opacity of this arrangement would always leave openings for demagogues. Then there was the fact that economic mismanagement was as old as the Islamic Republic, and probably much older than that.

Oil rendered Iranians dependent on the state, which controlled the resource, and the state independent of its people, who hardly needed to participate in the economy to keep it afloat. The middle class, with its disposable income, its professional expertise in fields like law and medicine, and its entrepreneurial potential, drives productivity in many of the world's economies, but in Iran it was practically superfluous. If the state had depended for its revenues on a taxable, productive middle class, it might have had to cultivate a relationship of trust and a climate of cooperation with these citizens. But with oil rents, the government saw no necessity or virtue in stimulating productivity.

The numbers told the story. Under Khatami, thanks to an oil boom, poverty had declined, inequality did not rise, and by 2005 the standard of living in Iran was the highest it had been since the mid-1970s. But oil rents tended to create unskilled jobs in sectors like construction. During Khatami's two terms, unemployment among illiterate men declined from 17 to 8 percent; among men with advanced degrees, it leaped from 15 to 23 percent. And among the most educated women, it was a stunning 43 percent.

The Islamic Republic was becoming a victim of its greatest success.

The postrevolutionary state had done much to promote social mobility, from modernizing the countryside and lowering the rural birthrate to expanding the country's university system. More Iranians than ever before climbed into the middle class, but once there, they found themselves adrift. The professions were heavily vetted for political orthodoxy, and there was not much private sector to speak of. Iran was by and large a middle-class country by the time Ahmadinejad took office, but to sustain a middle-class lifestyle required many Iranians to depend on unstable and ultimately unproductive sources of income: informal second jobs, the brokering of deals among third parties, the selling of family property. Middle-class Iranians complained, but even economists dismissed their complaints as so much entitlement or melodrama. The educated middle class was thought to be a prime reformist constituency, and the reformists were out: Ahmadinejad saw no political or economic cost to ignoring or antagonizing it.

Anyway, the president was in luck. He presided over the most dramatic spike in oil prices since the Islamic Revolution. He turned it into liquid cash, and loans upon loans. He'd come into the presidency offering patronage to the poor and spiritual exaltation to the gullible, but he had no interest in addressing the chronic insecurity of Iran's broad middle class, which, along with everyone else, now faced soaring prices and a real estate bubble. What should have felt like boom years felt more like a recession. When the price of oil declined, as it was sure to, the country would not even have its savings to fall back on.

The economic frustration that Ahmadinejad had tapped into with his 2005 campaign turned strongly against him by 2008. More than half of the deputies in the parliament had signed a letter blaming Ahmadinejad's policies for rising unemployment and inflation. In a parliamentary election that March, even Ahmadinejad's political allies could not run from his economic program fast enough, with many of them openly criticizing his contribution to inflation. The president's conservative critics carried the election by a comfortable margin. The conservative electorate was calling the president to heel.

. . .

BY THE TIME of the 2008 parliamentary election, Mosharekat, once the party of the ruling reformist majority, seemed a relic. It occupied a dilapidated pale brick town house in central Tehran, with a second-floor office designed for the wheelchair-bound visionary Saeed Hajjarian. While in the gleaming glass headquarters of the United Fundamentalist Front, not far from Haft-e Tir Square, candidates who differed by a hair's breadth tangled in lively and consequential debates about economic policy, Mosharekat theorists gathered for discussions so abstract they threatened to lift off the earth. Was Iran locked in a sultanistic system, or merely a sultanistic situation? Had official lies inured the populace to dishonesty and weakened the country's ethics? Were human rights enshrined in Islam? All of these were topics for discussion at a forum commemorating the anniversary of Hajjarian's shooting, but also coinciding with the parliamentary election campaign. One must have imagination, a reformist philosopher intoned at the gathering, without nurturing illusions.

The party still had a handful of members in the parliament, mostly from the provinces. The reformist minority leader, Nouradin Pirmoazen, a thoracic surgeon from a prominent family in Ardabil, happened to be at a conference in the United States when he heard that most of his colleagues, including many incumbents, had been disqualified by the Guardian Council from running for reelection. Pirmoazen spoke out in an interview on Voice of America, objecting that the election would be neither free nor fair. He soon found himself the subject of televised threats from the intelligence minister. Pirmoazen, marooned in Boston, would be one fewer reformist legislator for the fundamentalists to deal with.

By the fall of 2008, with the presidential election less than a year away, the reformists appeared to be spent. Their constituency was the one least likely to vote, because they were allowed so few candidates and had suffered such dispiriting experiences in power. To stand a chance of winning back the presidency the following year, reformists would need two things that seemed entirely quixotic to hope for: a galvanizing candidate and enormous voter turnout.

Toward the end of 2008, a declaration appeared, signed by an organization that called itself Setad 88. The group consisted of eighty-eight young reformist activists from across the country, and it announced its support for Mohammad Khatami if he were to run for president. Khatami was, the young activists felt, the only reformist who could handily defeat the incumbent. In spite of everything that had transpired during Khatami's eight years in power, the man was still widely loved and respected, the more so after the four years Iranians had just endured of Ahmadinejad's amusement park ride.

Setad meant business. It had already begun organizing a nationwide Khatami campaign without the former president's consent. It formed campaign teams, with eighty-eight members apiece, in every province. The provincial teams then organized township teams, and the big cities like Tehran had a team for each municipal district. There had never been anything like this in reformist politics. Setad was not a campaign run by a candidate. Khatami was a candidate recruited by a campaign.

Khatami had been a reluctant candidate in 1997; it was said that he shed tears upon agreeing, even more reluctantly, to run for reelection in 2001. Now he came to the fray, in February 2009, with what was undoubtedly a very heavy heart. But the situation in the country was dire, and the campaign preceded him. For the third time in his life, he took to the campaign trail, where the young people who'd once turned from him in disappointment now thronged his events. For all that he had failed to achieve, Khatami still represented something to his constituents—the better angels of their Islamic Republic, perhaps; the face of invitation rather than exclusion. Still, Khatami told his followers that he would step aside, gladly, for another reformist candidate, and that he would focus his energy on persuading the former prime minister, Mir Hossein Mousavi, to run in his stead.

MIR HOSSEIN MOUSAVI was a cipher. He had done something no other prominent member of the postrevolutionary nomenklatura had done:

he'd all but quit politics. From the very pinnacle of power under Khomeini, when he was Iran's wartime prime minister and favored son of the Supreme Leader; for twenty years, while his associates and his rivals battled over the legacy of the revolution they'd wrought; Mousavi largely retreated into private life. He was an architecture professor and a painter. He rebuffed all entreaties to run for office, even as he became an icon, to older Iranians, of a revolutionary competence and rectitude lost.

As a contemporary politician, said Khatami's former vice president Mohammad Ali Abtahi, Mousavi was "like an unopened melon; people don't have much information about what's going on inside." For those had been a crucial twenty years. Most of Mousavi's colleagues on the Islamic Left had made the dramatic and unforeseeable turn to liberal reformism. Then they had weathered the eight disappointing years of Khatami's presidency, and fallen along a spectrum of critique. Mousavi had not publicly accompanied his former allies on any part of this journey. By the company he kept, he was presumed to be a reformist. But by the history he embodied, he was still Khomeini's man.

Mousavi announced his candidacy on March 10, 2009. Khatami, as he'd promised, withdrew. He directed his supporters to embrace Mousavi instead. "I know that I would get the vote if I ran," said Khatami, "but the election is not just the voting on Friday. One also needs a candidate who on Saturday is strong enough to push his agenda. Mir Hossein is the man of Saturday."

For many young people, including those with Setad 88, this wasn't an obvious choice. They didn't know Mousavi, and his association with the revolutionary decade wasn't a credit to him in their eyes. Moreover, he was an ambiguous candidate. He distanced himself from Mosharekat's endorsement and suggested that if he was a reformist, he was equally a "principlist," which was the conservative faction's self-description. In an interview with *Der Spiegel*, Mousavi was hard put to distinguish himself from his rival on foreign policy, particularly regarding the nuclear issue, Israel, and relations with the United States; he even danced around a question about the Holocaust. But he did suggest that he would try to abolish the religious police.

Mainly, at first, Mousavi campaigned on a return to rational and responsible economic policy and planning. Under his premiership, Iran had suffered war, sanctions, and record-low oil revenues, but there had been neither shortages nor runaway inflation. Ahmadinejad, by comparison, looked profligate and unprofessional. And yet, Mousavi's ideological background marked him as a populist from the left, just as Ahmadinejad was a populist from the right. Like Ahmadinejad, Mousavi was also an ascetic who challenged official corruption with the very public humility of his lifestyle and character.

Mousavi was not the only reformist in the race. Mehdi Karroubi, by now a perennial candidate, had registered as well. Karroubi had made a very credible showing in 2005, and since that time he had come to speak out ever more boldly on rights and freedoms. Many of the old reformist intellectual elite supported Karroubi, mindful not only of his theoretical positions but of his consistently humane treatment of the families of political prisoners. Setad contemplated supporting Karroubi as the candidate most clearly in line with the demands of its young activists. But in the end it cast its weight behind the more visible candidate with the greater chance of winning.

Mousavi instantly inherited a campaign infrastructure that penetrated the entire country and that benefited from the energy of young people fed up with the status quo. For its posters and other campaign materials, Setad selected an image of Mousavi in a habitual pose, with his hand on his chest, an Iranian gesture of humility before one's interlocutor. The campaign adopted the color green, traditionally symbolic of Islam.

None of this suggested that the 2009 election would be an exciting one. Since Bani-Sadr, no elected president of the Islamic Republic had failed to serve two terms. Ahmadinejad was controversial and even unpopular among conservatives, if the midterm elections were any indication, but he faced no credible conservative rival. Mousavi was the de facto candidate of the reformists, but no one expected them to vote; so he was making a run for Ahmadinejad's voters, appealing to their nostalgia for early revolutionary ideology and the shared purpose of the Iran-Iraq War. So long as the reform-minded voters who'd sat out 2005, 2006, and 2008 remained on the sidelines, this election would be a narrow battle fought on Ahmadinejad's home turf.

SUPREME LEADER ALI KHAMENEI portrayed every election as an opportunity to demonstrate Iran's revolutionary steadfastness to the world by showing Iran's enemies that the Islamic Republic was vital and loved by its people. The country's high voter turnout was a matter of pride, as was the atmosphere of relative freedom that attended the campaign season, which officially lasted just two weeks prior to the vote. Given the lackluster turnout for the last three elections, the Islamic Republic was eager to "warm up the scene," as was often said in Tehran, to create a sense of excitement that would spur the fence-sitters to vote.

And so, in early June of 2009, the Islamic Republic tried something new: televised presidential debates in what would be described as the "American style." To any American viewer, however, the style was entirely foreign. The Iranian politicians did not speak in glib, focus group–tested sound bites but tended to ramble, interrupt themselves, and preface their remarks with prefaces to their prefaces. They spoke not to the public but to one another, unscripted and unrehearsed, and the combat was, at times, ferocious despite occasional exaggerated displays of Persian gentility. Iranian viewers were riveted.

Mousavi and Ahmadinejad squared off on June 3. It was the first chance many viewers had to get to know Mousavi as he spoke off the cuff, batting away what seemed at times to be a hail of missiles. The men faced each other at opposite ends of a large oval table in a television studio, across a centerpiece of white flowers. Mousavi was an elegant man in a professorial way. He was slender and white-haired, with wire-rimmed spectacles and a trimmed goatee. His gestures were restrained, his gaze cold. Across the table, Ahmadinejad looked more dapper than usual in a pressed gray blazer. He was also unusually serious, his mouth set in a line, his eyebrows parenthetical, a sheaf of papers in his lap and on the table before him.

The president's tone was bullying, self-pitying, and smarmy by turns. He opened by arguing that he faced not one opponent but the combined force of three: Mousavi, Khatami, and Rafsanjani had ganged up against a solitary, beleaguered Ahmadinejad in a relentless conspiracy. The public should not be fooled: Ahmadinejad ran not against Mousavi but against the whole past establishment, which felt its privileges threatened by Ahmadinejad's selfless service to the people. All the problems of the country had been laid at Ahmadinejad's feet. "Are these problems all created in the past four years?" demanded the president bitterly. "What about the twenty-four years before that? Does it mean that there was a heaven, and a utopia, and you delivered that to me, and I turned it to hell, and nothing positive has been done?"

Mousavi had complained that Ahmadinejad's foreign policy was reckless, the president groused. But during these four years Iran had made significant progress on its nuclear program and won the respect of Third World nations. "If Mr. Mousavi thinks that we should try to favor and please three or four major powers, this is against the late Imam's ideas and the values of the Islamic Revolution and our independence."

Ahmadinejad had many reasonable points to make, mainly about Mousavi's record, which the president claimed was not significantly better than Ahmadinejad's on civil liberties: in Mousavi's time, the president pointed out, there was but one newspaper that dared criticize the prime minister's proposed budget, and Mousavi had fulminated against it as an enemy of the revolution. Ahmadinejad, by comparison, tolerated a great deal more criticism. Could Mousavi speak of Ahmadinejad as dictatorial when his own government had stripped the president of his powers and used strong-arm tactics against its rivals in the parliament?

But the president came off as emotionally labile and thuggish. He lobbed criminal accusations at Rafsanjani's sons, and of their father he said darkly, "We believe he's actually the main player. We know who is running whose electoral campaign committee and what meetings, who's organizing those meetings and campaign." Toward the end of the debate, he displayed a photograph of Mousavi's wife, a former university chancellor. "I have a dossier from a lady," the president sneered. "You know the lady. She sits next to you in your campaign, which is against all the regulations." Ahmadinejad accused Mousavi's wife of having falsified her academic credentials. "*This* is lawlessness," Ahmadinejad remarked. The move would have been shocking anywhere, but in Iran it was especially brazen. To attack not only a respected cultural figure but the wife of a pious man, holding up her photograph no less, was the height of disrespect.

Mousavi did not shrink from the bullying or pretend that he and Ahmadinejad agreed more than they differed, nor did he respond in kind to Ahmadinejad's many saccharine protestations that he sought only to educate Mousavi because he liked him so much. There were two ways to govern the country, Mousavi stated. One was on the basis of "adventurism, instability, exhibitionism, raising slogans, imaginative moves, superstition, selfishness, self-centeredness, and not abiding by the rule of law, and also on the basis of going to extremes." If this didn't sound good, Mousavi offered the path of "collective wisdom" and "moderation." He'd decided to run for president, he explained, because the country had gone so far off course that he considered the situation dangerous.

Ahmadinejad had a tendency, Mousavi alleged, to flout the law when it got in his way. He set a bad precedent by doing so and a pernicious example for the people. He ignored parliamentary legislation he disagreed with and had dissolved the Management and Planning Organization on a whim. And wherever Mousavi went, he heard that university students were arrested, humiliated, and expelled, publishers banned or forced into bankruptcy by the censorship of their titles, artists and even clerics suppressed. Ahmadinejad had needlessly turned countless Iranians, including the cultural elite, against the government by dividing people into insiders and outsiders.

Ahmadinejad's erratic approach to foreign policy had undermined Iran's dignity and created tensions with other countries, Mousavi said. His extremism was a particular boon to Israel, which could now credibly claim to feel threatened by Iran. This was a "calamity," according to the former prime minister. As for the claim that he, Mousavi, was three candidates in one, the candidate openly scoffed. "Mr. Khatami is not just an unknown person; he has been a president for eight years; Mr. Hashemi too. So you can talk to them. . . . [The state broadcasting network] is at your disposal; you can invite them to a round table and talk to them. [How] are they related to me? It has nothing to do with me. I say that your foreign policy has inflicted damage on the country and on us, and Iran has been caged as a result of your economic and foreign policies."

Maybe it was his incontestable stature, as a former prime minister from the storied past, or his twenty-year absence from the scene, or maybe it was just his character, but Mousavi came off as a man who refused to be intimidated. Rumor had it that Mousavi had left politics at Khamenei's command, because the Leader feared his obstinacy. The former prime minister's performance on live television gave credence to such rumors. Iranians were watching, and many were persuaded that night to vote.

THIRTY-FIVE-YEAR-OLD ASIEH AMINI was just such a viewer. She was not a reformist. She had little use for grand ideas or factional politics. But she had given over her life, during Ahmadinejad's term, to battling just the sort of lawlessness Mousavi described. If the four years of hardline rule were a winter for Iranian activism, Asieh was one of its few hardy evergreens.

The activists of the Khatami era had been beguiled by visions and persuaded by theories. Their individual labors were threads in a larger tapestry designed by men like Hajjarian. Moreover, they imagined that they had powerful backers—that they were doing the bidding of a president who had called them forth as pioneers. Their sufferings in prison had been unexpected, and compounded by feelings of betrayal and abandonment. Asieh Amini was an activist for a different movement and a different time.

In the spring of 2009, Asieh Amini resolved not to vote. She imagined few Iranians would. They had no reason to trust the regime or to believe in its potential for reform. And the reformist candidates were, at first blush, uninspiring. Mehdi Karroubi had never interested her. She didn't think he stood a chance of winning, and even if he did win, she doubted he had the will or the muscle to change much. Mir Hossein Mousavi's twenty-year silence bothered her. He was a politician, a former prime minister. How could he have been so close to the system all those years and said nothing? And what leverage could such a person have if he gained power?

On a trip to her hometown in northern Iran, Asieh was surprised to find her family and friends abuzz about the former prime minister. Mousavi's history of conflict with Khamenei made him attractive to voters critical of the Leader. That he brought his wife, the artist and intellectual Zahra Rahnavard, into his campaign was particularly thrilling. No Iranian politician had ever campaigned with his wife before. By doing so, Mousavi vividly demonstrated his respect for his wife—and, by extension, for the political agency of women. Still, Asieh was not persuaded.

In Tehran, Asieh met with a group of women's rights activists to discuss an election strategy. The most honest thing they could do, Asieh argued, was to refrain from endorsing any candidate but to make it clear that they would vote women's rights. Whoever wanted their support had to earn it on the issues that concerned them. They put forward two in particular. They wanted Iran to ratify the United Nations Convention on the Elimination of All Forms of Discrimination Against Women. And they wanted four specific articles of the Iranian constitution revised. They pressed the candidates to answer these demands, bringing the matter of gender equality to the foreground of the presidential campaign.

The women's movement would vote on its issues. But this turned out to be an ambiguous stance. Could women's rights be served by voting for a candidate congenial on the issues but who had no chance of winning? Asieh didn't think so. Politics, in the end, was unavoidable. Some women's rights activists embraced Karroubi as the candidate with the most satisfactory answers to the movement's demands. Others, including, in the end, Asieh, embraced Mousavi as the candidate likeliest both to win the presidency and to leverage it strongly against the hard-liners.

For Asieh, the televised debate between Mousavi and Ahmadinejad was the turning point. She had never heard a reformist politician speak to a hard-liner the way Mousavi did to Ahmadinejad. Khatami and his people had been deferential, conciliatory, cautious. But Mousavi did not disguise his criticism. He spoke directly, without fear. He lambasted the president's performance on the economy. He practically called Ahmadinejad a madman. Asieh came away certain that if anybody would stand up to Khamenei, it was Mousavi.

FIFTEEN

ASIEH

Eve was not tall enough
I'll pick all the apples.

—ASIEH AMINI

NOT FAR FROM SHAHSAVAR, in Mazandaran province, where the
Alborz Mountains career toward the Caspian coast, Asieh Amini grew up
in an orchard of kiwis and clementines, her family's farms running into
gardens running to the banks of a bordering stream. Asieh was the third
of four sisters. When she was very young, before the revolution and the
war, her family still owned animals and employed gardeners and house-
keepers. After the revolution, Shahsavar became Tonekabon, and the Aminis became middle-class.

They came from the old gentry of feudal times. Asieh understood that
her grandmother was an important person because everyone, including
Asieh's father, had to sit up straight in her presence. In the north of Iran,
women could wield social power, hold high status, and work uncovered on
farms. But many men still had multiple wives. Because of that, Asieh's
extended family sprawled. Her cousins were so legion that they sometimes
seemed to populate all of northern Iran. Her father was a teacher. He had
been a solitary boy, given to prayer; he learned to perform his *namaz* when

he was only nine years old. He taught his daughters about Islam, but his touch was light, his faith voluntary, not conducive to force or to politics.

Asieh was five when the revolution came. There were things she would always remember. That she was not allowed to wear white shoes or short socks when she started school, a half hour's commute from home. That she thought the required dark hijab ugly, and she cried, but her mother gently explained that this was a rule no one could disobey. Most of all, Asieh remembered the three sons of a maternal aunt. They were revolutionaries, all three of them imprisoned under the shah. When they were released before the monarchy fell, they came to stay near Asieh's family, up north where they would be safe, hidden in the countryside among relatives who were not engaged in political fights. Asieh loved the oldest of those three boys. When they stayed with the Aminis, the house on the farm outside Shahsavar streamed with visitors, who came to hear the news from Tehran.

Asieh and her sisters spun themselves a cocoon of nature and literature. When they weren't playing outdoors, they followed the lead of the oldest sister, who loved to read, write stories, and paint. The second sister, Afsoon, two years ahead of Asieh, adored classical Persian poetry; she memorized the verse of Hafez and pursued her own writing with obvious talent. Asieh wrote poetry, too, but she kept it to herself. She imagined she would one day be a painter, and after that a writer. She had a relentless intelligence and indefatigable drive.

The landscape of her youth was rugged, perilous, and awesomely beautiful. In the house on the farm, with the orchard and the stream, in the divan of Hafez and the paint and the page, in the mountains and the sea and the embrace of her family, Asieh was shielded from the convulsion of her country: the war, the sanctions, the revolution, the political violence. The country was beggared, young men returned from the front without limbs; many did not return at all. Within Asieh's extended family were some loyal and some opposed to the new regime. There were young men in prison, and relatives who believed other relatives had murdered their very children. And then there were the three brothers from Tehran.

Their father, the husband of Asieh's aunt, was Ayatollah Mohammad

Mohammadi Gilani, a member of the Assembly of Experts and, for a time, the head of the Guardian Council. He was Iran's chief justice at the time of the prison massacres. He signed the execution orders for many of the new regime's opponents, and he was the judge who sentenced Abbas Amirentezam to life imprisonment for espionage. He defended the use of the bastinado and believed that the execution of dissidents and corrupt elements was necessary to rid the body politic of toxins that would otherwise adulterate its purity. Relatives of Asieh's father imagined that the family's link to Gilani might help them—that Mr. Amini could influence his wife's brother-in-law to help young relatives in trouble with the law. But Gilani was resolutely impartial. He told Asieh's father to ask him for nothing, even when an eighteen-year-old cousin was sentenced to death after a ten-minute trial because of a flyer he carried in his bag.

The judge's oldest son, the one Asieh loved when she was small, had died in a car accident in 1978. The other two joined the Mojahedin. They did it partly to rebel against their father. But Gilani was a man of terrible integrity. He loved his children, Asieh was certain of this. And she believed that he was not a cruel man. But he insisted that, before the law, he could not hold his children to a different standard from other people. In 1980 he signed an order for the execution of his remaining two sons. If the boys straightened out, Gilani said—if they became loyal to the state and its vision of Islam—he could guarantee their safety. But they didn't. They fled their father's home, hiding in Mojahedin safe houses. They evaded capture and execution, only to die, it was rumored, one of them during an attack on the safe house, the other in the street clashes that brought the country to the brink of civil war in 1981.

This story would become notorious in Iran. The name of Ayatollah Mohammad Mohammadi Gilani became synonymous with an era when the Islamic Republic was so rigid and bloodthirsty that it executed its very children. On a medical furlough, Abbas Amirentezam would visit the ayatollah in the hospital where he lay comatose for the last five years of his life, and he would offer Gilani his forgiveness and his prayers. But within Asieh's family, the saga was all but unspeakable. Asieh's aunt, the boys' mother, supported her husband. In death the three brothers receded behind a scrim of silence that only darkened their shadows, the more present for their memory's refusal. Even the boys' six sisters, who had loved them, grieved in silence. Many years later, when Asieh was released from a brief prison stint of her own, the silence fractured for a split second. If she'd been in Evin, a relative said, perhaps she had smelled the brothers there.

WHILE ALL AROUND THEM RAGED a political war that sundered their very family, Asieh and Afsoon spent their Thursday afternoons at a poetry circle that met at the Shahsavar public library. It was Asieh's first taste of literary life, and she adored it. But when the time came to choose her subjects in school, she chose mathematics and physics. She was good at these, and they would prepare her for the sort of career everyone wanted in the austere eighties, in engineering or medicine. After four years of study, she would take the *concours*, a competitive exam to determine her university placement. But in the run-up to the exam one evening, after studying late, she and her sister fell asleep in front of the family's woodstove. When her sister stoked the fire in the middle of the night, the burning logs tumbled out of the stove and onto a sleeping Asieh. She nursed her burns for a month, and missed her exams. She wouldn't have another opportunity to take them until the following year.

Asieh's father decided that, rather than sit at home and study, Asieh should go and live independently, just as if she were starting university on schedule at eighteen. She would spend the year in Mashhad, supported financially by her parents while she studied for her *concours* with a tutor and gathered the strength and resourcefulness she would need to become an independent adult. Two of her friends came with her. The three young women shared lodgings, lessons, and one of the best years of Asieh's life.

Mashhad's poetry circles were legendary. Ali Shariati once met a young Ali Khamenei in a poetry circle in Mashhad. Now Asieh Amini joined such a circle. It consisted mainly of old men, classical poets in their seventies and eighties. Asieh was a nearly comical misfit. She was only eighteen; she wrote in modern free verse, and her energy was frenetic. She clamored for a turn to read. The elderly poets brushed her off for as long as they could. When at last she read, the older poets reacted with disdain. They didn't care for the modern style. One of them sneered that these were not poems but essays. Furious, Asieh left and resolved never to return.

Days later, however, one of the older poets tracked her down. He apologized for the rough treatment she'd endured. That poetry circle had nothing to offer a young person, he explained. But her work was very good. He offered his instruction, support, and criticism. And so her time in the city was a poet's education, despite the hours she spent on math. Asieh wrote in verse and read in philosophy. She devoured the works of the pre-revolutionary Islamic philosopher Allameh Tabatabai, and she learned about Western philosophy by reading Will Durant's 1926 survey, *The Story of Philosophy*.

Durant's legacy in his native America was a vanishing one, even as it took root in faraway Iran. He was a middlebrow American favorite in the early to mid-twentieth century, when his sweeping histories, many of them written together with his wife, Ariel, topped bestseller lists and won a Pulitzer Prize. Like Popper, Durant was a former socialist turned liberal whose worldview tracked comfortably with the U.S. State Department during the Cold War. That might have been one reason his work appealed to the Franklin Book Programs, a nonprofit publishing effort that the American Book Publishers Council and the American Library Association established in seventeen developing countries in 1952, with an initial grant from the State Department.

The Franklin Book Programs were a classic American export—part public diplomacy, part market colonization, and part high-minded endeavor to promote literacy and cultural expression in developing countries allied with the United States. The editors in each country were local intellectual figures who selected the publications—mostly translated American works—to suit their countries' literary appetites. By far Franklin's most ambitious outpost was in Iran. There the program published some eight hundred titles, about fifty of which were original works in Persian. The schoolbooks that the short-story writer Samad Behrangi had railed against in the 1960s were Franklin publications: under the shah, the majority of the textbooks used in Iranian elementary schools were Franklin books translated from English and replete with irrelevant or inscrutable cultural references.

Traditionally, Iranian book publishers were also retailers: their storefronts were boutiques selling their own wares. Franklin introduced national book retailing to Iran by mass-producing cheap paperbacks and selling them everywhere, on stands that popped up near bus stops and grocery stores or wherever they might catch a passerby's notice. The appetite for these affordable, broadly available, mostly translated works was vast. Long after the Franklin Book Programs dissolved in 1977, and long after the Islamic Republic nationalized its local assets, certain improbable American authors and titles remained in the Iranian canon. Will Durant, whose breezy, readable surveys provided Iranian readers with a painless introduction to the Western philosophical tradition, was one of them.

FOR ASIEH, DURANT CAME FIRST; then she read Tabatabai; only later, Soroush. In the meantime, not quite by accident, she allowed math to languish. She flubbed the *concours*. She didn't qualify in math, and she didn't get into an elite public school. Asieh was too proud to go anyplace less prestigious than where her sisters had gone. She decided to repeat the *concours* the following year. And she would do it, this time, in the humanities.

She would have to master the equivalent of four years' studies on her own. She came back to the farm near Shahsavar and took up her studies behind the closed door of her bedroom, reading from morning until midnight. Finally her passions and her studies converged. She taught herself to speed-read until she could digest a book in just four hours. And she loved what she read. She placed seventeenth in the country in journalism on her *concours*. Soon she was off to the university that bore the name of her favorite philosopher, Allameh Tabatabai. It was among the top humanities campuses in Iran. She could read philosophy on her own, she thought; but to be a social and political journalist was a vocation, and this she would learn at school.

ASIEH WAS NOT THEN and would never become a political creature. But she would find politics, always, just beneath her fingertips, like a banister that ran alongside the steep staircase she climbed. To be a journalist was to scale the structure of politics and to grasp onto politics for support, even involuntarily, and even when the journalism was not itself about politics. In 1993, when she moved to Tehran, there was not yet a term in common parlance for the space she would come to occupy, there in the hollows of the structures of the state, by whose prerogatives her work would suffocate or flourish. Later she would understand this as civil society, and it was her natural home. Politics, she surmised, was by contrast little more than the pursuit of power, which did not interest her at all.

She was a freshman in journalism at Allameh Tabatabai when she went to a journalism fair with some of her friends, determined to convince an editor to give her a chance to write for a real newspaper. If she had been a political creature, Asieh would have cared first and foremost which newspaper that might be. But she did not. And so she stumbled upon *Kayhan*, the hardline newspaper that was practically an arm of the security forces. Asieh little knew, at the time, that *Kayhan* had denounced and threatened many of the writers whose work she loved. An editor who ran a yearly supplement for the newspaper gave Asieh her first assignment. When he left *Kayhan* for *Iran*, a centrist government newspaper, he invited Asieh to write for him there.

Iran was less strident than the hardline papers, and very large. Asieh felt lucky to find herself there. She did not much like the dress code: the strictest hijab, either a chador or a loose coat with the enveloping headdress called *maghnae*, was required in all government offices. Nor did she appreciate the gender segregation in the newsroom. But she was happy. The job slaked her ambitions. She was there to excel, not to wage futile battles with the world as it was. She was learning her trade; she respected her teachers and her boss; and she took an interest in sociology on the side, especially in John Locke and contemporary theorists of civil society.

One day, a colleague invited her to come with him to interview a famous writer: Javad Mojabi, a poet, satirist, and editor of one of the few literary magazines that had survived the first revolutionary decade. Asieh thrilled to the prospect of meeting this man. She didn't know that he lived under mortal threat, like so many writers in the period before the chain murders were exposed, or that he endured regular investigation and harassment. She was enthralled by his presence, and that of his chic and beautiful wife, and she was gobsmacked when, on learning that she wrote poetry, he asked her to recite some. She obliged. Mojabi invited the young stranger to join his writers' circle, even as his wife, protective and frightened for her husband's life, demanded to know: Was he sure he could trust Asieh?

The circle was very small and very critical, Mojabi told Asieh. She should be punctual, serious, disciplined, and strong. Yes, said Asieh, yes—anything. The meetings were not open, Mojabi continued. She could not bring anybody. The writers published nothing from these meetings, but they were very free within their confines. And the group needed another poet. Asieh would be that poet. And Mojabi would be her most important mentor, the person from whom she learned how, as a writer, to be free.

WHEN ASIEH'S BOSS TOOK OVER *Iran-e Javan*, a youth-oriented supplement to *Iran*, he made Asieh its cultural editor. It was a bold appointment. She was female, single, and very young, in a male-dominated workplace. And now she had a job that made her responsible for twenty-eight pages of content. Her supervisor thought she could do it, and Asieh thought so, too. But she felt herself surrounded by colleagues looking for her to fail. She supervised men who were older than she was and resented reporting to her. The paper's chief editor found fault with her every move. She put her head down and worked harder. Her days were often thirteen or fourteen hours long; when they were over, she brought still more work home.

One day a young male colleague pulled her aside.

"I don't know how to explain this to you," he said miserably, "but please leave this job."

"Why?" Asieh demanded.

The young man seemed to be fighting back tears. Every day, he told her, their colleagues spoke ill of her. "People don't like for a young, single girl to be an editor here," he told her.

"That may be true," Asieh replied, "but it's their problem, not mine."

IN LATE 1996, Asieh took little notice of the coming presidential election. Rafsanjani would go, she expected, and Nategh-Nouri would replace him. She never imagined that this decision was made by anyone but the Leader. But she was friendly with one of her professors at the university, a reformist intellectual named Hadi Khaniki, who kept her vaguely apprised of the political scene. She found him sad one day in the run-up to the election. Mir Hossein Mousavi had just declined the reformists' entreaties to run, he informed her. Mousavi preferred to remain an artist, outside of politics. Now the reformists had no candidate to offer.

Asieh didn't much care one way or the other about the election. But she wanted to cheer up Khaniki, and she thought, suddenly, of a rather lovely cleric who was a librarian she'd recently interviewed for her newspaper.

"You have somebody better than Mousavi," she told Khaniki. "You have, for example, Khatami."

Khaniki laughed. "Asieh," he said, "you're a poet. You should stick to poetry." If she knew politics, he explained, she would understand that Khatami was the wrong man for that job. He was a cultural figure who'd left politics years earlier because he didn't like to fight.

"Okay," said Asieh. "I just think people would like him."

Some weeks later, in a university corridor, Khaniki came charging toward Asieh with a newspaper in his hand.

"How did you know?" he practically shouted.

Khaniki was to become a speechwriter and adviser to President Khatami. During the campaign, he asked Asieh a favor. Khatami's press office badly needed an editor. Out of loyalty to Khaniki, Asieh volunteered her services at the Khatami campaign at night, after she left *Iran-e Javan*.

She would never know for certain, but she suspected that her moon-lighting for the Khatami campaign sealed her fate at *Iran*, which had favored Nategh-Nouri. In the month after Khatami was elected, the tension between Asieh and her boss mounted until she felt she had no choice but to resign. She would always joke that the new president's gift to her, in thanks for her volunteer work, was unemployment.

Khaniki found her work in the president's office, but Asieh lasted only a day. She was a journalist and wanted to remain one. And journalism was flourishing. There were new publications on the scene, including a news-paper called *Zan* (Woman). Asieh saw no utility in segregating news by gen-der. She even rather opposed it. But a former colleague from *Kayhan* had gone to *Zan* and wanted Asieh to work with him. She liked the colleague and needed a job. As it happened, Asieh would work for *Zan* for the short duration of the newspaper's existence. She met her husband there.

Javad Montazeri was a photojournalist. He had a broad, round face, kindly eyes, and a long beard that melted into his long hair. He cut a recog-nizable figure on the streets of Tehran with his mane and his camera. Like Asieh, he came from Mazandaran. Within a month Javad left *Zan* to work for *Khordad*, a newspaper run by Khatami's erstwhile interior minister, Abdollah Nouri, who was chased from office by hard-liners in 1998.

On Asieh's wedding day in April 1999, a friend called her at the beauty salon with bad news. *Zan* had been banned. Her job was gone. But Asieh could hardly react. Javad still had work, and she was still happy. More than five hundred wedding guests were waiting.

ASIEH WASN'T OUT OF WORK FOR LONG. She was an enterprising reporter, covering demonstrations in Kurdistan and an earthquake in Shi-raz for first one newspaper and then another. The work gave her energy and a feeling of incontestable purpose. Around her, the Iranian press was changing. More young women were entering journalism. The reformist papers weren't free, but they were far more daring than the old papers had been. The Eighteenth of Tir would test the limits of the independent press, and of Asieh's detachment.

Asieh was on her way to a meeting when her taxi driver informed her that the roads were closed because of a disturbance at the University of Tehran. She canceled her meeting and called Javad, telling him to meet her at the university entrance. They found the gate locked. Beyond it, they could see students and staff milling about in shock and in tears. A journalism student who'd attended occasional meetings at Asieh's newspaper recognized her. "I know her," he called out. "Let her in." It was early morning, and they were the first reporters to enter the blasted campus.

Javad's photographs that day became iconic ones. A small dorm room lay in cinders from a grenade strike, the mattresses burned from metal bed frames, the paint stripped from the walls. In other rooms, television sets had been smashed, belongings ransacked, air conditioners hurled to the street below; a student in a ruined corridor showed his back hatched with red welts. A window was broken where a student had been thrown.

Their attackers, the students told Asieh, said they did all this for their imams. But the attackers had come upon them in their dormitory as they slept. Asieh was not a party to this fight: she was a journalist covering a story. But she could not tear herself away. For the next week she and Javad were among the students, documenting a battle between unmatched adversaries, and a story that had been distorted beyond recognition in the state press.

A few days into the unrest, Asieh and Javad heard gunshots. They understood that a student had been shot. At the nearest hospital, they connived to see him, posing as family members. The photo was perhaps Javad's most daring. Officially, no students had been injured. But there in the limpid green light of a hospital room, a student lay intubated, unconscious, with bandages patching his abdomen and chest. An oxygen mask obscured his face, and a childish cartoon bedsheet covered his lower body.

Abdollah Nouri, the publisher of *Khordad*, viewed Javad's photos and reminded him gravely that he published them at his own risk as well as the newspaper's. But the images were too important to hold back. Javad insisted. *Khordad* splashed the pictures across its cover and ran two pages of photos inside as well. The demonstrating students held copies of the issue aloft like protest placards. They had been given little, Asieh understood. Every day they told her that they wanted to talk with President Khatami. Although the president sent his ministers, he never came.

Wednesday was the hardline counterdemonstration. Asieh and Javad stopped at a phone booth on the street so that Asieh could call her editor. While she was talking, she saw four or five big men in white shirts and kaffiyehs approach and begin to lead Javad away. She dropped the phone.

"Where are you taking him?" she demanded.

"That's his wife," one of the men said. "Arrest her, too."

The men did not take Asieh and Javad to a detention center or a police station. They took them to a dress shop in a duplex on Fatemi Square. They ordered the shopkeepers to leave as they led Asieh and Javad up a spiral staircase.

One of the men had a gun. He pushed the barrel into Asieh's abdomen and said to Javad, "Do you work for Abdollah Nouri?"

"Yes," Javad said.

The man rammed the gun harder into Asieh. He asked Javad, "Do you believe that Abdollah Nouri, Behzad Nabavi, Mostafa Tajzadeh, and Saeed Hajjarian work with Israel?"

"I don't know," Javad said.

"How is it possible you don't know?" fulminated the man with the gun to Asieh's stomach. "You work with them, and they work for Israel, and they made this demonstration this week. They killed the students because of Israel."

"How should I know?" said Javad. "I just work as a photographer."

"No," said the man. "You're a photo editor."

This was true. Asieh, the gun beneath her ribs, thought fast.

"Let me explain something to you," she interjected. "This is our job. I could be a teacher. A teacher just teaches students. A teacher doesn't make decisions about the education system. I could be someone who works in a bank. Not someone who makes decisions for the bank. We're journalists. We don't make decisions about the system. Your problem is with the system."

The man considered this. She might be right, he conceded. But in that case she could as easily work for the hardline press as for the reformists. Would she come over to the other side?

"I'll think about it," Asieh offered. She tried to sound natural. "But I'd have to leave the job I have now. I need to think."

"So think," the man commanded.

One of the men had taken Asieh's bag from her. Now he shook out its contents. Asieh's stomach lurched. A few days back, a friend had given her a Xerox copy of a photo that showed a cleric kissing the hand of Shah Mohammad Reza Pahlavi. As a joke, someone had written below the image the name of a high-ranking cleric in the judiciary. Asieh had slipped the paper into her bag. Now it could cause her untold trouble.

The captors found a notebook where she'd kept notes for a freelance project on antiquities for a cultural television program. The television network belonged to hard-liners.

"What is this?" one of her captors demanded.

Asieh felt a rush of relief. "It's for television," she said. "For your side."

The notes were exactly what she needed: proof positive that she was nothing but a journalist on assignment, neutral toward her subject, neutral even toward the politicized press, taking notes on historical objects for hardline television.

"Go to Abdollah Nouri," one of the white shirts told Javad before letting the couple go, "and tell him that we will arrest him and the others, and we will sentence them. We have a lot of evidence that they work with Israel."

Out on the street, Asieh rummaged through her bag. The picture of the cleric and the shah, mercifully, had been tucked into a zippered compartment the men had never checked. Asieh collapsed on the sidewalk with relief.

. . .

THE FIRST PHONE CALL WOKE Asieh from sleep the very next morning.

"Yesterday I asked you to work for us instead of for your newspaper," said the voice on the other end. Asieh hung up.

But the calls kept coming. "We know where you live. We know everything about you. Just think about how you can work with us."

Javad went back to work, but Asieh brooded, afraid to leave their apartment. She wrote a long, frank letter to President Khatami. She was not herself a believer in reform, she wrote, but surely the president was. Someone needed to protect people like her. She and her husband were in danger. The security forces wanted her to work for them. She didn't want to do it. What recourse did she have?

Asieh gathered her courage and left home. She went to *Khordad*. It was evening. Javad was surprised to see her there.

"I've come to see Abdollah Nouri," she told him simply. She waited hours outside Nouri's office. When at last he read her letter, she saw tears in his eyes.

"I'll bring it to President Khatami," he said.

He did better than that: he read her letter to the National Security Council. Maybe that was why the phone calls stopped. Or maybe her harassers simply lost interest. Whatever the reason, Asieh could breathe again. But Javad couldn't sleep. Often he woke in terror from nightmares of being followed; he had not only the demonstration photos to worry about but photos he'd taken at the mourning ceremonies of the victims of the chain murders. He implored Asieh to consider leaving Iran. But Asieh couldn't imagine a life in a country that wasn't her home, in a language that wasn't Persian.

They considered moving to another city instead. They decided on Chabahar, the southernmost city in Iran, in the remote province of Sistan-Baluchestan. But before they could leave, Asieh got another job offer in

Tehran. This one was from *Sobh-e Emrouz*, Hajjarian's newspaper, where Ganji also wrote. It was the hottest property in the Iranian media. Asieh took the offer. They would think about Chabahar another time.

ASIEH HAD NOT BEEN on the job for six months when she learned that she was pregnant. She wasn't ready. Her life was already overfull. When she wasn't working at the paper, she painted, wrote poetry, or played music on her tanbur, a traditional long-necked lute. She never imagined herself a mother. Only after long thought and searching talks with Javad did she resolve to see the pregnancy through.

Asieh was prepared for many things in life, but not this. To begin with, it wasn't fair. There was Javad, going about his life and his work just as before. Asieh's body grew cumbersome, volatile, somnolent, captive to sudden needs. She would not slow down. She would prove to herself and her colleagues that she could work as hard as before, accomplish as much as before. One day she was out in the street for sixteen hours, covering a police roundup of homeless people. About a week later she started leaking amniotic fluid. Her doctor ordered bed rest for the final three months of her pregnancy.

Asieh was confined to her home and no longer at home in her body. She had an engine inside her that churned the very air if there was no place for it to take her. She knew by now that she loved her unborn daughter and wanted to keep her well. But she herself was not well. She cried every day. She saw Javad as though from an unbridgeable distance. He tried to console her. The baby was fine. There was no problem. Why did she cry?

Asieh was not much better after her daughter was born. During her trimester of bed rest, the judiciary had shut down *Sobh-e Emrouz* and *Khordad*. Javad found work first with a Brazilian magazine and then with Abdollah Nouri's next venture, a newspaper called *Fath*. But Asieh was tied down. She had a baby, and the baby didn't sleep through the night for seven months. Sleep deprivation unraveled Asieh's mind and left her enervated, uninterested in the things she used to do and the people she used to see. She cared for her daughter and felt that the rest of her life was finished. The past was unrecoverable, and with it, the person she used to be.

Ava was a year old when Javad came home from work one day and asked his wife, "Do we have a cup of tea?"

"No," said Asieh.

"Is there anything to eat?"

"No," said Asieh.

"What did you do today?"

"Nothing," said Asieh wanly. "I just took care of the baby. I have a baby."

"I thought I married a person who was a poet and a journalist," said Javad. "I didn't know I married a housewife like you."

Asieh shed her last tears of self-pity that day. The next morning she started looking for a babysitter and a job.

SOON ASIEH HAD again not one job but two. An editor with whom Asieh had worked at *Iran* pulled her over to *Etemad*, where she was social editor, handling special reports and interviews. Most days, she worked from eight-thirty until it was time to pick up Ava at preschool at four. At night, when Ava slept, Asieh managed a website called Women's News in Iran. She still objected to gender-specific news, but some friends from *Zan* had asked for her help, and she took it on as a favor to them.

Asieh began to travel again for her reporting, leaving Ava with her sister, Afsoon, or other family members. She felt that she had returned to her own skin after an intolerable absence. She went to Bam, in southern Iran, to cover a devastating earthquake there. And then she heard that the United States was planning to invade Iraq. Early in 2003, reporters the world over began converging on Iraqi Kurdistan, often crossing through Iran; but so far as Asieh knew, the Iranian press hadn't approached the story.

Asieh went. She fell in with a crew from Al Jazeera, some German reporters, and Kaveh Golestan, an eminence among Iranian photojournalists. Golestan had a magnificent mustache and a storied career that spanned the twentieth century. In the 1960s he'd worked for the Franklin Book Programs, photographing Iranian schoolchildren using Franklin texts. In the 1970s his photos of Iranian poverty displeased the queen; in the 1980s his documentation of revolutionary censorship enraged the mullahs. He stilled the heaving flux of Iranian life in iconic black-and-white, and he taught photography at the University of Tehran, where Javad had been his student. To Asieh, he was avuncular and kind. In the Iraqi Kurdish cities of Erbil, Sulaimaniya, and Halabja, Asieh returned to her hotel at night and bantered amiably with Golestan and the other reporters about the likelihood of the American invasion.

From Sulaimaniya, Golestan urged Asieh to venture up the mountain that divided Iran from Iraq. Three groups of hardline Islamic militants camped on that mountainside. She could approach without setting them on edge if she wore the full hijab of their women, hands and face covered. Asieh looked into it. She learned that the mountain was so heavily laced with mines left over from the Iran-Iraq War that only the extremists themselves knew how to pass safely through. Asieh didn't go. But Kaveh Golestan did. He stepped on a land mine and was instantly killed on April 2, 2003.

WHEN ASIEH RETURNED TO TEHRAN, she understood that she was pregnant again. Her first pregnancy had been complicated, the aftermath disorienting. She had only just become herself again. Moreover, the life she and Javad led was a precarious one. They traveled on no notice, at their own risk, and their employers flickered in and out of existence. This was her primary self, the life she knew. She could not conceive of carrying another baby to term.

Asieh's doctor refused to help her abort the pregnancy. She had two friends who were doctors, one of them a gynecologist, but they refused as well—not, they explained, because the procedure was illegal but because they disapproved. One of them told Asieh she had two options. One was to find a doctor—however unscrupulous and expensive—who was willing to perform the surgery underground. The other was to take some pills so that she would start to bleed and damage the pregnancy. At that point an emergency room would be obliged to perform a dilation and curettage.

Asieh chose the second route. There was no way to proceed but blindly. The medicine she purchased on the black market came not as pills but as an injection. She would never know what it was. She hired a woman to administer it. The woman knew instantly what the injection was for, and she demanded that Asieh pay her the fetus's *diyeh*, or blood money, up front, to indemnify her in case Asieh demanded it later. Asieh paid.

She passed the night in terrible pain. But the blood didn't come. She knew now that she could not carry the fetus; she'd already harmed it beyond salvation. But no hospital would evacuate her uterus if she wasn't bleeding. So she injected herself a second time. Again the pain. Her doctor friend told her to walk or run to bring on contractions. Asieh did, continuously, despite the pain. But the blood didn't come. She had no choice now but the underground surgery, whatever its price.

The abortion doctor was very old, and Asieh believed he was a drug addict. He had no patients and seemed to perform no surgery other than abortions. His rooms were filthy. He told Asieh that in addition to the steep fee she'd owe him, she would have to pay an anesthesiologist and a nurse, whom he would hire. She agreed. On the day of her procedure, they showed up, the anesthesiologist with a vividly yellow face, Asieh imagined from drink, the nurse in towering heels and heavy makeup. Asieh delivered herself into the hands of sinister strangers in dirty rooms. Javad, supportive but very worried, asked again and again if she was sure. Asieh didn't see that she had any other choice.

In the days that followed, she bled and bled. Her body quaked with shock. She could not seek medical care or advice anywhere or tell anyone, other than Javad, what she had done. She told *Etemad* she was sick and took a few days off. Then she returned to life as she had known it, until everything changed.

. . .

IN THE SUMMER OF 2004, a news item from the town of Neka in her home province of Mazandaran brought Asieh up short. She'd been combing the country's media for stories about women to post to the women's news website. Now she saw that a sixteen-year-old girl had been executed for "acts incompatible with chastity." Or maybe, according to a different news source, the girl was twenty-one. Which was it? Asieh wondered. Why the discrepancy? And why was a young girl hanged? She pressed the matter at the website's next meeting. They should send someone to Neka to find out, she said. But no one wanted to go. Asieh took it on.

On the streets of Neka, men told Asieh that Atefah Sahaaleh was not a good girl. She sold her body, one man explained; a lady like Asieh shouldn't pursue such a story. Asieh wheeled on him. Could he really speak of killing a girl in the name of respecting her body? And who was he to tell Asieh what she should do? Another man told Asieh that Atefah had a psychological disorder.

At length Asieh found a small wooden gate that stood open. Over it hung black clothing and placards of mourning. This must be Atefah's family's home. It was half built and derelict. A young man appeared to have passed out on a flight of stairs within, his eyes half lidded and rolled back, drool pooling on his chin, flies swarming his face.

"Mister? Mister?" Asieh called out fearfully. "Are you okay?"

"Who are you?" someone asked her from behind. Asieh spun around. A muscle-bound young man regarded her warily.

"I'm a journalist," she replied.

"You came too late," said the young man, who turned out to be Atefah's cousin. "We lost her."

Over the days that followed, Asieh located the girl's living relatives and pieced together her story. Atefah was five when her mother left her father for another man, then died in a car accident. The father, heartbroken, turned to drugs and neglected his children. One of Atefah's brothers drowned in a river. Another became a drug addict. Atefah, eight years old, went to live with her grandparents, who were too old and poor to care for her.

When she was nine, a neighbor raped her. He paid her money for her silence. Then he came back, again and again. He brought other men to her. She was repeatedly raped, and given money to tell no one. That money was her subsistence. When she was thirteen, the Revolutionary Guards arrested her for the first time. Judge Haji Razaei sentenced her to a hundred lashes—the punishment for sexual crimes. Under the Iranian penal code, a woman could be sentenced to a hundred lashes three times. On the fourth arrest, she would be executed.

Asieh had never known about these laws. She lived in a world where they were never applied. Everyone had sex outside of marriage. The whole society was guilty. Why should anyone be hanged? Why, especially, a sixteen-year-old girl with mental problems and a childhood lost to the neglect, depravity, and violence of others? The girl was definitely sixteen: Asieh found her identity card. International law forbade the execution of minors under eighteen, regardless of the fact that the Iranian penal code made the age of criminal responsibility nine for girls and fifteen for boys. And so far as Asieh could ascertain, Atefah had been arrested only twice, not three times, before being sentenced to death.

Judge Haji Razaei in Neka had wanted Atefah dead, Asieh imagined. He'd placed the noose around the child's neck himself before she was hoisted on a crane in the town square. This was the typical Iranian execution method, which took longer and caused more pain than a trapdoor hanging. He'd falsified her age in order to circumvent the law. Had he raped her himself? Some reports suggested that Atefah had ripped off her hijab in the courtroom in an act of rage, and Razaei was determined to punish her for her backtalk. Asieh would never know. But something was wrong, and it wouldn't let her go.

Asieh had covered earthquakes, demonstrations, the rumors of war. But nothing would seize her the way that Atefah did. Was she a sister, an alter ego, a daughter Asieh might have had, or never had, in her life of relative privilege and safety, of literature and ambition, a life that had begun so close to where Atefah had suffered and died? Atefah was, maybe, all those things. She was the restless spirit of injustice done, a wrong Asieh could never right, although she would devote much of her life—and even her poetry—to Atefah, in ways no one had bothered to while the girl lived. Forever after, Asieh spoke of Atefah tenderly, by her first name, as of an intimate friend. Asieh would say that Atefah changed her life.

Back in Tehran, Asieh went over and over the notes and documents she'd gathered in Neka: Atefah's identity card, interviews with the father and aunts, even report cards from the brief time Atefah spent in school. But Asieh couldn't write and she couldn't sleep. Every time she'd try to set the story to the page, she cried until morning. When at last she pulled the report together, her newspaper wouldn't publish it.

"Why not?" Asieh demanded. "I have all the documents."

"Because you're fighting with sharia law," her editor in chief replied. "You're fighting the judiciary, and we can't do that."

Asieh sent the report to another newspaper, which also declined it. Finally, *Zanan* magazine, a women's publication that had long shared space and traded ideas with *Kiyan*, agreed to publish an edited version of Asieh's piece.

Asieh couldn't return to the life she had lived before Atefah. She found herself wondering how many other girls were in prison, awaiting execution for sexual crimes. She had a friend, Shadi Sadr, who was a human rights lawyer. Asieh brought Atefah's father and brother to Tehran to meet with her. Surely they could press charges against Judge Haji Razaei for hanging a juvenile. But Razaei, as a clergyman, would have to be tried by the Special Court of the Clergy. When Shadi brought the case there, the Special Court's chief justice, the ultra-hardline Gholam-Hossein Mohseni-Ejei, ordered the case permanently closed and sealed.

SCANT DAYS AFTER PUBLISHING her report on Atefah, Asieh heard about another girl sentenced to death. The city was Arak, southwest of

Tehran, and the girl was nineteen-year-old Leyla Mafi, developmentally delayed with a mental age of eight. She, too, had been sentenced to death on account of offenses against chastity. And she, too, was a victim of child rape. Asieh heard about the case at nine at night. By four a.m. she was on a bus bound for Arak. This time she was not too late. Leyla was still alive and in prison.

Leyla had been a child—some sources said eight, others five—when her mother first prostituted her, to a sixty-year-old man. From then on her mother and brother prostituted her every day, living off the money. Leyla gave birth for the first time at the age of nine, and again, to twins, at fourteen. At ten, after the first baby, she received her first hundred lashes for prostitution. By the time she was sentenced to death at nineteen—for incest, among other things, because her brothers were among the many townsmen who had raped her—she couldn't talk, care for herself, or live as a normal person in any way.

At the courthouse, the judge who had sentenced Leyla to death was polite and respectful, sending everyone out of the room so he could speak with the journalist from Tehran. The law, he told Asieh, was the law. It was his job simply to apply it. And the law looked darkly on Leyla because her sexual availability was destructive to family life. If society were an apple, the judge explained to Asieh, Leyla Mafi would be a worm.

"Do you have children?" Asieh demanded.

"Yes," said the judge.

"Boys? Girls?"

"Both," said the judge.

"My daughter is four years old," said Asieh. "In three or four years, somebody could rape her, and you would sentence her as a worm for society. How is that possible? What do you make of that?"

"I sentenced Leyla Mafi at nineteen, not at eight," the judge replied.

Sure, said Asieh, but from eight to nineteen, the girl had been enslaved; she had known no other life.

Asieh had with her a retainer from Shadi Sadr's office. What she wanted more than anything was to visit Leyla in prison and get her signature on that form. Then Leyla would have a lawyer, and a fighting chance. Asieh spent an hour with the judge, interviewing him and arguing with him. He should let Asieh take Leyla away and remake her life, she pressed him. Then he could judge whether or not Leyla was good for society.

The judge laughed. "Go," he said finally, dismissively. "Go and see what you want to see." He wrote a note to the prison ordering the wardens to admit Asieh as a visitor to Leyla Mafi.

Asieh was elated. She would do for Leyla everything she hadn't managed to do for Atefah. The wardens took the judge's note. But they didn't read it carefully. They assumed that Asieh was Leyla's lawyer. And so they brought the condemned girl before Asieh: a tall, beautiful young woman with the affect of a baby, a woman who could not speak or read or write, and who looked at Asieh in simple confusion.

Asieh put her arms around Leyla and spoke quietly in her ear.

"I am your sister," said Asieh. "I want to help you. Your situation is not good. You have to trust me. And I promise you that I will help you."

She took out Shadi Sadr's retainer: "I just need you to sign this."

But Leyla could not sign her name. So Asieh painted Leyla's finger with ink and stamped it on the signature line. A guard exploded in anger. Asieh had lied to them. The guard understood now that Asieh was not Leyla's lawyer—that Leyla had not had a lawyer until the moment Asieh stamped her finger on the form.

"This girl is sentenced to death!" the guard exploded. "She will be executed very soon. You can't do this. Get out of here!"

Asieh didn't care. It was done. Back in Tehran she told Shadi to go to Arak and see her new client. Asieh published an account of Leyla's case in *Zanan*, and it landed like a bomb. Her e-mail box lit up with well-wishers wondering what they could do for Leyla Mafi. Push for the girl's retrial and release, Asieh replied. The prison officials filed charges against Asieh, who had not known that it was illegal for her to bring a lawyer's retainer into the prison. But because it was the judge himself who'd signed the note granting her entry, he ordered the charges dropped.

Leyla's story became known not only within Iran but internationally, with press reports that started with Iranian journalists and bloggers abroad and ricocheted through the international media and human rights organizations. When President Khatami paid a state visit to Norway, the prime minister, who had read about Leyla Mafi in the Norwegian papers, raised the matter with the Iranian president. In due time Leyla had a second trial with a younger, more sympathetic judge.

Asieh was there, pacing outside the courtroom door while the judge deliberated.

"Relax," the judge popped out and told her. "She'll be free."

But Asieh was worried, she told the judge. Just to be free would not be enough for Leyla. If her family forced her back into the sex trade, there would be nothing Asieh or anyone else could do for her.

"I can have her sent to Tehran as her punishment," the judge offered. "But then what will you do?"

"Just do it," Asieh said. And he did.

Asieh and Shadi found an organization for indigent young women that took Leyla into its care. They raised money to support Leyla's needs, which included a nanny, for she could not care for herself; a psychologist to help heal her lifelong trauma; and a private tutor who taught her to read and write and to pass the equivalent of fifth grade. Asieh brought Leyla to her own home as often as she could, so that she could play with Ava and experience family life. Leyla's psychologists told Asieh that the girl's exposure to Javad was especially important, as she lacked any normal experiences interacting with men.

"You're like a mother to me," Leyla told Asieh once. "You should find me a husband."

Asieh filmed Leyla often. When she had enough of these clips, she planned to edit them together to send to Leyla's first judge, with a question: Was Leyla good for society now?

A YOUNG WOMAN IN QAZVIN faced the death penalty for murdering a man whom she claimed was trying to rape her. Again Asieh found the judge to be a decent man. But the young woman had not convinced him that she'd acted in self-defense. There was, under Iranian law, an alternative to the death penalty in such cases: *diyeh*—blood money—paid by the accused to the family of the victim. The girl in Qazvin could never afford the man's *diyeh*. So Asieh published a plea on the women's news website and on a weblog she had started to keep. In less than fifteen minutes, she raised the money to buy the Qazvin girl's life. She rented a car with two friends. They drove to the victim's family's home in the mountains outside Hamadan with a box of candy and a check.

Asieh was changing. She was still the high-powered newspaper editor, running sixteen pages of *Etemad* daily now, and still a poet. She was also becoming something else: someone possessed by the stories of underage prisoners on death row, of impoverished young women convicted of crimes against chastity, lives rendered cheap before they began. All the paradox of her country, in its decency and its cruelty, lay upon her conscience. Colleagues reproved her. She couldn't be a journalist and an activist at once, and these were death penalty cases, lost causes, not worth her reportorial time. Asieh knew only that she had work to do. If she, as a journalist, had not known about these laws or their enforcement, what might she owe to the better education of her 70 million countrymen?

At the beginning of Khatami's first term, Asieh had fought with her old professor, Hadi Khaniki, then a presidential spokesman, about civil society. He spoke of it as of a program that could be instated from above. Asieh protested that, by definition, civil society should come from the people, not the government. The argument grew heated. Asieh told Khaniki that he no longer spoke to her as her sociology professor but as the occupant of the chair he sat in, which happened to belong to a government office. Khaniki sent her away and cut their ties. Now, years later, she saw him at a meeting. The very best things in civil society, he conceded publicly, were those done by people like her.

But Asieh didn't know where President Khatami and the reformists stood on the issues that mattered to her. Given the choice, she preferred to work with reformists rather than their rivals. But she neither trusted nor expected to trust politicians. When Shirin Ebadi, the human rights lawyer, won the Nobel Prize for Peace in 2003, President Khatami's comments belittled Ebadi's achievement. Iran could be proud of a Nobel Prize in science or literature, he said, but the prize for peace was not important. Asieh replied in a column arguing that Ebadi's recognition honored the nation.

Asieh had never considered herself a feminist. She saw her activist work in the frame of children's rights. Iran had a nasty habit of sentencing juveniles for capital crimes, holding them in prison, and then executing them once they turned eighteen. Iran also had one of the highest rates of execution in the world, second only to China. But as her work on death penalty cases became better known, women's rights activists pulled her increasingly into their orbit. They included Asieh in a gathering to discuss what should be done to mark Shirin Ebadi's return to Iran with her prize.

The meeting impressed Asieh with its breadth of representation. Some of the women there were strict Muslims and Islamists; others were secular. Their work spanned a wide gamut of concerns. They turned out an enormous crowd at the airport when Shirin Ebadi's flight touched down. Their presence was celebratory, but it was also protective. No harm could come to Shirin Ebadi under such a glaring light. And the very work of organizing that display was the start of something. Iran's women's rights activists had forged a network. The same group would go on holding those meetings weekly or biweekly for the following year and a half. Through them, they came to a consensus that the most important overarching issue facing Iranian women was the discriminatory nature of the law.

Under Iranian law, women did not have equal rights in marriage, divorce, or inheritance. Men could marry multiple wives and engage in something called temporary marriage that was a kind of legal prostitution. Children inherited their nationality from their fathers but not their mothers. A woman's life and limb were worth less, in blood money, than a man's; a woman's testimony weighed less than a man's in court; honor killings, in which a male relative might kill a woman for bringing dishonor to her family through her sexual behavior, were not regarded as murders under the law. Then there was the six-year gender difference in the age of criminal responsibility.

At the very end of Khatami's presidency, in the summer of 2005, the women's rights activists who'd first begun convening to honor Shirin Ebadi organized a silent protest. Thousands of demonstrators massed in front of the University of Tehran. Javad took photos; Asieh wrote. This was the first demonstration for women's rights in Iran in twenty years. The last one had been to protest Khomeini's imposition of mandatory hijab. This one set itself against the fundamental inequities in the law.

ASIEH AMINI WAS NOT AFFLICTED with the anguish that troubled those who had believed in Khatami's promise. But more than in 1997, she found that she cared very much who won the presidential election in 2005. She wasn't expecting a miracle: democracy, a free press, a liberated civil society. She didn't imagine a coordinated confrontation with the hard-liners from within, or a showdown between human rights supporters and the judiciary. She just wanted a government she could work with—one that left a few threads loose for her to tug, a few pinpricks in the heavy lid of the state that would allow activists like her to breathe. Her work—for women, for juveniles, for the sanctity of life under Iranian law—was a long, slow trudge through territory that would be hostile no matter who was president. For that very reason, it made a world of difference if the presidency was hostile, too.

Nobody wanted to vote for Mostafa Moin, Khatami's education minister and the candidate of the reformist party, Mosharekat. If Khatami had accomplished so little, Asieh's friends and relatives told her, what might they expect from the far less charismatic Moin? What strength could he possibly martial that Khatami had not already eclipsed, to little avail? Still, Moin did something Asieh respected. He had his campaign invite women's activists, human rights activists, and journalists to come and consult with him. Asieh was there in all three roles. And she saw the candidate listen while the activists voiced their frustrations and their desires.

He had begun by pontificating on gender equality, quoting from the Quran in its support. But a very young women's rights activist interrupted him.

"Stop talking to God," she said. "Answer me, instead. You aren't a messenger from God to us. If we vote for you, you have to do something for us."

After the election, Asieh heard from a friend of Moin's that the candidate called the meeting the best thing that had happened to him during his campaign. From the women's rights activists, he told his friend, "I heard something that in thirty years I never heard."

Asieh felt certain, after that meeting, that a Moin presidency would offer the space she needed to continue her work, and that it would be far more congenial than a return to the Rafsanjani era she remembered so well. At a time when die-hard reformists called for an election boycott, nonpolitical Asieh Amini implored her friends and family to vote, with her, for Moin. But she couldn't persuade Javad or any of her sisters. When Ahmadinejad squeezed into the second round, she turned on her loved ones in anger. They, and the others who'd boycotted the first round, were responsible for the terrible choice before them now, she insisted. They should hold their noses and vote for Rafsanjani, because the alternative was intolerable.

WHEN AHMADINEJAD ASSUMED THE PRESIDENCY, a chill descended almost immediately on the remaining reformist press. As Asieh would recall, some censorship was internal and anticipatory. This was not the time to do battle with the prosecutor's office. Asieh's editor told her to stop publishing so many things about women; *Etemad* was not a feminist newspaper. After several disputes, Asieh left *Etemad* to work for the same nongovernmental group Omid had once worked for, promoting civil society. She would organize its website and go on researching death penalty cases on her own time. Now she had fully emerged as more activist than journalist. And her work lay all the more squarely within the new administration's sights.

Ahmadinejad's intelligence minister was the former head of the Special Court of the Clergy, Gholam-Hossein Mohseni-Ejei—the man by whose direct order Atefah Sahaaleh's judge had been protected from prosecution.

Shortly after his appointment, Mohseni-Ejei announced that "civil society" was nothing short of a strategic tool of the enemy, by which he meant the United States. Activists like Asieh knew by now that this was how the security forces laid their groundwork for a coming sweep.

Shirin Ebadi called Asieh shortly after Mohseni-Ejei's statement. "We know each other from afar," the Nobel laureate began. But Iranian rights activists now needed to draw closer. Ebadi gathered a group of about ten leaders, including Asieh, in her office. They and their organizations were the remnants of the once vital civil society scene cultivated and marooned in Khatami's time. Now they were isolated and imperiled. They would need to defend one another if and when they faced arrest. They organized a secret network that met regularly in Ebadi's office until they couldn't, and then they met online.

For Asieh, that network was a source of strength and sustenance. She went on with her research and her advocacy despite the gathering gloom. She took on cases of minors charged with capital crimes. She could not adjudicate the defendants' guilt or innocence. She simply believed that whatever these young people had done before the age of eighteen, the state should not kill them. Under international law, if not Iranian law, they were children.

Delara Darabi, in the city of Rasht, was a painter from the age of four, intelligent and favored by her father. But at seventeen she'd taken up with a nineteen-year-old boy named Amir Hossein Sotoudeh. He wanted to marry her, and he was anxious to raise the money to support their life together. By Delara's later telling, one night in 2003, Amir Hossein lured her to the home of her father's wealthy female cousin. There, she claimed, he drugged Delara with a sedative so that she could not resist while he killed the cousin and burglarized the home. If they should be caught, Amir Hossein pleaded, Delara should confess to the crime in his stead, because she was only seventeen and could not be executed. At nineteen, he would surely face the death penalty.

A friend of Amir Hossein's tipped off Delara's father. Mr. Darabi called Delara before him and demanded to know if what he'd been told was true.

It was, she admitted. Her father, incensed, did not wait to hear another word. He called the police to have his daughter and her boyfriend taken away. For two weeks he heard nothing from Delara. And then he heard that she had confessed to committing the murder.

Delara's father went to see her in prison. Was it true that she had murdered the cousin?

"How can you believe it?" Delara replied. "Am I capable of killing someone?"

Contrary to Amir Hossein's alleged prediction, when the case came before a judge in February of 2005, Delara's age at the time of the crime earned her no mercy. Although she retracted her confession, she was sentenced to death. Her lawyer pursued a retrial for the three years that followed, and he brought Asieh to Rasht to research and publicize the case.

Every time he talked to Asieh about his daughter, Delara's father cried. If only he had listened to Delara and dissuaded her from that first and fateful confession to what he sincerely believed was her boyfriend's crime. Asieh asked to see Delara's paintings, expecting little more than a competent adolescent display. But the paintings, many of them made in prison with nothing but Delara's fingers for a brush, most of them in black-and-white with accents in red, were brilliant and terrifying. The figures that populated them were skeletal or blindfolded, incarcerated or facing the noose; they were incandescent in darkness, penned in by barbed wire and bars, their faces full of wreckage. Delara painted death, prison, and her impression of injustice, and she would have been a prodigy anywhere in the world.

"I can write about your daughter," Asieh told Mr. Darabi at length. "But I'd prefer to show her paintings to people. They're better than any explanation of mine."

IN MAY 2006, Asieh got a baffling phone call. An old friend in Mashhad had read about Asieh's work on juvenile execution. Did Asieh work on other forms of judicial killing? the friend wanted to know. For example, stoning?

Stoning was an antiquated Islamic punishment, usually for adultery, that involved burying a married woman and her lover in pits with their hands tied behind their backs and pelting their heads and torsos with rocks until they died. Surely the Iranian penal system authorized nothing so barbaric. In fact, Asieh had asked Shadi Sadr about it once, as she'd seen this sentence noted on some case files. Shadi assured Asieh that, in 2002, Ayatollah Shahroudi, the chief justice, had ordered a moratorium on stoning. Maybe some prisoners still carried this sentence, Shadi said, but it was an empty threat, impossible—indeed, illegal—to fulfill.

Asieh explained to her friend in Mashhad what Shadi had explained to her. The couple could not possibly have been stoned. But the friend insisted. Asieh should come to Mashhad and see for herself.

Friends and colleagues warned Asieh to let this one drop. If there had been a stoning, it had been done in secret, and whoever had ordered it would go to great lengths to keep it hidden. But Asieh went to Mashhad and found a source. He was the neighbor of an old friend from her year in Mashhad. He worked for the intelligence service of the Revolutionary Guard, and he had witnessed everything.

Asieh and a colleague invited him into their car and had him lead them to the location of the stoning. The guardsman had a wireless radio for the Revolutionary Guard intelligence service. Every time it crackled, Asieh felt her skin prickle. She had no way of knowing if she could trust this man. But then he spoke. He used to be a very serious Muslim, the guardsman told Asieh. After that day at Behesht-e Reza cemetery, he didn't know if he believed in anything anymore.

The couple's names were Mahboubeh M. and Abbas H. The judge who had sentenced them sent a letter to the Revolutionary Guard's intelligence office, to the governorate, to the Basij, and to the local bus depot, announcing that there was to be an Islamic ceremony at the cemetery and asking for volunteers. Many people registered. Some were Revolutionary Guardsmen and Basijis; some were bus drivers. None knew what sort of ceremony this would be.

Abbas H. and Mahboubeh M. were brought to the spot alive, but dressed for burial. They were lowered into pits that had been dug into the ground. But the woman's pit was not deep enough: it was important that her breasts be concealed by the earth. So she was removed and the hole dug deeper.

A high-ranking cleric who was an important judge in Mashhad addressed the crowd with poetry. Each stone they cast at this couple, he informed them, was a stone to build their own homes in paradise. He cast the first stone himself.

Abbas H. was silent. Maybe he was already dead. Or maybe his soul had taken leave of his still-living body. But the woman cried, and she spoke. "Please cut off my hands," she said, "cut off my feet. But don't do this to me."

They had arrived at the cemetery. Asieh's colleague stumbled from the car and vomited. The guardsman continued his story. He had not wanted to participate, he told Asieh. The judge called to him and told him to cast a stone. The guardsman protested that his job was to protect the crowd. He was not a volunteer and could not abandon his post. But what he really felt was something else. This judge, this cleric, was talking about God and the Prophet. And the guardsman did not know what to do with such a God or such a prophet.

"There's a film of the stoning," the guardsman told Asieh.

"Where is it?" she asked. "I'll do anything for access to it."

He said, "I have a copy. If you can guarantee that a country will give me and my family safe refuge, I will give it to you."

Asieh had no means of making such a guarantee. But she was afraid of the guardsman. Now he knew her, and knew what she knew. She told him that she would look into it. But she was never able to meet his demand.

THERE WAS NO QUESTION in her mind that the stoning had taken place, and that it was done in secrecy. She brought her knowledge to the judge in the case. He refused to be interviewed. That was fine, Asieh said, but could he tell her if he'd issued the sentences?

He'd followed the law, the judge replied. He didn't make the law, but he was bound to impose it.

Asieh reminded the judge that the head of the judiciary had ordered an end to stoning. The judge scoffed. Sharia law was supreme, he explained, not the judiciary. As a judge, he was answerable not to any official in Tehran but to the law itself. He would make his own decisions, independent of treaties or legislation or the policies of Shahroudi.

Asieh would take this statement, and the insight it offered into the function of the judiciary, back to her friends in the Iranian women's rights community. They had made discriminatory law the focus of their protest. And now they understood something they hadn't understood before. They could take their demands to the government, and even to the head of the judiciary, where they might find a responsive hearing. But under the Iranian system, judges were clerics trained in Islamic jurisprudence. The most hardline judges believed they answered to a higher law than the legislation approved by the parliament. Asieh would soon learn that the Iranian constitution and penal code, in their infinite ambiguity, supported both this view and its opposite.

ASIEH HAD WORKED WITH THE LAWYER, Shadi Sadr, informally on all her cases. Asieh did the research and made contact with the defendants. Shadi offered legal advice and defense. Now Asieh came to Shadi with what she'd learned in Mashhad. She was sure that this stoning had taken place. But she had no documentary evidence. If she published a story, the judiciary would say it was a lie, and Asieh would be able neither to prove her case nor to protect herself from reprisals. Those responsible would seek to silence her before she uncovered more evidence. Under Khatami, to publish such a story would have been risky; now, with the increasing repression and opacity of hardline rule, it would be foolhardy.

Asieh had met some Pakistani women's rights activists at a conference in Lahore earlier that year. She'd talked to them about stoning in their country, before she'd understood that it still took place in her own. In Pakistan, stoning was not a judicial punishment but a vendetta voluntarily carried out by villagers. The Pakistani feminists had started a campaign to eradicate it through exposure and condemnation. Asieh proposed that she and Shadi try something like this. They wouldn't publish anything; they would talk to people, and meanwhile Asieh would go on researching the Mashhad case until they could bring it before the public.

Shadi liked the idea, and she brought in a third partner who was a well-known older feminist with roots in the revolutionary movement and the Islamic Left. The three women founded the Stop Stoning Forever campaign together with two women living abroad who could broadcast their findings and raise their international profile at less risk.

Asieh would remember the campaign's early days as among the best of her life. Now her solitary work on execution cases had gravity, company, larger purpose—and now she had a fierce knot of solidarity gathered around her. She and her partners worked on cases every bit as harrowing as the earlier ones. But they expended their anxiety and energy after hours in giddy parties where they danced and drank and sang. Once the three of them rented a bus and took their children north to Kelardasht, a lush valley in Mazandaran. They spent the weekend at the vacation home of a friend of Asieh's, relaxing but also planning for the campaign's future.

When women staged a sit-in outside a soccer stadium to protest their exclusion, Asieh and one of her partners were there. Her partner's foot was badly injured by the attacking police. When other groups organized a women's rights protest in Haft-e Tir Square in Tehran on June 12, 2006, Asieh went to show her support. The women confronted a cordon of security and police, who fought them off with batons, pepper spray, and colored paint that they used to mark fleeing protesters for arrest. Seventy people were arrested that day. Asieh was not one of them. Of those who were, fourteen were to be tried and sentenced to prison terms for "acting against national security" or "disturbing the public order."

The time was as dark as any Asieh had known. But it was also the time when Iran's women's movement coalesced. The movement was of a piece with its hardships, like a city built into a granite mountainside. After the demonstration in Haft-e Tir Square, some women's rights activists launched what they called the One Million Signatures campaign. They printed pamphlets detailing laws that discriminated against women. Activists distributed the pamphlets among women in private, explaining their contents and collecting signatures for the repeal of those laws.

Asieh and her partners worked differently. Their weapon was transparency, and so their campaign relied on media. They also shouldered a reporting burden: they needed real evidence that the judiciary had not complied with the moratorium on stoning.

Asieh had one of the campaign's expatriate partners publish an interview with her in which Asieh mentioned that she'd heard about a case of stoning in Mashhad and was researching it. That interview finally provoked the response Asieh had hoped for: a friend of one of the victim's families came forward and offered to take Asieh to the stoned woman's children.

Asieh went back to Mashhad for the full story and a couple of relevant documents. According to the family, Mahboubeh M. was married to an abusive man who beat her bloody and brought other women into the home. She had never wanted to marry this man; her father had insisted. When she tried four times to divorce her abuser, her father told her she would have no place to go if she did, because he would not support her. Abbas H. loved Mahboubeh M. and killed her husband. Under torture, Mahboubeh M. was forced to confess that she and Abbas H. had a sexual relationship, and that this was the reason for the murder. Asieh would never know for certain whether this was true. The family denied it. But it was the pretext for stoning both of them.

The family gave Asieh two documents. One was from the court, confirming the sentence. The other was a forensics report confirming the cause of death. Now Asieh published what she knew on her blog. It was a story no newspaper dared to touch. The minister of justice, Jamal Karimi-Rad, gave a press conference. This stoning story was a lie, he said, spread by feminists who wanted to be famous. They took money from foreign countries and spread fictions that served Western prejudices about Islamic law.

STONING WAS NOT TECHNICALLY a women's issue. The sentence was levied at least as often on men accused of sexual relations with married women. But adultery was, in the end, a women's issue. Men could legally have up to four wives and many lovers. There was only limited recourse for a woman who objected. Women didn't have equal rights in initiating divorce, and they automatically lost custody of all children over the age of seven if they did manage to leave. Married women could not so much as hold jobs without permission from their husbands. Those who took lovers could be stoned, with their lovers, for adultery. Asieh and her partners in the campaign hoped to hold the whole battery of discriminatory family laws up to the light by exposing the persistence of stoning.

The campaign's founders gave interview upon interview. Asieh canvassed the country from north to south, east to west, city to city, prison to prison. She spent only two weekends with her family in the summer of 2006. She and her partners located seventeen people sentenced to be stoned, and they tracked down their families and their lawyers. Shadi set up a network to help those who had no lawyers. Soon the campaign had a big advisory board. Asieh did the legwork; Shadi did the legal work; and their third partner ran the activist campaign. When they couldn't publish inside, they got word of their cases outside, to groups like Amnesty International, and the information boomeranged back into Iran.

ASIEH WAS BUSY PLANNING Delara Darabi's exhibition in the fall of 2006. By now she had met Delara in prison, and she had met Delara's judge. For some reason, like Atefah's judge before him, he seemed determined to execute the delicate girl, Asieh believed. She hoped she could forestall him by making Delara an artistic celebrity.

Asieh found Delara a gallery. It belonged to Lili Golestan, the sister of Kaveh Golestan, the photographer killed by a land mine in Kurdistan. When Asieh and Javad brought the paintings to Lili Golestan, she was floored. She had not cared one way or the other about their quality; she was donating space for a cause she considered important. But the paintings were, Lili told Asieh now, "amazing." On the merits alone, Delara deserved a showing.

The opening was like nothing the Golestan Gallery had ever seen. Five ambassadors came, along with a crowd of filmmakers, journalists, and activists. The press coverage was global. Delara's likeness, in a blue head-scarf and with downcast gaze, her knuckles to her lips in contemplation, appeared on placards of demonstrators as far away as Italy and Burkina Faso. So did the haunting images from her show.

"The paintings in front of you are not wordless images and colors, they are the painful photo realities of our life," Delara wrote in a statement posted on the gallery wall. "The only face I see in front of me every day is a wall. For three years, I have been defending myself with colors, forms and words. These paintings are an oath to a crime I did not commit. Unless the colors bring me back to life, I greet you who have come to view my paintings from behind that wall."

Delara remained behind the wall for another two and a half years. Then the judge proceeded in secret, with no witnesses and no notice. Delara Darabi called home at seven o'clock on the morning of May 1, 2009. The last words anyone heard her speak were these:

"Oh, Mother," she said, "I see the hangman's noose in front of me. They are going to execute me. Please save me."

JAMAL KARIMI-RAD, the justice minister, had all but named Asieh and her colleagues in his weekly press conferences. Certain forces inside the country dared to threaten the judiciary, he intimated darkly, and they would be dealt with. The minister was gunning for Asieh's arrest, she heard from others; her work enraged him. If anything or anyone gave Asieh pause, it was he. But she pursued her stoning cases.

In the city of Takestan in the province of Qazvin, a man named Jafar
Kiani and his alleged lover, Mokarrameh Ebrahimi, had been sentenced to
stoning for adultery nearly ten years earlier. The court was preparing only
now to carry out the sentence. The campaign sprang into action, publiciz-
ing the case every way it knew how. Asieh heard, at length, that the sentence had been dropped—a victory for the campaign. But three days later
she heard something else: Kiani had been taken in secret to a mountain
outside town, where he was stoned.

Asieh went to that mountain, where a villager showed her the bloodied
stones. She gathered them to bring to Tehran as evidence. She took photos
and videos and interviewed the villagers. Then she stopped in Qazvin to
see a local activist who had summoned her. That activist had an important
document. Someone had surreptitiously taken a paper from the desk of the
judge in Kiani's case and scanned it. The scan was on a CD. Asieh was to
read the document, its pilferer directed, and then destroy the disc.

The document was a letter from the Takestan judge to Shahroudi,
explicitly defying the moratorium on stoning. No decree of Shahroudi's
would stop him from issuing the sentence, the judge declared. Islamic law,
he claimed, was on his side. And he cited the text of a law Asieh had never
seen before. This law granted judges discretion over stoning and the hundred lashes punishment for crimes against chastity. Any judge who deemed
these punishments justified could impose them independent of the system.
For although one article of the constitution demanded that courts make
decisions only in accordance with the laws of the state, another stipulated
that if the state provided no relevant law, the judge should refer to "Islamic
sources and credible fatwas." A similar inconsistency could be found in the
penal code. Ayatollah Shahroudi might be the head of the judiciary, the
Takestan judge concluded, but there was nothing he could do in the case of
Jafar Kiani.

Asieh broke the CD, as she was told. But she committed its contents to
memory. She understood now that a profound battle was raging inside the
judiciary. Some judges decided their cases based solely on the country's

penal code, while others went beyond it, appealing to sharia. A growing number of fundamentalist judges did not accept Shahroudi's authority. And Shahroudi kept publicly silent, which was, Asieh felt, an unfortunate boon to his enemies.

Asieh would not be silent. She gave interviews to Deutsche Welle and the BBC in the taxi that took her home to Tehran. She awaited the consequences. But some days later, on December 27, 2006, Jamal Karimi-Rad died in a car accident. Asieh was ashamed to admit that she felt a smidgen of relief.

ASIEH GOT A LETTER from some of her activist colleagues in the early spring of 2007. Five of the women arrested at the previous year's demonstration in Haft-e Tir Square were scheduled to go on trial on March 4. The community of women's rights activists should show their support for these women, the letter suggested, by appearing in front of the courthouse in silent protest.

The police began arresting the silent protesters almost as soon as they converged on the courthouse. They handled Asieh so roughly that they ripped her manteau. The defendants and their lawyers, including Shadi Sadr, walked out of the courtroom in coordinated protest. They were arrested, too. Asieh and thirty-two other women were taken first to Vozara, the detention center normally used by the morality police. The police holding them were women, and the activists saw an opportunity.

"We're here because of *you*," one of the activists told the policewomen, "because of your daughters, your nieces. You should support us."

The police and their detainees erupted in discussion. Some of the policewomen confided that they did support the women's activism and regretted detaining them; others barked at the sympathizers to shut up. The detainees were moved to Evin Prison, and all discussion came to an end.

Asieh could see, from the bottom of her blindfold, that her interrogator had a thick file in his hands. On top she thought she saw printouts from her blog. The interrogator complained one day that her incarceration had attracted a lot of news coverage. What could she say? Asieh tossed off; she and her colleagues were important. But from the tone and the line of his questioning, she understood something else. She wasn't supposed to be in prison just yet. The security forces had meant to keep her and the other women activists under surveillance, to track their network and their activities and spring the trap later on. But the protest outside the courtroom was a provocation, and now here she was.

Her interrogator knew that the activists planned a women's rights demonstration in front of the parliament for the following week. Asieh should cancel it, he instructed her. But she couldn't do that from prison, she pointed out. She'd be out in time, he told her. And she was. Asieh and most of the other prisoners were released five days after their arrest. Only two remained in prison, and they were Asieh's two partners in the Stop Stoning Forever campaign.

All the released women were under the same instructions: to cancel the demonstration. But if they did so, there was a good chance not everyone would hear in time. The women who showed up would be vulnerable to brutal reprisals, and the organizers would be responsible. But if they didn't call it off, Asieh was certain her friends would suffer in prison.

Asieh came up with a plan. They should call the demonstration off. But then they should go to the parliament at the appointed time, ostensibly in order to tell anyone who mistakenly showed up to go home. They were there, they told the security forces ingenuously, to cancel the demonstration. The security forces beat them with batons. Asieh took pictures of a fellow activist's foot, black with bruises.

The remaining two prisoners were released on March 15. One posted $220,000 bail; the other, $280,000. Organizations each of them ran had been shut down. But not the Stop Stoning Forever campaign.

Their work, they understood, was closely monitored now. So were their lives. Asieh knew her phones were tapped and her comings and goings watched. One day a stranger dropped in on one of Asieh's neighbors. He said he was researching an accident report for insurance purposes. He asked the neighbor about all the families in the building and their cars. He left but some minutes later rang the neighbor's bell again. Through the intercom he said, "I forgot to ask you about Mrs. Amini's car. Which one is hers?"

The neighbor had never given Asieh's name. And everyone in the building knew her by her married name, as Mrs. Montazeri.

ONE EVENING, Asieh found herself at home alone. Ava was at a friend's house; Javad was working. The apartment was dark. Suddenly Asieh felt that she couldn't breathe. She had an overwhelming urge to weep, but she couldn't make a sound. She thought she might die. She took a shower. And then she checked her e-mail. She found a nice note from a journalist friend in exile. For some reason, it unlocked her. She sobbed so violently and long that her neighbors came to check on her. She'd lost a relative, she lied.

Her e-mail was flooded now with terrible stories from far-flung towns, from relatives and lawyers of the condemned who had no recourse and had heard of Asieh's work. Three men in Semnan province, she was told, were to be executed. She referred the case to another activist group. But one morning at five, it was Asieh their lawyer called, to say that the men were about to be hanged. Asieh's hand was paralyzed in that moment. She couldn't move it. She observed her body as though from without. The moment passed. Then she went to see Delara's mother in Rasht. On her return she felt her body quake, as though feverish, in the night. This happened once a week now. She had fevers she could not explain. She figured they were viruses. She took pills, but still the shivering returned.

There was trouble within the campaign. Asieh's partners flew at a higher altitude than she did: they were more internationally connected and preoccupied at times with matters of theoretical framing that seemed to Asieh a distraction. There were divisions and disagreements among them even as their caseload grew. Asieh was on the phone one afternoon, in a tense discussion with one of her partners, when she fell. The phone dropped. She wasn't asleep. She could hear the room around her. But she couldn't move. For an hour or two she lay there.

Headaches came: immense, pulverizing headaches that responded to no pill, no therapy. Asieh's partners were not returning her calls or e-mails. There was work to be done, desperate people who depended on them. Finally Asieh went to see a neurologist. She'd had some kind of nervous shock, he surmised. There was nothing to do but rest. Every day and every night the shivering convulsed her body, a fever she could not shake. And then one day she couldn't move her eyes, her shoulders, her neck. She went to the hospital.

For a week, Asieh was tested for everything from meningitis to AIDS to malaria. She had an MRI, a spinal tap. Everything came back normal. But the pain in her head and now her eyes was unendurable. She felt as though her eyes would leave her skull. But the hospital could not admit her, because according to her test results she was healthy. Maybe she should see an eye doctor, one of the emergency room doctors suggested. She left in a fury of disbelief. And the next morning she woke up blind.

Two red bulbs had replaced her eyes, as though her eyelids had turned inside out and swelled to the size of grapes. She visited a very famous professor of ophthalmology, who told her she had no problem. She was crazed with frustration. How could she be blind, she demanded, and have an eye doctor tell her she was normal?

"My daughter," the professor said, "I can see your eyes. But the problem is not with your eyes."

Asieh went now to the top neurologist in Tehran. He confirmed what the first neurologist had said. A psychological trigger had sent her body into shock, and this had set off an earthquake in her nervous system. Her syndrome was extremely rare. Maybe one in a million bodies would respond as Asieh's had to extreme stress. But when he understood the nature of Asieh's work, he became convinced of his diagnosis. He prescribed her high doses of cortisone to relieve the swelling. The drugs blurred her memory and dulled her mind. Sometimes when she left home, she couldn't find her way back.

Asieh, fogged and enervated, had a bad feeling about the campaign. She could not get through to Shadi. But she reached the campaign's contact person in Montreal, at an international organization under whose umbrella the campaign had recently decided to work. The woman told her to relax. No one would do anything without her.

But something drastic had already been done. While Asieh was sick, her colleagues had dissolved the Iranian campaign entirely into the Montreal-based contact's organization. Like that, everything Asieh had built disappeared. She would never know why or by whose hand.

As she convalesced, Asieh was summoned for questioning by the intelligence ministry. Her interrogator knew the campaign well. Intelligence agents had broken into its offices and searched her files. Her interrogator asked after her health, specifically her eyes, as if to let her know he knew all about that, too. Even her body, it seemed to Asieh, was subject to malevolent scrutiny. But most of all, they wanted to know about that network of civil society activists she had helped forge in the office of Shirin Ebadi.

LONG, DARK MONTHS HURTLED DOWN ON HER. Asieh had lost her campaign, her vocation, her friends—even, it seemed at times, her body and mind. The latter two were the first to return to her. The swelling in her eyes receded. By March 2009, Asieh was well enough to travel to New York to give a speech about juvenile execution before a group affiliated with the United Nations. But when she thought of the families of the condemned who had placed dim and fragile hopes in her, and she knew no way to explain to them the collapse of the campaign, she became depressed.

Asieh wrote poems to her interrogator: "How many times have I asked you / 'Don't come to my dreams with a gun.'" And she wrote a moving letter to an expatriate friend in the United States about the need for human rights workers to have training, counseling, and periods of rest she'd never thought to carve out. The friend published a translation of Asieh's letter on an English-language website called Iranian.com, and she included photographs of Asieh's eyes, squeezed into their sockets by the shocking red protuberances that looked like nothing any of Asieh's doctors had ever seen.

Were human rights workers in other countries better prepared, better trained? Asieh didn't know. But she couldn't imagine circumstances more chaotic than those that prevailed in Iran. She had become deeply enmeshed with the subjects of her research, she reflected in her letter. Delara, Atefah, and others peopled her dreams. She had sat alongside mothers at the scaffolds of their sons. She had no models, no mentors, no handbook to follow that might have cautioned her to keep her distance or flagged the signs of her coming collapse.

"The truth is that we work on a remote island," she wrote. "We are alone. I realized this while I was staring at the ceiling for two months with painful eyes."

SIXTEEN

THE EPIC OF DIRT AND DUST

The destiny of each generation must be in its own hands.

—AYATOLLAH RUHOLLAH KHOMEINI,
February 2, 1979

AT THE END OF MAY 2009, Tehran exploded with a strange, political nightlife. Its color was green, for the candidacy of Mir Hossein Mousavi, and its eruption was a surprise to anyone who'd watched cynicism set in with reformist voters since Khatami's time. What came to be called the Green Wave could not be explained, at first, as a groundswell for the uncharismatic, backward-looking candidate that Mousavi was when he entered the race. Nor was it a sudden resurgence of investment in the vision the reformist intellectuals had once set forth. Rather, it was a groundswell against Ahmadinejad, its fuel as much anger as hope.

Mousavi was at first an unlikely vehicle for that anger. Those who were drawn in 2005 to Ahmadinejad's asceticism and old-school revolutionary rhetoric knew Mousavi as the real thing—a font of Islamic Left ideology and a religious ascetic without Ahmadinejad's eclecticism and showmanship. Only as he absorbed the demands of his burgeoning support base after the debates did Mousavi come to stand for other values, including civil rights and freedoms and, above all, the rule of law. He did not speak of "political development" or "civil society." He was not nearly as progressive, intellectually, as Khatami had been. But his campaign speeches railed against official lies, crookedness, and favoritism, and against what Mousavi described as the president's lack of respect for the rights of those outside his own circle. Iran's martyrs had not died for this.

Much later, Mousavi would say of the color green that his supporters had chosen it, and he had fallen in behind them. This statement—"I followed you"—would affix itself to the former prime minister. Most everyone would forget that he did not say it in reference to the Green Movement itself. He might as well have. For by dint of little more than character and happenstance, Mousavi was all but conscripted to travel a road well beyond the fallow fields Khatami once plowed.

ASIEH AND JAVAD WENT into the streets of Tehran before midnight and stayed there until after dawn. Crowds of people in green danced, linked arms, and loosed a wild happiness that was alien to those streets. They traded poems, and jokes upon jokes about Ahmadinejad. They debated, almost civilly, with Basijis who ventured into the green crowds to press the case for Ahmadinejad. For all the world, it looked like the germ of democracy. Asieh was concerned, she confided to Javad. Things were not normal.

On June 8, Mousavi supporters, organized by Setad 88, planned to form a human chain eighty-eight kilometers long, with links in cities throughout the country. They would stand single file, each holding fifty centimeters of green ribbon upraised as a symbol. In Tehran, the chain would stretch the length of Valiasr, Tehran's longest boulevard, from Tajrish Square in the north to Rah Ahan Square in the south. In the area near Fatemi Square, by the interior ministry, so many people showed up that no cars could pass. Asieh, who brought Ava into the streets that day, was stunned. She'd never expected to see such an outpouring for Mousavi.

Even Mousavi's campaign volunteers were surprised by what they'd helped unleash. One young volunteer saw her mother in the middle of a square, chanting slogans with the young people at one in the morning. She'd been a leftist in 1979. She'd helped Khomeini come to power. She'd caused her children terrible trouble, she told her daughter now, and she wanted to make it right.

On the Chamran Expressway in the north of Tehran, a local jounalist observed one night in late May, the crowd was too thick to drive through, and people parked their cars in the middle of the road, getting out to mill among the crowds of young people who sang and danced. The crowd belonged to Mousavi, and within it rage was as palpable as hope. "One week, two weeks, three weeks, Ahmadi hasn't had a shower," sang the children. A popular brand of Cheetos-like snacks had a monkey on its logo, and a woman waved a bag of them out her car window, pointing at the monkey and yelling, "Don't vote for him!" The Basijis on their motorbikes just smiled serenely.

When Khatami spoke at the Azadi soccer stadium, the atmosphere was electric: there was not a spot left to sit on the grass or in the aisles. Days later, the journalist attended a women's rally for Ahmadinejad at the same stadium. The crowd was immeasurably thinner and a great deal older, the attendees dutiful, their energy subdued. The journalist counted sixty busloads of women from Qom, and there were buses from Lorestan as well. A famous female athletic personality was horrified when the journalist approached her. She pushed up the sleeve of her manteau to show her green shirt beneath. "Our manager said we had to come here," she confided. "We had no choice."

The campaign worker who'd seen her mother in the square would recall traveling to Islamshahr and Shahr-e Rey—incorporated suburbs in the south of Tehran, presumed conservative strongholds—and finding such strong support for Mousavi that she thought she'd driven the wrong direction. In Tabriz, where the ethnic Azeri population was traditionally distrustful of central government and disinclined to vote, Mousavi, an ethnic Azeri, filled the soccer stadium, with people tripping over one another to get in.

The town of Birjand, in South Khorasan province, had been an Ahmadinejad stronghold in 2005. A foreign reporter who covered Ahmadinejad's "rock star" treatment there during a 2007 provincial tour returned in 2009 and found the town wild for Mousavi, with roaring green-clad crowds of thousands straining to brush their fingertips against the candidate's white hair. In 2007, one said, residents had been forced to turn out for Ahmadinejad; but this time "these are real people in this place. For love we will give our lives."

No one, it seemed, was working in June 2009. The clock had stopped. That this festival took place in the wee hours of the mornings contributed to its aura of enchanted unreality. Older observers would liken those nights to the headiest days of 1979; younger ones thrilled to a sneak preview of a freedom they were all the more determined now to grasp. But for Asieh Amini, the excitement was tempered with foreboding. Why, she wondered, was the Islamic Republic allowing this?

THE ISLAMIC REPUBLIC, it transpired, was worried. So recounted the Revolutionary Guard Corps' top commander, Mohammad Ali Jafari, when he explained the summer's events to an audience of clerics and uniformed guardsmen some months later. (A video of his address would leak to the Iranian expatriate press in 2014.) The reformists could not be allowed to return to power. This was a "red line"—whether for the Revolutionary Guard or the Leader, Jafari did not specify. But Mousavi absolutely had to be stopped. When the Green Wave crested, the reformists called explicitly on the Revolutionary Guard and the Basij not to interfere in the election. The reason for this plea was clear, Jafari said: without the security forces' interference, the election would likely go to a run-off. The Revolutionary Guard couldn't allow that, because there was no guarantee Ahmadinejad would win. Exactly how the Revolutionary Guard had resolved this crisis, and at whose command, Jafari left blank except to praise the initiative's success.

On June 9, three days before the election, the Mousavi and Karroubi campaigns wrote to the Guardian Council to warn of possible irregularities afoot. They said they had learned from sources inside the interior ministry that the number of ballots printed was vastly greater than the number of potential voters, and that twice the necessary number of validation stamps had been made and distributed as well. These materials could be put to untoward purposes, the candidates suggested, particularly in the smaller precincts, where the polls closed earliest. But their entreaty was seemingly lost in the preelection tumult.

On June 11, the night before the election, Asieh and a friend had a minor car accident near Vanak Square. No one was hurt, but the women had to wait at the police station behind the square. There, Asieh noticed something different from the previous nights. The Basijis did not venture into the crowd to argue for Ahmadinejad. They hung back behind the square on their motorcycles. Asieh saw that one was bleeding from the head.

"What happened to you?" she asked in her gentlest, most maternal tone.

"Some Mousavi supporters beat me and broke my head," he told her.

Surely, she said, they didn't beat him just to express their support for Mousavi. Had he gotten into a fight?

"It's finished," the Basiji replied.

"What's finished?" Asieh asked.

The Basiji laughed. Another Basiji who'd been listening laughed, too. "Everything is finished," they told her. "And Doctor," which was what they called Ahmadinejad, "will come tomorrow."

Now Asieh laughed. "The election is tomorrow," she chided, "not tonight."

"No," one of the Basijis said meaningfully. "The election was tonight."

ON ELECTION DAY, Asieh couldn't help feeling happy and expectant. She had never seen the polling stations like this. Voters waited as long as three hours on snaking lines to cast their ballots, and the mood on those lines was exuberant for Mousavi.

Rumors of fraud wafted through the crowds, some of them—like the one suggesting that the pens at the polling stations were loaded with disappearing ink—clearly preposterous. Others were more credible, as they allegedly originated within the interior ministry. But the reformists had assured their supporters that the most the security forces could possibly falsify would be two to four million votes. With a turnout as big as it clearly was in Tehran, four million votes hardly mattered. The election might go to a run-off, and then Mousavi's advantage would only swell.

In the afternoon, some polls closed precipitously. Others had run out of ballot papers. Text messaging service had been shut down throughout the country since the night before, and in the afternoon many reformist websites suddenly went dark. Asieh felt certain now that something wasn't right. By evening she was fielding ominous and confused reports. And then something strange happened just as the polls closed.

Mir Hossein Mousavi called a press conference in which he claimed that there were indeed irregularities in the election's administration. He declared himself the winner with by far the greater share of the vote, and he called on the Supreme Leader to intercede.

It was a bizarre move. Mousavi could not possibly have known the election's outcome. But from his words and his manner, it was clear that he anticipated something, and he was sending up a preemptive flare.

The polls had barely closed when the interior ministry announced the results based on partial returns: Ahmadinejad would be the winner by a commanding margin—69 percent at the time of the announcement, although in the end the official tally would give him 63 percent to Mousavi's 34.

The speed of the initial announcement was unprecedented. Tabulating Iran's handwritten paper ballots normally took twelve to forty-eight hours, and this year's turnout was much higher than normal—officially 85 percent, or 39 million voters. The interior ministry said its calculation was based on five million of those votes. Even this was far more than was normally counted so instantaneously, and to announce preliminary results with such finality was unheard-of in Iran. The capital was locked down, with communications jammed, Revolutionary Guardsmen and Basij forces dispatched into the streets, the interior ministry sealed off like a bunker.

AIDA SAADAT WAS a thirty-five-year-old women's rights activist from the city of Qazvin. She was a friend of Asieh's, the daughter of a factory technician and a carpet weaver. She'd supported herself since she was eighteen, sometimes commuting eight hours a day between Qazvin and Tehran, and often, like Asieh, working multiple jobs.

Although her degree was in English translation, Aida had devoted her twenties to eradicating child abuse in the villages of Qazvin province. She believed that Iran's problems were as much cultural as political. People needed to learn not to accept violence as a normal condition of life, she felt. Aida was divorced, with a child of her own. After years working in the villages, she came to Tehran and worked with the One Million Signatures campaign and with a human rights group that defended the rights of prisoners.

In 2009 she cast her lot with Karroubi. He was courageous and kind, Aida felt, and an unambivalent supporter of causes she held dear. Karroubi, far more than Mousavi, was the election's outspoken advocate for women's rights, human rights, and political freedom. He had traveled an enormous distance over the four years of Ahmadinejad's presidency, and he had done so following only his alert humanitarian conscience.

For Aida, the two weeks before the election had been an experience apart. For four years, under Ahmadinejad, her organizations could not so much as hold meetings without someone getting arrested. Now there were no repercussions, there was no fear. Only when she tasted this freedom did Aida truly know how hungry she had been for it. She had never lived like this in her life.

She was at the Karroubi campaign headquarters the night of June 12. The students, journalists, and activists who had gathered there were puzzling over the announced returns, calling their counterparts in the provinces, when the office manager told them to vacate the building. Threats had come in from the police, and security forces had raided Karroubi's office in a different building, destroying everything they didn't seize.

As Aida left the building, she saw that a cordon of police on motorbikes surrounded it. Security agents swore at the exiting campaign workers and yelled at them to leave or face arrest. Aida ventured into streets that just two nights before had pulsed with unaccustomed freedom. Now she saw Basijis beating and insulting young people who carried green or white signs from the Mousavi or Karroubi campaigns.

Security forces had invaded one of Mousavi's campaign offices before five that evening, and his headquarters at around eight. They attacked the Setad 88 headquarters with tear gas and batons just before dawn. The activists poured down the stairs, scrambling to get out, a father separated from his crying child, some of the volunteers injured and limping. Was this a coup d'état? the volunteers asked one another. Why attack a campaign office with tear gas in the middle of the night?

It was two in the morning when Asieh Amini took a phone call from a prominent journalist.

"Sleep tonight," the journalist told Asieh and Javad, "because it's finished. They called all the newspapers and told them to change their headlines. Ahmadinejad will be announced the winner."

"I know," Asieh heard herself saying. "I heard it last night."

THE SPEED OF THE COUNT, followed by the communications blackout, the threatening atmosphere, the raids and arrests and attacks on civilians, did not give the impression of a confident, law-abiding republic that had just reelected its president by a two-thirds majority. The numbers, too, raised questions. Mousavi was alleged to have lost even in his hometown. Karroubi, after coming in a close third in 2005, pulled less than 1 percent of the vote—fewer than the number of spoiled ballots. Ethnic minorities and rural voters dramatically changed their voting patterns. Many precincts reported more votes than they had eligible voters, and while this was somewhat normal in Iran, where people can vote anywhere they happen to be, the numbers suggested the presence of hundreds of visitors in villages where such an influx would surely have been noticed.

Mousavi complained that many of his election observers had been prevented from carrying out their work. A researcher in a village near Shiraz reported that ballot boxes were sealed and swept from the polling station before the ballots could be counted in the presence of observers. Similar allegations were reported in Azerbaijan province. Employees of the interior ministry continued to loose vexing rumors. One told *The New York Times* on June 13 that for weeks the ministry had prepared itself by purging potential skeptics and packing its ranks with Ahmadinejad loyalists from around the country. The employee showed the reporter his ministry badge and explained, "They didn't rig the vote. They didn't even look at the vote. They just wrote the name and put the number in front of it."

These and other oddities could, and would, be dismissed or explained away by those who accepted the election results as valid. In an effort to resolve what was becoming a rancorous global dispute, foreign statisticians would pore over the election figures, wrenched from any context, looking for mathematical evidence of anomalies or the lack thereof. But on the evening of June 12, for a great many Iranian voters, the disbelief was swift and visceral. Turnout, Ahmadinejad's opponents had believed, was the game, and they had won it, which meant they could not have lost. For Ahmadinejad to have won against Mousavi two to one, he would have needed to retain all of his voters from 2005, despite his disappointing and polarizing term in office and the conservative disenchantment with him that was evident in the 2006 and 2008 elections. He would also have needed seven million new votes. But the Iranians who had sat out the 2005 election were very unlikely hardline conservatives. Not only did hardline conservatives have a horse in that race—Ahmadinejad—but their Supreme Leader called them to the polls as a duty to God and country. By definition, they were the ones who did not abstain.

Ahmadinejad's supporters would point out that the Mousavi camp could muster no hard evidence of fraud. The reformists, they would say, were simply full of themselves, unaware that a few photogenic young people in North Tehran did not represent the nation. Why was it so hard for them to accept that they were a minority after all? That the leap in voter turnout was no Green Wave but an expression of confidence in the president? Opinion polls, notoriously unreliable in Iran, did show Ahmadinejad ahead prior to the election (except when they didn't). The Greens had swept one another up in a shared narcissism that blinded them to the greater enthusiasm for Ahmadinejad.

Those who had waited on those long lines for hours to cast their votes knew for whom they voted, Mousavi said in a statement. Together with Karroubi and Mohsen Rezaie, Ahmadinejad's sole challenger from the right, Mousavi petitioned the Guardian Council to nullify the election and hold it anew. The three candidates called on their supporters to remain calm.

"I personally strongly protest the many obvious violations, and I'm warning I will not surrender to this dangerous charade," Mousavi declared. "The result of such performance by some officials will jeopardize the pillars of the Islamic Republic and will establish tyranny."

MOUSAVI AND KARROUBI requested permission to hold a demonstration. The interior ministry said no, as it would to every such request Mousavi and Karroubi put forth. But demonstrators came anyway. Some ten thousand protesters took to the streets in Tehran on June 13, the day after the vote. By dusk, there were clashes. Young people had set fires in plastic garbage cans all around, perhaps to ward off the tear gas that was now pouring into squares the Basij and riot police had cleared of protesters. Enghelab Square was packed with people, some of them shouting "Down with the dictator!" Others chanted a song about judgment day. Some demonstrators threw stones at the Basij, who fought back with batons, rubber hoses, and cables.

On his way to a meeting at Mosharekat headquarters, the former deputy interior minister Mostafa Tajzadeh, who was one of Mousavi's campaign managers, spoke to his son-in-law by phone. Tajzadeh said he was certain from the sources he maintained inside his old ministry that the election results were fraudulent.

The son-in-law told Tajzadeh to be careful. But Tajzadeh just laughed. No interrogator could get a phony confession out of him, he said, and they knew it: "But you can bring me cigarettes in prison."

Tajzadeh's meeting at Mosherakat was interrupted by a raid. Along with several other high-profile reformists, Tajzadeh was arrested and brought to Evin.

MAHMOUD AHMADINEJAD was never one for subtlety. Even when his hand was strong, he had a tendency to overplay it. The president held a victory rally on Sunday, June 14, in Valiasr Square. His supporters should pay no heed to the sore losers from the other side, he told the crowd. They were like fans of a losing soccer team: "Those whose team has lost are angry and will do anything to vent their anger. Forty million people participated in the elections in Iran. . . . Now four or five dirt or dust creeping from the corners may do something. But you must know that the pure river that is the Iranian nation will not allow them to put themselves on display."

Later, under pressure even from conservatives who thought the "dirt or dust" remark had gone too far, Ahmadinejad would walk it back, claiming that he was referring only to those who rioted and started fires: those people, he clarified, "are nothing, they are not even a part of the nation of Iran."

But whatever he had actually meant by the remark, it was a spark to a tinderbox. *Etemad Melli*, Karroubi's newspaper, ran a photograph of protesters carrying a banner with the words "The Epic of Dust and Dirt" in green. It was a reference to the phrase for Khatami's 1997 win, "The Epic of the Second of Khordad." "We are not dust and dirt," read another placard, "we are the nation of Iran." Mohammad Reza Shajarian, a wildly popular singer, asked the regime's broadcasting agency to please stop playing his songs because, as he said, "this is the voice of dirt and dust and will always remain so."

The night of the victory rally, in an eerie replay of a night not so long past, security forces armed with riot gear burst into the dormitory at the University of Tehran. They lobbed tear gas canisters into dorm rooms, broke windows, beat students, shot them with pellet guns, and arrested more than a hundred of them. They beat five students to death with their batons and shot two dead. Five others were hospitalized for twenty days or longer.

Security forces raided dormitories in other cities as well: Tabriz, Babol, Mashhad, Zahedan, Isfahan, Shiraz. Two students were reportedly killed in Shiraz. The university chancellor resigned in protest. Even the conservative speaker of the parliament was scandalized and demanded an investigation. Another conservative parliamentarian reproached Ahmadinejad for his earlier remarks, adding that those who assaulted university students in the middle of the night were the ones who were dirt and dust. But the investigation would go nowhere, except to lay blame on unnamed saboteurs who sought to blacken the face of the regime.

IRAN WAS NOT A COUNTRY of frivolous street protests. The price was simply too high, for too little return. The reformists around President Khatami had studiously avoided calling their supporters to the streets during their time in power. Mousavi did no differently, but the times were different, and on Monday, June 15, 2009, a dam broke. More Iranians flooded the streets than at any time since the 1979 revolution, and the tactic they chose came directly from the women's rights activists' playbook. They would stand together in silence, many holding placards with a simple slogan: "Where is my vote?"

As Asieh got ready to leave the house, Javad told her not to expect much. He had not forgotten the Eighteenth of Tir, nor should she. The people would come to the streets, sure. But Mousavi and Karroubi wouldn't. The politicians would do what Iranian politicians always did: they would set the people up to face the brutal security establishment alone.

But Mousavi and Karroubi did show up, and the people, if they were alone, were alone in their multitudes.

Tehran was a city truncated and divided, literally and invisibly, by the walls that set off private spaces of safety from public ones of menace. Now it seemed to have turned inside out, its residents shoulder to shoulder across the fifty-thousand-square-meter expanse of Azadi Square and the streets beyond. From bookshop-lined Enghelab Square near the university, to Azadi with its distinctive arch-shaped monument and hexagonal gardens, the people—ordinary Iranians of every age and type, alongside activists and reformists who had fought all those years—pressed together so tightly they literally took Asieh's breath away. Tehran's conservative mayor estimated the crowd at three million; engineers Asieh knew at the university capped it at four. The crowd vibrated with a vast, univocal silence, and with the exhilarating, surreal absence of fear.

The show of power and unity in that crowd was unlike anything Asieh had known. Even years later, the thought of it would bring tears to her eyes. As she passed Sharif University, she saw a van driving slowly with the crowd, Karroubi standing on its roof.

"Javad," Asieh said when she got home. "You're a big loser. Because that is the most important thing that has happened to me in all my life."

The security forces hung back, maybe under orders, or maybe because the crowd was just too big. But toward the end of the day, gunshots pierced the silence of the demonstrators and the restraint of the security forces. Video footage would show militiamen shooting into the crowd from the roof of their headquarters near Azadi Square. At least eight people were killed in Tehran. It was a day when a young woman who came to those streets found herself holding a stranger's corpse, her manteau soaked in blood, the dead man resting against her in her nightmares for addled nights to come.

FAMOUS REFORMISTS WERE DISAPPEARING. They were arrested in their homes and offices, then spirited off to Evin, where most were held incommunicado for at least a month. They were the middle level of reformist leadership: people who had name recognition, networks, political vision, or organizing know-how. Many were major national figures from the time of the revolution. All had held responsible positions in the government.

There were former cabinet ministers, deputy ministers, and members of the parliament; hostage takers, city councilmen, a former presidential spokesman, associates of Rafsanjani and Khatami alike, even the seventy-eight-year-old foreign minister under Bazargan. Some of these men, like Mostafa Tajzadeh and Khatami's vice president Mohammad Ali Abtahi, had been targeted for nearly a decade. Then there was Saeed Hajjarian, who still required round-the-clock nursing care and many medications.

Even for the Islamic Republic, this was new. The entire leadership of a mainstream political faction had been rounded up as criminals. The family members knew little and could say less, but what news emerged was disturbing. Hajjarian, his daughter alleged, underwent interrogation under the blazing sun, with buckets of ice water occasionally dumped on him to elicit shock. Mohammad Ali Abtahi told his wife he was drugged: "In the last few days, they have been giving me a pill that separates me from the noise and tumult of this world." Soon enough, a number of the detainees, including Hajjarian and Abtahi, issued statements describing the excellent treatment and quality of life they enjoyed in Evin. They would not be seen publicly until August 1, when they would be paraded on television in shocking condition, to deliver their forced confessions and stand in trumped-up show trials.

FOREIGN JOURNALISTS WERE EJECTED from the country. Internet speeds slowed to a crawl when connections weren't blacked-out altogether. When SMS service functioned, Javad Montazeri got text messages from *Ershad*. He was not authorized, the messages said, to take photos of protests. Similar messages had gone out to all the photojournalists. Javad didn't stop photographing, and he didn't stop sending images and videos to friends abroad, no matter how slowly the Internet functioned or how heavily it was monitored. Asieh reported from the streets for a website called Roozonline, using five different pseudonyms.

Thousands of demonstrators continued to turn out daily, although plainclothes militias beat them with abandon. Aida Saadat walked whole days armed with a water bottle and cigarettes and lighters, which were said to ward off tear gas. She was on the phone all the time, telling reporters what she saw—here on Valiasr, there at Haft-e Tir Square, wherever she happened to be. She was beaten so often that her friends made jokes about not wanting to stand near her. Once she bit the Basiji who assailed her. She wasn't sure he felt it through his uniform, but it was better than doing nothing. Sometimes she was tagged with green and yellow paint balls that the security forces used to identify activists for arrest.

When Aida wasn't haunting the streets, she could be found in front of Evin Prison. Thousands of people had been arrested, and many of them were now missing. Aida and some activist colleagues were looking for the family members, in order to build an information network. She was also looking for the sheets Evin posted outside with lists of recent detainees. When the lists went up, even though there were security cameras trained on her, Aida would read the names aloud into a voice recorder. Then she would go home, transcribe the lists, and send them to human rights organizations. She collected some two thousand names. They accounted for, at most, half of those who'd disappeared.

Some Iranians repaired to their rooftops at night, where they sent up calls, one roof to another: *Allahu Akbar! Allahu Akbar!* Such, in 1979, had been the midnight call and response of the revolutionary multitudes. Back then, it signaled resistance to the shah in the name of God. Now it signaled the persistence of the protest movement in the face of violence and its refusal to be cast as irreligious or counterrevolutionary. It reclaimed the past and reproached what the Islamic Republic had become.

ONCE UPON A TIME, in Ayatollah Khomeini's day, the government's warring factions had appealed to the Supreme Leader to arbitrate their disputes. Khomeini was never exactly neutral. He had winnowed the governing factions to a narrow band within a single party. But within that inner circle of government, Khomeini was a balancer of interests and a settler of conflicts. He was never so much missed in that role as he was in 2009.

Khamenei was no Khomeini. He had been a factional player from the start, a party to the disputes Khomeini had arbitrated—usually between himself, as president, and Mousavi, as prime minister. As Leader, Khamenei's hardline allegiances were explicit, his preference for Ahmadinejad common knowledge, and his Guardian Council, led by the aging Ayatollah Ahmad Jannati, was as hardline and partial as he was.

Still, if only in fantasy, the Leader had a role to play. There was no one else in a position to unite the country, to curtail the security forces' excesses, or to soothe the wounded dignity of the Green Movement. Ahmadinejad was committed to the harsh course he'd chosen, but Khamenei could still unwind the noose. The Leader was to speak at Friday prayers at the University of Tehran on June 19, and the country awaited him tensely.

The prayer hall was packed tightly with devoted followers. Ahmadinejad was there. Mousavi and Karroubi were noticeably absent. Khamenei spoke for an hour. He began by praising the nation for participating in the election despite the usual foreign plots to discourage it. Iran had once again showed the world that it loved and trusted its Islamic Republic. All four candidates, Khamenei insisted, belonged to the system and upheld its legitimacy. Khamenei knew them well, and while he favored Ahmadinejad, he assured the hardline crowd that there was no true opposition in the race, and that the voters had made their selections within the boundaries of the constitution.

Khamenei spoke at length about the televised debate between Ahmadinejad and Mousavi. He reprimanded Ahmadinejad for accusing Rafsanjani and his sons of corruption, even while clarifying that in the 2005 election, he himself preferred Ahmadinejad, whose views on domestic and foreign affairs were closer to his own. He also expressed grave sadness that Mousavi had assailed the honesty and character of the president and exaggerated the country's current difficulties.

The election results were legitimate, the Leader asserted: "The Islamic Republic does not betray the votes of the people." A million votes or fewer could be fraudulent, but not 11 million. Those who had doubts should lodge their complaints with the Guardian Council. Street pressure would be counterproductive. To submit to it would be the beginning of tyranny. Moreover, said the Leader, protests furnished cover for infiltrating terrorists. When such elements then provoked violence among the people, and the Basij reacted appropriately, who was to blame?

"One's heart is torn apart when one sees such events," the Leader lamented, "when one sees that they raid university dormitories and harm young students, not rioting students but the pious students, and then chant slogans in support of the Leader, too. One's heart is torn apart by such events."

In his wisdom and kindness, his solidarity with his people, his profound sorrow for their sufferings, Khamenei reserved his most ominous words for Mousavi and those who would follow him in protest:

> Those—the politicians, heads of parties, and directors of political currents—who can exert some influence on the public and are listened to by some groups, should be very careful of their conduct. They should be very careful of what they say. If they show the slightest extremism, the repercussions will be felt by the body of the people and can lead to a very sensitive and dangerous situation, which even they cannot control. . . . If the political elite ignore the law, or cut off their noses to spite their faces, whether they want to or not, they will be responsible for the bloodshed, violence, and chaos to follow.

MOUSAVI AND KARROUBI HAD LODGED their complaints with the Guardian Council, which promised a random review of some ballot boxes; but they expected little from the high clerical body, given its biases and those the Leader had just expressed. Mousavi was famous for his obstinacy, however, and he was true to his reputation now. He responded to Khamenei's speech with a statement striking in its continual evocation of the 1980s as a wellspring of ideology and of hope.

He had come to the election, Mousavi said, to assure Iran's people that the revolution had not been in vain and that it was still possible to live spiritually in the fallen modern world. "I had come to say that bypassing the law results in tyranny; to remind that attention to human beings' generosity does not weaken the foundation of the regime, but strengthens it," Mousavi said. "I had come to say that people expect truth and honesty from their servants, and a lot of our troubles have arisen from lies. I had come to say that backwardness, poverty, corruption, and injustice are not our destiny."

Mousavi, like Khamenei, praised the participation of the people, although he suggested that voters had poured forth in hope of righting a crisis of administration. And he directly answered Khamenei's attempt to lay the regime's violence at his door: "If this good faith and trust coming from the people is not answered by protecting their votes, or the people cannot react in a civil and peaceful way to defend their rights, there will be dangerous pathways ahead, responsibility for which lies with those who can't stand peaceful behaviors."

Mousavi dismissed Khamenei's argument that the sheer volume of votes in Ahmadinejad's favor made fraud impossible. The Leader was in effect suggesting that the magnitude of the alleged fraud was evidence that no fraud had taken place. Such sophistry insulted the republican foundations of the state and gave comfort to those who all along thought Islam incompatible with republicanism. Khomeini had left Iran a better legacy than this.

To his followers, Mousavi pledged that he would stand by their side at all times. He urged them to let no one steal from them the flag of the Islamic Republic or the heritage of the revolution their fathers had wrought. He told them to "continue your social movements based on freedoms explicitly stated in the constitution and stay away from violence, as you have been doing." And he staked out his territory within the orthodoxy of the revolution and under the supposed protection of its security forces:

In this road, we are not up against the Basij members; Basijis are our brothers. In this road, we are not up against the Revolutionary Guard members; they are the protectors of our revolution and regime. We are not up against the military; they are the protectors of our borders. We are not up against our sacred regime and its legal structures; this structure guards our independence, freedom, and Islamic Republic. We are up against the deviations and deceptions and we want to reform them; a reformation that returns us to the pure principles of the Islamic Revolution.

KHATAMI HAD ONCE CALLED MOUSAVI "the man of Saturday." He had meant the Saturday after being elected president. But Mousavi was a man for Saturdays no one had imagined. No politician under the Islamic Republic had spoken up for the masses on the streets as he had. The Saturday that followed Khamenei's speech was June 20, and it would be known forever after as Bloody Saturday. Mousavi did not call off his supporters, as the Leader had told him to, and his supporters did not stay home. They came to the streets, by some estimates in the tens of thousands, specifically to show that they were not afraid. Security forces met them there with knives, razors, and guns. More than twenty people were shot to death, untold numbers beaten to death or seriously wounded.

Between Valiasr Square and Enghelab was an inferno, young people on the ground with Basijis beating their heads with clubs until their brains bled. Asieh was on her way to Enghelab Square with two of her friends when a tide of people came barreling toward them in flight. Asieh felt herself carried by the crowd and then pulled from it by two large men in black uniforms with big batons. They flattened her against a wall and beat her shoulders, back, and head. When she crumpled to the ground, her assailants were swept away by the stampede. Asieh's friends had turned against the current to find her. But Asieh couldn't run, and they needed to. She released their hands and threw herself into the nearest alleyway on her hands and knees.

The shouted slogans and gunfire drew nearer, and the sky darkened with a thick cloud. Asieh's eyes burned and she choked on her breath. She dragged herself along the ground to the nearest doorbells. It was a long time before anybody answered. A man cracked a gate and beckoned her to come in. In his courtyard he doused her with water to cleanse the tear gas. It didn't help much, but later she was grateful, because it helped conceal the fact that she lost control of her bladder as she slept in that courtyard. Asieh was the first of many wounded the man ushered in.

The Basij were out in the alley, loudly discussing whether or not they should search all the homes on the block. The wounded protesters in the courtyard kept their voices low, worried they would bring violence on their host. Asieh spotted a colleague from *Etemad*, and there was a father with his college-aged son, whose face was bloodied and his shoulder broken. The son was a poet, the father told her eagerly, and he had the battered young man pass the time by reciting his poems for Asieh. Her head still swimming, Asieh took out her voice recorder and let it run. Crimes had been committed here, she thought woozily. Maybe one day she would need evidence.

When evening fell, Asieh started for home. Traffic was heavy. A stranger gave her a ride halfway, and she found a taxi for the rest. Wherever she looked from the windows, she saw fires burning. She heard gunshots.

For the second time in her life, Asieh needed an emergency room but did not dare go. Security forces lay in wait at all the hospitals. A friend of hers had gone from emergency room to emergency room with a gaping head wound and found no safety in any of them. At last he got his stitches at a dental clinic. Asieh found a doctor who would come to her home. She was lucky, the doctor said. The club had hit the hard part of her skull. She needed to rest. Her concussion would heal. But her bruises were impressive. He photographed them and prescribed a painkiller for her neck.

NEDA AGHA-SOLTAN, twenty-six years old, was a middle-class girl from Tehran who had studied philosophy, tourism, and voice. Her name, in fact, meant "voice." But in the final video of her, the one that would make her an international symbol, Neda was silent. She had already spoken her last words—"I'm burning!"—before the film began.

Shot in the chest on Bloody Saturday, Neda bled to death with her eyes seemingly locked to the viewer on the other side of an anonymous camera phone at the scene. The clip showed her splayed on the sidewalk in gray pants and a black manteau, men bent over her, frantic to stanch her bleeding chest. She stared, a gaze unblinking but full of fear, until it was emptied of everything as blood spidered and then gushed from her nose and mouth.

Neda was not the first to die that week, nor the only one that day. But she was the only one to die on camera, in a video clip that would be seen all over the world. Something about the occlusion of her beauty by that dark mask of blood captured a particular horror—of things that did not go together, untimeliness, the triumph of death over life. Inside Iran, where the culture of martyrdom ran deep, Neda became a vessel for the anger and grief of millions.

The young woman was unarmed. She had exited a car and walked into the street at the wrong moment. Two men had tried mightily to save her. One of them was a doctor. He could be heard in the video clip shouting at the others to apply pressure to her wound. Another voice—that of Neda's music teacher, who had accompanied her that day—cried, "Neda, don't be afraid! Neda, stay with me." They tried to resuscitate her breathing, then they loaded her, well past hope, into a car bound for a hospital.

The doctor remained behind at the scene and saw the crowd mob a militiaman who exclaimed, "I didn't mean to kill her!" The crowd ripped the Basiji's shirt and took his weapons and his identity card. Then they debated what to do. They could hardly hand him to the police, and while some people hungered for immediate revenge, they resolved not to make themselves murderers, too. Instead they kept his identity card and set him free.

The doctor who witnessed all this fled to Britain. He told the BBC that the bullet had entered Neda from the front, rupturing her aorta and probably her lung. There was no exit wound. The look in her eyes, he said, was of surprise and frank confusion. The innocence behind that look haunted him ceaselessly. For three nights he didn't sleep. He felt guilty because he hadn't managed to save her and because, after she had gone, when he rose from her body and understood that he stood in the spot where she had been shot, he felt afraid for his own life.

The other documented witness, Neda's music teacher, spoke to the press of his anguish and sorrow for the loss of a young woman he described as joyful and vibrant. "This is a crime that is not in support of the government," he said. "This is a crime against humanity." Then he was imprisoned and apparently coerced into challenging the doctor's testimony. Neda was shot not from the front but from behind, he would allege; there had been no militiamen on the scene. He died on the fifth anniversary of Neda's death, reportedly a depressed and broken man.

The Islamic Republic variously blamed Neda's death on fellow demonstrators, the Mojahedin, the BBC, and the doctor who tried to save her life. Mousavi would have none of it. On June 21 he spoke up for the present and even for the past: "Had those responsible for the murders at the student dormitory on the Eighteenth of Tir, 1999, been confronted under the law and in an appropriate manner, today we wouldn't have to bear witness to the same type of tragedies on a larger scale, and wouldn't have to hear the truth being bent in a more brazen fashion." The same criminals, Mousavi asserted, were responsible for manipulating the election as for brutalizing the people, and now they dared to deny what hundreds had witnessed and even documented.

"I am not ready to stop standing, even for a second," Mousavi insisted, "in the shadow of the green tree of restoring the rights of the people of Iran, that has been unjustly fed with the blood of the youth of this country."

WHEN ASIEH SAW THE VIDEO of Neda's death, she wondered why the young woman's family had not come forward. And were there other demonstrators killed? Had they returned to 1988, when political massacres, carried out in secret, were not spoken of, even as the bodies vanished into mass graves?

One day, a women's rights activist called Asieh's home. She needed a new manteau, the activist said; would Asieh care to go shopping with her? Asieh understood at once that this was code. Of course, she said. She needed a new manteau, too.

A group of six activists gathered. They had all heard terrible, unconfirmable things. Some demonstrators had been shot; others might have died under torture. But none of the families were coming forward. Maybe they were still looking for their loved ones in the chaos, hoping to find them in prisons and hospitals. The women decided that the time had come for them to reactivate their network. They would search for the victims and offer solace to the families, encouraging them to speak out. They would try to organize memorials for the fortieth day after each death, according to tradition.

Their first lead came from within their own network. Parvin Fahimi belonged to a group called Mothers for Peace, of which Asieh was also a member. Fahimi had been searching in vain for her nineteen-year-old son, Sohrab Arabi, since he disappeared at the June 15 protest in Azadi Square. They'd gone there together and were separated by the crowd. Cell phone communications were jammed that day. For nearly a month, Fahimi haunted the prisons and the hospitals until at a police station she was allowed to view photographs of the unidentified deceased. Sohrab was "Picture Number 12." A perfunctory coroner's report gave June 19 as the date of death but no cause, and no accounting for Sohrab's whereabouts from June 15 to 19. When the family recovered the body, they saw that Sohrab had taken a bullet in his chest.

Fahimi summoned her friends in the women's network to a ceremony at Behesht-e Zahra. Asieh went with Aida Saadat. Their group was surrounded by Basijis and Revolutionary Guards, but Parvin Fahimi held nothing back on their account. She was, and would remain, so outspoken that she would become a celebrity of sorts in her grief and rage, known everywhere as "the mother of Sohrab," holding a dark mirror to a state that did not see her child as its own.

Asieh published a report about Sohrab on Roozonline. Within twenty-four hours the news was everywhere. Parvin Fahimi held ceremonies at the cemetery and in her home. At one such gathering, three days after Asieh's report was published, a stranger arrived at the Fahimi residence. She was a handsome, gray-haired woman with an arresting presence, dressed from head to toe in black. Her name was Hajar Rostami.

"I am Neda's mother," she told the assembled mourners, who embraced her and cried.

Rostami had apparently kept silent at the behest of a young lawyer who'd sought her out after her daughter's death. He'd promised the family that he could help them so long as they kept their heads down. The authorities had forbidden Rostami from so much as hanging a black banner outside her home. But now she was ready to shed the lawyer and speak out.

Rostami told the activists not to organize a ceremony for her daughter's fortieth day: she would do that herself. But they helped her publicize it. When mourners converged at Neda's gravesite, the riot police dispersed them with tear gas and beatings, arresting at least fifty. Karroubi attended the ceremony, but Mousavi was barred from exiting his car.

SOUTH OF TEHRAN, past Shahr-e Rey and just outside the Behesht-e Zahra cemetery, in a small city called Kahrizak, lay a detention center designed in 2001 for the abuse of drug addicts, rapists, and so-called thugs. Kahrizak Detention Center was built to hold fifty prisoners in underground cells and metal containers that superheated in the summer months. The holding pens were airless. There were no toilets. The facility had been flagged as substandard back in 2007, but the treatment and fate of the criminals imprisoned there were little remarked, except by Iran's indefatigable human rights activists, before the summer of 2009.

On July 9, the tenth anniversary of the Eighteenth of Tir, in a police station courtyard in Tehran, Saeed Mortazavi's deputy informed 147 detained demonstrators that they were to be bused to Kahrizak. Most of the detainees had already sustained injuries in clashes with militiamen during the demonstration or been beaten in the police yard. Some had broken arms and legs, blood clots, or eye infections. They would not receive medical care. Rather, on arrival in Kahrizak, they were packed tightly together in a metal holding pen fetid with vomit, urine, and human waste. The guards were exceptionally brutal, by one account beating several prisoners comatose and killing four before morning. This same account held that there were as many as 200 people in that single metal cell—the 147 demonstrators, plus common criminals of the roughest sort.

The July heat cooked the tin container, and the only water the prisoners were given smelled of urine. They were denied food or given scraps of leftovers to distribute among them. Guards burned detainees' hands and feet with molten tar, broke their teeth, put them through mock executions, and raped and sodomized them violently and repeatedly. At times the air in the crowded cell was poisonously polluted by exhaust from the generator just outside it. On the second day of the demonstrators' detention, the guards transferred a dozen new inmates into the cell. They'd come from a place called "the cage," where men with infectious diseases were held. "They were zombies more than human beings," a witness told the *Los Angeles Times*.

Prisoners from Kahrizak were transferred to Evin on overcrowded buses in the heat of the day. The regular prison authorities balked at the sight of them. They had to log the physical condition of prisoners on admittance, and these prisoners arrived missing toenails and teeth, with extensive bruising to their rectums, some of them in critical condition after just five days in Kahrizak. One, twenty-four-year-old Amir Javadifar, died on the bus. Two others, eighteen-year-old Mohammad Kamrani and twenty-five-year-old Mohsen Ruholamini, were transferred to hospitals. Kamrani was chained to a bed, even though he was comatose, and inadequately cared for, while in Ruholamini's case, the transfer came too late. Both young men died of injuries sustained in Kahrizak. The victims' families were forbidden to hold proper funerals.

While Kamrani lay comatose, a visitor to another patient helped change his bandages and told a reporter that she would never forget what she saw. The young man was missing all but two of his top teeth and a number of his nails; his head was bashed in, his kidneys wrecked, and the stitching around his rectum suggested sexual torture. Ruholamini's father was told his son had died of meningitis. But when he recovered the body and the medical records, it was clear that the young man did not have meningitis. He did have a massive infection that had invaded untreated wounds administered by his torturers; and he apparently died from cardiac arrest and bleeding to the lungs as a result of severe physical stress and repeated blunt trauma. His mouth, his father noted, had been "bashed in," his jaw broken.

LATE ONE SUMMER NIGHT, Aida Saadat got a strange e-mail from a woman she didn't know. The woman had access to the office of the medical examiner at the city morgue. She and others from the morgue had seen evidence that eight detained demonstrators had been raped and killed. They did not know what to do with this information. A mutual friend had persuaded them to approach Aida about arranging a meeting with Karroubi. Aida set up the meeting for the following day.

Karroubi listened to the report without obvious emotion. The allegations were probably not the first he'd heard, and they would certainly not be the only ones. In a July 29 open letter to Rafsanjani, Karroubi made clear that he had spoken to sources who knew the detention centers from the inside. Officials who held "sensitive positions in the country," he wrote, some of them even veterans of the Iran-Iraq War, had informed him that some detained women had been raped so brutally that their uteruses had ruptured. "Young boys held in detention have also been savagely raped. . . . The young boys are suffering from depression and serious physical and mental damage since their rapes," the cleric wrote. These reports were so awful, lamented Karroubi, that "if even one of them is true, it would be a tragedy for the Islamic Republic" and would "overshadow the sins of many dictatorships including that of the deposed Shah."

To talk about rape, let alone about rape carried out by the supposedly pious guardians of the Islamic Republic, was to shatter a taboo. And there was no one better, or more shocking, to do it than a man of the cloth. The security forces were prepared for him: the day after he met with some of the witnesses, they raided his office. And the witnesses were prepared, too: at least one of those Aida knew left her job and fled to the provinces.

Karroubi's letter called for the parliament to investigate the rape charges and the abuses at Kahrizak. He found support for this request in unlikely places, for the Kahrizak abuses turned out to have been visited upon the wrong people. Kamrani was the nephew of an Ahmadinejad aide. Ruholamini's father was a close adviser to conservative presidential candidate and former Revolutionary Guard commander Mohsen Rezaie. These were the sons of the hardline elite, and their families' complaints could not be dismissed as sedition. Khamenei himself ordered Kahrizak temporarily closed at the end of July, around the time of Karroubi's letter.

The hardline judge Gholam-Hossein Mohseni-Ejei had recently been appointed prosecutor general of Iran. He headed a judicial inquiry into the rape charges and summarily dismissed them as unfounded. Tehran's police chief conceded that mistakes were made at Kahrizak, but brushed them off as minor. As for the parliament, it, too, dismissed the sexual assault charges out of hand, quite possibly under pressure. But it did take up Rezaie's call for an investigation into other abuses at Kahrizak. The parliamentary deputies who insisted on that investigation were fundamentalist conservatives, but they would be the ones to carry the flag for civil liberties in years to come.

Mohsen Ruholamini's medical records and death certificate bore the signature of a young doctor about the same age as the deceased. The doctor had been assigned to Kahrizak for his military service. When the investigation began, the bosses at Kahrizak pressed the doctor to alter Ruholamini's records so that it would appear the young man had died of meningitis. The doctor did no such thing. Instead he told the committee: "He was brought to me after being physically and severely tortured. He was in a grave physical condition and I had limited medical supplies, but I did my best to save him. It was then that I was threatened by the authorities of Kahrizak that if I disclose the cause of death and injuries of the detainees, I will cease to live."

Former inmates from Kahrizak were skeptical. That doctor had been cruel to them, they told the *Los Angeles Times*, refusing them treatment and beating prisoners himself. Regardless, the doctor died under mysterious conditions in November. First, police claimed the twenty-six-year-old had died of a heart attack, but when no medical evidence supported this, the story changed to poisoning and finally to suicide. A different doctor who had also examined Kahrizak inmates was mysteriously shot to death the following September.

Not for the first time, a parliamentary investigation fingered Saeed Mortazavi. The prosecutor had signed the order sending demonstrators to Kahrizak. He was also the source of the story that the three young men had died of meningitis there. He was alleged to have ordered false documents drawn up to this effect. Later he would say that the deaths were the result of overcrowding and that the prisoners had arrived with their injuries. But as the Kahrizak investigation closed in on Mortazavi in 2010, Ahmadinejad swept him out of the way, removing him from the prosecutor's office and appointing him to an antismuggling post.

The parliamentary committee on Kahrizak issued its final report in January 2010. It would definitively refute the claims about meningitis, and it would even establish that Mortazavi had falsely claimed that prisoners were taken to Kahrizak because Evin was full. In fact, Evin wasn't full, but Kahrizak was. The committee members excoriated the judiciary for claiming ignorance of the conditions in one of its facilities. The detainees, they said, had died of "lack of space, weakness of health services, inappropriate nutrition, lack of air conditioner . . . and as a result of beating and neglect."

However, the committee hastened to add, the ultimate fault lay with the reformists. None of this would have happened if Mousavi and Karroubi "did not attempt to break the law and incite the emotions of the people." The presidential candidates should "be accountable and the judicial system must not be dismissive of such criminal acts."

IT COULD BE SAID THAT when Ayatollah Khomeini rejected his heir apparent for defending the rights of prisoners and objecting to the massacre of thousands back in 1988, he set the Islamic Republic's course. His anointed successor, Ali Khamenei, would exhibit no such compunction about the use of violence against political enemies. And the man who would have been Leader, Ayatollah Hossein Ali Montazeri, would end his life as the voice of conscience from outside the system he had helped create.

Montazeri was eighty-seven years old in the summer of 2009. Of the election, he remarked that "nobody in their right mind" could believe that the votes had been fairly counted. "This is neither Islamic, nor a republic," Montazeri stated. He reminded the security forces who beat unarmed protesters that "receiving orders will not excuse them before God." On the matter of Kahrizak, Montazeri would admonish Khamenei that to close the facility was not enough. The building had committed no crime, but those who had would go on to torture and kill another day.

In a fatwa of July 11, 2009, the ayatollah addressed those who demanded that Mousavi furnish evidence of fraud. The burden of proof was on the other side. It was the duty of public servants, Montazeri insisted, to convince the public that they deserved its trust, and to do so before a truly impartial judge. As for the people, if they believed their government was illegitimate and that it persisted in power "by force or deception," they had a positive obligation to demand its dismissal. Just as Khomeini had done in 1979, he quoted Imam Ali, the leader of the Shiites: "Do not abandon the principle of 'enjoining to righteousness and dissuading from evil' for then the worst among you will dominate you and your prayers will not be heard." The Islamic morality police had long insisted that by flogging women for improper hijab, they were "enjoining to righteousness and dissuading from evil." Now Montazeri reclaimed that principle as a call for resistance against an unjust state.

When the regime abandoned its commitment to justice, Montazeri wrote, its people were no longer obliged to protect it. The real attack on Islamic rule was the one carried out from within the regime: "How is it imaginable that through injustice and un-Islamic acts, a just and Islamic regime would be secured and strengthened?" Montazeri reminded the clerics in power that the Prophet Mohammad would not have accorded "one iota of legal or religious value" to confessions attained in prison, and that as servants of the people, politicians had no business abridging the freedoms of speech and assembly. Said Montazeri:

> A regime that is based on club-wielding, injustice, violation of rights, usurpation and adulteration of votes, murder, subjugation, incarceration, medieval and Stalinist tortures, repression, censorship of newspapers and means of communication, imprisonment of the thinkers and elites of the society on trumped-up charges and extraction of false confessions—especially when these are extracted under duress—is condemned and unworthy before religion, reason and the world's wise observers.

AYATOLLAH MONTAZERI DIED in his sleep some five months later, on December 19. The Green Movement would pour forth to mourn him from Tehran to Qom, Najafabad to Zanjan, meeting the Basij and riot police even inside of mosques, in its last major confrontations, the largest and most violent since June 20.

The grand ayatollah's mourning period coincided with Ashura. But the security forces of the Islamic Republic were well past worrying about any injunctions against violence on the holiest of all Shiite holy days. Amateur videos showed them running over protesters with police vehicles, and eyewitnesses alleged that they opened fire into crowds. Demonstrators, inflamed, assailed security agents and set police property on fire. Hundreds of demonstrators—by some reports well over a thousand—disappeared into Iran's prisons that day, and hospitals reported scores of head injuries and gunshot wounds. Ali Habibi Mousavi, nephew of the presidential candidate and a forty-three-year-old father of two, was not even protesting but was shot in the chest in Tehran. He was one of thirty-seven people one official news source reported killed on Ashura. There would be no consensus on this figure and little reliable reporting on the day's events, due to a heavy pall of censorship. Of the protest videos posted to YouTube, one showed university students chanting, "Montazeri, you are finally free."

SEVENTEEN

THE END OF THE DIRTY WARS OF INTELLECTUALS

*The pliable, the satellites, the soul slaves, the
camp-followers of any big movement, do not
suffice a dictator. Never will he be content until
the free, the few independents, have become his
toadies and his serfs; and, in order to make his
doctrine universal, he arranges for the state to
brand nonconformity as a crime.*

—STEFAN ZWEIG, *The Right to Heresy*

PAYAM FAZLINEJAD, the young man who had come to Shahram and
Roozbeh seemingly suicidal and alone, and almost certainly to entrap
them, had hardened by now into a fully established propagandist for the
hardline judiciary. He worked for Fars, the news agency of the Revolutionary Guard, and *Kayhan*, the newspaper associated with the Supreme
Leader.

It was in *Kayhan* that Fazlinejad published an explosive five-part series
in early June 2009. His treatise was called "Mohammad Khatami's Mission
for a Velvet Coup d'État," and it purported to lay bare an elaborate international plot to overthrow the Islamic Republic using a nefarious force called

"civil society." The current unrest, by Payam's telling, had long been planned as the endgame of this Western conspiracy.

Fazlinejad used the reformists' own language against them. From grains of truth, he nurtured whole orchards of fantasy: scholarly exchanges became clandestine meetings with Western philosophers who were really covert operatives; theories about the development of civil society became plots to surround and upend the revolutionary state. Curiously, Fazlinejad proceeded from the assumption that civil institutions, independent media, and voter participation would inevitably empower secularizing forces, and so these things were inherently subversive and had to be blocked. Authoritarianism, by these lights, was the very essence of the regime, and authoritarian measures were the only means for protecting it.

Fazlinejad traced the "velvet coup" plot to the CIA and MI6, acting through think tanks in the United States, Britain, and Germany. As far back as 1988, these foreign elements, together with Iranian expatriate royalists and Zionists, had unleashed the *Kiyan* Circle and the Center for Strategic Research to do their bidding inside Iran. Abdolkarim Soroush was charged with priming the intellectual field for secularism, while Hossein Bashiriyeh would formulate a political strategy under the guise of "political development." They had recruited a circle of political operatives including Saeed Hajjarian, Mostafa Tajzadeh, Mohammad Ali Abtahi, Mohsen Kadivar, and, of course, Mohammad Khatami, who was to spearhead the operation.

Once the conspirators had installed Khatami in power, they held elections for city and local councils, supposedly in order to create "participatory democracy" and a "culture of civil society," but in fact as a scheme to confiscate local resources and "spread secularism at all social and cultural levels." Then, at Bashiriyeh's alleged insistence, the reformist interior ministry set aside a budget to finance "civil institutions," or NGOs, that would become a subversive social force capable of overthrowing the regime.

For reasons Fazlinejad did not specify, however, the reformist project foundered in 2001. The CIA, concerned, supposedly dispatched its agent, the German philosopher Jürgen Habermas, to Iran "to assess the conditions of the American project of 'transition to democracy.'" Habermas did, in fact, travel to Iran in 2002 at the invitation of the reformists. His lectures attracted staggeringly large crowds, and Iranians engaged him in lively discussions about the place of religion in the public sphere. In Fazlinejad's version, Habermas came to deliver directives to Kadivar, Hajjarian, and others. He advised the reformists to build democratic institutions, working particularly within universities and political parties, and to "prepare for a civil struggle." Of course the reformist operatives did his bidding. But the reformists lost the city councils in 2003 and the parliament in 2004, plunging their "civil society" project into disarray.

That was when the West dispatched its next "security and intelligence theorist." The late American pragmatist philosopher Richard Rorty, Fazlinejad wrote, "is known as the greatest American philosopher, but he is in fact one of the oldest leaders of covert operations of the CIA in the field of thought, who joined the CIA in its managing staff for a project known as 'dirty wars of intellectuals' in the 1950s." (In fact, Rorty was a graduate student at Yale in the 1950s, writing a dissertation called "The Concept of Potentiality.") When Rorty visited Tehran in June 2004, Fazlinejad contended, he told the reformists to jettison their local debates and concerns. They would achieve their goals only with "complete dependence on American traditions and following the philosophy of pragmatism." Like Habermas, Rorty suggested organizing "democratic institutions" that could be unleashed at the moment of crisis in order to establish American democracy.

But the conspirators saved their big guns for the fall of 2004. The Australian political theorist John Keane was, according to Fazlinejad, the "master key" and "the brain of the British MI6." Keane, the author of a 1988 book called *Democracy and Civil Society*, was apparently the mastermind behind the fall of communism in Czechoslovakia and Poland. His book returned the term "civil society" to the lexicon of Western political philosophy after 130 years of disuse, and it reimagined civil society as "militant," Fazlinejad revealed. Keane was also the agent of a secret $900 million CIA and MI6 project to infiltrate and subvert Shiite religious institutions and communities in order to depoliticize the religion. The existence of this plan, Fazlinejad reported, was documented in a book called *A Plan to Divide and Desolate the Theology*, by a former CIA agent named Michael Brant. But this book seems to exist only in a blogpost in Urdu by one Liaquat Raza, who claimed that Brant was the "right hand of Bob Woodwards, CIA's ex-chief [*sic*]."

Keane had visited Tehran in 2004. At the time, Fazlinejad asserted, Bashiriyeh and Soroush had just returned from an important meeting with former U.S. secretary of state George Shultz and "Pentagon Strategist" Francis Fukuyama (a political scientist at Johns Hopkins at the time), who apprised the Iranians of their role in "Polandising" Iran. Keane supposedly met with Hajjarian, instructing him in "soft subversion" and the latest "models of democratization." Keane, too, allegedly advised the reformist government to subsidize NGOs, independent media, and civil institutions in order to challenge the regime and eventually bring it down in a velvet coup.

Fazlinejad implicated George Soros and the United States Congress in this plot, but not all the malefactors were American or British. According to Fazlinejad, a Dutch parliamentarian of Iranian extraction instructed Shirin Ebadi to hitch a feminist movement to the civil rights strategy. It was in accordance with the Dutch plan that Iranian feminists had launched the One Million Signatures campaign, "which was in a way openly in the service of producing and distributing naked prostitution in Iran." (Fazlinejad thereafter identified it as "the campaign to spread prostitution.")

The planning of the "green coup d'état project for the tenth presidential elections," Fazlinejad assured the reader, was a matter of such layered complexity that he could not explain all its strategic and intelligence dimensions. But in the final phase, the reformists mobilized Mir Hossein Mousavi ("no one knew why he had been put in hiding for such a long time"), who concluded his "breathtaking election campaign" with a meeting with a British envoy, in which he declared the civil struggle about to begin.

On the finer points of civil struggle, Fazlinejad's language turned convoluted and vague. The plan was for a defeated presidential candidate to gin up a legitimacy crisis. The organized, trained agents of civil society would go into the streets with an agenda of "vandalism, terrorism and creating crisis," and the tumult would be made to appear much more widespread than it truly was. In Iran, there was no social mass in the streets, Fazlinejad asserted, only a band of trained subversives, whose aim was to "paralyze the nervous system of the country," leading to the collapse of the regime.

Mousavi, by Fazlinejad's account, set the civil struggle phase in motion, but the key figure inside Iran was really Khatami. Fazlinejad provided an itinerary of Khatami's international travels, which very suspiciously had the former president out of the country for much of the 2009 campaign season. Perhaps most suspiciously of all, Khatami had visited Tunisia at the very same time that United States president Barack Obama set foot in Egypt, which is also in North Africa. In a June 14, 2009, statement, Khatami had damningly "used terms such as demonstrations, civil protests seven times."

THE FAZLINEJAD TREATISE was but a foretaste of the judiciary's case against the reformist leadership. On August 1, 2009, the televised trial of what appeared to be an auditorium full of defendants opened in Tehran's Revolutionary Court. Rows of former high officials in prison pajamas, sallow-complected and hollow-eyed, flanked by men in uniform, listened first to the prosecutor's twenty-five-page indictment and then to one another's self-denunciations.

The deterioration of Mohammad Ali Abtahi's physical appearance was perhaps the most dramatic. The once rotund and smiling cleric, now defrocked, seemed to have lost half his weight, and his face was drawn and haunted as well as sweaty and confused. But it was Saeed Hajjarian's confession that brought the proceedings to a climax at once chilling and absurd.

Hajjarian was too ill to read, so a young Mosharekat member who was also an inmate was obliged to read Hajjarian's forced confession for him. Published by Fars News, the confession ran to six pages. In it, Hajjarian

renounced Max Weber's theory of patrimonialism, which he now understood could not possibly apply to the Islamic Republic. Weber's theory was
meant to describe countries where "people are treated as subjects and
deprived of all citizenship rights," Hajjarian noted. Of course, this was not
the case in Iran, the political theorist with the bullet in his spine conceded
under duress.

The Islamic Republic was a revolutionary system, Hajjarian noted.
Weber had nothing to say about that. The Iranian regime held elections,
and it drew "legitimacy from the expectation of the return of the missing
twelfth imam." Weber accounted for none of these particulars, which
meant that his schema was meaningless for Iran. Hajjarian, in his ignorance, had once "fallen blindly into the trap of these misguided theories."
Now he saw the light, and he apologized.

Hajjarian regretted, he continued, having uncritically disseminated the
ideas of Western social scientists, including Max Weber. In the wake of the
tenth presidential election, "we now know that many of these ideas were at
the root of the protests that threatened national unity." The ideas of Habermas and the American sociologist Talcott Parsons were particularly to
blame. "Theories of the human sciences contain ideological weapons that
can be converted into strategies and tactics and mustered against the country's official ideology," wrote Hajjarian apologetically.

THE INDICTMENT BY THE OFFICE of the prosecutor, Saeed Mortazavi, linked dangerous Western ideas to a covert foreign plot, much as
Fazlinejad's essay had done. Read by Mortazavi's deputy, it began with long
quotations from the confession of a supposed spy held in custody, and
arranged itself almost entirely around a narrative attributed to this source.

According to the indictment, the spy spelled out for the prosecution the
complex structure of the conspiracy Fazlinejad had sketched. The conspirators included the Open Society Institute, the Rockefeller Institute, the
Ford Foundation, the German Marshall Fund of the United States, Freedom House, the Council on Foreign Relations, the German Council on

Foreign Relations, and the Centre for the Study of Democracy (run by John Keane) in England. The Dutch foundation Hivos had propped up the women's movement, while the Berkman Center for Internet & Society at Harvard University supported Iranian bloggers.

Not surprisingly, the prosecution fastened onto the work of Gene Sharp, an elderly American theorist of nonviolent struggle whose pamphlet on civil resistance to dictatorship had been found at the scene of "velvet" revolutions around the world. According to the indictment, those revolutions, too, had been the work of American operatives. In Iran, the deputy prosecutor alleged darkly, more than 100 of the 198 steps laid forth in Sharp's manual had already been executed. The models for Iran were, according to the alleged spy, Georgia, Poland, the Czech Republic, Serbia, Croatia, Ukraine, and Kyrgyzstan. The inclusion of Croatia, which had no such revolution, betrayed either the source's or the prosecutor's indifferent grasp of world events.

The supposed spy asserted that velvet coups always proceed according to a single plan. Preparations begin about two years before a presidential election. The foreign conspirators select their candidate. Then "they heavily invest in him, such that supporters of the candidate begin to educate people via networks similar to business models such as the pyramid scheme (which are a proven way of attracting supporters in campaigns)." If their candidate loses, they allege fraud, demanding that new elections be held with foreign observers. The presence of foreign observers, the indictment implied, assured the chosen candidate's victory.

Iran's network of collaborators, according to the indictment, included Shadi Sadr and Shirin Ebadi; the New York–based human rights researcher Hadi Ghaemi, who had worked for the "Zionist organization" Human Rights Watch; and the former student activist Ali Afshari, now in exile. Of course the most important intellectual operative was Abdolkarim Soroush, whose job was to undermine Iran's resistance to Westernization by attacking the sacred pillars of the Islamic Republic, like *velayat-e faqih* and the unity of religion and politics.

Soroush and other religious intellectuals "slowly targeted the cultural foundations of the Revolution and began destroying them," the deputy prosecutor alleged. "From that time, their intellectual discussions were marked by inept training and intellectual tyranny—something that they kept secret." Once the intellectual groundwork was laid, the conspirators were to build institutions in the form of NGOs. Then they would link those institutions into a network.

The role of the reformist political parties was particularly nefarious. Mosharekat's platform had the audacity to depict the Islamic Republic as despotic and antidemocratic, and to urge that reformists seek positions within every elected institution, from the parliament and the city councils to the Assembly of Experts. The indictment cited a line in the platform that read, "So that the democratic segment of the leadership will be able to use the crises that threaten the whole political system in favor of solidifying democracy and gaining more bargaining power," and then asked, presumably rhetorically, "Can this sentence be deemed to be anything other than treason?" The prosecution also cited unnamed sources claiming that Mosharekat chapters in Isfahan and Arak had polled their members about whether they would give up the Supreme Leader to the Americans if the Americans invaded.

From here it was a short leap to the conclusion that a cynical and perfidious plot had unfolded around the tenth presidential election. Quoting heavily from the prison confessions of the men gathered in the courtroom, particularly Abtahi and Tajzadeh, the deputy prosecutor alleged that the conspirators knew full well that there was no fraud, but that they had planned before the vote to erode the public's trust in the electoral system. To that end, the prosecutor alleged, the reformists had forged a letter from interior ministry officials raising concerns before election day. The prosecutor quoted Tajzadeh as stating in prison that his own figures tracked with the official ones the night of the election: "I never said that cheating had taken place. The allegations they make have nothing to do with me and I was not involved, but of course my party has issued a statement and I should also be punished."

The "illegal gatherings" that followed the vote were part of the plan, the indictment claimed, and they had been organized by the defendants, including the ones who were arrested well before any protest took place. Also preplanned was the dissemination to foreign media of photographs and videos that seemed to show a brutal crackdown on unarmed demonstrators. The prosecution stated: "Among the pictures and videos there are many scenes of distraught faces from inside the country, suggesting to viewers that the agitators are the people of Iran who have come to the streets in protest of the elections."

Fortunately, Iran's security forces had intercepted the terrorists that the Americans had dispatched to plant bombs at polling stations, the prosecution alleged. But chaos was widespread. Conspirators built homemade grenades and then dressed up in pilfered Revolutionary Guard uniforms to detonate them. Famous human rights lawyers were hiding stashes of weapons and drugs in their offices. Daftar Tahkim and other treasonous elements among the students attacked their own dormitories in order to elicit popular sympathy. For the victims of those raids, the prosecutor shed the most audacious of crocodile tears: "A review of the reports and statistics of the beaten and injured lying on hospital beds reveals that the planners and agents of this disruption and sedition project were willing to sacrifice the innocent lives of the children of this land in order to achieve their goals."

THE ALLEGED SPY WHOSE ACCOUNT was the basis for the indictment was an ambitious young blogger who had undergone a curious series of transformations. Hossein Derakhshan, an Iranian émigré living in Canada during Ahmadinejad's first term, was a hustling self-promoter who peppered the American media with submissions and often credited himself with introducing blogging to Iran. In early posts he identified himself as an atheist and openly advocated a secular government for Iran. His friends and colleagues in the West remember him as a hard-living bon vivant motivated above all by a desire for fame.

Derakhshan would later explain that he'd embraced reformism under Khatami as a form of teenage rebellion; he came from a wealthy conservative family close to the regime. He would claim that after he emigrated to Canada, his experience of Western capitalism and his revulsion for the neoconservative foreign policy of United States president George W. Bush alarmed him into rejecting reform. Iranian reformists, he concluded, were giving aid and comfort to the neocons. They'd been corrupted by Enlightenment rationality. He embraced postcolonial theory and the work of Edward Said, Jacques Derrida, and Judith Butler. His former friends and colleagues suspected him of rather more sinister motives when he embraced a hardline defense of the Islamic Republic and began writing in praise of Ahmadinejad, parroting official talking points and denouncing reformists and human rights advocates.

Derakhshan's revised political commitments were still not clear when, in a brash and ill-considered publicity stunt, he traveled to Israel in early 2006 and again in 2007, publicly defying the Iranian ban on such travel. He called it a mission of freelance diplomacy. He'd hoped to influence Israeli public opinion against a war with Iran, he'd claim, and by doing so, to influence American foreign policy as well. He basked in a fleeting limelight and posed for photographs in the streets of Tel Aviv wearing an "I ♥ Tehran" T-shirt.

Upon his return to Iran in 2008, Derakhshan was taken into custody. His interrogators didn't trust his conversion any more than his former friends among the reformists did. They figured he was trying to infiltrate the Iranian regime on behalf of Mossad or the CIA. He'd later claim that, returning as a loyal subject who chose to submit to the law of his country, he expected to serve three years for his violation of the travel ban. Instead, he was eventually dealt two death sentences and a nearly twenty-year prison term. He was, he said, like a soldier mistakenly bombarded by his own air force. (Khamenei would pardon him in late 2014.)

Derakhshan would later insist, perhaps self-servingly, that when it came to the words attributed to him in the indictment of the reformist leadership, he'd been grievously used. They were taken from an analysis he was asked to write in December 2008, explaining how the ideas and actions of the reformists served imperial interests. He had never meant to outline a

CIA-directed plot or to speak authoritatively as a witness to one. In any case, at the time of his writing, the election was still six months away and Mousavi had not even announced his candidacy.

PAYAM FAZLINEJAD'S *KAYHAN* TREATISE was hallucinatory and, as John Keane would note in response, potentially libelous, with its claims of treasonous conspiracy. That its author had himself quite possibly come by his hardline views in prison added a layer of pathos to its balefulness. The fact that its themes also animated the prosecution's official indictment of the reformist leadership suggested that these were not narratives devised solely of opportunity or expedience. They spoke to a presentiment, among the hard-liners, that was deep-seated and not entirely irrational.

Even paranoids, it's often said, have enemies, and that was certainly true of the Islamic Republic of Iran. Perhaps the security establishment wished for so simple an enemy as a foreign power pulling marionette strings among the dissident factions and civic activists of Iran. Surely, if it were possible to bring down the Islamic Republic by holding seminars and sending checks to reformist politicians and civil society groups, Washington would have eagerly done so. But the ethos of Iranian independence from foreign powers ran deep, and it was not solely the property of conservatives. When the administration of George W. Bush set aside money for the Iranian opposition, the Iranian opposition, aghast, refused it. The Islamic Republic never supplied a shred of evidence, apart from forced confessions, to the contrary.

What the Islamic Republic feared was already inside it. Iran's reform movement had indeed borrowed from Weber, Habermas, and Rorty, but its ideology was self-taught, as authentic an outgrowth of the revolution as Ansar-e Hezbollah. Far from being guided by foreign masterminds, the reformist theorists grappled publicly and contentiously with the strategic conundrums Iran's unique political system had placed in their path. The West had neither philosophers nor spymasters so capable of navigating that labyrinth, or so invested in the outcome, as men like Mostafa Tajadeh and Saeed Hajjarian.

These men, and others like them, had presumed that their Islamic Republic was dynamic and responsive, capable of shedding its autocratic elements. Khamenei had a different view of what was essential and what was not.

The language of the second indictment—for there would be five show trials and five indictments—was in some ways starker than the first in its revelation of the regime's self-definition. Among the nefarious aims of foreigners were "exposing cases of violations of human rights," training reporters "towards the end of gathering information and analysis," and "creating websites and training for holding elections and presenting full information on the 2009 electoral candidates." After the election, American agents were further guilty of providing software and servers that allowed Iranians to get around Internet filters imposed by their government. The listener was apparently meant to consider it self-evident that the true national interest, protected by the regime, lay in censoring the press, filtering the Internet, concealing human rights abuses, and obfuscating the electoral process.

FOR ANOTHER YEAR AND A HALF, Mir Hossein Mousavi would not be silenced. In statements regularly released to his followers, the former prime minister drew ever more sharply and eloquently into focus. He was not a creature of the reform movement, with its sociological jargon and its bitter experience in power. Mousavi's language was simple and spiritual, morally decent and frankly nostalgic. He spoke of Ayatollah Khomeini as of a lost father whose wisdom gleamed all the more brightly as the father's image receded behind the son's. Everything that was good and just in the Islamic Republic, and in Mousavi himself, originated with the imam. No matter that the opposite was probably also true. The revolution's best intentions had gone astray, and everyone knew it.

For Mousavi, the Green Movement's objective was to reclaim that lost purity. In this, rhetorically and emotionally, he echoed Shariati, who in the 1970s exhorted Iranians to reclaim a past that had never existed and to "return" to an aspirational self. "We demand the Islamic Republic, not a word more, and not a word less," Mousavi said in late September, echoing Khomeini's words from the time of the revolution. He resurrected a Khomeini who respected the results of elections even when they didn't go his way. "It's okay, let them take Isfahan," Khomeini had said with a smile when his desired candidate lost that city. Mousavi's Khomeini urged honesty on politicians and held the public in high regard: "Never do anything that you can't explain to the people," he admonished the heads of the three branches of government when they were forced to reveal the Iran-Contra dealings. The country's founding father had been desecrated, first by foreigners who misunderstood him, but second and just as gravely by hard-liners who imagined Khomeini an advocate of the oppression they had wrought.

The Iranian nation wanted and deserved respect, Mousavi insisted. "A great nation doesn't tolerate degraded elections with fixed results," he said. "When a nation becomes great, its public servants can no longer tell the people what to eat, where to go, whom to elect and whom or what to trust." Iranians wanted sound economic management. They did not want a state that attacked laborers for demanding wages or assaulted women for demanding rights. "The majority of people here *like* one another," he said. "They do not want to be divided into the Party of God and the Party of the Devil, nor into humans on one side and dirt and animals on the other."

Mousavi called on the regime to release political prisoners, free the press, allow political parties and demonstrations, revise the country's election laws, and make the president accountable. These demands became the Green Movement's charter, and they defined the movement as a civil rights campaign. Five respected reformist intellectuals outside the country signed their names to Mousavi's demands, appending additional calls for the independence of the universities, the seminaries, and the military from politics, and for an elected judiciary and elected leaders at all levels. The signatories included Akbar Ganji and Abdolkarim Soroush.

What Mousavi demanded of the regime was basic. What he demanded of his followers was transcendent. In an October statement, Mousavi included a meditation on the dignity of the oppressed that deserves a place in the global canon of resistance literature. The formal structures of the state, Mousavi reminded his followers, were but a small share of reality. The lives of Iranians gave those structures meaning and substance. Symbols could be forced on people, but meanings were inalienable.

"The superficial structures can arrest the children of this revolution and imprison them like criminals and dress them up in degraded clothing, but the people can look at those images and feel pride, and create heroes out of those very images," Mousavi observed. "Who is the winner in this confrontation? . . . The superficial structures can sentence these families to isolation, and the people can embrace them. Truly, which of these will triumph?"

By the force of their moral and intellectual integrity, Iranians could correct the inner substance, if not the outer scaffold, of their country's political life. And they had done so. Said Mousavi: "In the past few months, we have changed society not by breaking this external order but by changing its meaning. We have no need to break order when it is we who give it direction in every circumstance." Because of this, Mousavi had hope for the future. "There are so many nations who do not choose to exercise this power, who choose to leave power in the hands of the powerful," he noted. "They will not lead their societies, but we will."

IN FEBRUARY 2011, the house on Pasteur Street where Mir Hossein Mousavi lived with his wife, Zahra Rahnavard, became a prison, its doors and windows welded shut and floodlights, cameras, and surveillance devices installed around it. According to a 2013 Reuters report, the authorities removed handles from the interior doors so that the couple had no privacy, and they confiscated personal papers, artwork, telephones, radios, and computers. Mousavi and Rahnavard were not permitted to read the newspaper or to access their own library except on rare occasions. They had so little fresh air that Rahnavard developed breathing problems and Mousavi broke a window with his fist.

Sources close to the Mousavi family told Reuters that the guards who took up residence in the couple's home were coarse and violent. Mousavi's health was poor. He visited the hospital more than once for circulatory problems. He had lost twenty-six pounds by the spring of 2013; Rahnavard lost thirty-seven.

Mehdi Karroubi had no security in his home. In a 2010 interview he recounted, "Recently, for five days in a row, there were rocks and grenades thrown at my house. Our neighbors have been frightened, their property burned and destroyed." He had expected no less, he reflected. "But I am concerned about Islam, and I am afraid that these people who are attacking and harassing people in the name of Islam are doing serious damage to our religion in the eyes of the world." He would not back down from his defense of Iran's political prisoners. "I will say it clearly," he insisted. "They raped people in detention in the early days of the movement, and they continue to torture dissidents in brutal ways in prison."

By 2011, Karroubi was also under house arrest, in an intelligence ministry safe house in central Tehran; he, too, languished for want of fresh air. None of the three opposition leaders was ever charged with any crime, let alone sentenced by any court. But rumor held that they would not be released until they publicly repented.

Mousavi could no longer issue statements. What he did, at first, was recommend books. They were books that conveyed messages. First was *News of a Kidnapping*, Gabriel García Márquez's account of a spate of celebrity abductions by Colombian drug cartels. The book quickly sold out in Iran as Mousavi's followers plumbed it for relevant meanings. Second was an obscure but resonant book by Stefan Zweig, about a sixteenth-century theologian who challenged John Calvin. It was called *The Right to Heresy*.

Zweig, an Austrian Jew, fled Europe in 1934, shortly after Hitler rose to power. He published *The Right to Heresy* in 1936. Six years later he committed suicide with his wife in Brazil, "the world of my own language having disappeared from me and my spiritual home, Europe, having destroyed itself," as he wrote in his suicide note. Among Zweig's works, *The Right to Heresy* was little-known, having lapsed out of print in English almost immediately. The author could little have imagined the book's second life in Iran, which began when it was published in Persian in 1997.

The Right to Heresy portrayed John Calvin as a cruel theocrat who imposed a joyless asceticism on Geneva, enforced slavish conformity to his own theology, and pursued personal vendettas with a cold, self-righteous fanaticism. The hero of Zweig's book was a dissident theologian and humanist named Sebastian Castellio, who objected when Calvin burned an alleged heretic at the stake with his writings. The state had no dominion over the inner lives of men, Castellio insisted: "To burn a man alive does not defend a doctrine, but slays a man." Tolerance, and not persecution, was the proper Christian response to dissent. "When I reflect on what a heretic really is," Castellio wrote, "I can find no other criterion than that we are all heretics in the eyes of those who do not share our views."

Calvin responded to criticism of his policy on heresy by trumping up charges of conspiracy and torturing political opposition leaders until they confessed to having plotted his overthrow. Castellio, who was not a politician but an intellectual, turned the other cheek as Calvin published calumnies against him. He died of natural causes before he could himself be burned as a heretic. "The eternal tragedy of despots is that they continue to fear persons of independent mind even when these have been disarmed and gagged," wrote Zweig. "The very fact that a crushed adversary says nothing, but refuses to enroll himself among the toadies and servants of the tyrant, makes his continued existence a source of irritation."

IN AUGUST 2009, Ayatollah Khamenei denounced the social sciences. Speaking to university students and faculty, the Leader remarked that these fields of study produced doubt, uncertainty, and secularism: "Many of the humanities and liberal arts are based on philosophies whose foundations are materialism and disbelief in godly and Islamic teachings," he asserted. Teaching such disciplines would lead to a loss of faith. Right-minded thinkers should review the country's university curriculum.

Abdolkarim Soroush responded with an idea. "The theocrats expect the human sciences to use concepts such as God's will, spirit and other intra-religious teachings in their explanations about human beings and societies," he explained, "and since the human sciences do not comply with these expectations, the theocrats and the *ulema* [Islamic scholars] view them with distaste." This problem was as old as the Cultural Revolution, and Soroush knew it firsthand. Back then, the suspicion sprouted from ideological rigidity, ignorance, and fear of the purchase Marxism held on Iranian students. Now the call for Islamizing the humanities and social sciences had a more directly political cast. A secular political science, Soroush surmised, seemed to Khamenei "just a short step away from a secular politics." Anyone who doubted this, Soroush referred to the show trial of Saeed Hajjarian.

The clergy's effort to Islamize academic knowledge in the 1980s had ended in defeat. But if Khamenei wanted to try again to produce Islamic social sciences, Soroush suggested, Iran's intellectuals should not stand in the way. Rather, they should encourage the Leader to assign his best minds to this project, and to steep those minds in the fields of knowledge as they existed, so that they might "witness the painful birth of knowledge from the womb of observation, mathematics, criticism, reflection, intuition, luck and good fortune, so that they do not go out on a limb or expect to pick the fruits before they have planted the tree." Then, when their work was done, they should stack their ideas boldly next to those produced by secular rationality, the better to measure their success and so that these two forms of knowledge could "distill and refine one another."

Soroush offered just a word of caution to his "science-sowing" friends. They would encounter an irresolvable circularity in their project, for the very tools they required in order to extract social sciences from the Quran were secular and worldly ones. For example, they could hardly study the history and culture of the Arabs without historical anthropology and sociology; and without understanding the Arabs, they would not understand the Quran. Far from being "futile and unproductive," Soroush stressed, the secular human sciences were the "imperative, golden key for unlocking religious knowledge."

This was not Soroush's first word of advice to Khamenei since the election, but it was surely his most civil. Like many prominent Iranians in exile, he had watched events unfold in his native land with largely impotent grief and fury. He had addressed a series of letters, each more purple than the last, to the Supreme Leader, blasting him for turning tyrant, surrounding himself with sycophants, and brutalizing his critics. Religious despotism had burned itself out in Iran, Soroush observed, and when it fell, Soroush would be among the first to celebrate. "O God, be my witness: I, who have cared about religion all my life and who have taught religion, dissociate myself from this tyranny-worshipping system," he wrote. "And if there was ever a day when, by some oversight or error, I assisted the oppressors, I beg for forgiveness and absolution."

Khamenei might have prevented much had he freed the press and listened to his critics, Soroush lamented. The economic corruption the Leader claimed to condemn might have been exposed by reporters before sinking its roots. Khamenei might have been sobered before his hubris engulfed him. In any case, wrote Soroush, "Ruling over joyful, free, knowledgeable, nimble people is something to boast about; not over captive, grief-stricken serfs."

Soroush was beyond reach, but his daughter, Kimia, and son-in-law, Hamed, who were neither public figures nor political activists, were not. Agents of the security establishment closed in on Hamed and held him naked in a freezing room all night long, threatening his life and attempting to force him to condemn his wife as a loose woman and divorce her, and to denounce his father-in-law as a foreign spy. Instead he fled with his wife to the United States.

MOSTAFA TAJZADEH, sentenced to six years in prison, wrote letters of his own. One, smuggled from prison, was an open letter to Khamenei. Most were to his wife. She posted a loving exchange between them on her blog, in a public display of private intimacy that was itself an act of defiance in the conservative culture of Iran under the Islamic Republic.

"I have been anxious since yesterday when you told me that finally after

170 days you saw the sky and the moon," she wrote in her letter. "How naïve I was. Every night I stared up at the grayish-blue sky of our city, looking for your eyes, thinking that your blindfold had been removed for your half-hour outdoor stroll and you too were staring into the sky." Tajzadeh closed his reply by writing, "I am proud of you for being such a wonderful wife—more than what I deserved. . . . I wish I had all your letters here in prison, could enjoy reading them and show off to my friends in prison that this is my Fakhri! I kiss your beautiful face and wish you health and happiness. Your love, Your Mostafa."

In the beginning, Tajzadeh studied his interrogators. Maybe, he thought, the long sessions of coercive questioning would furnish opportunities for debate. But the chasm that divided him from his captors was immense, and he and they shared not a spit of solid ground on which to grapple. In an open letter smuggled from Evin in 2010, Tajzadeh enumerated all the ways his ideal political system differed from that of his interrogators, beginning with his desire for debate and theirs for forced confessions and repentance under duress. His interrogators, he understood, saw dissent as conspiracy. Every idea he held dear was, in their eyes, a threat to be quashed. And so their prisons were populated with the very people Tajzadeh thought most fit to rule the country.

That letter of Tajzadeh's was a document of historic importance, not for its reflections on the present, but for its bold accounting for the influence of the past. Unlike Mousavi or virtually any other prominent reformist, Tajzadeh evinced no romantic illusions about the 1980s. Although he believed that the revolutionary decade had a positive legacy to offer, he also recognized it as a wellspring of violence and repression. The hard-liners, he charged, had built on the revolution's mistakes instead of its achievements. But the reformists had to answer for their own role in institutionalizing violence. He and others on the Islamic Left had responded to the revolutionary courts with "consenting silence" even as the judiciary executed unknown numbers of political opponents, Tajzadeh lamented. "Thus," he wrote, "we must confess, but not in show trials or in the way the interrogators want us to confess to offenses that we have not committed, but in front of the nation and based on facts. The Revolution generation must confess, not for its current efforts to expand democracy and human rights" but for its past mistakes.

Tajzadeh repented now, on behalf of the reformists, for failing to defend the first persecuted dissident cleric and for failing to take a strong, early stand for human rights. If, Tajzadeh wrote, "we are to confess and ask for forgiveness, which we must, we must apologize for the wrong treatment that Bazargan . . . received; and also apologize to all those political activists who wanted to be legally active in politics, but their rights were ignored by making various excuses. We must apologize to the citizens for imposing on them a certain lifestyle and interfering in their private lives."

Those who, like Tajzadeh, now found themselves subject to the violent persuasion of prison interrogators had a duty to expose and condemn their torturers. But they should begin, he said, by asking "for forgiveness from those who were truly oppressed, and accepting the fact that if we had fulfilled our moral and national duty at the right time, we would not have been trapped in the forced confession and repenting."

In his letter Tajzadeh spoke not to the Revolutionary Court that demanded his contrition, but to the younger generation of Iranians who had waited, so far in vain, for a revolutionary of his stature to take responsibility for the system he'd helped forge. Tajzadeh broke his generation's "consenting silence." To the empty symbolics of confession, he appended the meaning of the history he had lived.

THROUGHOUT THE FALL OF 2009, demonstrators used official gatherings for cover. They would never get permission for protests of their own, but when the regime marked al-Quds Day, or the anniversary of the American embassy seizure, or Student Day, some of the hardiest Greens lifted their heads, usually to have them smacked down.

The Mourning Mothers met every Saturday at Laleh Park, which was the park nearest where Neda was shot, at the hour when Neda was killed. They dressed in black and carried photos of the slain demonstrators, speaking about the dead to passersby. The police confronted them so aggressively, even beating seventy-year-old women who participated, that the group drew more media attention than it ever anticipated.

Aida Saadat was summoned for interrogation one day and questioned for fourteen hours. She was banned from leaving the country; she was banned from leaving the city; she was all but banned from using her car. She was forced to stop working and had already stopped going home: for a month she'd stayed with friends. Walking back to her friend's apartment from the intelligence ministry late that night, Aida was jumped by baton-wielding men who beat her face, hands, and foot bloody and told her that next time they would kill her.

She could see where she was headed, like the others before her whose families struggled to put up bail with the deeds to their homes, whose networks and secrets lay open to their interrogators unless they put up a terrible resistance. Was she someone who could resist like that? Most people weren't.

Aida had a child, an eleven-year-old son who now fielded calls from security agents looking for his mother. She felt everything she'd worked for, all her years in Qazvin, receding beyond her reach: the impossibly long days at multiple jobs, driving perilous roads late at night, building her country. She'd linked poor rural families with psychologists to break cycles of abuse and violence. She'd set up a free day care center to keep the children of working parents from neglect. She stopped an honor killing once. Now, in Tehran, she'd helped organize the Mourning Mothers and publicize the post-election abuses. She was the link between Karroubi and some of the early rape allegations. She was a member of one of the country's most secretive and fierce human rights organizations, the Committee of Human Rights Reporters, which smuggled information about political prisoners out of the jails. She knew things, and she imagined the damage that information could do when it was wrested from her.

Her passport had expired. She couldn't apply for a new one while she was banned from leaving the country. But there were smugglers known to lead people illegally across the Turkish border. December was very cold in the mountains that divided Turkey from Iran. Chances were fifty-fifty that she would pass safely or that she would be arrested or freeze to death, the smugglers told Aida.

There was no time to hesitate or to nurse her fears. She had no time, even, to go home to pack a bag. She took as many warm things as her friend could give her, bought a bus ticket to Orumiyeh in the far northwest of Iranian Azerbaijan, and stopped in Qazvin to say good-bye to her parents in the night.

"Don't do this," her father implored her. He'd been to those mountains and knew how frigid they were in winter.

"This is the only way," Aida told him. "I can't take a plane, I can't take a bus. I can't even go legally because I don't have a passport. This is the only way."

Aida was the only woman on the smuggling route. She had given herself into the care of dangerous men, people she would normally have been afraid even to speak to. The other refugees in their hands were also men, mainly Afghans and Pakistanis. Aida feared for her life and she feared assault. She clutched her hijab closely around her and kept apart from the others. The only ones she talked to were an Afghan man and his young son, Abdollah, who reminded Aida of her own child. She helped care for Abdollah, and the father wept to her about his late wife, who had died in a suicide bombing. His suffering reminded Aida that her own was nothing in the greater scheme. She would manage.

Abdollah's father watched over her, but when he slept, and she, too, was expected to sleep in a small room with all those men, she was afraid to close her eyes. She felt herself stiffen with every move, every audible breath among the rugged strangers, until she couldn't stand it anymore, and she left. She sat outside in a cold that seemed to freeze her very blood. And in the morning she and the Afghan and Pakistani men had to scurry like animals, ducking to hide behind bushes and hillocks, at an altitude that crushed the breath from Aida's lungs.

She couldn't go on. She sat gasping on the ground, and a smuggler came to stand over her.

"You are putting the rest of our lives in danger because you can't take it?" he demanded. "You can't tolerate it? You can't breathe? I could simply leave you right here and you'll be killed by animals. Are you coming or staying? Make a decision now."

Aida couldn't stand up. An Afghan went to her, took her bag and her hand, and helped her to join the others. After almost half an hour, they were near the border. The smugglers had paid off a border guard. There were two groups of refugees. Aida's was in front. The boy, Abdollah, and his father were in the one behind hers. A river lay before them. Aida was not a swimmer; she feared the water. Now she couldn't hesitate. They would walk across, on a winter night. It was not so bad while she was submerged. But when she reached the shore and stepped out into the frigid air, she might have taken a knife to her skin.

The smugglers had made a mistake. The first group was paid off to cross the border; the second group was not. The border guards shouted at the second group of refugees to stop. Then they started shooting. Aida was only a short distance away when she saw Abdollah fall. She was on Turkish territory, frozen in wet clothes, and she could not move or even cry until later that night, when she couldn't do anything else.

PEOPLE ASIEH AMINI KNEW were disappearing. Often they were arrested in the middle of the night, spirited off to prison for unknown terms. Asieh had visions of her own midnight arrest, before the terrified eyes of nine-year-old Ava. Sometimes she felt that she was waiting for this. She was back in touch with Shadi Sadr, who told her it was obvious which pseudonyms were Asieh's on Roozonline. Anyone who knew her style of writing could figure it out. Surely someone in the intelligence ministry had an eye as keen as Shadi's.

When she saw the show trials and forced confessions on television, Asieh cried. Her friend, the journalist and filmmaker Maziar Bahari, was gaunt. He seemed a broken man, hardly recognizable. Mohammad Ali Abtahi was a specter. If these people had broken in prison, what would happen to her?

Early one Friday morning, Asieh's doorbell rang. It was a colleague of Javad's. She had been arrested at a small demonstration in Valiasr Square and released from prison two days earlier. Thirty-six women were held in her cell, she said, and half of them had been interrogated about Asieh Amini. Asieh should leave her house, the woman insisted. She should probably leave the country.

Before the election, Asieh had been invited to a poetry festival in Sweden. She responded to the Swedish ambassador now. She would go to the festival, she told him, but she needed to bring her daughter. At the airport, she left her cell phone open, connected on a call to Javad, so that he could listen and know if she was stopped. But she got through.

Every day, Javad told Asieh when she spoke with him from Sweden, things were getting worse. The defendant in one of her cases, Behnoud Shojaie, seventeen when he killed another man in a fight, was executed. Their friends in prison had been swallowed into the system; there was nothing anyone could do for them. When Maziar Bahari was released, he sent Asieh a short note: Don't come back, it said. She understood that he'd been forced to speak about her in prison.

Everything Asieh was and everything she did was in one or another way tied to her country—its complexities, its language, its terrors, and its splendors. She was not an engineer, with skills transferable anywhere in the world. She would carry, always, a weight of work unfinished, a sense of being needed in a place where she couldn't live. On cell walls in the women's section of Evin, she was told, prisoners had etched lines from her poems.

Asieh was one of the lucky ones. Through a program for writers at risk, she landed in Trondheim, Norway, as the poet in residence at the public library. Javad joined her and Ava there. She published two books of poetry and started work on a memoir, studied Norwegian, and regarded her new compatriots with a warm and gentle quizzicality. The landscape, in its jagged immensity and its brilliant blues and greens, its rock-faced coast and glassy fjord, reminded her and Javad of Mazandaran. In Trondheim in summer, the sun never set, and in winter it never rose. The light had a

broad, flat quality, and life, an element of unreality. Even the airport highway cut through spectacular, unspoiled scenes of undulating land and satu-
rated color. Off the road to Asieh's apartment building was a recreational
sight of singular frivolity: beach volleyball courts. As though the world
were such a place, and Asieh such a person as to live in it. For now, she was.

EPILOGUE

I LAST VISITED IRAN at a dark time, in February 2012. Almost three years had passed since the Green Movement was subdued, and the hardliners who'd consolidated power called reform by a new name: *fetneh*, or "the sedition." Some reformists were still in prison. Others had retreated into private life, at least for the moment, their movement now beyond the pale of legitimate, even legal, opposition. Young people who had once found an outlet for their civic energies and their grievances in the reform movement now faced largely unpalatable options—among them, acquiescence, apathy, or outright defiance of a state that would not tolerate it.

In my past experience, Iran's repressive apparatus had the presence of a snake coiled out of view. You trod a bland, well-tended path through a landscape of surpassing beauty, knowing that if you set foot off the trail, you risked disturbing something hostile and watchful you couldn't see. In 2012 the menace was in the open, the subject of jokes and cynical asides even among compliant bureaucrats. Iranian analysts spoke of the "securitization" of the state. There was a measure of relief in this—an end to the gaslight, a new clarity about where the lines were drawn. But of course it was also grim. Those lines seemed to encircle an ever narrower realm of elite opinion as the only permissible arena for debate.

And yet, debate there was. One of the delicious paradoxes of the Islamic Republic is its seemingly endless capacity to produce internal opposition to its own authoritarianism. No matter how many people or groups are cast out of the circle of power, those who remain continue to divide and to challenge one another. That challenge is built into the state Khomeini wrought, with all its calculations and compromises, and it is a veritable life force. When I visited Iran in 2012, I could not meet with any reformists. But among the hard-liners then campaigning for seats in the parliament and fulminating from the pages of newspapers and websites, I heard lively, energetic discussions of everything from the economy to *velayat-e faqih*, all within the boundaries of relative ideological orthodoxy.

If there was one figure teetering on the edge of that inner sanctum, it was Ahmadinejad. Like Khatami before him, the populist president was fighting for his political life at the end of his second term. He had gotten big for his britches, overtly challenging Khamenei on cabinet appointments and going into public sulks when he didn't get his way. *Kayhan* began a drumbeat against the president, labeling his faction a "deviated current" and suggesting that his chief of staff was an agent of velvet revolution. You might say it couldn't have happened to a nicer guy. Still, Ahmadinejad was besieged and isolated. Conservative parliamentarians called for the president's impeachment and summoned him to the legislature for aggressive questioning about his management of the economy. I will never forget meeting the president's bewildered media adviser shortly after he was sentenced to prison for insulting the Supreme Leader, whom he revered. Another close Ahmadinejad ally, the infamous prosecutor Saeed Mortazavi, was indicted for his role in the Kahrizak affair. (In the end Mortazavi would be acquitted—yet another only-in-Iran story of authoritarian self-policing and impunity at once.)

Out on the streets, people wanted to talk about chicken. Inflation had been a chronic complaint, but now it was acute, as nothing reflected more clearly than the rising price of food. Chicken was normally the affordable meat, even when lamb was out of reach. But now chicken was becoming a luxury, and this was an assault on the dignity of people living in a resource-rich country. The national police chief urged television networks not to broadcast images of chicken for fear of setting off social unrest. This stricture resulted mainly in a new strain of chicken humor on social media. But the economic malaise was a serious business. The conservative establishment variously denied it or blamed it on Ahmadinejad, because at that time one could not yet talk about the ferocious trade sanctions that were beginning to choke Iran's oil industry and financial sector.

In 2012, Iran was above all a country under pressure. International tensions over its nuclear program had reached a nearly intolerable peak. The worst of the sanctions were just then taking hold, and the possibility of a military confrontation was never far from anyone's mind. Iranians lived as though under a swollen cloud that never burst and never passed. They got no relief from their own government, which had squeezed the air out of the country's political and expressive spaces. Inflation spiraled. In scant months, the value of the currency would take a vertiginous dive. The situation didn't seem sustainable, but the more frightening possibility was that it was.

BY NOW IT WILL PROBABLY BORE YOU to hear that there is no such thing as a boring presidential election in Iran. But I submit that this is true. In 2013, it seemed that the Leader had handpicked a candidate who was as rigid as he was extreme. Saeed Jalili was the head of the country's foreign policy–making body and a former nuclear negotiator for Ahmadinejad. A European diplomat described him to me as little more than a robotic dispenser of talking points. *Kayhan* praised him as a "super-hezbollahi" in what many took to be an endorsement.

I can't say for sure that the Leader had committed himself to Jalili's support. I've always wondered whether Khamenei had for his own reasons entertained the idea of changing course. He had the upper hand now, having decisively crushed his domestic opposition. He could afford to be flexible. At the very least, he left an opening.

In the first presidential debate, a close aide of Khamenei's—himself not a very convincing candidate—tore into Jalili's stance on foreign policy, pointing out that intransigence on that front had won Iran nothing but sanctions. After that, foreign policy, usually off-limits to public debate, was fair game. The field opened to the race's dark horse, Hassan Rouhani, a pragmatic foreign policy hand who was so close to the disfavored Rafsanjani that hardly anyone believed he stood a chance.

More than any other candidate, Rouhani was the face of diplomatic engagement with the world. He had agreed to freeze Iran's nuclear program back in 2003, when he was Iran's lead negotiator under Khatami. (Ahmadinejad, presumably with the Leader's blessing, had reversed that stance.) Rouhani was no reformist. He was a long-standing pillar of the security establishment, well remembered for his hostility to the student movement in 1999, and never sympathetic to the reformist intellectual project. But he spoke of national unity at a time when Iran needed nothing more. He pledged to draw up a civic charter delineating the people's rights, and he even said he would work to secure the release of the Green Movement leaders from house arrest.

"Just let go of reformism," Saeed Hajjarian is said to have advised his former Mosharekat colleagues. "We are Iranian and Muslim. Let's participate in the elections to decrease the suffering of the people.'" Both Khatami and Rafsanjani endorsed Rouhani. Three days before the vote, they persuaded the only reformist in the race to stand down in Rouhani's favor. The dark horse surged.

I later heard from a source close to the Iranian regime that Khamenei voted for Jalili, but that he instructed the security apparatus to accept the outcome of the election, whatever it might be, because he did not want another 2009. If this was true, it was remarkable, not least as a backhanded admission that there had indeed been interference in 2009. In any case, Rouhani carried the election in a single round, with a commanding 51 percent of the vote. The conservative vote splintered among the hardline candidates, with Jalili coming in third. This time, the results were declared not Friday night, upon the closure of the polls, but Saturday afternoon, as usual. And they met with jubilation rather than protest.

. . .

ROUHANI REKINDLED MANY IRANIAN HOPES. They were not the same hopes Khatami once stirred. Perhaps, as one analyst told me, the reformists had at last been chastened: once they had traded revolutionary utopianism for liberal utopianism, but now they saw that real politics is compromise. Or maybe they were playing the long game. They wouldn't have been the first. The Rouhani administration made it clear that any domestic agenda must await the resolution of the nuclear file, which promised relief from sanctions and a factional win for the president.

The nuclear accord between Iran and six world powers held out hope not only for bringing Iran's nuclear program under significant international oversight, but ultimately, for ending the country's isolation and ratcheting down the tensions that had ensnared Iran and the United States for more than three decades. An Iran that was connected to the world, rather than severed from it, would surely be a safer, better place for its citizens. By most measures, Iranian civil society, along with the overwhelming majority of the populace, supported that outcome. So did many in the United States who believed, as I did, that there was no possible solution to Iran's problems, or to America's problems with Iran, that would come at the barrel of a gun. Bloodshed and privation would do less to stymie Iran's hard-liners than to damage its most promising resource, which was the goodwill and civic energy of its people.

Under Rouhani, by many accounts, the spectrum of public debate widened, with new moderate and centrist newspapers filling the space. But the needle did not move much on human rights. In a record year for executions in the Islamic Republic, 753 Iranian prisoners were put to death, nearly half of them drug offenders and at least thirteen juveniles. By a 2014 tally, Iran held thirty journalists in prison, second only to China. Mir Hossein Mousavi, Zahra Rahnavard, and Mehdi Karroubi were still under house arrest. The two major reformist parties, Mosharekat and Etemad Melli, had been banned since 2009. When a new reformist party emerged after six years, within a week one of its members was arrested. In February

2015, the judiciary pronounced it illegal to publish former president Mohammad Khatami's image or even his name.

In times of renewed optimism and civil peace, it became inconvenient, not to say impolite, to talk about human rights or democratic reform. Too much had been vested not just in the diplomatic process but in the pragmatic centrism of the Rouhani administration. To some extent, this was the counterintuitive legacy of 2009 and the years of polarization that followed. To go on participating in the Iranian political system and hoping for it to produce constructive change—to go on, in the strictest sense, being a reformist—meant, for many, making peace with the events of 2009 and finding a new equilibrium.

And yet, to the extent that the reform movement of the late twentieth century has now passed into history, it is a history of dignity and sacrifice that encompasses Iran's revolution and stretches forward, beyond the visible horizon. Iran does not have a culture of passive citizenship, despite the best efforts of its rulers, past and present, to produce one. What it does have in many quarters is a restless determination to challenge injustice and to seize control of its destiny.

The Iranians whose stories I've told in this book did not try to overthrow the Islamic Republic. Rather, they endowed it with their dreams. They imagined it could accommodate their philosophical challenges and electoral participation, their efforts to organize communities and their insistence on speaking their minds. They believed there were truths that needed to be told and dead who deserved to be grieved. Some of them envisioned an Iran freed of its demons because it had confronted its past. Nearly all of them were eventually forced to leave Iran. But there will be others. Because the impulse that moved them is one that rarely rests for long. Like a little fish of any color, it darts on, and then on, and on.

ACKNOWLEDGMENTS

I owe a special debt to those Iranians who shared their stories with me in detail for publication, among them Ali Afshari, Asieh Amini, Hossein Bashiriyeh, Akbar Ganji, Alireza Haghighi, Mostafa Rokhsefat, Aida Saadat, and Abdolkarim Soroush. To say that Omid Memarian, Roozbeh Mirebrahimi, Shahram Rafizadeh, and Solmaz Sharif spent innumerable hours in interviews with me, and made themselves available for often wrenching follow-ups, would not begin to do justice to what they allowed me to put them through, together and separately, as they repeatedly relived the most painful experiences of their lives for the public record. I am grateful for their candor, their courage, and so much more.

This book would not exist without *The New Yorker*, which in 2005 took a chance on a little-known reporter who was determined to go to Iran. I am indebted to David Remnick for placing that trust in me, and to Daniel Zalewski, my friend and editor, for setting it all in motion and seeing me through the human and reportorial complexities. I am grateful to Dorothy Wickenden, also at *The New Yorker*, and to Scott Malcomson, who sent me to Iran for *The New York Times Magazine* at the end of 2006. My agent, Sarah Chalfant of the Andrew Wylie Agency, helped me conceptualize this book in 2007 and has been an unflagging source of support, good counsel, and sanity since.

I feel enormously lucky to have landed at Riverhead, where my editor, Becky Saletan, has given this book—and me—the great benefit of her clear vision, literary sensitivity, warm friendship, and enthusiasm for history and the ideas that move it. Thanks to her, a sprawling, obsessive manuscript became a book. I am grateful to many others at Riverhead too, particularly Anna Jardine, Katie Freeman, Jynne Martin, Kate Stark, Karen Mayer, Hea Eun Grace Han, and Marysarah Quinn.

Over the course of my research, many Iranians and Iran experts shared their time and expertise with me, offering advice, insight, introductions, translation, analysis, and the benefit of their research or experience. I cannot name the friends and sources who still reside in Iran, but I hope they know who they are and how deeply they are appreciated. Here I extend my thanks to Mahboubeh Abbasgholizadeh, Morteza Abdolalian, Ervand Abrahamian, Anisa Afshar, Ramin Ahmadi, Masih Alinejad, Maryam Amuzegar, Bahman Baktiari, Amir Barmaki, Mehrzad Boroujerdi, Kaveh Ehsani, Haleh Esfandiari, Hadi Ghaemi, Hossein Ghazian, Roya Hakakian, Kevan Harris, Masood Hooman, Mohsen Kadivar, Hosein Kamaly, Mahdis Keshavarz, Nika Khanjani, Azam Khatam, Abbas Milani, Maryam Mirza, Shaya Mohajer, Manouchehr Mohammadi, Afshin Molavi, Javad Montazeri, Nahid Mozaffari, Nouradin Pirmoazen, Ali Rahnema, Ahmad Sadri, Mahmoud Sadri, Karim Sajadpour, Djavad Salehi-Isfahani, Mohsen Sazegara, Nahid Siamdoust, Evan Siegel, Ebrahim Soltani, Kambiz Tavana, Roberto Toscano, Parvaneh Vahidmanesh, and Lila Azam Zanganeh.

This project has benefited from the support and generosity of the Dorothy and Lewis B. Cullman Center for Scholars and Writers at the New York Public Library, where Jean Strouse was wise and wonderful; the American Academy in Berlin, where Gary Smith's enthusiasm buoyed my work at crucial moments; and the Institute for Advanced Study, where Joan Scott offered guidance and challenge.

Thanks, too, to Stephen Heintz and William Luers for including me in the edifying meetings of their Iran Project; to David Patterson, now of the Stuart Krichevsky Literary Agency; and to Justin Vogt at *Foreign Affairs*.

Thank you, Carol Jack. And a huge thanks to my resourceful and exacting fact-checkers: Matthew Sherrill, Darragh McNicholas, and Lara Zarum.

I am grateful to all my friends, but especially those who have listened at length to tales of Iranian intrigue and bucked me up through periods of writer's block: Kira Brunner Don, Sonia Katyal, Nicholas Kulish, Daniel Bergner, Gary Bass, Alexander Star, Amy Waldman, Susie Linfield, Alissa Quart, Alissa Levin, Rinne Groff. Most of all, Eyal Press, who read the manuscript from beginning to end and offered valuable support and feedback.

My love and thanks to my family, for everything: Marie Secor, Robert Secor, Anna Secor, Nancy Packer, Ann Packer. My children, Charlie and Julia Packer, for making me happy.

There remain two people to whom I am grateful above all. Mohammad Ayatollahi Tabaar has been beyond generous with his knowledge and insight. He lent this work meaning and purpose and kept me company in the forest of its details. I only hope the finished product is worthy of all he has given me.

I come now to thank my husband, George Packer, my inspiration and ballast, my love. And yet, having spilled so many words in the foregoing pages, here I find that every last one fails.

NOTES

A NOTE ON SOURCES

With a very few exceptions, I have not included citations for material that comes from my own reporting and interviews, some of which were the basis of my previously published articles on Iran for *The New Yorker*, *The New York Times Magazine*, and other publications. I traveled to Iran five times between 2004 and 2012, and have conducted interviews with more than one hundred sixty Iranians residing inside and outside the country—intellectuals, politicians, journalists, activists, clergymen, economists, businesspeople, and ordinary citizens. I was able to directly observe rallies, panel discussions, speeches, and polling stations related to elections in 2005, 2006, 2008, and 2012.

CHAPTER ONE. LITTLE BLACK FISH

4 *The Little Black Fish*: Samad Behrangi, *The Little Black Fish and Other Modern Persian Stories*, trans. Eric Hooglund and Mary Hooglund (Washington, DC: Three Continents Press, 1976), 1–19.

5 **Behrangi noted in an early essay:** Brad Hanson, "The 'Westoxication' of Iran: Depictions and Reactions of Behrangi, Al-e Ahmad, and Shariati," *International Journal of Middle East Studies* 15, no. 1 (Feb. 1983), 1–23.

5 **"I don't desire that aware children":** Ibid., 2.

7 **It was Al-e Ahmad who floated:** Abbas Milani, *Eminent Persians: The Men and Women Who Made Modern Iran, 1941–1979* (Syracuse, NY: Syracuse University Press and Persian Book World, 2008), vol. 2, 842.

7 **"Now we must mourn":** Jalal Al-e Ahmad, "Samad and the Folk Legend," in *Iranian Society: An Anthology of Writings*, ed. Michael Hillmann (Lexington, KY: Mazda, 1982), 141.

9 **"I completely forgot all the memories"**: Ali Rahnema, *An Islamic Utopian: A Political Biography of Ali Shari'ati* (London and New York: I. B. Tauris, 2000), 192.

9 **"During his lectures"**: Ibid., 177.

10 **"a student who is more educated"**: Ibid., 38.

12 **"stinking mud"**: Ibid., 292.

12 **"A futureless past"**: Ibid., 107.

13 **"Shariati's work was a type of revivalism"**: Ali Mirsepassi, *Intellectual Discourse and the Politics of Modernization: Negotiating Modernity in Iran* (Cambridge, England: Cambridge University Press, 2000), 118.

14 **religion was the last line of defense:** Ali Gheissari, *Iranian Intellectuals in the 20th Century* (Austin: University of Texas Press, 1998), 101.

14 **Shariati was still a nationalist:** Rahnema, *An Islamic Utopian*, 125.

14 **Shariati looked at secular, even nihilistic, postwar Europe:** Farzin Vahdat, *God and Juggernaut: Iran's Intellectual Encounter with Modernity* (Syracuse, NY: Syracuse University Press, 2002), 143–45.

16 **At a meeting during that visit:** Rahnema, *An Islamic Utopian*, 191.

16 **"the staircases, the yard"**: Interview with Alireza Alavi Tabar in Ali Mirsepassi, *Democracy in Modern Iran: Islam, Culture, and Political Change* (New York: New York University Press, 2010), 128.

16 **"revolutionary society"**: Rahnema, *An Islamic Utopian*, 236.

16 **Motahhari was uneasy:** H. E. Chehabi, *Iranian Politics and Religious Modernism: The Liberation Movement of Iran Under the Shah and Khomeini* (London: I. B. Tauris, 1990), 205.

17 **"Our society is neither intellectually"**: Rahnema, *An Islamic Utopian*, 133–34.

17 **the country's new Bastille:** Ervand Abrahamian, *Tortured Confessions: Prisons and Public Recantations in Modern Iran* (Berkeley and Los Angeles: University of California Press, 1999), 105.

18 **"the martyr is the pulsing heart"**: Rahnema, *An Islamic Utopian*, 315.

18 **"Wage jihad and kill if you can"**: Ibid., 356.

18 **forced to parrot that argument in public recantations:** Abrahamian, *Tortured Confessions*, 116.

19 **"pressed to the wall like frightened sparrows"**: Reza Khojasteh-Rahimi, "We Should Pursue Shariati's Path but We Shouldn't Be Mere Followers: An Interview with Abdulkarim Soroush," June 19, 2008, http://www.drsoroush.com/English/Interviews/E-INT-Shariati_June2008.html.

20 **"He had long hair, down to his shoulders"**: Ibid.

CHAPTER TWO. ISLAMIC REPUBLIC

22 **"So our city will be governed"**: Plato, *The Republic*, trans. Paul Shorey, in *Plato: The Collected Dialogues, Including the Letters*, eds. Edith Hamilton and Huntington Cairns (Princeton, NJ: Princeton University Press, 1989), 752.

28 ***Revelation of Secrets:*** Saïd Amir Arjomand, *After Khomeini: Iran Under His Successors* (New York: Oxford University Press, 2009), 20. Various dates are given for the publication of this work, spanning from 1941 to 1944.

28 **a cover to allow Bahais:** Hamid Ansari, *The Narrative of Awakening: A Look at Imam Khomeini's Ideal, Scientific and Political Biography (from Birth to Ascension)*, trans. and ed. Seyed Manoochehr Moosavi (Qom, Iran: Institute for

Compilation and Publication of the Works of Imam Khomeini, International Affairs Division, 1994), 55.

28 **"If some American's servant":** Ruhollah Khomeini, "A Warning to the Nation" (1941), in Ruhollah Khomeini, *Islam and Revolution I: Writings and Declarations of Imam Khomeini (1941–1980)*, trans. and ed. Hamid Algar (Berkeley, CA: Mizan Press, 1981), 181–82.

29 **"from the streetsweeper . . . associated vices":** Ibid., 171.

29 **Khomeini argued for a state:** Ibid., 37.

29 **"The governance of the *faqih*":** Ibid., 63.

30 **"the opium of the masses":** Ibid., 214.

31 **The nationalists even forged a relationship:** Mohammad Ayatollahi Tabaar, "From Womb to Tomb: Religion, the State and War in Iran," unpublished thesis shared by author.

34 **"The government I intend to appoint":** Khomeini, "A Warning to the Nation," 269.

34 **"Those who imagine":** Ibid.

34 **"You who have chosen a course":** Ibid., 270.

35 **"sowing corruption on earth":** Ervand Abrahamian, *Tortured Confessions: Prison and Public Recantation in Modern Iran* (Berkeley and Los Angeles: University of California Press, 1999), 124.

35 **more than seven times the number of political prisoners:** Ibid., 169.

36 **terms he found divisive:** H. E. Chehabi, *Iranian Politics and Religious Modernism: The Liberation Movement of Iran Under the Shah and Khomeini* (London: I. B. Tauris, 1990), 64.

36 **"Don't expect me to act":** Ibid., 258.

37 **Khomeini defended their work:** Khomeini, "A Warning to the Nation," 330–32.

37 **Bazargan's government tried and failed:** Chehabi, *Iranian Politics and Religious Modernism*, 258–59.

37 **"In theory, the government is in charge":** Ervand Abrahamian, *The Iranian Mojahedin* (New Haven, CT: Yale University Press, 1989), 48.

37 **"darkly as in a dream":** Plato, *The Republic*, 752.

37 **"Yes" carried the day:** Asgar Schirazi, *The Constitution of Iran: Politics and the State in the Islamic Republic*, trans. John O'Kane (London: I. B. Tauris, 1998), 27.

38 **rife with irregularities:** Ibid., 31–32.

38 **the assembly was packed:** Hossein Bashiriyeh, *The State and Revolution in Iran: 1962–1982* (New York: Palgrave Macmillan, 1984), 151.

38 **"Now the Constitution makes some provision":** Khomeini, "A Warning to the Nation," 342.

39 **"seriously prejudicial to our interests":** James G. Blight, Janet M. Lang, Hussain Banai, Malcolm Byrne, and John Tirman, *Becoming Enemies: U.S.-Iran Relations and the Iran-Iraq War, 1979–1988* (New York: Rowman & Littlefield, 2012), 299–300.

40 **In his final televised address:** Chehabi, *Iranian Politics and Religious Modernism*, 273.

40 **ratified by a popular referendum:** Abrahamian, *The Iranian Mojahedin*, 58.

40 **Khomeini publicly averred:** Bashiriyeh, *The State and Revolution in Iran*, 156.

41 **"The president should be in charge":** David Menashri, *Iran: A Decade of War and Revolution* (New York: Holmes & Meier, 1990), 133.

41 **"enemy of the clergy"**: Ibid., 134.

41 **"Bazargan with a different face"**: Abrahamian, *The Iranian Mojahedin*, 60.

41 **"along with the revolution"**: Bashiriyeh, *The State and Revolution in Iran*, 158.

41 **This was no minor border skirmish**: Blight et al., *Becoming Enemies*, 73.

42 **Mojahedin-e Khalq, whose ranks were swelling with young people**: Bashiriyeh, *The State and Revolution in Iran*, 161.

42 **"This is not a republic"**: Abrahamian, *The Iranian Mojahedin*, 66.

42 **He even asked Khomeini**: Menashri, *Iran*, 171.

42 **demonstrators clashed in the streets**: Ibid., 176.

42 **"I am very sorry"**: Ibid., 181.

43 **"democratic Islamic Republic"**: Bashiriyeh, *The State and Revolution in Iran*, 160–61.

43 **"Thank God the enemies"**: Scheherezade Faramarzi, "Executions Continue as Opposition Mounts Underground Campaign," Associated Press, June 28, 1981.

44 **"are not merely permissible"**: Abrahamian, *The Iranian Mojahedin*, 68.

48 **"Did you ask for a defense lawyer?"**: Reuters, "No Need for Defence Attorney, Iran Judge Tells Former Official," *Globe and Mail*, March 19, 1981.

48 **"The Americans gave us plenty"**: "Still Feuding, Fighting, Fussing," *Newsweek*, U.S. ed., March 30, 1981, 44.

49 **"They have turned me into a devil"**: Reuters, "Former Iran Official Seeks Defence Right," *Globe and Mail*, April 28, 1981,

49 **"opportunists and criminals"** . . . **"The time has come"**: Menashri, *Iran*, 178.

CHAPTER THREE. THE PERIOD OF CONSTANT CONTEMPLATION

59 **Soroush read Khomeini's treatise on Islamic government**: Farhang Rajaee, *Islamism and Modernism: The Changing Discourse in Iran* (Austin: University of Texas Press, 2007), 226.

63 **"We always have a duty"**: Reza Khojasteh-Rahimi, "We Should Pursue Shariati's Path but We Shouldn't Be Mere Followers: An Interview with Abdulkarim Soroush," June 2008, http://www.drsoroush.com/English/Interviews/E-INT -Shariati_June2008.html.

66 **"banishing the power of cool and critical judgment"**: Karl Popper, *The Open Society and Its Enemies*, vol. 2, *Hegel and Marx* (New York: Routledge, 2003), 216.

66 **"The dogma that economic power"**: Ibid., 139.

66 **"It is high time . . . 'how much power is wielded?'"**: Ibid., 178.

68 **"we are pleased now"**: Behrooz Ghamari-Tabrizi, *Islam and Dissent in Postrevolutionary Iran: Abdolkarim Soroush, Religious Politics and Democratic Reform* (London: I. B. Tauris, 2008), 127.

68 **"Otherwise, God forbid"**: Ibid., 127.

68 **"masked dogmatism"** . . . **"improper" hijab**: Ibid., 104.

69 **"restructuring . . . higher education"**: Ibid., 112.

70 **"conspirators and other agents"**: Ibid., 116.

70 **"We should neither limit social liberties"**: Ibid., 189.

71 **"After a few sentences"**: "The Story of the Cultural Revolution: 'Right to the End They Didn't Know Where They Were Meant to Be Going,'" interview with Abdolkarim Soroush, published in *Lowh*, Oct. 1, 1999, available at http://

www.drsoroush.com/English/Interviews/E-INT-19991000-The_Story_of_the
_Cultural_Revolution.html.

72 **"He did not shed any tears":** Ghamari-Tabrizi, *Islam and Dissent in Postrevolutionary Iran*, 117.

74 **"The prophets were not sent to angels":** Farzin Vahdat, *God and Juggernaut: Iran's Intellectual Encounter with Modernity* (Syracuse, NY: Syracuse University Press, 2002), 199.

75 **"Modern man sees his own image":** Ibid., 195.

75 **Davari believed that the political problem with the West:** The explanation of Davari's thought owes much to Vahdat, *God and Juggernaut*, chapter 5.

77 **"the only thinker whose ideas are consistent":** Ghamari-Tabrizi, *Islam and Dissent in Postrevolutionary Iran*, 191.

77 **a former student recalls:** See Mahmoud Sadri, "Fardid: Passionate and Genuine but Deeply Flawed Intellectual," http://nilgoon.org/archive/mahmoudsadri/pages/mahmoudsadri_002.html.

77 **"Every spring I buy grass seed":** Ibid.

78 **everything said outside Iran . . . aims with violence:** Maryam Kashani, "Never in Iran's History Has Philosophy Been So Political: An Interview with Abdulkarim Soroush," Jan. 30, 2006, http://drsoroush.com/en/never-in-irans-history-has-philosophy-been-so-political/.

78 **"If these people attack liberalism":** Ibid.

78 **In his lectures in the 1980s:** Ali Paya, "Karl Popper and the Iranian Intellectuals," *American Journal of Islamic Social Sciences* 20, no. 2 (Spring 2003), 61.

78 **"What is this rubbish they advocate":** Ghamari-Tabrizi, *Islam and Dissent in Postrevolutionary Iran*, 191.

79 **"Who is Popper?":** Ibid., 190.

79 **Popper's pseudophilosophy served:** Paya, "Karl Popper and the Iranian Intellectuals," 61–63.

80 **"are identical to those of Khomeini":** David Menashri, *Iran: A Decade of War and Revolution* (New York: Holmes & Meier, 1990), 218.

CHAPTER FOUR. BAPTISM OF BLOOD

82 **190,000 combat dead:** *Iran Times*, Oct. 17, 2014, 2, cited in Lawrence G. Potter, "New Casualty Figures for Iran-Iraq War," message posted Oct. 16, 2014, to Gulf 2000 electronic mailing list, archived at https://members.gulf2000.columbia.edu. Iran-Iraq War casualty figures are contentious and vary widely among sources. See also http://kurzman.unc.edu/death-tolls-of-the-iran-iraq-war/.

83 **Iran's gross domestic product:** Djavad Salehi-Isfahani, "Poverty, Inequality, and Populist Politics in Iran," *Journal of Economic Inequality* 7, no. 1 (March 2009), 5–24.

83 **Decline on this scale:** Ibid.

84 **This radical faction:** Bahman Baktiari, *Parliamentary Politics in Revolutionary Iran: The Institutionalization of Factional Politics* (Gainesville: University Press of Florida, 1996), 81.

84 **His account has been called into question:** It has been challenged in Persian here: http://www.irajmesdaghi.com/page1.php?id=395.

86 **Mousavi briefly helmed the foreign ministry:** United Press International, "Personality Spotlight: Mir Hossein Mousavi, Iranian Prime Minister," Oct. 29, 1981.

86 **He supported nationalizing:** David Menashri, *Iran: A Decade of War and Revolution* (New York: Holmes & Meier, 1990), 306, 327, 356.

86 **"the flames of this fire":** United Press International, "Iran Warns War Could Spread," Dec. 20, 1982.

86 **"cancerous tumor":** Reuters, "Annihilate Israel: Iran," *Sydney Morning Herald*, Nov. 18, 1988.

86 **"to honor the brave resistance":** "700 Protest Prison Death of Israeli Tourists' Killer," *Chicago Tribune*, Jan. 9, 1986, 5. The quote is from Tehran Radio.

86 **Mousavi spoke from the roof:** Reuters, "Iran Marks Anniversary of Embassy Takeover," *Globe and Mail*, Nov. 5, 1983.

88 **Iran would need seven times:** For Khomeini's letter published after the cease-fire, summarizing the reports of the chief of armed forces, see http://www.aftabnews.ir/vdceeo8jho8zn.html.

88 **"I know it is hard on you":** Dilip Hiro, *The Longest War: The Iran-Iraq Military Conflict* (New York: Routledge, 1990), 243.

88 **"Taking this decision . . . for his satisfaction":** Robert Pear, "Khomeini Accepts 'Poison' of Ending War with Iraq; U.N. Sending Mission," *New York Times*, July 21, 1988.

90 **a cell so crowded:** Ervand Abrahamian, *Tortured Confessions: Prisons and Public Recantations in Modern Iran* (Berkeley and Los Angeles: University of California Press, 1999), 135, 169, 140.

90 **most severely persecuted religious minority:** Reza Afshari, *Human Rights in Iran: The Abuse of Cultural Relativism* (Philadelphia: University of Pennsylvania Press, 2001), 119–28.

91 **They would twist and crush:** Abrahamian, *Tortured Confessions*, 139.

91 **In 1994 he estimated:** Ibid., 140.

91 **Another former prisoner recalls being suspended:** Houshang Asadi, *Letters to My Torturer: Love, Revolution, and Imprisonment in Iran* (Oxford: Oneworld, 2010).

91 **More than 7,900 Iranian political prisoners:** Abrahamian, *Tortured Confessions*, 169.

92 **"as painful as observing an actual death":** Ibid., 154.

92 **"something snapped inside of all of us":** Ibid.

92 **The *tavob* enjoyed:** Ibid., 168.

93 **"truly crazy":** Afshari, *Human Rights in Iran*, 105.

93 **By mid-1986, political prisoners:** Abrahamian, *Tortured Confessions*, 174–75.

94 **Khomeini wrote him a letter:** Afshari, *Human Rights in Iran*, 105.

94 **"contrary to the expediency of Islam":** Iran Human Rights Documentation Center, "Deadly Fatwa: Iran's 1988 Prison Massacre," Aug. 2009, 16, http://www.iranhrdc.org/english/publications/reports/3158-deadly-fatwa-iran-s-1988-prison-massacre.html.

94 **The regime boasted:** Abrahamian, *Tortured Confessions*, 129.

95 **force of seven thousand fighters:** Iran Human Rights Documentation Center, "Deadly Fatwa," 9–10, 12–13.

95 **"those who remain steadfast . . . implementation of the verdict":** Ibid., 88 (translation of entire fatwa and answers to questions).

97 **At Evin, according to one former prison official:** Christina Lamb, "Khomeini Fatwa 'Led to Killing of 30,000 in Iran,'" *Daily Telegraph*, Feb. 4, 2001. See also Iran Human Rights Documentation Center, "Deadly Fatwa," 27.

97 **The executioners complained of overwork:** Abrahamian, *Tortured Confessions*, 211.

97 **Some former inmates at Gohardasht Prison:** Ibid., 211–12.

97 **"Hajj Amjad, a guard":** Iran Human Rights Documentation Center, "Deadly Fatwa," 28.

97 **Montazeri would later estimate:** Ibid., 8, citing Montazeri's memoir.

98 **The site was heavily patrolled:** Ibid., 52–53.

98 **"baptism of blood":** Abrahamian, *Tortured Confessions*, 219.

98 **Speaker Rafsanjani claimed:** Amnesty International, "Iran: Violations of Human Rights 1987–1990" (1990), 11, https://www.amnesty.org/en/documents/MDE13/021/1990/en/.

98 **"Do you think we should hand out":** Iran Human Rights Documentation Center, "Deadly Fatwa."

99 **"to execute people who have been sentenced":** Ibid., Appendix 5, 96.

99 **Montazeri tried again in a missive dated August 4:** Ibid., Appendix 6, 100.

100 **"I have received more blows . . . it will not be solved but spread":** Ibid., Appendix 7, 104.

100 **"We will cause irreparable injustice":** Baktiari, *Parliamentary Politics in Revolutionary Iran*, 172.

101 **He disinherited Montazeri:** Abrahamian, *Tortured Confessions*, 220.

101 **"the appropriate political and managerial skills":** Karim Sadjadpour, *Reading Khamenei: The World View of Iran's Most Powerful Leader* (Washington, DC: Carnegie Endowment for International Peace, 2008), 6.

101 **Rafsanjani saluted this decision:** Ibid.

102 **"We need a focus for people's emotions":** Menashri, *Iran*, 349.

102 **"I am an individual":** Sadjadpour, *Reading Khamenei*, 7.

CHAPTER FIVE. EXPANSION AND CONTRACTION

109 **"the whole record of past revolutions":** Hannah Arendt, *On Revolution* (New York: Penguin Books, 2006), 102.

113 **Close to 80 percent:** Behrooz Ghamari-Tabrizi, *Islam and Dissent in Postrevolutionary Iran: Abdolkarim Soroush, Religious Politics and Democratic Reform* (London: I. B. Tauris, 2008), 194.

115 **These were the Mutazilites:** The summary of Mutazilite theory and history taken largely from Richard C. Martin and Mark R. Woodward, with Dwi S. Atmaja, *Defenders of Reason in Islam: Mu'tazilism from Medieval School to Modern Symbol* (Oxford: Oneworld, 1997).

116 **it led some clerics in Qom:** Mohammad Ayatollahi Tabaar, "Who Wrote the Quran?," *New York Times Magazine*, Dec. 5, 2008.

116 **"We say that the cherry is the fruit":** "Mohammad's Word, Mohammad's Miracle: An Interview with Abdulkarim Soroush by Kargozaran Newspaper," Feb. 9, 2008, http://drsoroush.com/en/mohammads-word-mohammads-miracle/.

118 **"the spread of thoughts"**: Ghamari-Tabrizi, *Islam and Dissent in Postrevolutionary Iran*, 217.

119 **Popper wrote him two letters in response**: Ali Paya, "Karl Popper and the Iranian Intellectuals," *American Journal of Islamic Social Sciences* 20, no. 2 (Spring 2003), 68.

120 **Soroush gave just two lectures and two interviews on the "woman question"**: Ziba Mir-Hosseini, *Islam and Gender: The Religious Debate in Contemporary Iran* (Princeton, NJ: Princeton University Press, 1999), 217–46.

122 **"Dr. Soroush issue"** . . . **"Iranian national independence"**: Ghamari-Tabrizi, *Islam and Dissent in Postrevolutionary Iran*, 217.

122 **"enemies of the revolution" were "exploiting naïve people"**: Ibid., 218.

122 **"we will throw these fashionable ideas"**: Ibid., 219.

123 **"I have come to you in humility"**: Ibid., 220.

123 **"The triumph of worshippers"**: Ibid., 222.

CHAPTER SIX. THERMIDOR

127 **"These revolutions are not worms turning"**: Crane Brinton, *The Anatomy of Revolution* (New York: Vintage, 1965), 250.

128 **"What differentiates this ideal world"**: Ibid., 47.

129 **"If it becomes a cultural phenomenon"**: Mehdi Moslem, *Factional Politics in Post-Khomeini Iran* (Syracuse, NY: Syracuse University Press, 2002), 145.

129 **"Asceticism is necessary"**: Ibid., 144.

129 **"through suppression, pressure and threat"**: Ibid., 169.

131 **"shed no blood for the United States"**: Bahman Baktiari, *Parliamentary Politics in Revolutionary Iran: The Institutionalization of Factional Politics* (Gainesville: University Press of Florida, 1996), 212.

137 **"And though of so unlimited a power"**: Thomas Hobbes, *Leviathan*, 20:18 (Oxford: Oxford University Press, 1996).

146 **"If you think we will fall"**: Ali Mirsepassi, *Democracy in Modern Iran: Islam, Culture, and Political Change* (New York: New York University Press, 2010), 140.

CHAPTER SEVEN. THE SECOND OF KHORDAD

152 **"To make our society stable"**: Mohammad Khatami, *Islam, Liberty and Development*, trans. Hossein Kamaly (Binghamton, NY: Global Academic Publishing, 1998), 115.

152 **"We can only critique tradition"**: Ibid., 34.

152 **"The cultural strategy of a dynamic and vibrant"**: Ibid., 112.

152 **"The legitimacy of government stems from people's vote"**: Ibid., 150.

156 **"cultural onslaught"** . . . **"corruption, decadence and idleness"**: David Menashri, *Post-Revolutionary Politics in Iran: Religion, Society and Power* (Portland, OR: Frank Cass, 2001), 84.

157 **campaigned in the American style**: Genieve Abdo and Jonathan Lyons, *Answering Only to God: Faith and Freedom in Twenty-first-Century Iran* (New York: Henry Holt, 2003), chap. 3.

157 **the entire machinery of the Tehran municipality at his disposal**: Ibid., 70–71.

158 **"Less than a week before the election"**: Ibid., 73.

158 **"I shall not allow anyone"**: Ibid., 74.

158 **some 80 percent of Iranian voters:** Iran Data Portal, http://www.princeton.edu/ irandataportal/elections/pres/1997.

161 **"degraded . . . infantile":** A summary of Montazeri's speech is in Ziba Mir-Hosseini and Richard Tapper, *Islam and Democracy in Iran: Eshkevari and the Quest for Reform* (London and New York: I. B. Tauris, 2006), 103–108.

161 **Even its budget was overseen:** Mirjam Kunkler, "The Special Court of the Clergy and the Repression of Dissident Clergy in Iran," in *The Rule of Law, Islam, and Constitutional Politics in Egypt and Iran,* ed. Saïd Amir Arjomand and Nathan J. Brown (Albany: State University of New York Press, 2013), 57–100.

162 **"If I were you":** Mehdi Moslem, *Factional Politics in Post-Khomeini Iran* (Syracuse, NY: Syracuse University Press, 2002), 256.

CHAPTER EIGHT. THE CHAIN MURDERS

170 **the family's lawyer would recount:** Shirin Ebadi with Azadeh Moaveni, *Iran Awakening: A Memoir of Revolution and Hope* (New York: Random House, 2006), 137.

172 **"I see him off with his weapon":** Hammed Shahidian, "Writing Out Terror," Jan. 8, 1999. Unpublished manuscript posted on Oct. 8, 2005 (after the author's death), on Iranian.com, http://iranian.com/BTW/2005/October/Terror/index .html.

173 **"Wherever religion and government . . . own religious beliefs and knowledge":** Ziba Mir-Hosseini and Richard Tapper, *Islam and Democracy in Iran: Eshkevari and the Quest for Reform* (London and New York: I. B. Tauris, 2006), 69.

173 **"Now that the fervor has subsided":** Ibid., 67.

174 **The inclusion of the old literary elite:** Reza Afshari, *Human Rights in Iran: The Abuse of Cultural Relativism* (Philadelphia: University of Pennsylvania Press, 2001). See particularly chapter 13, "The Right to Freedom of Opinion, Expression, and Press," 185–216.

174 **They opened their consensus meetings:** Mehrangiz Kar, *Crossing the Red Line: The Struggle for Human Rights in Iran* (Costa Mesa, CA: Blind Owl Press/ Mazda, 2007), 125–29.

174 **"We are the writers!"** Hammed Shahidian, trans., "We Are the Writers!," *Iranian Studies* 30, nos. 3–4 (1997), 291–93,

175 **"Killing hypocrites does not require a court order":** "Rafsanjani to Succeed Khamenei?," Iran brief, Info-Prod Research (Middle East), no. 64 (Oct. 4, 1999).

176 **An unbridgeable divide:** Afshari, *Human Rights in Iran,* 206.

176 **"[A] society in which religion":** Mir-Hosseini and Tapper, *Islam and Democracy in Iran,* 71.

180 **They released a videotape in which Emami's wife:** Ebadi with Moaveni, *Iran Awakening,* 139.

180 **"Directing everyone's eyes . . . flag of terror on religion's dome":** Akbar Ganji, "Assassination's Directors," in *Writers Under Siege: Voices of Freedom from Around the World,* ed. Lucy Popescu and Carole Seymour-Jones (New York: New York University Press, 2007), 152–53.

181 **Ganji wrote in *Sobh-e Emrouz*:** Akbar Ganji, "The Questions Raised by a Suicide," in *Writers Under Siege,* 153–55.

CHAPTER NINE. THE EIGHTEENTH OF TIR

190 **"What need is there . . . forces act as mere spectators?":** David Menashri, *Post-Revolutionary Politics in Iran: Religion, Society and Power* (Portland, OR; Frank Cass, 2001), 136.

193 **debated a sweeping new law:** A. W. Samii, "The Contemporary Iranian News Media: 1998–1999," *Middle East Review of International Affairs (MERIA) Journal* 3, no. 4 (Dec. 1999), available online on Rubin Center for Research in International Affairs website, http://www.gloria-center.org/1999/12/samii-1999-12-01/.

194 **"We have to create laws . . . let us take measures":** FDI: Foundation for Democracy in Iran, "Hard-liners Close Salam Newspaper," News Flash, July 8, 1999, http://www.iran.org/news/bbc990708.htm.

194 *Salam* **published an explosive story:** Abbas Samii, "The Internal Struggle over Iran's Future," in *Crises in the Contemporary Persian Gulf*, ed. Barry Rubin (New York: Frank Cass, 2002), 277–313.

197 **Khamenei condemned the attack:** "Iran's Tiananmen Square, or 1979 Revisited?," *Mideast Mirror*, 13, no. 131 (June 12, 1999).

198 **"We will resolutely and decisively quell":** Geneive Abdo, "Khatami Abandons Student Protesters: Iran's Pro-Democracy Activists Left Stunned, Confused As President Sides with Hard-liners," *Globe and Mail* (Canada), July 15, 1999.

200 **"fast-talking self-promoter":** Elaine Sciolino, *Persian Mirrors: The Elusive Face of Iran* (New York: Free Press, 2005), 242.

201 **"was administered an unspecified 'medicine'":** "Islamic Republic of Iran: Iran: Akbar Mohammadi's Death in Custody Signals Need for Justice Reform," Amnesty International, Aug. 9, 2006, http://www.amnesty.or.jp/en/news/2006/0809_551.html.

202 **"the true children of the revolution" . . . violence to Islam:** Menashri, *Post-Revolutionary Politics in Iran*, 147.

203 **"among the best supporters":** Tarek Al-Issawi, "After Protests, Khatami Pledges to Continue Reform Program," Associated Press, July 28, 1999.

203 **"There is no split":** "Iran Riots a 'Declaration of War' Against Me: Khatami," Agence France-Presse, July 28, 1999.

203 **"an ugly and offensive incident" . . . "no matter who they are":** Ibid.

203 **"My dear ones":** Geneive Abdo and Jonathan Lyons, *Answering Only to God: Faith and Freedom in Twenty-first Century Iran* (New York: Henry Holt, 2003), 219.

208 **"I felt like a lonely and vulnerable child" . . . "untied me from the bed":** Iran Human Rights Documentation Center, "Witness Statement: Ali Afshari," 2008, 14, http://www.iranhrdc.org/english/publications/witness-testimony/3175-witness-statement-ali-afshari.html.

CHAPTER TEN. MASTER PLANS

213 **"Who wants to sit":** Jeffrey M. Hardwick, *Mall Maker: Victor Gruen, Architect of an American Dream* (Philadelphia: University of Pennsylvania Press, 2010), 151.

214 **"graft and corruption":** Ibid., 188.

214 **"The world of postwar America":** Ibid., 215.

215 **Tehran sloped sharply:** Ali Madanipour, *Tehran: The Making of a Metropolis* (New York: John Wiley & Sons, 1998), 103.

215 **Tehran's population grew from 160,000 to 5 million:** Asef Bayat, *Street Politics: Poor People's Movements in Iran* (New York: Columbia University Press, 1997), 25.

215 **top 12 million in 2004:** Tehran Municipality, "Tehran, Social Situation," http://en.tehran.ir/Default.aspx?tabid=99.

215 **fully 35 percent of Tehran's population:** Bayat, *Street Politics*, 29.

216 **"There are few examples of a megacity":** Wouter Vanstiphout, "The Saddest City in the World: Tehran and the Legacy of an American Dream of Modern Town Planning," in *The New Town*, a research and exhibition project by Crimson Architectural Historians, Rotterdam, March 2, 2006, http://www.thenewtown.nl/article.php?id_article=71.

217 **"centuries went by and generations followed":** Ibid.

217 **The Islamic Republic brought electricity:** In 1977, only 16 percent of rural homes had electricity; by 1984, 57 percent did. Now rural families could purchase refrigerators (up from 7 to 35 percent of rural homes in the same period) and television sets.

217 **Under the shah, rural women:** Djavad Salehi-Isfahani, "The Revolution and the Rural Poor," *Radical History Review*, no. 105 (Fall 2009), 139–44.

218 **"Neither east nor west!" . . . "neither water nor electricity!":** Bayat, *Street Politics*, 86.

219 **Gholamhossein Karbaschi called for flowers:** Fariba Adelkah, *Being Modern in Iran* (New York: Columbia University Press, 2000), 22.

221 **Karbaschi quintupled the city's budget:** Kaveh Ehsani, "The Politics of Property in the Islamic Republic of Iran," in *The Rule of Law, Islam, and Constitutional Politics in Egypt and Iran*, ed. Saïd Amir Arjomand and Nathan J. Brown (Albany: State University of New York Press, 2013), 162.

221 **Karbaschi created six hundred new parks:** Asef Bayat, *Making Islam Democratic: Social Movements and the Post-Islamist Turn* (Stanford, CA: Stanford University Press, 2007), 56.

222 **Ayatollah Khamenei warned Karbaschi:** Ibid., 58.

224 **"primarily as sources of revenue":** Kaveh Ehsani and Sai'id Hajjarian, "'Existing Political Vessels Cannot Contain the Reform Movement': A Conversation with Sai'id Hajjarian," *Pushing the Limits, Iran's Islamic Revolution at Twenty*, special issue of *Middle East Report*, no. 212 (Autumn 1999), 42.

225 **Karbaschi's trial opened in June:** Information on the trial comes from "Tehran Mayor Denies Stealing 'a Single Rial' As Trial Resumes," Agence France-Press, June 11, 1998.

226 **"You've set up a group":** Afshin Valinejad, "Tehran Mayor Accuses Authorities of Torture," Associated Press, July 5, 1998.

228 **he told reporters that he'd learned:** John Daniszewski, "Shooting Leaves Iranian Reformist Seriously Hurt," *Los Angeles Times*, March 13, 2000, A1.

228 **"religious duty":** Susan Sachs, "2 Trials Focus Attention on Iranian Justice," *New York Times*, May 3, 2000, A12; BBC Summary of World Broadcasts, May 5, 2000, English text of report from Vision of the Islamic Republic of Iran, Network 4, May 3, 2000.

229 **"The enemies of freedom":** Scott Peterson, "Are Hardliners Taking Aim at Reformists?," *Christian Science Monitor,* March 13, 2000, 7.

230 **"certain internal organizational problems":** BBC Monitoring Middle East, "Iran: Two Tehran Municipality Deputies Resign," text of report from *Kayhan* website (in Persian), Jan. 17, 2002.

231 **"During the past four years":** Hoseyn Shariatmadari, "Note of the Day" column on *Kayhan* website (in Persian), Jan. 9, 2003, 2. Translated for BBC Summary of World Broadcasts, Jan. 10, 2003.

231 **Another commentator in *Kayhan*:** Mohammad Mohajeri, "This Council Was Disbanded Four Years Ago" on *Kayhan* website (in Persian), Jan. 15, 2003, 2. Translated for BBC Summary of World Broadcasts, Jan. 16, 2003.

232 **some 95 percent ... low 10 percent:** Figures cited by interior ministry spokesman Jahanbakhsh Khanjani in Ali Akbar Dareini, "Local Election Turnout in Tehran 10 percent, Conservatives in Lead," Associated Press Worldstream, March 1, 2003.

232 **Conservatives took fourteen ... by carrying between 85,000 and 190,000 votes:** "Khatami Worried About Low Turnout at Iranian Municipal Elections," Deutsche Presse-Agentur, March 3, 2003.

232 **"safeguarding the achievements":** Reuters, "Conservatives Crush Reformers in Iran; 14 of 15 Seats on Tehran Council Go to Hardliners," *Chicago Tribune,* March 3, 2003, 3.

CHAPTER ELEVEN. THE MIRACLE ROOM

235 **By later accounts, she was hardly ever alone there:** Iran Human Rights Documentation Center, "Impunity in Iran: The Death of Photojournalist Zahra Kazemi," Nov. 2006, http://www.iranhrdc.org/english/publications/reports/3148-impunity-in-iran-the-death-of-photojournalist-zahra-kazemi.html.

237 **On July 10 she was removed:** Ibid., Appendix 4, 1–3.

238 **He became a key outspoken witness:** Ibid., Appendix 6, "Khoshvaght Letter," 1–4.

238 **"In view of Ms. Zahra Kazemi's inhumane treatment":** Ibid., Appendix 4, 1.

239 **There were oddities:** Ibid., Appendix 7, "Abdol Karim Lahiji's Statement on the Special Presidential Commission Report," 1–2.

240 **"How could it be":** Ibid., Appendix 2, "Report of the Parliamentary Article 90 Commission," 4.

240 **He replied to the commission's questions:** Ibid., Appendix 2, 4–6.

240 **lambasted Mortazavi in a speech and in an open letter to the prosecutor:** Ibid., Appendix 2 and Appendix 8, "Mohsen Armin Letter: Mortazavi Must Stand Trial."

252 **"We think like Kadivar":** Mehdi Moslem, *Factional Politics in Post-Khomeini Iran* (Syracuse, NY: Syracuse University Press, 2002), 263.

253 **In 2001 the court handed the deputy interior minister:** Muhammad Sahimi, "Patriotists and Reformists: Behzad Nabavi and Mostafa Tajzadeh," Tehran Bureau, *Frontline,* PBS.org, Aug. 11, 2009, http://www.pbs.org/wgbh/pages/frontline/tehranbureau/2009/08/patriots-and-reformists-behzad-nabavi-and-mostafa-tajzadeh.html.

CHAPTER THIRTEEN. POSTMORTEM

314 On December 6, 2004, President Mohammad Khatami . . . "stop the beating of students": "Iranian President Heckled During Speech to Students," BBC Monitoring International Reports, Dec. 8, 2004. Khatami's speech, with English subtitles, can be found at https://www.youtube.com/watch?v=qrZw-yGlyTk.

317 Five reformist luminaries convened . . . "no state can survive": Saeed Hajjarian, Abbas Abdi, Mostafa Tajzadeh, Hamidreza Jalaeipour, and Alireza Alavitabar, *Reformation vs. Reformation: A Critical Dialogue* (Tehran: Tarh-e No, 2006). Selected translations by Massood Hooman, commissioned by the author.

322 "The goal of the system": A translation of this letter can be found at http:// www.europarl.europa.eu/meetdocs/2004_2009/documents/dv/ ganjiletter100705_/ganjiletter100705_en.pdf.

323 "If civil disobedience needs leadership and planning": freeganji.blogspot.com, accessed July 17, 2005.

323 "Forcing repentance letters on prisoners": Ibid.

328 "Lack of vision theoretically leads": Dariush Sajjadi, transcript of interview with Abdolkarim Soroush, broadcast on Homa TV, March 9, 2006, file:///Users/ macbook/Desktop/Book/Interview%20notes/Intellectuals/Soroush/Dr.%20 Soroush.webarchive.

328 "All the important, modern, political institutions": Ali Asghar Seyyedabadi, "The Muddled Dream of Returning to Tradition: An Interview with Abdulkarim Soroush," Nov. 19, 2006, http://drsoroush.com/en/ the-muddled-dream-of-returning-to-tradition/.

331 "the relatively free atmosphere": Sajjadi, transcript of interview with Abdolkarim Soroush.

331 Rafsanjani easily led the first round of voting . . . national totals: Election data can be found at http://www.princeton.edu/irandataportal/elections/pres/2005/.

CHAPTER FOURTEEN. A COMMON MAN

339 Iran never had a politician: Biographical details on Ahmadinejad are from Kasra Naji, *Ahmadinejad: The Secret History of Iran's Radical Leader* (Berkeley and Los Angeles: University of California Press, 2008).

340 After the revolution, Ahmadinejad . . . lead to lawlessness: Ibid. See also Alireza Haghighi and Victoria Tahmasebi, "The 'Velvet Revolution' of Iranian Puritan Hardliners," *International Journal*, Autumn 2006, 961.

341 he was active in those years against Khatami: Naji, *Ahmadinejad*, 46.

343 "Immediately these people say": Ibid., 234.

344 "Economics, like any other science": Ibid., 233.

344 He even invited German chancellor Angela Merkel: Ibid., 181.

345 Ahmadinejad undertook the most far-reaching governmental housecleaning: Haghighi and Tahmasebi, "The 'Velvet Revolution' of Iranian Puritan Hardliners," 970, n. 13.

346 In the first year of his presidency alone: Ali Rahnema, *Superstition as Ideology in Iranian Politics: From Majlesi to Ahmadinejad* (New York: Cambridge University Press, 2011), 59.

347 The elected institutions, Mesbah believed: Jahangir Amuzegar, "Iran's Theocracy Under Siege," *Middle East Policy* 1, no. 10 (March 21, 2003), 135.

347 **"We shall wait to see":** John Ward Anderson, "Iran's Conservatives Face a Growing Split; Extremist Clerics Blamed for Rise in Secularism," *Washington Post*, June 2, 2001.

347 **"It doesn't matter what the people think":** Afshin Molavi, *The Soul of Iran: A Nation's Struggle for Freedom* (New York: W. W. Norton, 2005), 105.

347 **"just as it checks the distribution":** John Ward Anderson, "Islamic Democracy's Power Politics; As Iran's Election Nears, Key Issue Is Accountability—to the Public, or to God?" *Washington Post*, May 25, 2001.

347 **He called for the violent elimination:** "Rafsanjani to Succeed Khamene'i?," Iran brief, Info-Prod Research (Middle East), no. 64 (Oct. 4, 1999).

347 **Ahmadinejad, too, scorned all efforts:** Naji, *Ahmadinejad*, 70.

347 **they worried that the president and Mesbah undermined Islam by toying:** For Mesbah-Yazdi and Ahmadinejad (excluding Mesbah-Yazdi's quotations on politics), see Rahnema, *Superstition as Ideology in Iranian Politics*, 54–99.

350 **More Iranians than ever before climbed:** On the expansion of the middle class under the Islamic Republic, see Kevan Harris, "A Martyrs' Welfare State and Its Contradictions: Regime Resilience and Limits Through the Lens of Social Policy in Iran," in *Middle East Authoritarianisms: Governance, Contestation, and Regime Resilience in Syria and Iran*, ed. Steven Heydemann and Reinoud Leenders (Stanford, CA: Stanford University Press, 2013). See also Kevan Harris, "The Brokered Exuberance of the Middle Class: An Ethnographic Analysis of Iran's 2009 Green Movement," *Mobilization: An International Journal* 17, no. 4, (2012), 435–55.

352 **Toward the end of 2008:** See Arash Ghafouri, "Setad 88—Iran's Greatest Campaign in Support of Mirhossein Mousavi," in *Election Fallout: Iran's Exiled Journalists on Their Struggle for Democratic Change*, ed. Marcus Michaelson, trans. Evan J. Siegel (Berlin: Verlag Hans Schiler, 2011), 50–61, http://library.fes .de/pdf-files/iez/08560.pdf.

353 **"like an unopened melon":** Ibid.

353 **"I know that I would get the vote if I ran":** Muhammad Sahimi, "The Political Evolution of Mousavi," Tehran Bureau, *Frontline*, PBS.org, Feb. 16, 2010, http:// www.pbs.org/wgbh/pages/frontline/tehranbureau/2010/02/the-political -evolution-of-mousavi.html.

353 **In an interview with *Der Spiegel*:** http://www.spiegel.de/international/world/ iranian-elections-the-answer-to-ahmadinejad-a-622225.html.

355 **Mousavi and Ahmadinejad squared off:** A transcript of their debate can be found at http://www.irantracker.org/analysis/mousavi-ahmadinejad-june-3 -presidential-debate-transcript; video with English subtitles at https://www .youtube.com/watch?v=9DNmR15Lui8.

CHAPTER FIFTEEN. ASIEH

365 **The Franklin Book Programs:** Datus C. Smith, Jr., "Franklin Book Program," *Encyclopædia Iranica*, vol. 10, fasc. 2, 187–90 (Dec. 15, 2002; last updated Jan. 31, 2012). Accessed online at http://www.iranicaonline.org/articles/franklin-book-program. See also Louise S. Robbins, "Publishing American Values: The Franklin Book Programs as Cold War Cultural Diplomacy, *Library Trends* 55, no. 3 (Winter 2007), 638–50.

397 **"The paintings in front of you":** Quoted in Robert Tait, "Dead Woman Painting," *Guardian*, Oct. 25, 2006, http://www.theguardian.com/world/2006/oct/25/worlddispatch.arts.

397 **The last words anyone heard her speak:** Claire Soares, "Delara Darabi, 'Oh Mother, I Can See the Noose,'" *Independent*, May 4, 2009, http://www.independent.co.uk/news/world/middle-east/delara-darabi-oh-mother-i-can-see-the-noose-1678543.html.

CHAPTER SIXTEEN. THE EPIC OF DIRT AND DUST

405 **"The destiny of each generation":** Ruhollah Khomeini, "Address at Bihisht-i Zahra," in Ruhollah Khomeini, *Islam and Revolution I: Writings and Declarations of Imam Khomeini (1941–1980)*, trans. and ed. Hamid Algar (Berkeley, CA: Mizan Press, 1981), 255.

408 **"these are real people":** Scott Peterson, *Let the Swords Encircle Me: Iran— A Journey Behind the Headlines* (New York: Simon & Schuster, 2010), 476.

408 **A video of his address:** http://www.al-monitor.com/pulse/originals/2014/06/leaked-video-accuses-2009-election-fraud.html#; video (in Persian): https://www.facebook.com/photo.php?v=870388962988721&set=vb.153044948056463&type=2&theater.

412 **Ethnic minorities and rural voters:** Ali Ansari, ed., "Preliminary Analysis of the Voting Figures in Iran's 2009 Election," Chatham House and Institute of Iranian Studies, University of St. Andrews, June 21, 2009, 11.

413 **the numbers suggested the presence:** Iran Human Rights Documentation Center, "Violent Aftermath: The 2009 Election and Suppression of Dissent in Iran," Feb. 2010, 10, http://www.iranhrdc.org/english/publications/reports/3161-violent-aftermath-the-2009-election-and-suppression-of-dissent-in-iran.html.

413 **A researcher in a village near Shiraz:** Eric Hooglund, "Iran's Rural Vote and Election Fraud," Tehran Bureau, *Frontline*, PBS.org, June 17, 2009, posted June 21, 2010, http://www.pbs.org/wgbh/pages/frontline/tehranbureau/2010/06/irans-rural-vote-and-election-fraud.html.

413 **Similar allegations were reported:** Iran Human Rights Documentation Center, "Violent Aftermath," 10.

413 **foreign statisticians:** See Thomas Lotze, http://thomaslotze.com/iran/.

414 **"I personally strongly protest":** Reuters, "Angry Mousavi Says Iran Vote Result a Fix," June 13, 2009, http://mobile.reuters.com/article/idUSTRE55C1K020090613.

415 **The president held a victory rally:** CNN, "Ahmadinejad Says Remarks Taken out of Context," June 18, 2009, http://www.cnn.com/2009/WORLD/meast/06/18/iran.ahmadinejad.comments/index.html?iref=24hours.

416 **"this is the voice of dirt and dust":** Robert Tait, "The Dust Revolution—How Mahmoud Ahmadinejad's Jibe Backfired," *Guardian*, June 18, 2009, http://www.theguardian.com/world/2009/jun/18/iran-election-protests-mahmoud-ahmadinejad.

416 **Another conservative parliamentarian:** Ibid.

420 **Khamenei spoke at length . . . "chaos to follow":** Juan Cole, "Supreme Leader Khameini's Friday Address on the Presidential Election," *Informed Comment*, June 19, 2009, http://www.juancole.com/2009/06/supreme-leader-khameneis-friday-address.html.

422 **He responded to Khamenei's speech with a statement:** Mousavi's speech can be found translated at http://iranfacts.blogspot.com/2009/06/my-translation-of -mousavis-latest.html.

425 **But in the final video of her . . . "This is a crime against humanity":** Borzou Daragahi, "From the Archives: Family, Friends Mourn 'Neda,' Iranian Woman Who Died on Video," *Los Angeles Times*, June 23, 2009, www.latimes.com/ world/la-fg-iran-neda23-2009jun23-story.html#page=1.

426 **Then he was imprisoned and apparently coerced:** "Key Witness Disputes Hejazi Account of Neda Death," Press TV, July 29, 2009, http://edition.presstv .ir/detail/101954.html.

426 **"Had those responsible for the murders":** Mir Hossein Mousavi, "Public Response to the Election Fraud and Protests," June 21, 2009, http://www .princeton.edu/irandataportal/elections/pres/2009/candidates/mousavi/ 21-june-2009/.

426 **"I am not ready to stop standing":** Ibid.

429 **by one account beating several prisoners:** http://loln.wordpress.com/2009/07/28/ first-hand-testimonials-of-a-21-year-old-iranian-protester-who-was-arrested-on-18 -tir-protests-in-tehran-and-taken-to-kahrizak-camp/.

429 **"They were zombies":** Borzou Daragahi and Ramin Mostagim, "Imprisoned Iranian Protesters Share a Bond Forged in Hell," *Los Angeles Times*, Feb. 14, 2010, http://articles.latimes.com/2010/feb/14/world/la-fg-iran-prison14 -2010feb14.

429 **They had to log the physical condition . . . proper funerals:** Iran Human Rights Documentation Center, "Violent Aftermath," section 3.1, Kahrizak Detention Center.

429 **a visitor to another patient . . . told a reporter:** Borzou Daragahi, "Iran Roiled by Prison Abuse Claims," *Los Angeles Times*, Aug. 12, 2009, http://articles .latimes.com/2009/aug/12/world/fg-iran-abuse12.

430 **"bashed in":** Ibid.

430 **In a July 29 open letter to Rafsanjani:** Stories quoting Karroubi's letter can be found at http://www.rferl.org/content/Two_Months_Later_Truth_About _Irans_Postelection_Crackdown_Still_Unknown/1796492.html; http://www .nytimes.com/2009/08/13/world/middleeast/13iran.html?_r=0. A full translation of the letter, which uses slightly different wording for the same quoted portions, can be found at http://khordaad88.com/?p=75.

431 **"He was brought to me after being physically and severely tortured":** Physicians for Human Rights, "Rights Groups Call for Independent Autopsy of Iranian Doctor Who Treated Tortured Prisoners," Nov. 25, 2009, http://physiciansforhumanrights.org/blog/iranian-doctor -autopsy.html.

432 **they told the *Los Angeles Times*:** Ramin Mostaghim and Borzou Daragahi, "Was Kahrizak Prison Doctor a Victim or Villain?," *Los Angeles Times*, Feb. 14, 2010, http://articles.latimes.com/2010/feb/14/world/la-fgw-iran-prison-doctor14 -2010feb14.

432 **"lack of space, weakness of health services":** Iran Human Rights Documentation Center, "Violent Aftermath," citing Complete Text of the Special Report of the Majlis, Jan. 10, 2009.

432 **"did not attempt to break the law":** Iran Human Rights Documentation Center, "Violent Aftermath," 54.

433 **"nobody in their right mind" . . . "receiving orders":** Warren P. Strobel and Jonathan S. Landay, "Iran's Senior Ayatollah Slams Election, Confirming Split," *McClatchyDC*, June 16, 2009, http://www.mcclatchydc.com/news/nation-world/world/article24542242.html.

433 **In a fatwa of July 11, 2009 . . . "the world's wise observers":** Ahmad Sadri and Mahmoud Sadri, "Delegitimizing the Islamic Republic of Iran with a *Fatwa*: The Significance of Ayatollah Montazeri's Post-Election Legal Ruling of July 2009," in *The People Reloaded: The Green Movement and the Struggle for Iran's Future*, ed. Nader Hashemi and Danny Postel (Brooklyn, NY: Melville House, 2011), 165.

434 **"Montazeri, you are finally free":** Richard Spencer, "Grand Ayatollah Montazeri Death Sparks Protests," *Telegraph*, Dec. 20, 2009, http://www.telegraph.co.uk/news/worldnews/middleeast/iran/6851224/Grand-Ayatollah-Montazeri-death-sparks-protests.html.

CHAPTER SEVENTEEN. THE END OF THE DIRTY WARS OF INTELLECTUALS

435 **an explosive five-part series:** Payam Fazlinejad, "Mohammad Khatami's Mission for a Velvet Coup d'État." English translation available at docstoc.com.

437 **Habermas did, in fact, travel to Iran in 2002:** Christiane Hoffmann, "The Unrest Is Growing: Habermas in Iran; Interview with Jürgen Habermas on His Visit to Iran," *Frankfurter Allgemeine Zeitung*, June 18, 2002, English translation available at www.pubtheo.com/page.asp?pid=1073.

439 **Hajjarian's forced confession . . . ran to six pages:** Quotations are from Charles Kurzman, "Reading Weber in Tehran," *Chronicle of Higher Education*, Nov. 1, 2009, http://chronicle.com/article/Social-Science-on-Trial-in-/48949/.

440 **The indictment by the office of the prosecutor:** The full text of the indictment in English is available via Evan Siegel at www.qlineorientalist.com/IranRises/the-indictment/#Indictmentt6.

446 **The language of the second indictment:** Text of the indictment in English can be found at http://www.iranhrdc.org/english/human-rights-documents/indictments/3342-second-indictment.html.

447 **"We demand the Islamic Republic":** Mir Hossein Mousavi, "Violence Is Not the Solution," Sept. 28, 2009, http://www.princeton.edu/irandataportal/elections/pres/2009/candidates/mousavi/28-september-2009/.

447 **"It's okay, let them take Isfahan":** "Mousavi's Meeting with Reformist Parliament Opposition Delegates," http://www.parlemannews.ir/?n=9919; "Reformist Delegates of the Opposition in Parliament Meet Mousavi," http://khordaad88.com/?p=1519.

447 **"Never do anything that you can't explain to the people":** From the Mousavi Facebook page, "Mir Hossein Mousavi in His First Video Interview After the Election: Explaining the National Unity Plan," Oct. 19, 2009, http://www.facebook.com/note.php?note_id=160862192605&ref=mf.

447 **"The majority of people here *like* one another":** Mir Hossein Mousavi, "Interview with Kaleme: The Green Movement Is Standing Firm on Its Rightful

Demands," Feb. 27, 2010, http://www.princeton.edu/irandataportal/elections/pres/2009/candidates/mousavi/27-february-2010/.

447 **In an October statement, Mousavi included:** Mir Hossein Mousavi, "The Significance of the 13th of Aban," Oct. 31, 2009, http://www.princeton.edu/irandataportal/elections/pres/2009/candidates/mousavi/31-october-2009/.

448 **According to a 2013 Reuters report:** Yeganeh Torbati, "Insight: Ahead of Vote, 'Kidnapped' Iran Reformists Imprisoned at Home," June 11, 2013, http://www.reuters.com/article/2013/06/11/us-iran-election-opposition-insight-id USBRE95A0OH20130611.

449 **"Recently, for five days in a row":** Laura Secor, "Iran's Green Movement: An Interview with Mehdi Karroubi," in *The People Reloaded: The Green Movement and the Struggle for Iran's Future*, ed. Nader Hashemi and Danny Postel (Brooklyn, NY: Melville House, 2011), 408–14.

449 **"the world of my own language":** On Zweig's biography, see Leo Spitzer, *Lives in Between: Assimilation and Marginality in Austria, Brazil, West Africa, 1780–1945* (Cambridge, England: Cambridge University Press, 1989). See also Leo Care, "The Escape Artist: The Life and Death of Stefan Zweig," *The New Yorker*, Aug. 27, 2012.

450 **"To burn a man alive":** Stefan Zweig, *The Right to Heresy: Castellio Against Calvin*, trans. Eden and Cedar Paul (London: Cassell, 1936), 216.

450 **"When I reflect on what a heretic really is":** Ibid., 188.

450 **"The eternal tragedy of despots":** Ibid., 228.

450 **"Many of the humanities and liberal arts":** Michael Slackman, "Purge of Iranian Universities Is Feared," *New York Times*, Sept. 1, 2009, http://www.nytimes.com/2009/09/02/world/middleeast/02iran.html.

450 **Abdolkarim Soroush responded with an idea:** All the quotations of Soroush here are from: Abdolkarim Soroush, "A Word of Advice to the Advocates of Islamic Human Sciences," Oct. 9, 2010, http://drsoroush.com/en/a-word-of-advice-to-the-advocates-of-islamic-human-sciences/.

452 **She posted a loving exchange:** Nazila Fathi, "To Reza in Jail: Love and Unity," *New York Times*, Week in Review, May 15, 2010, http://www.nytimes.com/2010/05/16/weekinreview/16fathi.html.

453 **In an open letter smuggled from Evin in 2010:** Quotations from the Tajzadeh letter are discussed in Muhammad Sahimi, "Tajzadeh: Reformists Should Ask Nation for Forgiveness," Tehran Bureau, *Frontline*, PBS.org, June 15, 2010, http://www.pbs.org/wgbh/pages/frontline/tehranbureau/2010/06/tajzadeh-reformists-should-ask-the-nation-for-forgiveness.html.

EPILOGUE

463 **"Just let go of reformism":** Arash Karami, "Former Tehran Mayor Reveals Why Reformists Decided to Support Rouhani," *Al-Monitor*, April 8, 2014, http://www.al-monitor.com/pulse/originals/2014/04/former-tehran-mayor-explains-reformists-support-rouhani.html#ixzz3k2ryhelx.

464 **In a record year for executions:** "Report of the Special Rapporteur on the Situation of Human Rights in the Islamic Republic of Iran, Ahmed Shaheed," March 12, 2015, http://shaheedoniran.org/wp-content/uploads/2015/03/HRC-2015.pdf, 6.

464 **By a 2014 tally:** Committee to Protect Journalists, "2014 Prison Census: 221 Journalists Jailed Worldwide," Dec. 1, 2014, https://www.cpj.org/imprisoned/ 2014.php.

465 **making peace with the events of 2009:** In general, I find Iranian opinion polls to be suspect. Iranians are careful what they say on the phone to loved ones, let alone to strangers, because there is good reason to fear retribution for political speech. So when a pollster calls to ask your views on the events of 2009, if your opinions don't track with the official line, maybe you decline the call, or maybe you dissemble, or maybe you brazenly tell the truth. We can't know why people answer the way they do, but we know that they are weighing sensitivities other than their own. Hence I relay these numbers with substantial doubt as to what they tell us: In a 2015 opinion poll, 59 percent of respondents said they now believed there was no fraud in the 2009 election. Forty percent said that the protesters had no right to demonstrate, and 40 percent approved of the police response. Still, when they were asked who the protesters were, 41 percent of respondents said the demonstrators were ordinary people; 21 percent said they were students or youth. Only 9 percent said the protesters were rich people, despite state propaganda to that effect. And the smallest group of all— 6 percent—bought the idea that they were a conspiracy guided by foreigners. See iPOS (Information and Public Opinion Solutions) Poll, "Iranians' Views on the Green Movement Legacy," June 22, 2015, https://www.ipos.me/en/; IranWire, "View from Iran, The Green Movement," June 23, 2015, http:// en.iranwire.com/features/6576/.

SELECTED BIBLIOGRAPHY

THIS BOOK OWES A GREAT DEBT to the vast, challenging, and fascinating scholarly literature on Iran. I have included here the books and journal articles that substantially contributed to my understanding of this country and its politics. Many of the authors also generously fielded my phone calls and inquiries specific to their areas of expertise. Not included are the great many contemporaneous newspaper articles and websites that are cited in the endnotes, along with the invaluable resources compiled by the Iran Human Rights Documentation Center in New Haven, Connecticut; the Iran Data Portal at Princeton University; and *Encyclopædia Iranica* at Columbia University.

Abdo, Geneive, and Jonathan Lyons. *Answering Only to God: Faith and Freedom in Twenty-first-Century Iran.* New York: Henry Holt, 2003.

Abrahamian, Ervand. *The Iranian Mojahedin.* New Haven, CT: Yale University Press, 1989.

———. *Khomeinism: Essays on the Islamic Republic.* Berkeley and Los Angeles: University of California Press, 1993.

———. *Tortured Confessions: Prisons and Public Recantations in Modern Iran.* Berkeley and Los Angeles: University of California Press, 1999.

Adelkah, Fariba. *Being Modern in Iran.* New York: Columbia University Press, 2000.

Afshari, Reza. *Human Rights in Iran: The Abuse of Cultural Relativism.* Philadelphia: University of Pennsylvania Press, 2001.

Al-e Ahmad, Jalal. *Occidentosis: A Plague from the West.* Translated by R. Campbell and edited by Hamid Algar. Berkeley, CA: Mizan Press, 1984.

———. "Samad and the Folk Legend." In *Iranian Society: An Anthology of Writings,* ed. Michael Hillmann. Lexington, KY: Mazda, 1982.

Ansari, Hamid. *The Narrative of Awakening: A Look at Imam Khomeini's Ideal, Scientific and Political Biography (from Birth to Ascension).* Translated and edited by Seyed Manoochehr Moosavi. Qom, Iran: Institute for Compilation and Publication of the Works of Imam Khomeini, International Affairs Division, 1994.

Arendt, Hannah. *On Revolution.* New York: Penguin Books, 2006.

Arjomand, Saïd Amir. *After Khomeini: Iran Under His Successors.* New York: Oxford University Press, 2009.

Asadi, Houshang. *Letters to My Torturer: Love, Revolution, and Imprisonment in Iran.* Oxford: Oneworld, 2010.

Axworthy, Michael. *Revolutionary Iran: A History of the Islamic Republic.* New York: Oxford University Press, 2013.

Bahari, Maziar, with Aimee Malloy. *Then They Came for Me: A Family's Story of Love, Captivity, and Survival.* New York: Random House, 2011.

Baktiari, Bahman. *Parliamentary Politics in Revolutionary Iran: The Institutionalization of Factional Politics.* Gainesville: University Press of Florida, 1996.

Bashiriyeh, Hossein. *The State and Revolution in Iran: 1962–1982.* New York: Palgrave Macmillan, 1984.

Bayat, Asef. *Making Islam Democratic: Social Movements and the Post-Islamist Turn.* Stanford, CA: Stanford University Press, 2007.

———. *Street Politics: Poor People's Movements in Iran.* New York: Columbia University Press, 1997.

Behrangi, Samad. "The Little Black Fish," in *The Little Black Fish and Other Modern Persian Stories.* Translated by Eric Hooglund and Mary Hooglund. Washington, DC: Three Continents Press, 1976.

Blight, James G., Janet M. Lang, Hussain Banai, Malcolm Byrne, and John Tirman. *Becoming Enemies: U.S.-Iran Relations and the Iran-Iraq War, 1979–1988.* New York: Rowman & Littlefield, 2012.

Boroujerdi, Mehrzad. *Iranian Intellectuals and the West: The Tormented Triumph of Nativism.* Syracuse, NY: Syracuse University Press, 1996.

Brinton, Crane. *The Anatomy of Revolution.* New York: Vintage, 1965.

Brumberg, Daniel. *Reinventing Khomeini: The Struggle for Reform in Iran.* Chicago: University of Chicago Press, 2001.

Buchan, James. *Days of God: The Revolution in Iran and Its Consequences.* New York: Simon & Schuster, 2013.

Chehabi, H. E. *Iranian Politics and Religious Modernism: The Liberation Movement of Iran Under the Shah and Khomeini.* London: I. B. Tauris, 1990.

Dabashi, Hamid. *Theology of Discontent: The Ideological Foundation of the Islamic Revolution in Iran.* New Brunswick, NJ: Transaction, 2008.

———, and Peter Chelkowski. *Staging a Revolution: The Art of Persuasion in the Islamic Republic of Iran.* New York: New York University Press, 1999.

Ebadi, Shirin, with Azadeh Moaveni. *Iran Awakening: A Memoir of Revolution and Hope.* New York: Random House, 2006.

Ehsani, Kaveh. "The Politics of Property in the Islamic Republic of Iran." In *The Rule of Law, Islam, and Constitutional Politics in Egypt and Iran,* ed. Said Amir Arjomand and Nathan J. Brown, 153–79. Albany: State University of New York Press, 2013.

Ganji, Akbar. *The Road to Democracy in Iran.* Cambridge, MA: MIT Press, 2008.

———. "Who Is Ali Khamenei? The Worldview of Iran's Supreme Leader." *Foreign Affairs* 92, no. 5 (Sept./Oct. 2013), 24–48.

Ghamari-Tabrizi, Behrooz. *Islam and Dissent in Postrevolutionary Iran: Abdolkarim Soroush, Religious Politics and Democratic Reform.* London: I. B. Tauris, 2008.

Gheissari, Ali. *Iranian Intellectuals in the 20th Century.* Austin: University of Texas Press, 1998.

———, and Vali Nasr. *Democracy in Iran: History and the Quest for Liberty.* New York: Oxford University Press, 2006.

Hakakian, Roya. *Assassins of the Turquoise Palace.* New York: Grove Press, 2011.

Hanson, Brad. "The 'Westoxication' of Iran: Depictions and Reactions of Behrangi, Al-e Ahmad, and Shariati." *International Journal of Middle East Studies* 15, no. 1 (Feb. 1983), 1–23.

Hardwick, Jeffrey M. *Mall Maker: Victor Gruen, Architect of an American Dream.* Philadelphia: University of Pennsylvania Press, 2010.

Harris, Kevan, "The Brokered Exuberance of the Middle Class: An Ethnographic Analysis of Iran's 2009 Green Movement." *Mobilization: An International Journal* 17, no. 4 (Dec. 2012), 435–55.

———. "A Martyrs' Welfare State and Its Contradictions: Regime Resilience and Limits Through the Lens of Social Policy in Iran." In *Middle East Authoritarianisms: Governance, Contestation, and Regime Resilience in Syria and Iran,* ed. Steven Heydemann and Reinoud Leenders, 61–80. Stanford, CA: Stanford University Press, 2013.

Hashemi, Nader, and Danny Postel, eds. *The People Reloaded: The Green Movement and the Struggle for Iran's Future.* Brooklyn, NY: Melville House, 2011.

Hedayat, Sadegh. *The Blind Owl.* Translated by D. P. Costello. New York: Grove Press, 1994.

Hobbes, Thomas. *Leviathan.* Oxford: Oxford University Press, 1996.

Jahanbakhsh, Forough. *Islam, Democracy and Religious Modernism in Iran, 1953–2000.* Leiden, Netherlands: Brill, 2001.

Kadivar, Mohammad Ali. "Alliances and Perception Profiles in the Iranian Reform Movement, 1997 to 2005." *American Sociological Review,* published online Oct. 2013. http://asr.sagepub.com/content/early/2013/10/30/000312 2413508285.

Kar, Mehrangiz. *Crossing the Red Line: The Struggle for Human Rights in Iran.* Costa Mesa, CA: Blind Owl Press/Mazda, 2007.

Keddie, Nikki R. *Modern Iran: Roots and Results of Revolution.* New Haven, CT: Yale University Press, 2003.

Keshavarzian, Arang. *Bazaar and State in Iran: The Politics of the Tehran Marketplace.* New York: Cambridge University Press, 2007.

Khatami, Mohammad. *Hope and Challenge: The Iranian President Speaks.* Translated by Alidad Mafinezam. Binghamton, NY: Institute of Global Cultural Studies, Binghamton University, 1997.

———. *Islam, Liberty and Development.* Translated by Hossein Kamaly. Binghamton, NY: Global Academic Publishing, 1998.

Khomeini, Ruhollah. *Islam and Revolution I: Writings and Declarations of Imam Khomeini (1941–1980).* Translated and edited by Hamid Algar. Berkeley, CA: Mizan Press, 1981.

Kunkler, Mirjam. "The Special Court of the Clergy and the Repression of Dissident Clergy in Iran." In *The Rule of Law, Islam, and Constitutional Politics in Egypt and Iran,* ed. Said Amir Arjomand and Nathan J. Brown, 57–100. Albany: State University of New York Press, 2013.

Madanipour, Ali. *Tehran: The Making of a Metropolis.* New York: John Wiley & Sons, 1998.

Martin, Richard C., and Mark R. Woodward, with Dwi S. Atmaja. *Defenders of Reason in Islam: Mu'tazilism from Medieval School to Modern Symbol.* Oxford: Oneworld, 1997.

Menashri, David. *Iran: A Decade of War and Revolution.* New York: Holmes & Meier, 1990.

———. *Post-Revolutionary Politics in Iran: Religion, Society and Power.* Portland, OR; Frank Cass, 2001.

Michaelson, Marcus, ed. *Election Fallout: Iran's Exiled Journalists on Their Struggle for Democratic Change.* Translated by Evan J. Siegel. Berlin: Hans Schiler, 2011. http://library.fes.de/pdf-files/iez/08560.pdf.

Milani, Abbas. *Eminent Persians: The Men and Women Who Made Modern Iran, 1941–1979.* 2 vols. Syracuse, NY: Syracuse University Press and Persian Book World, 2008.

———. *The Shah.* New York: Palgrave Macmillan, 2011.

Mirgholami, Morteza, and Sidh Sintusingha. "From Traditional Mahallehs to Modern Neighborhoods: The Case of Narmak, Tehran." *Comparative Studies of South Asia, Africa and the Middle East* 32, no. 1 (2012), 214–37.

Mir-Hosseini, Ziba. *Islam and Gender: The Religious Debate in Contemporary Iran.* Princeton, NJ: Princeton University Press, 1999.

———, and Richard Tapper. *Islam and Democracy in Iran: Eshkevari and the Quest for Reform.* London and New York: I. B. Tauris, 2006.

Mirsepassi, Ali. *Democracy in Modern Iran: Islam, Culture, and Political Change.* New York: New York University Press, 2010.

————. *Intellectual Discourse and the Politics of Modernization: Negotiating Modernity in Iran.* Cambridge, England: Cambridge University Press, 2000.

Molavi, Afshin. *The Soul of Iran: A Nation's Struggle for Freedom.* New York: W. W. Norton, 2005.

Moqadam, Afsaneh. *Death to the Dictator! A Young Man Casts a Vote in Iran's 2009 Election and Pays a Devastating Price.* New York: Sarah Crichton Books/Farrar, Straus and Giroux, 2010.

Moslem, Mehdi. *Factional Politics in Post-Khomeini Iran.* Syracuse, NY: Syracuse University Press, 2002.

Mottahedeh, Roy. *The Mantle of the Prophet: Religion and Politics in Iran.* Oxford: Oneworld, 2000.

Mozaffari, Nahid, and Ahmad Karimi Hakkak, eds. *Strange Times, My Dear: The PEN Anthology of Contemporary Iranian Literature.* New York: Arcade, 2005.

Nabavi, Negin, ed. *Intellectual Trends in Twentieth-Century Iran: A Critical Survey.* Gainesville: University Press of Florida, 2003.

Naji, Kasra. *Ahmadinejad: The Secret History of Iran's Radical Leader.* Berkeley and Los Angeles: University of California Press, 2008.

Nohmani, Farhad, and Sohrab Behdad. *Class and Labor in Iran: Did the Revolution Matter?* Syracuse, NY: Syracuse University Press, 2006.

Paya, Ali. "Karl Popper and the Iranian Intellectuals." *American Journal of Islamic Social Sciences* 20, no. 2 (Spring 2003), 50–79.

Peterson, Scott. *Let the Swords Encircle Me: Iran—A Journey Behind the Headlines.* New York: Simon & Schuster, 2010.

Plato. *The Republic.* In *Plato: The Collected Dialogues, Including the Letters*, ed. Edith Hamilton and Huntington Cairns, trans. Paul Shorey. Princeton, NJ: Princeton University Press, 1989.

Popescu, Lucy, and Carole Seymour-Jones, eds. *Writers Under Siege: Voices of Freedom from Around the World.* New York: New York University Press, 2007.

Popper, Karl. *The Open Society and Its Enemies*, vol. 2: *Hegel and Marx.* New York: Routledge, 2003.

————. *Unended Quest: An Intellectual Autobiography.* Chicago and LaSalle, IL: Open Court, 1990.

Rahnema, Ali. *An Islamic Utopian: A Political Biography of Ali Shari'ati.* London and New York: I. B. Tauris, 2000.

————. *Superstition as Ideology in Iranian Politics: From Majlesi to Ahmadinejad.* New York: Cambridge University Press, 2011.

Rajaee, Farhang. *Islamism and Modernism: The Changing Discourse in Iran.* Austin: University of Texas Press, 2007.

Rejali, Darius. *Torture and Modernity: Self, Society, and State in Modern Iran.* Boulder, CO: Westview Press, 1994.

Saberi, Roxana. *Between Two Worlds: My Life and Captivity in Iran.* New York: HarperCollins, 2010.

Sadjadpour, Karim. *Reading Khamenei: The World View of Iran's Most Powerful Leader.* Washington, DC: Carnegie Endowment for International Peace, 2008.

Salehi-Isfahani, Djavad. "Poverty, Inequality, and Populist Politics in Iran." *Journal of Economic Inequality* 7, no. 1 (March 2009), 5–24.

———. "The Revolution and the Rural Poor." *Radical History Review*, no. 105 (Fall 2009), 139–44.

Schirazi, Asgar. *The Constitution of Iran: Politics and the State in the Islamic Republic.* Translated by John O'Kane. London: I. B. Tauris, 1998.

Sciolino, Elaine. *Persian Mirrors: The Elusive Face of Iran.* New York: Free Press, 2005.

Soroush, Abdolkarim. *Reason, Freedom, and Democracy in Islam: Essential Writings of Abdolkarim Soroush.* Translated by Mahmoud Sadri and Ahmad Sadri. New York: Oxford University Press, 2002.

Tabaar, Mohammad Ayatollahi. "From Womb to Tomb: Religion, the State and War in Iran." Unpublished thesis shared by author.

Tajbakhsh, Kian. "Political Decentralization and the Creation of Local Government in Iran: Consolidation or Transformation of the Theocratic State?" *Social Research* 67, no. 2 (Summer 2000: Iran Since the Revolution), 377–404.

Vahdat, Farzin. *God and Juggernaut: Iran's Intellectual Encounter with Modernity.* Syracuse, NY: Syracuse University Press, 2002.

Vanstiphout, Wouter. "The Saddest City in the World: Tehran and the Legacy of an American Dream of Modern Town Planning." In *The New Town*, research and exhibition project by Crimson Architectural Historians, Rotterdam, March 2, 2006. http://www.thenewtown.nl/article.php?id_article=71.

Wright, Robin. *The Last Great Revolution: Turmoil and Transformation in Iran.* New York: Alfred A. Knopf, 2000.

Zweig, Stefan. *The Right to Heresy: Castellio Against Calvin.* Translated by Eden and Cedar Paul. London: Cassell, 1936.

INDEX

trade sanctions, 83, 354, 462–64
Tudeh Party (communist), 11, 68, 84
twelve imams, 13, 27, 29, 63

underground press, 52
United Fundamentalist Front, 351
United Nations
  funding of NGOs from, 270
  Iran-Iraq War and, 86, 88
  prison observers from, 93
  refugees and, 311
  women's rights and, 359
United States
  attitudes toward, 131
  Bazargan working with, 48–49
  "civil society" as tool of, 389
  coup against Mossadegh, 11
  hostage crisis at embassy of, 39, 41–42, 69, 83–84, 86, 247, 340
  influence on shah, 28
  Iran-Contra affair and, 87, 447
  Islamic nationalists and, 31
  Khomeini view of, 28–29
  shah and, 39
  shooting down airliner, 88
  "velvet coup" plot and, 436–38, 441, 444
  viewed as aggressor, 236
Universal Declaration of Human Rights, 30, 75
universities
  attacks after election of 2009, 416
  closing of, 69
  insecure atmosphere in 1980s, 71
  in Mousavi era, 139
  purges, 44, 69, 71
  under Rafsanjani, 132–33, 187–89, 246
  reopening, 70
  See also Eighteenth of Tir campus crisis; names of individual universities
University of Mashhad, 15
University of Tehran, 194–98, 416
utopianism, 12, 15, 64, 74, 95, 127, 464

Vanstiphout, Wouter, 217
velayat-e faqih (rule of Islamic jurisconsult)
  in constitution, 40, 85
  Ganji on, 322, 323
  as incompatible with republic, 322
  as Islamized monarchy, 142
  Khomeini's theory of, 15
  revision of role, 101
  Revolutionary Council and, 34
"velvet coup" conspiracy
  alleged collaborators in, 441–42
  confessions in, 439–40, 445
  Fazlinejad treatise on, 435–39
  trials and, 439–43, 446
Voice of America, 351

"We Are the Writers!" (open letter), 174, 176–77
Weber, Max, 319, 323, 439–40
websites
  based in Europe, 311
  Iranian.com, 403–4
  Roozonline, 419, 427, 457
  suppression of reformist, 410
  "velvet coup" trial and, 267, 410, 446
  Women's News, 376, 379, 385
West and Western culture
  Al-e Ahmad and, 7–9
  cinema and, 24
  Heidegger and, 77
  Iranian elites and, 5
  Khatami rejecting, 151–52
  Soroush and, 70–71
  support for reformists in, 440–41
Western thought
  humanism in, 75
  Khatami on, 151–52
  political theory and, 137–38
  Soroush and, 59–63
  "velvet coup" plot and, 439–41
westoxication, 26, 77, 115, 151
Westoxication (Al-e Ahmad), 7–9, 75
"What Is Enlightenment?" (Kant), 80
What Is Science? What Is Philosophy? (Soroush), 67
Where Are You, Hasanak? (Parnian), 166–67
White Revolution, 28
women
  in Basij militia, 45
  charged with sexual crimes, 380–81
  as political prisoners, 96–97
  rights of, 120, 386
  rural, 217–18
  suffrage for, 28, 36
Women's News (website), 376, 379
women's rights movement
  Amini and, 359, 386
  demonstrations and, 399–400
  in election of 2009, 359
  stoning and, 393–95
Wright, Frank Lloyd, 213

Yas-e No (newspaper), 241
Yazdi, Ebrahim (politician), 21

Zalzadeh, Ebrahim (editor), 177
Zan (newspaper), 370
Zanan (journal), 119–20, 374, 381
Zavarei, Reza (judiciary official), 156
Zaydis (sect), 117
Zibakalam, Sadegh (student), 72
Zweig, Stefan, 435, 449–50